YEATS: An Annual of Critical and Textual Studies

Etching by Jack Coughlin

In memoriam Liam Miller (24 April 1924–17 May 1987), maker of beautiful books. He served Irish culture and was devoted to Yeats studies: author of *The Noble Drama of W. B. Yeats,* general editor of the *Yeats Centenary Papers* and *New Yeats Papers,* designer and producer of Yeats's plays at the Lantern Theatre, publisher at the Dolmen Press of a generation of Yeats scholarship. —David R. Clark

> Shall we in that great night rejoice?
> What do we know but that we face
> One another in this place?

YEATS

An Annual of Critical
and Textual Studies

Volume VI, 1988

Edited by Richard J. Finneran

Ann Arbor
The University of Michigan Press

Grateful acknowledgment is made to Macmillan Publishing Company and A. P.
Watt Ltd., on behalf of Michael B. Yeats and Macmillan London Ltd., for
permission to reprint the poems "Closing Rhyme" from *Responsibilities*,
"Vacillation," and "Politics," by W. B. Yeats. Reprinted by permission from
W. B. Yeats, *The Poems: A New Edition*, edited by Richard J. Finneran. "Vacilla-
tion" copyright 1933 by Macmillan Publishing Company, renewed 1961 by
Bertha Georgie Yeats. "Closing Rhyme" copyright 1916 by Macmillan Publish-
ing Company, renewed 1944 by Bertha Georgie Yeats. "Politics" copyright 1940
by Georgie Yeats, renewed 1968 by Bertha Georgie Yeats, Michael Butler Yeats
and Anne Yeats.

Contents

REVIEW ESSAYS

REVIEWS

Editorial Information

EDITOR: Richard J. Finneran
REVIEW EDITOR: Mary FitzGerald
EDITORIAL ASSISTANT: Gwenn de Mauriac

We welcome submissions of articles, notes, and editions of fugitive or unpublished works. Although we generally follow the *MLA Handbook for Writers of Research Papers*, 2d ed. (New York: MLA, 1984), we do not include a list of works cited; intending contributors are advised to request a style sheet from the editor at Department of English, University of Tennessee, Knoxville, Tennessee 37996, U.S.A. Submissions received by 15 May are assured of consideration for publication in the following year. The editor is grateful to the Graduate Council on Research, Tulane University, for a grant to aid in the preparation of this volume. All quotations from Yeats's writings, both published and unpublished, are made with the permission of the copyright holders. We are particularly indebted to Anne Yeats; Michael B. Yeats; A. P. Watt Ltd.; Macmillan, London; and Macmillan Publishing Co., Inc., New York.

This publication is affiliated with the Conference of Editors of Learned Journals and is indexed as *Yeats* in the *MLA International Bibliography*.

Contributors

Ronald Bush, Professor of Humanities, California Institute of Technology

David R. Clark, Professor Emeritus of English, University of Massachusetts

Jack Coughlin, printmaker and sculptor, has done many portraits of Irish writers and exhibited widely in the United States and Ireland

Keith Cunningham, Professor of English, Northern Arizona University

Terence Diggory, Associate Professor of English, Skidmore College

Ralph Harding Earle completed his dissertation on Yeats's syntax at the University of North Carolina, Chapel Hill

Edward Engelberg, Professor of Romance and Comparative Literature, Brandeis University

Mary FitzGerald, Professor of English, University of New Orleans

Ian Fletcher, Professor Emeritus of English, Arizona State University

George Mills Harper, Professor of English, Florida State University

Margaret Mills Harper, Assistant Professor of English, Ohio State University at Marion

Connie K. Hood, Assistant Professor of English, Tennessee Technological University

K. P. S. Jochum, Professor of English, Universität Bamberg

Phillip L. Marcus, Professor of English, Cornell University

Gwenn de Mauriac, graduate student in English, Tulane University

Jeffrey Meyers, Professor of English, University of Colorado

Raeburn Miller, Professor of English, University of New Orleans

Brendan O Hehir, Professor of English, University of California at Berkeley

James Olney, Professor of English, Louisiana State University
Donald H. Reiman, Editor, *Shelley and His Circle: 1773–1822*
David Rogers, Professor of English, Seton Hall University
David S. Thatcher, Professor of English, University of Victoria
Anca Vlasopolos, Associate Professor of English, Wayne State
    University

Editor's Notes

Under the direction of Artistic Director Vincent Dowling, the Abbey Theatre has launched a project to perform the entire dramatic canon of Yeats within the next five years. To assist in that laudable endeavor, James W. Flannery has been appointed an associate international artist; he will teach at the Abbey School of Theatre and will direct the five-play Cuchulain cycle.

The cataloguing of the Yeats microfilm collection at the State University of New York at Stony Brook has now been completed (as far as funding will allow), under the direction of Peggy L. McMullen. By this time a Preliminary Finding Aid should be available. The old style of citation (e.g., SB00.00.00) has been replaced by frame numbers from the microfilms. The former numbers can be converted to the new with but little difficulty; unfortunately, collating the Stony Brook materials with the originals in the National Library of Ireland still must be done by individual scholars on a page-by-page basis.

Three major projects are nearing completion: a Census of Yeats manuscripts by Conrad A. Balliet (Department of English, Wittenberg University, Springfield, Ohio 45501); a new primary bibliography by Colin Smythe (P.O. Box 6, Gerrards Cross, Buckinghamshire SL9 8EF, England); and an expanded edition of *W. B. Yeats: A Classified Bibliography of Criticism* by K. P. S. Jochum (Universität Bamberg, Postfach 1549, D-8600 Bamberg, West Germany). Readers with relevant information are requested to contact the appropriate individual.

The biographies of Yeats by Roy Foster and Mrs. Yeats by Ann Saddlemyer continue in progress.

By this time two volumes in the Collected Edition of the Works should have been published: *Letters to the New Island*, edited by George Bornstein and Hugh Witemeyer; and *Prefaces and Introductions*, edited by William H. O'Donnell. Scheduled for publication early in 1989 are a revised edition of *The Poems: A New Edition*, edited by Richard J. Finneran, as well as an abridged edition, also edited by Finneran, which will contain the canonical poems only and be available in paperback.

A Yeats Club was founded in Oxford in 1986. Despite the title, Yeats would seem to be only one of their varied interests. *The Yeats Club*

Review was issued once as a separate publication (1.1 [Summer 1987]), but no. 2 (Spring 1988) was incorporated into the first issue of *Celtic Dawn* (Spring 1988). Address: P.O. Box 271, Oxford OX2 6DU, England.

We note with a deep sense of loss the death in 1987 of Richard Ellmann and of Liam Miller. After his two seminal studies of Yeats, Ellmann devoted most of his time first to Joyce and then to Wilde, with the result that he will surely be remembered as one of the greatest literary biographers of this century. Yet he continued to teach us about Yeats, as witnessed by the volume reviewed in this issue by James Olney. Liam Miller's contribution to Yeats studies was of a more varied kind: not only a scholar of the plays, Miller was also a major force in Irish publishing for several decades, and many important monographs on Yeats owe their existence to his efforts.

Richard Ellmann has already had many memorials—and deservedly so. Remembering Yeats's fondness for the passage in which Spenser laments that the Earl of Leicester's fame "is worn alreadie out of thought," we take this opportunity to pay tribute through our frontispiece to Liam Miller.

Abbreviations

The following abbreviations are used throughout the volume, on the model of (Au 181) to refer to page 181 of *Autobiographies*. In addition, some of the essays use special abbreviations, as indicated in the notes. To distinguish these from the abbreviations listed below, they are italicized (unless an author's name).

Au	*Autobiographies*. London: Macmillan, 1955.
AV-A	*A Critical Edition of Yeats's* A Vision *(1925)*. Ed. George Mills Harper and Walter Kelly Hood. London: Macmillan, 1978.
AV-B	*A Vision*. London: Macmillan, 1962.
B	Allan Wade, *A Bibliography of the Writings of W. B. Yeats*. 3d ed. Rev. Russell K. Alspach. London: Rupert Hart-Davis, 1968.
CLI	*The Collected Letters of W. B. Yeats: Volume One, 1865–1895*. Ed. John Kelly. Oxford: Clarendon Press, 1986.
E&I	*Essays and Introductions*. London & New York: Macmillan, 1961.
Ex	*Explorations*. Sel. Mrs. W. B. Yeats. London: Macmillan, 1962; New York: Macmillan, 1963.
JSD	*John Sherman and Dhoya*. Ed. Richard J. Finneran. Detroit: Wayne State University Press, 1969.
L	*The Letters of W. B. Yeats*. Ed. Allan Wade. London: Rupert Hart-Davis, 1954; New York: Macmillan, 1955.
LDW	*Letters on Poetry from W. B. Yeats to Dorothy Wellesley*. Intro. Kathleen Raine. London & New York: Oxford University Press, 1964.
LMR	*Ah, Sweet Dancer: W. B. Yeats [&] Margot Ruddock, A Correspondence*. Ed. Roger McHugh. London & New York: Macmillan, 1970.
LNI	*Letters to the New Island*. Ed. Horace Reynolds. Cambridge: Harvard University Press, 1934.
LRB	*The Correspondence of Robert Bridges and W. B. Yeats*. Ed. Richard J. Finneran. London: Macmillan, 1977.
LTSM	*W. B. Yeats and T. Sturge Moore: Their Correspondence, 1901–*

	1937. Ed. Ursula Bridge. London: Routledge & Kegan Paul; New York: Oxford University Press, 1953.
LTWBY	*Letters to W. B. Yeats.* Ed. Richard J. Finneran, George Mills Harper, and William M. Murphy. London: Macmillan; New York: Columbia University Press, 1977.
Mem	*Memoirs.* Ed. Denis Donoghue. London: Macmillan, 1972; New York: Macmillan, 1973.
Myth	*Mythologies.* London & New York: Macmillan, 1959.
OBMV	*The Oxford Book of Modern Verse, 1892–1935.* Chosen by W. B. Yeats. Oxford: Clarendon Press, 1936.
P	*The Poems: A New Edition.* Ed. Richard J. Finneran. New York: Macmillan, 1983; London: Macmillan, 1984. [Cited from the corrected second printing (1984) or later printings.]
SB	*The Speckled Bird, with Variant Versions.* Ed. William H. O'Donnell. Toronto: McClelland and Stewart, 1976 [1977].
SS	*The Senate Speeches of W. B. Yeats.* Ed. Donald R. Pearce. Bloomington: Indiana University Press, 1960.
TB	*Theatre Business: The Correspondence of the First Abbey Theatre Directors: William Butler Yeats, Lady Gregory, and J. M. Synge.* Ed. Ann Saddlemyer. Gerrards Cross: Colin Smythe; University Park: Pennsylvania State University Press, 1982.
UP1	*Uncollected Prose by W. B. Yeats.* Vol. 1. Ed. John P. Frayne. London: Macmillan; New York: Columbia University Press, 1970.
UP2	*Uncollected Prose by W. B. Yeats.* Vol. 2. Ed. John P. Frayne and Colton Johnson. London: Macmillan, 1975; New York: Columbia University Press, 1976.
VP	*The Variorum Edition of the Poems of W. B. Yeats.* Ed. Russell K. Alspach. New York: Macmillan, 1957. [Cited from the corrected third printing (1966) or later printings.]
VPl	*The Variorum Edition of the Plays of W. B. Yeats.* Ed. Russell K. Alspach. London & New York: Macmillan, 1966. [Cited from the corrected second printing (1966) or later printings.]

Articles

The Modernist under Siege

Ronald Bush

In the mid-sixties, when Frank Kermode suggested in *The Sense of an Ending* that modernism's conservative social stance was at least in part the result of imposing aesthetic notions of order onto politics, the idea seemed worth considering.[1] The modernists, Kermode reasoned, were fiercely dedicated to ending "the hegemony of [the] bourgeois . . . and all the 'Bergsonian' attitudes to time or human psychology, all the mess which makes up a commonplace [twentieth-century] view of reality." Thus it was hardly surprising that their passionate conceptions, though forged in the context of "poetry or . . . a theory of poetry," occasionally spilled over to alarming fantasies in which "a police and a civil service" accomplished a comparably masterful "final solution" (*SE* 111). Nevertheless, Kermode was careful to add, although the modernist writers sometimes extended dangerous fictions beyond their proper sphere, the fictions themselves were specifically designed "to know by and not to live by," and in the major literature of the period an ingrained skepticism ensured that the myths did not run riot (*SE* 112, 104).

Ten years after Kermode's speculations, however, when antimodernism had reached a boiling point, the Marxist Terry Eagleton in *Criticism and Ideology* would assert without qualification that the connection between modernist poetics and repressive politics was thoroughgoing and necessary.[2] Indeed, Eagleton argued, both were simply ideological expressions of the same cultural situation. "Confronted with world imperialist crisis, severe economic depression and intensifying working-class militancy, English society stood in urgent need" of an ideology that would seem to "eradicate the last vestiges" of liberalism and Romantic individualism and yet really only reinforce the individual consciousness and the individual artifact (*CI* 146–47). In Eagleton's argument, modern-

---

1. Frank Kermode, *The Sense of an Ending: Studies in the Theory of Fiction* (1966; rpt. New York: Oxford University Press, 1968). Hereafter cited in the text as *SE*.
2. Terry Eagleton, *Criticism and Ideology: A Study in Marxist Literary Theory* (1975; rpt. London: Verso, 1985). Hereafter cited in the text as *CI*.

ist form even as it seemed to mime the contradictions of the time was by necessity closed, elitist, and totalizing. So in the case of *The Waste Land,* the masterpiece of the movement's most effective spokesman, what appeared to be a fragmented presentation of cultural disintegration in fact comprised a "closed, coherent, authoritative discourse" whose "totalising mythological forms" and "elaborate display of esoteric [reference]" "silently allude[d] to a transcendance" of its own content (*CI* 148–50).

And however novel or provocative Eagleton's position may have struck readers in 1975, in 1988 it looks anything but eccentric. On the contrary, as American and European *literati* ascribe to postmodernism and poststructuralism more and more of the oppositional values that were once seen as essentially modernist, and as modernism begins to seem more conservative and less interesting, Eagleton's voice takes on a representative status. His attitudes can be found scattered through a number of recent studies, some of which present genuine surprises. One would, for example, expect to find them reflected in Andrew Ross's 1986 *The Failure of Modernism,* a young turk's book that lives up to its title by arguing that modernism's factitious categories (the "true, natural, or ego-less") correspond to a "cultural will that sought to translate abstract theory into political fact through the self-asserted autonomy of its medium."[3] But what about Richard Poirier? Once a champion of modernist writing, Poirier in 1987 called it "a snob's game" and "a privileged and exclusive form of discourse."[4] And a few months later Sandra Gilbert, who began her career with a book extolling Lawrence's poetry, published an essay that contended, "from James to Pound and Eliot to Joyce . . . male modernists attempted to achieve what Lawrence called 'the mastery that man must hold' by an occulting of language through the deliberate and elaborate deployment of allusions, puns, deconstructions and reconstructions, an occulting that would transform the mother tongue itself into a kind of 'father speech.' "[5]

These developments should first be pursued in respect to Eliot, who

---

3. Andrew Ross, *The Failure of Modernism: Symptoms of American Poetry* (New York: Columbia University Press, 1986), 211–19.

4. Richard Poirier, *The Renewal of Literature: Emersonian Reflections* (New York: Random House, 1987), 98–99.

5. Sandra Gilbert, "Woman's Sentence, Man's Sentencing: Linguistic Fantasies in Woolf and Joyce," *Virginia Woolf and Bloomsbury: A Centenary Celebration,* ed. Jane Marcus (London: Macmillan, 1987), 221.

remains the primary target for such criticism because of his onetime eminence and because the criticism he wrote in middle age set a pattern for connecting modernist writing and conservative ideology. Having treated Eliot elsewhere, though,[6] I would here like to address the similar but in some ways more interesting case of Yeats.

Yeats, of course, could seem even more reactionary than his contemporaries. After all, he frequently dissociated himself from the techniques of modernist fragmentation[7] and just as frequently proclaimed that his poetry, like all true literature, drew its power not from the internal conflicts of a particular person or a particular era but, Centaur-like, found "in the popular lore its back and its strong legs" (Au 129). Yet despite these celebrations of tradition and national mythology, there is no gainsaying the profoundly skeptical and dramatic (that is to say, dialectical) procedures of his work: his fondness for dialogues and interrogatives, for instance, and above all his deepseated and very Nietzschean reliance on the doctrine of the mask, an exercise in self-overcoming in which man strives to become what is "of all imaginable things / The most unlike" (P 162). In one of his most famous apothegms Yeats wrote that "we make out of the quarrel with others, rhetoric, but of the quarrel with ourselves, poetry" (Myth 331). And the vividness of his poetic quarrels were what attracted some of the earliest and best of his critics. F. R. Leavis, recall, noted in 1932 that there was "always an ironical overtone" in Yeats,[8] and Denis Donoghue based his study of Yeats on the assertion that Yeats's "sense of consciousness as conflict is the most important article in [his] faith as a poet."[9] Hence despite Yeats's conservative themes, it was from the beginning clear to at least some readers that his art was rooted not in totalitarian poetics but in structures enacting the competition of value. In the recent words of Balachandra Rajan, Yeats's "world exhibits the play of energies rather than the play of purposes. Instead of proceeding from closures to larger closures, he proceeds from closures into that underlying openness

---

6. See "But is it Modern?: (T. S. Eliot in 1988)," *Yale Review* 77.2 (Winter 1988): 193–206; and "Turned toward Creation: T. S. Eliot 1988," in *T. S. Eliot: Man and Poet,* ed. Carroll F. Terrell (Orono: National Poetry Foundation), forthcoming.

7. See the author's "Yeats, Spooks, Nursery Rhymes, and the Vicissitudes of Late Modernism," *Yeats* 3 (1985): 17.

8. F. R. Leavis, *New Bearings in English Poetry* (1932; rpt. Ann Arbor: University of Michigan Press, 1964), 46.

9. Denis Donoghue, *William Butler Yeats* (New York: Viking, 1971), 34.

from which endeavors at closure seek to protect themselves by the pro-
pitiation of a further succession of stances. . . . The quarrel within the self
is the basis of his poetry, not a condition the poetry amends."[10]

Which is not to say that there were not other readers who took the
poet's pronouncements about tradition more seriously. These critics are
for the most part associated with New Criticism, a movement more
univocally conservative than modernism ever was. The keynote of the
New Critical response to Yeats was sounded by R. P. Blackmur in 1936
and echoed in 1939 by John Crowe Ransom, who acknowledged Black-
mur's lead.[11] Both stressed Yeats's "religious insight," and Ransom as-
serted that although he had once believed "there can be no more poetry
on the order of its famous triumphs until we come again upon a time
when an elaborate Myth will be accepted universally. . . . Yeats has
disproved it. We have no common religion but we have not stopped
being religious. . . . [Yeats] was a tireless religious eclectic and im-
provisor of religious imagery, and this strategy, which was perhaps the
only strategy, succeeded."[12] Then in the winter 1942 "Special Yeats
Issue" of *The Southern Review,* Allen Tate, Austin Warren, and others
expanded on this line of praise, characterizing Yeats's use of myth as
essentially traditional.[13] Finally a group of *The Southern Review* essays,
along with Blackmur's, Ransom's, and an earlier piece of Cleanth
Brooks's, were enshrined in a volume of selected criticism entitled *The
Permanence of Yeats* (1950) which for many years remained a standard
Yeats companion.

Considering this reception history, the interesting thing about many
recent Marxist and postmodernist critics of Yeats is that rather than
questioning the New Critics' assumptions, they accept them and reverse
their valence. Citing Yeatsian phrases about rootedness and tradition,
they arrive at conclusions similar to Blackmur's and Ransom's, this time
not to praise the poet, but to bury him. To illustrate, I wish to take up

---

10. Balachandra Rajan, "Its Own Executioner: Yeats and the Fragment," *Yeats* 3
(1985): 83.

11. See R. P. Blackmur, "The Later Poetry of W. B. Yeats," *The Southern Review* 2.2
(1936); and John Crowe Ransom, "Yeats and His Symbols," *The Kenyon Review* 1.3
(1939). For reasons made clear below, I cite from reprintings in *The Permanence of Yeats,* ed.
James Hall and Martin Steinmann (1950; rpt. New York: Collier, 1961), 38–59 and 85–96.

12. *The Permanence of Yeats,* 86.

13. *The Southern Review* 7.3 (Winter 1941–42). Other contributors included Black-
mur, L. C. Knights, F. O. Matthiessen, Delmore Schwartz, Kenneth Burke, and T. S.
Eliot.

two examples at some length, both of which assume that Yeats's modernism is at heart a mystified traditionalism and is ultimately totalitarian. The first and the more influential of the two is the discussion of Yeats in Eagleton's *Criticism and Ideology.*

Eagleton begins by suggesting that Yeats's position was more complicated than Eliot's because of his Irish nationality. Not being American or English, Eagleton says, meant that rather than needing to write his way out of "the dwindling resources of [bourgeois] Romantic individualism," Yeats started in an earlier cultural phase. His task was instead to affirm an *aristocratic* Romanticism against a crude but still vital Irish middle class (*CI* 151), Yeats's alienation combined with his idealism and drove him to become like Blake a "mythologer of bourgeois revolution"; he did so, however, by creating "massive symbolic totalities" that mystified his bourgeois purpose (*CI* 153). His characteristic gesture—the poetic mask—belongs to one of these symbolic totalities. It simulates "the organic unity of personal identity and social function" that western bourgeois society had just destroyed and it shares in the same ideological pressures that impelled Yeats to "restore the organic unity of Irish society" and flirt with the corporate "political mould of fascism" (*CI* 153, 154). In sum, for Eagleton the forms of Yeats's modernism are no more conflicted than they were for Ransom or Blackmur, nor does he wish to deemphasize the importance of Yeatsian tradition. And tellingly he views the Yeatsian doctrine of the mask not as a device employed to include antagonistic values but as a way of converting competition into totality.

W. J. McCormack's *Ascendancy and Tradition in Anglo-Irish Literary History from 1789 to 1939* (1985)[14] is a good example of how Marxist work of the last ten years has responded to the implicit weaknesses of Eagleton's abstractions even as it continues to rely on relatively naive notions of modernist form. McCormack's is a long and impressive book that takes as its subject Ireland since 1789, and I cannot hope to respond here to all of it. (It argues, for example, that the tendency to idealize the eighteenth-century Irish Protestant Ascendancy that we ordinarily associate with Yeats was in fact common to a large segment of the nineteenth-century Irish middle class, and that here and elsewhere Yeats was conditioned by his historical situation far more than he would have us

---

14. W. J. McCormack, *Ascendancy and Tradition in Anglo-Irish Literary History from 1789 to 1939* (Oxford: Oxford University Press, 1985). Hereafter cited in the text as *AT.*

believe.) What concerns me especially is McCormack's concluding dis-
cussion of the way Yeats's *Purgatory* reveals the values of modernism, a
discussion which explicitly denies that the critic "has gone over to the
view that all literature is ideology and not more" (*A T* 400).

Following Donald Torchiana,[15] McCormack asserts that *Purgatory*
incorporates the political unpleasantness of Yeats's late social criticism
and integrates "much that had appeared casual in Yeats's prose" (*A T*
371). But McCormack also makes a stronger claim—that the play's
"source *and style* . . . combine most effectively to point to the nine-
teenth-century origins of that historical movement which reached its
apotheosis in European fascism" (*A T* 372, emphasis mine). As far as I
can untangle it, his account of the ideological implications of *Purgatory's*
style (it is clear he also has in mind its form and structure) proceeds like
this. McCormack first notices that Yeats alters his sources and that the
play reorients the Old Man's motivation "by the deliberate elimination
of the psychological rationale of [his] drunken fury—his suspicion that
[his son is in fact] not his." For this Yeats substitutes attitudes rooted in
"class hatred" (*A T* 371)—i.e., the Old Man's desire to end the degrading
social consequences of his mother's misalliance by killing his father and
son. McCormack then links Yeats's decision, which makes it harder to
distinguish the Old Man's distress from his mother's, to a structural
decision to conflate the Old Man's story with his mother's, a formal
strategy in which morally comparable actions at different times are pre-
sented simultaneously. In McCormack's view, both decisions are related
to the way the play simplifies the Old Man's house into a metaphor for
his experience, and to the way Yeats's syntax achieves the "effect of
drawing past and present, event and re-enactment, into a single image by
the elision" of ambiguous connectives (*A T* 386). All, he suggests, com-
bine to idealize the historical roots of a class hatred which we would
recognize as the play's major theme if it weren't for the obfuscations of
the conflated stories. In fact, McCormack argues, the modernist's ide-
alistic romantic philosophy of history is at the heart of his "preference for
synchronic order at the expense of diachronic logic" (*A T* 391). Wishing
away the real dynamics of history, the modernist creates works like
Purgatory in which cause and effect disappear and events are arranged

---

15. See Donald Torchiana, *Yeats and Georgian Ireland* (Evanston: Northwestern Uni-
versity Press, 1966), 344–52.

under the aspect of eternity. Thus bad faith is at the heart of "an aesthetic justifying the text as autonomous" (*AT* 378).

McCormack's last claim is that the text of *Purgatory* finally reacts to its own false consciousness and, transcending its modernist form, rises from fascism pure and simple to "critical fascism" (*AT* 399). The play ends after the Old Man murders his son in what McCormack reads as a ritual moment of social purification. It is at that point that his final words call out to God for his mother's release and his own. In these final lines, McCormack argues, the Old Man realizes the futility of his judgments and the text breaks out of the false structure in which these judgments are founded: "Those final lines are seen," he insists, "as a cry of despair from within the self-regulating modernist art-work, an appeal for release from the sovereignty of the text" (*AT* 379). *Purgatory* thus becomes a herald of its own postmodernist critique.

The problem with McCormack's reading of *Purgatory*, and with the notions of modernism embedded in it, is that they don't fit the play we see emerging from Yeats's drafts. Sandra F. Siegel's 1986 edition of the *Purgatory* manuscripts[16] makes it clear that although Yeats did originally saturate the play in the kind of hatred for the Irish middle class that colors "On the Boiler," the essay he paired it with, he soon complicated his theme. Subsequent to his initial scenario, for example, what had been an endorsement of the Old Man's social attitudes changed considerably as Yeats overlayed it with a strong dose of revulsion. Where in the scenario a stage direction exonerates the Old Man's murder/euthanasia of his son by showing the boy "[submit] to the authority of his father and willingly [offer] himself as though in ritual," in succeeding drafts starting with the first verse version it is clear that the Old Man murders his son "neither to purify the house, nor to save his mother's soul, nor to terminate the lineage polluted by an evil curse" (*PM* 6). Instead Yeats subjects the Old Man to increasing irony as revision after revision diminishes his level of self-knowledge and calls his professions of outrage over the moral and social decline of his family into question. Siegel concludes that "as Yeats presents the Old Man in the final version, his moral rage, so strongly directed in the first half of the play toward the purification of the great house, subsides in the second half as his lust is directed toward the

---

16. W. B. Yeats, *Purgatory: Manuscript Materials including the Author's Final Text*, ed. Sandra F. Siegel (Ithaca: Cornell University Press, 1986). Hereafter cited in the text as *PM*.

mother. The themes interlock as though to account for and provoke one another." And so, she adds, the finished play "dramatizes two conflicting impulses in the Old Man, who understands both but fails to recognize that they conflict with one another" (*PM* 12–13). Her evidence thus leads to a view of both the theme and the structure of the play diametrically opposed to McCormack's but consonant with the one Helen Vendler provides in *Yeats's Vision and the Later Plays*. Far from supporting the Old Man's antidemocratic impulses in any simple way, Vendler writes, the play from the beginning undermines them. As it nears its end, Yeats makes us understand that "the Old Man's proper function is to forgive his mother and father since the real consequence in him is his mad hatred of them both, not the coarse son he has begotten. In killing his son, he is intensifying the consequences of his mother's action, rather than abrogating them." And the Old Man's final appeal to God, rather than being a postmodernist gesture destroying the modernist symmetries and the fascist judgments of the play he has directed, is, again to quote Vendler, a cry "of frustration and incomprehension, as the Old Man discovers that lashing out at the world cannot cure an inner evil."[17]

Nor does the refutation of McCormack implicit in the *Purgatory* manuscripts end there. The Siegel edition goes on to suggest that not only may interpretations of the play based on its connection to "On the Boiler" be inadequate, but that there is something insufficient about too righteous a revulsion from the essay itself. The drafts, Siegel notes, show that while Yeats did explicitly link the two together, "in the process of revising the play, he continued to revise the essay." And she explains that "those revisions, of the play and also of the essay, seem to have had the effect of modifying the argument he proposed in the early drafts of both. If Yeats had revised neither the play nor the essay, it would probably be fair to say that *Purgatory* is the animation of his conservative beliefs about eugenic reform. The final versions of *Purgatory* and 'On the Boiler,' however, allow for a different reading" (*PM* 13).

As ugly as passages in *Purgatory* can appear, therefore, it is clearly improper to identify its form with a consistent ideology. The play dramatizes the conflicting intellectual positions of its author, and, as in most of Yeats's work, its essential power flows out of that very real intellectual drama. In *Purgatory,* Siegel tells us, "Yeats advances an argument and

---

17. Helen Hennessy Vendler, *Yeats's Vision and the Later Plays* (Cambridge: Harvard University Press, 1963), 200–201.

then proceeds to devalue or repudiate the view he seemed to uphold. He thus asserts both his convictions and his doubts" (PM 20). And yet, no less than New Critics far cruder than Blackmur, both Eagleton and McCormack contrive to mistake one facet of that dialectic for the whole, overlooking the radical and pervasive skepticism which was always a component of the modernists' conflicted philosophical program. As the searching scholarly studies of Sanford Schwartz and Michael Levenson have recently shown, modernism harbored more and not fewer contradictions than its proponents suggested.[18] Their conclusions, along with the brief analyses above, urge us now to return, not to the speculations about modernism and politics Frank Kermode advanced twenty years ago, but to Kermode's second thoughts. For even as he pointed to the unfortunate moments when the modernists aesthetisized politics, Kermode maintained that their best work was founded in continuous self-qualification. Yeats especially, he insisted, was "at bottom . . . sceptical about the nonsense with which he satisfied what we can call his lust for commitment. Now and again he believed some of it, but in so far as his true commitment was to poetry he recognized his fictions as heuristic and dispensable, 'consciously false.' . . . [Indeed,] the whole history of Yeats's style, which from earliest times, before the turn of the century, he was trying to move towards colloquial uncertainty, reflects [a] regard for the reality that will not be reduced" (SE 104, 106).

18. See Sanford Schwartz, The Matrix of Modernism: Pound, Eliot and Early Twentieth-Century Thought (Princeton: Princeton University Press, 1985), and Michael H. Levenson, A Genealogy of Modernism: A Study of English Literary Doctrine 1908–1922 (Cambridge: Cambridge University Press, 1984).

Into the Tradition: W. B. Yeats and Michael J. Murphy

KEITH CUNNINGHAM

The blurb on the back cover of Michael J. Murphy's *Tyrone Folk Quest* reads: "His story . . . will, I feel certain, become a classic of our literature."[1] Even granting that the nature and purpose of blurbs is such that they require heavy discounting, the statement is a rather sweeping claim to make about a literature which includes W. B. Yeats. Page nine of *Tyrone Folk Quest* incorporates an excerpt from a letter introduced by Murphy's statement that he had been thrilled to receive it:

> I have read your article . . . and I think we . . . share many thoughts, though you are young and I am so old and tired. I understand so well how some little thing like your head of shot grain can evoke a dream more vivid than what we sometimes call reality, and take one into the World where Time is not and you have the rare power of describing it. . . ."

The letter so introduced was from Maud Gonne MacBride, and linking Yeats and Murphy is not as farfetched as it might first appear. Brunvand observed, "Collected folklore texts . . . are of little use . . . until identified by category . . . or published."[2] For folklore to be of use, field observations must be translated into written form: dry bones must be covered with flesh. Both Yeats and Murphy were Irish writers who admired, and were in turn admired by, Maud Gonne, though one knew her when she was young and the other when she was old. Her description could as well refer to Yeats as to Murphy; her words serve to yoke the two together. Their definitions of folklore, their methods of present-

---

1. Michael J. Murphy, *Tyrone Folk Quest* (Belfast: Blackstaff, 1973). Hereafter cited in the text as Murphy.

2. Jan Harold Brunvand, *The Study of American Folklore: An Introduction*, 2d ed. (New York: Norton, 1978), 16. Hereafter cited in the text as Brunvand.

ing it, and their concepts of its uses evoke "a World where Time is not"; certainly they share a rare power of translating the hidden Ireland from their fieldwork to their written words.

Defining the field is an on-going, ever changing, constant brouhaha in folklore. Brunvand divides folklore research into two camps:

> From the humanistic point of view folklore research has tended to emphasize the "lore," usually taking a literary approach to the recorded "text" of verbal traditions; from the social science point of view folklore research has emphasized the "folk," taking an anthropological approach to the full cultural significance of traditions. (Brunvand 11)

However, a third possibility exists which seems to be particularly common among the Irish and certainly was found in Yeats and Murphy. Of course, the two men's views of folklore differ in important aspects. Murphy knew and employed O'Sullivan's 600-page *Handbook of Irish Folklore* (Murphy 81) and made distinctions between material in Community and Historical categories (Murphy 34) which probably would have infuriated Yeats. Murphy did a great deal of collecting of customary folklore (and material culture); Yeats certainly acknowledged the former genre (noting that the majority of the Irish peasants "still are adverse to sitting down to dine thirteen at table, or being helped to salt, or walking under a ladder"[3]), but almost completely ignored the later form. Both men, however, perceived folklore in Jungian terms.

In describing folklore collecting Yeats wrote:

> You must go adroitly to work, and make friends with the children, and the old men, with those who have not felt the pressure of mere daylight existence, and those with whom it is growing less, and will have altogether taken itself off one of these days. (*Tales* 4)

In describing folklore collecting Murphy wrote:

> He has to win the confidence of people adroitly, and patiently be able to ask them to confess to a knowledge which . . . can bring

---

3. W. B. Yeats, *Fairy and Folk Tales of Ireland* (1888; rpt. with *Irish Fairy Tales,* New York: Macmillan, 1973), 4. Hereafter cited in the text as *Tales.*

down . . . wrath. . . . He wants . . . their very thoughts and at-
titudes . . . as far back as the human memory can reach. . . . (Mur-
phy 16)

Murphy further said of that reach, "the folk mind . . . is still an astound-
ing survival of ideas and racial memories retained in depth and detail and
approach" (Murphy 17).

Yeats lovingly described Paddy Flynn smiling in his sleep and wrote,
"Assuredly some joy not quite of this steadfast earth lightens in those
eyes . . ." (*Tales* 9). Murphy described his experiences in Glenhull as
"eluding the smother of Time" and further described his informant
Francis McBride's self-predicted death: "There was something so impon-
derable about the passing of this man that it impeded thought. . . .
Something unanalytical still . . ." (Murphy 68, 90). Jung's description,
"Such a consciousness would see the becoming and passing away of
things simultaneously with their momentary existence in the present, and
not only that, it would also see what was before their becoming and will be
after their passing hence,"[4] describes Yeats's Paddy Flynn, Murphy's
Francis McBride, and the two folklorists' implicit definition of folklore as
"the World where Time is not." Murphy and Yeats thus defined folklore
in neither humanistic nor social science terms, but in terms of Jungian
psychoanalytic theory (Yeats before Jung, Murphy after both) and saw it
neither as text nor cultural artifact, but as, in Murphy's words, "the
seminal strains fundamental to the essential philosophy of the people"
(Murphy 10) or as manifestations of the Other as it continually revealed
itself in becomings and passings.

Just as they shared a basically Jungian concept of folklore, so Yeats
and Murphy shared similar views of how the Other could best be col-
lected and should best be translated. Yeats railed against what he called
folklore science and equated it with collectors who had "tabulated all
their tales in forms like grocers' bills" rather than having "caught the
very voice of the people, the pulse of life." Murphy too, in Yeats's
words, wished to tell "of the Irish peasantry rather than of the primitive
religion of mankind, or whatever else the folk-lorists are on the gad
after" (*Tales* 6). He, for example, concluded his telling of a story in

---

4. C. G. Jung, *Psychological Types,* vol. 20 in *The Collected Works of C. G. Jung,* ed. Sir
Herbert Read, Michael Fordham, Gerhard Adler, and William McGuire (Princeton: Prince-
ton University Press, 1971), 395.

which one of his informants gently, almost absentmindedly, told him
"My woman died just at 2.00 o'clock," with the observation that "this,
anyway, was folklore as valid as McCullagh's story of Cromwell and the
Irish dead" (Murphy 60).

Their shared emphasis on the folk in folklore apparently led Yeats
and Murphy to a similar emphasis on the importance of describing infor-
mants, contextual situations, and performance characteristics (though
the latter two terms became current in folklore scholarship after both of
them had done their major collecting). Yeats's portraits of Paddy Flynn
and Old Biddy Hart (*Tales* 5–6, 302–3) are masterpieces. Murphy specif-
ically stated that the purpose of *Tyrone Folk Quest* was "to deal mainly
with the storytellers," and he was correct when he concluded his book
with the assertion that the folk voices he had described will "now live
forever" (Murphy 5, 95). Because of Murphy's success, Francis Daniel
and Peter Pat Roe, Irishmen who would otherwise have remained un-
known, have joined a select group of people (including Yeats's Paddy
Flynn and Old Biddy Hart, Dorson's J. D. Suggs, and Lomax's Dink[5])
whose performances and personalities have been presented so vividly
that they persist beyond becoming and passing. Only rarely can human
beings translate the unknown to the known and by so doing bestow
immortality; Yeats and Murphy are among the few who have done so.

Yeats and Murphy also shared a surprisingly modern view of the
importance of presenting the far too often unknown collector (them-
selves) as a vital part of the collecting process. This ideal, presented
perhaps most persuasively in *People Studying People* by Georges and
Jones,[6] is very similar to Donoghue's description of Yeats's theories and
practices concerning autobiography:

> The Autobiography required not merely an act of memory on
> Yeats's part, but an approach to the meaning of the lives it recited,
> not least his own. . . . He does not scorn the private life, but he
> assumes that the available meaning of a man's life is the relation
> between that life and the society which, in part, it defines. (Mem 9–
> 10)

---

5. Richard M. Dorson, *American Negro Folktales* (Greenwich, Conn.: Fawcett, 1967),
59–64; John A. Lomax and Alan Lomax, *Folksong USA: 111 Best American Ballads,* ed. Alan
Lomax (New York: Duell, Sloan & Pearce, 1947), 39–40.

6. Robert A. Georges and Michael O. Jones, *People Studying People: The Human
Element in Fieldwork* (Berkeley: University of California Press, 1980).

Similarly, Murphy explained that a central purpose of *Tyrone Folk Quest*
was to give his and his wife's "own reaction to these people" (Murphy
5), and he, as an Irish collector of almost forgotten Irish lore, is a central
figure in his book.

More significant in making Murphy's book "a classic in our liter-
ature" and a worthy companion to Yeats's works is that both men not
only saw folklore as "a World where Time is not" and themselves and
their informants as important parts of this largely unknown oral Irish
world to be recorded and translated as accurately as possible, but also
shared "a rare power of describing it." Ronsley claims that Yeats's auto-
biography "evinces more the imaginative artist than the disinterested
biographer," and proves his claim by noting the book's unity, use of
dialogue, occasional insertion of verse, metaphors, scenes of "poignant
confrontation," sudden shifts from past to present tense, and sudden
shifts in atmosphere and tone.[7] All of these characteristics are a part of
Yeats's folklore writing as well as his autobiographical writing, and all,
except the insertion of verse, are also evinced in *Tyrone Folk Quest*.

Tyrone Folk Quest begins with Murphy and his family going to
County Tyrone for two years and ends with his making a return visit to
the area twelve years after his stay there. The apparent chronological
structure, however, is illusionary. Murphy reported that he had written
over a million words recording Tyrone folklore and had in addition kept a
daily journal during the two-year period he was there (Murphy 5, 88). His
use of this mass of material to produce a 95-page book shows the same
attitude toward experience and literature which characterizes Yeats's auto-
biography, and the book's unity is a tribute to his literary skills. " 'You
couldn't,' says Francis, as more snow began to fall, 'be of service to this
man. He's a man after folklore if you know what that means from the
University of Dublin' " (Murphy 86). As Ronsley says of Yeats, Murphy
used a great deal of dialogue, and he used it to good effect.

Unlike Yeats, Murphy rarely introduced verse into *Tyrone Folk
Quest;* his use of short traditional narratives is, however, structurally
similar to Yeats's use of verse, occurs even more frequently, and involves
well-chosen, well-told tales which reveal hidden character and culture
indirectly and succinctly, "where such articles as flails for threshing ex-
isted alongside threshing-mills drawn by steam traction-engines":

---

7. Joseph Ronsley, *Yeats's Autobiography: Life as Symbolic Pattern* (Cambridge, Mass.:
Harvard University Press, 1968), 4.

McBride asked the engineer in charge when the new bridge would be open as his own thresher was isolated. . . . So the work was rushed and the heads of the contracting firm from Derry came to watch McBride drive his thresher over the new bridge. . . .

Of course McBride calmly walked back over the new bridge with an old flail under his arm. . . . (Murphy 50)

Metaphor appears as frequently and as naturally in Murphy's writing as in Yeats's. For example, Murphy described Glenhull "as a green inkwell in the misshapen desks of the foothills of the Sperrins" and spoke of "a road like an old hat-band sliding up the crown" (Murphy 18, 46).

Murphy, like Yeats, included numerous poignant scenes where he and those from whom he collected confronted becoming and passing.

I chatted, then rose to go. He seemed disappointed because I had not got on to folklore. He began to tell a long piece of narration and was clearly tiring himself. I tried to stop him, said I would call again when he was better.

He said: "Sit and ask me whatever you want. I don't want to take anything of value to you or to anyone coming after away with me. Sit and ask me your fill: for I'm ploughing the head-rig anymore."

The head-rig of a field is the last to be ploughed: he was likening the life-span to a field. He knew his own was shortly to be finished. I sat and listened and wrote. (Murphy 51–52)

In an amusing story about one of his neighbors, who assumed Murphy was a tinker or worse and offered him a job as a manual laborer, Murphy ended with the comment:

I knew he was worried about possible local reaction in gossip to his blunder. When he left I saw him to the road. He apologised repeatedly and profusely and begged me not to mention the incident to anyone, as I knew he would. Until now I never had. (Murphy 22)

This ending is but one of the many examples in *Tyrone Folk Quest* of the sudden shift from past to present tense comparable to what Ronsley describes as a part of Yeats's artistry.

The last characteristic Ronsley mentions as a part of Yeats's literary skill is his use of sudden and dramatic shifts in atmosphere and tone. In

the same tradition Murphy ended chapter 26 with a one-sentence para-
graph announcing that his son had fallen down and split his head and
then devoted chapter 27 to the telling of an anecdote concerning mis-
taken identity. *Tyrone Folk Quest* contains many such sudden shifts in
atmosphere and tone.

The overall impression which emerges from comparing Yeats's and
Murphy's writing is that they both had a rare power of describing the
"World where Time is not" and of translating fieldwork to literature.
Their emphasis on the literary dimensions of collecting and presenting
folklore might well be an outgrowth of their common idea of the proper
use of folklore. F. S. L. Lyons seems to have been summarizing schol-
arship concerning Yeats when he wrote that "Yeats . . . shared the pas-
sionate belief that it would be possible so to use the rich resources of Irish
fairy-tale and folklore and heroic legend to create an Irish literature."[8]
Yeats's use of Irish literature in his own work is well-known. Murphy also
used folklore for literature. *Tyrone Folk Quest* mentioned the "evocative
prose poems," one of which inspired Gonne's letter, a short story attribut-
ing a malfunctioning chimney to the cutting of a fairy thorn, and a play
which was set "against the familiar rural forces" (Murphy 9, 35, 38).

In addition to viewing folklore as a valuable source for their own
writing and for a national literature, Yeats and Murphy both seem to have
been concerned with a responsibility to present the hidden Irish "World
where Time is not" to the Irish. In his introduction to *The Celtic Twilight*
Yeats wrote, "I have desired . . . to create a little world . . . and to show
in a vision something of the face of Ireland to any of my own people who
would look where I bid them" (Myth 1). His purpose, in other words, was
to go into the tradition and translate the hidden Irish experience into Irish
literature, making the hidden intelligible to the Irish. I think Murphy
would agree with this purpose.

Yeats and Murphy were linked by their Jungian view of folklore as
the "World where Time is not"; by their complex, and thoroughly mod-
ern, ideas as to how it, the people who performed it, and those who
collected it should be presented; and by their concepts of its uses. Mur-
phy defined folklore in *Tyrone Folk Quest* as "working in the present on
products and presentation of the past for purposes of the future" (Mur-
phy 75). I think Yeats would agree.

---

8. F. S. L. Lyons, "Yeats and the Anglo-Irish Twilight," *Irish Culture and Na-
tionalism, 1750–1950*, ed. Oliver MacDonagh, W. F. Mandle, and Pauric Travers (New
York: St. Martin's, 1983), 214–15.

Questions of Syntax, Syntax of Questions: Yeats and the Topology of Passion

RALPH HARDING EARLE

Although Yeats rarely discussed his processes of poetic composition, one statement on his attitude toward syntax has become relatively well-known: looking back on his career in the mid-1930s he stated "I discovered that I must seek, not as Wordsworth thought, words in common use, but a powerful and passionate syntax" (E&I 521–22). It is difficult to say precisely what Yeats meant by *passion,* or even by *syntax* in this context, but a systematic look at enough examples of his syntax will show the extraordinary qualities it is capable of bringing to his poetry. The power, effectiveness, and vitality of Yeats's syntax create for it a unique position in Yeats's system of poetics, and these qualities can easily be seen as the passion of which he spoke.

Rather than focus on the subjective effects of Yeats's syntax, for which it suffices simply to express admiration, the current study addresses the specific syntactic techniques that give rise to such effects. In this respect, the objective surface of the poem takes precedence over the subjective heights the poem attains. Because it structures the poetic surface by positioning words and images to generate passionate effects, syntax can be considered "the topology of passion."

Many critics—Ellmann, Parkinson, and Davie to name a few—have discussed the general implications of the phrase "powerful and passionate syntax" and some have examined the syntax of particular poems. But, with few exceptions, such studies run to general observations or single issues, and have rarely taken a comprehensive look at the details of Yeats's syntactic practice. The current study examines "passionate syntax" throughout Yeats's lyrical poetry, and assesses the importance of syntax in Yeats's overall system of poetics.

That syntactic ordering of meaning simultaneously creates new meaning has long been understood by linguistic theorists: Traugott and Pratt assert that syntax "does a great deal to support meanings, and sometimes even helps create them, especially when a sense of contrasts between appearance and reality is at issue."[1] According to Winifred Nowottny, a more specifically literary linguist,

> Syntax, however little it is noted by the reader, is the groundwork of the poet's art. . . . When a passage relies chiefly on its especially compelling and artful syntax to make its effect, the reader and the critics, who never expect syntax to be more than "a harmless, necessary drudge" holding open the door while the pageantry of words sweeps through, will be at a loss to understand why a passage affects them as it does and at a loss to do critical justice to its art.[2]

By carefully examining the syntax in enough examples of Yeats's poetry, we should attain a position from which to do "critical justice" to Yeats the poetic craftsman.

Thomas Parkinson devotes a full chapter of *Yeats: The Later Poetry* to the question of Yeatsian syntax.[3] His concern is mainly with the general effects of "passionate syntax" rather than with its specific mechanics. He reconstructs Yeats's personal views on syntax, a subject on which he concludes that Yeats was as taciturn as he was on all aspects of his personal composition process. Parkinson offers the following quotation from an unpublished manuscript among Yeats's papers to emphasize Yeats's concern with finding the right syntax: "We tolerate, or enjoy an artificial syntax and a rhythm that is neither speech, nor anything suggesting a song because our thought is artificial" (Parkinson 185). Parkinson argues that Yeats was working from intention rather than theory: he intended that his syntax esthetically reproduce the rhythms of thought, rather than literally mimic those rhythms. In other words, Yeats intended a syntax that is powerful and passionate, yet natural-sounding.

Yeats's unique contribution lies in his great syntactic virtuosity, so that although his syntax remains within the bounds of the acceptable, it achieves an uncommonly wide variety of effects. Perhaps the most striking feature of Yeats's syntax is his unusually long sentences. Stanza-long

---

1. Elizabeth Closs Traugott and Mary Louise Pratt, *Linguistics for Students of Literature* (New York: Harcourt Brace Jovanovich, 1980), 177. Hereafter cited in the text as Traugott and Pratt.

2. Winifred Nowottny, *The Language Poets Use* (New York: Oxford University Press, 1962), 10. Hereafter cited in the text as Nowottny.

3. Thomas Parkinson, *W. B. Yeats: The Later Poetry* (Berkeley: University of California Press, 1971), 181–231. Hereafter cited in the text as Parkinson.

sentences frequently occur. "Among School Children" contains sixty-four lines, but only eleven sentences. This seems to have been a characteristic from the start: the opening sentence of *Crossways* runs to ten lines and sixty-four words.

Such long sentences create a complex textual framework for the interplay of Yeats's other syntactic devices, providing ample room for the manipulation of word- and phrase-order that is the hallmark of his syntactic practice. Of course Yeats did not use long sentences exclusively: much of the effectiveness of the first stanza of "Sailing to Byzantium" rests in the contrast between the bold seven-word statement that opens the poem—"That is no country for old men" (P 193)—and the thirty-seven-word elaboration that follows, a sentence in which Yeats amply displays his virtuosity.

Many of Yeats's long sentences take the form of questions. The Lyrical section of *The Poems* contains over 300 questions in its 374 poems. This unusual frequency of questions, and particularly rhetorical questions, makes it necessary to consider the interrogative sentence structure itself as one of Yeats's habitual syntactic strategies.

While much Yeatsian syntax is unique and specific to individual poems, Yeats also tends to return time and again to certain fixed strategies. His syntax is by no means limited by these strategies or effects; rather they represent the core of his sense of syntax. The great virtue of his using syntax as a prosodic strategy lies in the breadth of possibility it makes available to him.

Yeats's syntactic strategies operate principally on the level of the sentence, affecting the order of major clausal and phrasal units. These strategies include the devices known as parataxis, hypotaxis, parallelism, and transposition. In addition Yeats frequently uses a number of more specific devices that cannot easily be categorized. One of these is the absolute construction, rare in the language as a whole, which occurs in some of his most memorable poems, such as "Among School Children," "The Second Coming," and "The Tower."

A related device centers on the technique known as enjambment. By playing the syntactic speech unit against the poetic verse unit, Yeats achieves an effect which Adelyn Dougherty has named *Speech-Unit Crossover.*[4]

---

4. Adelyn Dougherty, " 'Traditional Metres' and 'Passionate Syntax' in the Verse of William Butler Yeats," *Language and Style* 14.3 (Summer 1981): 17–18. Hereafter cited in the text as Dougherty.

Yeats often achieves similar effects through dissimilar devices; principal among these effects are ambiguity and compression. Ambiguity occurs on the level of word and phrase through what Joseph Adams has called the *Syntactic Mask,* and on the level of sentence by ambiguously-determined hypotaxis. Compression comes about through the use of absolute constructions and can also occur through omission and through certain forms of parallelism.

Since Yeatsian syntax is characterized by flexibility, fluidity, and variation, many of its strategies defy categorization. They can be enormously effective in context but impossible to generalize to any other situation. Naturally it would be fruitless to enumerate these variations; it is better to discuss them as they come up, and allow the specific examples to convey a feeling for the whole.

Perhaps the most pervasive of Yeats's specific syntactic devices is his manipulation of hypotaxis. According to linguistic theory, one of the most important ideational functions of syntax is to express connections and cohesiveness (Traugott and Pratt 169). Syntax often accomplishes this by means of subordination, in other words by ranking ideas within a sentence in terms of their relative importance, expressing them in clauses governed by connective words such as relative pronouns and subordinate conjunctions, which assert the relationship between the main idea of the sentence and the lesser ones. In classical rhetoric, this use of syntax is referred to as hypotaxis. It contrasts with parataxis, the sort of syntax we are familiar with in such material as *Beowulf,* in which sentence connectives rarely express the relationship of ideas. Parataxis generally consists of short, simple sentences or at most the use of the coordinate conjunctions, in particular *and.*

Interestingly, Yeats was a master of both styles. Although his habitually long sentences lent themselves to the syntactic convolutions of hypotaxis, he also structured many poems around simple clauses linked by coordinating conjunctions, particularly in the early stages of his career. These poems tend to be drawn from the folk material that interested him so much; they tend to take the ballad structure, and to be spoken by such homespun dramatic personae as Moll Magee, Father Gilligan, and the Fiddler of Dooney. Yeats maintained an interest in this variant of folk poetry throughout his career, and the late "Crazy Jane" sequence provides some of his most memorable poetry:

> I met the Bishop on the road
> And much said he and I.

'Those breasts are flat and fallen now,
Those veins must soon be dry;
Live in a heavenly mansion,
Not in some foul sty.'

(P 259)

Perhaps the ballad tradition or the unlettered personae require parataxis; perhaps this is Yeats's most sincere effort to live up to his often-cited claim that "I tried to make the language of poetry coincide with passionate, normal speech" (E&I 521).

When the persona is a literate man such as Michael Robartes, Raymond Lully, or some more obvious version of the poet himself, the syntax tends to hypotaxis. Pursuing the subject of "passionate, normal speech," Yeats claims that "I wanted to write in whatever language comes most naturally when we soliloquise, as I do all day long, upon the events of our lives or of any life where we can see ourselves for the moment" (E&I 521). The language is certainly that of soliloquy, but it is hard to accept as entirely natural; perhaps such creative hypotaxis comes most naturally only to people who, like Yeats, have dedicated much of their lives to the range of possibilities inherent in language.

The conscious literary use of hypotaxis is by no means unique to Yeats; as one of his links with the English poetic tradition, it sets his style, like Joyce's, apart from fellow modernists such as Hemingway and Stein. Creative hypotaxis permeates Yeats's poetry and achieves many different effects, depending on its ideational and prosodic contexts.

An untitled sonnet from *Responsibilities* demonstrates Yeatsian hypotaxis in a vivid and elegant manner. In it, Yeats succeeds at combining a full command of the structure with a full command of the syntax it contains. Richard Ellmann remarks:

Because his postures are never still, because his dignity suits him well and is always passionately provoked, Yeats is able to carry off fairly successfully even a *tour de force* like the concluding poem of the *Responsibilities* volume (1914), where he writes a fourteen-line poem in only one long, suspended sentence.[5]

---

5. Richard Ellmann, *The Identity of Yeats*, 2d ed. (London: Faber, 1964), 141–42; hereafter cited in the text as Ellmann. The original is italicized and serves with the opening "Pardon, old fathers . . ." as a frame for the volume. As this does not affect the analysis of the poem, I take the liberty of dispensing with it.

If the poem were not somewhat more vague and more personal than is common with Yeats, it would be better known:

> While I, from that reed-throated whisperer
> Who comes at need, although not now as once
> A clear articulation in the air,
> But inwardly, surmise companions
> Beyond the fling of the dull ass's hoof,
> —Ben Jonson's phrase—and find when June is come
> At Kyle-na-no under the ancient roof
> A sterner conscience and a friendlier home,
> I can forgive even that wrong of wrongs,
> Those undreamt accidents that have made me
> —Seeing that Fame has perished this long while,
> Being but a part of ancient ceremony—
> Notorious, till all my priceless things
> Are but a post the passing dogs defile.

                                                        (P 128)

The poem turns on the contrast between restful artistic fulfillment at Lady Gregory's Coole Park (Kyle-na-no) and the vicissitudes of the public life. Its basic argument can be paraphrased as follows:

> While I surmise loftier companions and find at Coole Park a sterner conscience and a friendlier home, I can forgive even those accidents that have made me notorious.

Although the single long sentence is based around a simple subject and verb ("I can forgive"), it contains several levels of subordination. Chief among these is the opening adverbial clause: "While I . . . surmise companions . . . and find . . . a conscience. . . ." Each of the two verbs governs one additional dependent clause ("who comes at need," "when June is come"). However, in typical fashion Yeats varies this hypotactical parallelism by allowing one of the subordinate clauses direct access to its governing verb while burying the other in a forest of prepositional phrases. Because the *while* clause ends with the eighth line, the poem's formal turn is also a syntactic turn. The apparent syntactic wildness of the opening lines is reined in by structure.

Line nine contains the crux of the poem, and fittingly the syntax comes into clearest focus here. But this clarity evolves out of complexity and dissolves again into complexity. It stands midway between the sub-

ordinated inner complexity of artistic inspiration and the outer complex-
ity, also subordinated, of the "notorious" poet's relationship with the
"passing dogs" of society.

Syntactically, the last five lines are simply an appositive that serves
to amplify "that wrong of wrongs" in line nine. However, in the elabo-
rate hypotaxis that Yeats develops out of "Those undreamt accidents"
lies much of the poem's power and nuance. Although his concern is with
those accidents that have made him notorious, subordination and trans-
position deemphasize that notoriety. Of course, he would rather have
become famous, but "Fame has perished this long while, / Being but a
part of ancient ceremony." By transposing this subordinate adverbial
clause to its unusual position between the direct object *me* and its requi-
site adjective *notorious,* he syntactically emphasizes the absence of fame
and underplays the presence of notoriety. This paves the way for a final
hypotactical flourish: the closing "passing dogs" clause is dependent on
the adjective "notorious," which itself is embedded in a previous depen-
dent clause. Thus the poem closes with a deeply subordinate, and there-
by deemphasized thought. The syntax emphasizes the forgiveness fea-
tured in the main clause. However, the closing couplet of a sonnet holds
a strong formal position, which allows the defiling dogs to achieve a
maximum impact even as Yeats dissociates himself from them syntac-
tically. The net effect is a vivid and memorable, if somewhat discourag-
ing, impression of what the poet is up against.

Written during Yeats's tenure at the Abbey Theatre, this poem is an
early example of his mature mastery over syntax. Therein lies a criticism:
the syntax calls attention to itself to such a degree that the actual subject
matter shrinks in importance and the poem is of interest *chiefly* as a
syntactic *tour de force.* Unlike later poems in which form, syntax, and
meaning are carefully balanced, this one sacrifices comprehensibility in
the interests of a form/syntax blend.

At certain points, however, the relative incomprehensibility gener-
ated by syntax can serve the poet well: for example, the "reed-throated
whisperer's" visits are described in three parallel adverbials: "who comes
at need, although not now as once / A clear articulation in the air, / But
inwardly." The parallelism is obvious between the prepositional phrase
at need, and the adverb *inwardly.* However, these are separated by "Al-
though not now as once / A clear articulation in the air." The precise
syntactic denotation (or in this case detonation) is ambiguous, though it
can plausibly be considered an adverbial clause compressed by elimina-

tion of the redundant subject/verb "it comes." The negativity of "not now" creates a disequilibrium that parallels the sense of loss Yeats is evoking, leading up to the straightforward adverb *inwardly* that not only resolves the parallel syntax, but also reconciles the poet to the shift in inspiration from external to internal. Yeats frequently employs syntax to create such ambiguity, though in many cases the ambiguity cannot be resolved within the context of the poem, as it can here.

Ambiguity of this sort can be created by many syntactic means, as demonstrated by Joseph Adams in *Yeats and the Masks of Syntax*. To Adams, a syntactic mask is a unit that is deliberately syntactically ambiguous, so that no single interpretation can dominate:

> It is as if the dominant meaning in one of Jakobson's multi-layered structures becomes unanchored and all the parts, both forms and meanings, are then free to combine and disperse. Form and meaning in the syntactic masks exhibit precisely this kind of disarticulation and play. A mask most often appears as a syntactic ambiguity, but as one having little to do with enriching the global interpretation of the poem where it occurs. The important thing about the ambiguity of the syntactic mask is that it is more or less unresolvable, so much so that an oscillation is set up between its alternative possibilities. With neither syntactic form becoming fully possible, no final meaning can be assigned. Form and meaning thus become radically dislodged from one another. Moreover, made up as they are of competing alternative forms, the syntactic masks never become integrated as complete syntactic units. In fact, they violate the very rules that normally allow a decision to be made as to the identity of a syntactic unit.[6]

Although Adams discusses longer, clausal structures in the later portions of his study, he spends much time on the ambiguity of single words, such as *that* used in the relative sense and the definite article used in a sense somewhere between anaphoric and situational. For example, he argues that the opening line of "Among School Children"—"I walk through the long schoolroom questioning;"—contains an unresolvable ambiguity created by the non-specifiable and thus anaphoric use of the

---

6. Joseph Adams, *Yeats and the Masks of Syntax* (New York: Columbia University Press, 1985).

definite article: is the reader supposed to already be familiar with the schoolroom or does Yeats intend it as a new experience? For purposes of the current study, ambiguity of this sort has little relevance. In only a minor way does it affect the relationship between syntax and significant meaning. The current study seeks not to address the ambiguity of individual words, which would seem to be a lexical rather than syntactic question, but rather the relationship between phrase- and clause-structure and meaning, in which units that can be construed as syntactic masks certainly do play a part.

Adams's study places Yeats in a post-structuralist theoretical framework in which syntactic ambiguity serves to dissociate form and meaning. However, in proceeding to his conclusions he displays precisely the type of pre-structuralist certainty that he feels syntactic masks make obsolete. If, as he says, "no final meaning can be assigned," then why should this necessarily diminish the alternate meanings? Rather, the ambiguity enhances the value of the two or more readings that are expressed simultaneously; it is the reader's mind, rather than the inanimate text, that actively works out the relationship between the possibilities. To say that Plato and Aristotle disagree is by no means to diminish either one. To say that "Among School Children" seems on one reading to be Platonic, on another to be Aristotelian, is only to enhance the value of the poem.

Yeatsian ambiguity allows form and meaning a greater independence from one another and prevents either from becoming dominant. One of the most significant contributions of Yeats's poetry is his reminder that the form-created "dance" of the poetry is as important as the "blear-eyed wisdom" it conveys, that any ultimate significance resides in the balance of the two. Throughout his mature work, passionate and innovative syntax dances with decorous and traditional form to maintain this balance.

In addition to structural ambiguity, one important means of balancing form and syntax stems from the common prosodic practice known as enjambment, the running-on of a syntactic unit across the boundary of the prosodic unit (the line or stanza). Dougherty has made an extensive analysis of Yeatsian enjambment:

> In the later verse, beginning with *The Wild Swans at Coole* (1919), Yeats crosses the verse-line, in a kind of rhythmic counterpoint, with a unit of language structure which I shall call the *speech-unit*. . . . By

speech-unit I mean simply a stretch of speech that is bounded by
pause-punctuation graphically indicated in the text. (Dougherty 217–
18)

In one sense, this is a complex way of saying that enjambment has
an effect on the poem's meaning. On the other hand, it emphasizes
Yeats's structured and calculated use of enjambment, coupled with inno-
vative syntax, to maintain the independence of metrical rhythm and
syntactic rhythm in his poems. According to Dougherty, "speech-unit
crossover" allows Yeats to establish, "however briefly," more complex
rhythms than traditional verse structure yields, by the addition of a
second potential rhythmic unit at odds with the verse structure (Dough-
erty 219). The subsequent rhythmic tension can heighten the dramatic
effect of the poem, and, by integrating everyday speech rhythms into the
verse structure, allow a freer range of expression than in poems whose
syntactic structure is bound to the verse structure.

One example Dougherty cites is the opening stanza of "Sailing to
Byzantium." The verse structure is the traditional ottava rima that
served Yeats so well in his mature years. However, the first emphatic
phrase establishes a contrapuntal rhythm that starts as iambic tetrameter
and modulates into trimeter. Here is how the poem would appear if
scanned according to this rhythmic counterpoint, with slashes indicating
the actual line breaks:

> That is no country for old men.
> The young / In one another's arms,
> birds in the trees, / —Those dying generations—
> at their song, / The salmon-falls,
> the mackerel-crowded seas, /
> Fish, flesh, or fowl,
> Commend all summer long /
> Whatever is begotten, born, and dies.
>
> (cf. P 193)

The short first sentence establishes a rhythmic pattern for the long one
that follows, so that a rhythmic tension is created that is only resolved
back into iambic pentameter when the long series of parallel subjects is
resolved into verb and object. Not only does this reflect the tension felt
by the old man himself, but it conveys a series of relatively static nouns

in a dynamic way. Neither structure, syntax, nor idea is allowed to dominate the passage; all work inseparably.

Dougherty concludes, "Clearly it is this counterpointing that transforms the 'traditional metres' Yeats compelled himself to accept into the 'powerful and passionate' syntax he sought" (Dougherty 224). While the current study argues that no single strategy imparts that passion to Yeats's poems, the expressive potential of speech-unit crossover is certainly a factor.

The "speech-unit" that "crosses over" in the beginning of "Sailing to Byzantium" derives its character from the long series of parallel subjects in the second sentence. This suggests another of Yeats's most striking syntactic strategies, his habitual use of syntactic parallelism. Long series of parallel subjects, verbs, objects, prepositional phrases, subordinate clauses, and even entire sentences populate his poetry. The following passage from "Byzantium" is particularly rich:

> At midnight on the Emperor's pavement flit
> Flames that no faggot feeds, nor steel has lit,
> Nor storm disturbs, flames begotten of flame,
> Where blood-begotten spirits come
> And all complexities of fury leave,
> Dying into a dance,
> An agony of trance,
> An agony of flame that cannot singe a sleeve.
>
> (P 248)

Besides increasing the lushness and sensuality of the imagery, such parallelism can serve a number of other strategic functions. For example, in many of Yeats's most syntactically complex poems, parallelism clarifies both syntax and meaning, enabling the reader to comprehend a potentially confusing construction by a comparison with a parallel one. A one-sentence stanza from "Ancestral Houses" will illustrate:

> O what if gardens where the peacock strays
> With delicate feet upon old terraces,
> Or else all Juno from an urn displays
> Before the indifferent garden deities;
> O what if levelled lawns and gravelled ways
> Where slippered Contemplation finds his ease
> And Childhood a delight for every sense,
> But take our greatness with our violence?
>
> (P 201)

The first of the stanza's three compound subjects, *gardens,* is separated from the single verb *take* by six and a half lines. This potentially confusing syntactic situation is made orderly and comprehensible by the self-evidently regular parallelism. The structure of the adjectival where-clause dependent on *gardens* is made evident by the rhyming of its two parallel verbs *strays* and *displays.* The similar where-clause modifying "levelled lawns and gravelled ways" has a structure emphasized by the alliteration of its two parallel subjects, *Contemplation* and *Childhood.* Furthermore the parallel nature of the subject noun phrases is emphasized by the repetition of "O what if" in the first and fifth lines. The effect is to make an eight-line sentence comprehensible in two units of four lines each.

Yeats manages to stretch the two subject clauses through seven of the stanza's eight lines, "foregrounding" the parallelism by fitting it to the verse form as noted above. What is not obvious is the finesse and variation with which he achieves this: in no case are any pair of parallel structures handled in exactly the same way. Line one contains a single subject, *gardens,* while line five counters with the compound "levelled lawns and gravelled ways" that further specify the concept of gardens. The subjects in lines one and five alike are modified by adjectival where-clauses; however, the first contains a simple subject and a compound verb while the second contains two separate sets of subject and object linked by one common verb. Of the three nouns—*peacock, Contemplation* and *Childhood*—that are ushered through the gardens via these where-clauses, only the peacock is concrete while the other two are abstract. Ironically, the flesh-and-blood bird is linked with the ephemeral trappings of classical mythology, while the dual abstractions of *Childhood* and *Contemplation* conjure up a very concrete visit by the aging poet and one or both of his young children.

The rhyme scheme also contributes to the sense of order achieved by this intricate sentence: the sibilants that end all eight lines bestow a unity that goes almost unnoticed beneath the variation of the rhyming vowels, and the voiced *s*'s of the first six lines resolve themselves into the more subdued voiceless *s*'s of the last two. This interweaving of form, sound, syntax, and meaning enables the poem to epitomize the formal English Garden that achieves order out of a seeming chaos of nature.

Two additional effects of parallelism in the stanza seem contradictory to one another: first, the proliferation of parallel units can serve to weaken the connective bonds of syntax by placing distance and verbiage between elements that syntactically belong together. However, parallelism can also enforce connections between ideas, for ideas expressed in syntactically parallel units are often perceived as ideationally parallel (a rhetorical fact well known to politicians and television commercial writers).

In the stanza in question, the syntax achieves a weakening of ideational bonds. The richness and balance of this syntax enlarge upon the "greatness" of the ancestral homes and contrast effectively with the sudden, violent verb phrase of the final line. It is hard to remember that the gardens, lawns, and walks are subjects of this long sentence, but the syntax asserts that it must be so. The garden setting is balanced and unified by means of parallelism; the same parallelism masks the violence that the poet perceives as inexorably connected with material greatness; the thoroughness of the illusion sadly masks (from all eyes but the poet's) the necessity to "take our greatness with our violence." Parallelism can also serve to weaken the sense of time in a poem. E. L. Epstein explores this device in discussing Yeats's use, in five poems, of "a catalogue of nominal phrases without finite verbs."[7] This particular type of parallelism weakens the time sequence enforced by finite verbs, evoking a sense of timelessness in order to distill lasting value out of a hectic and predominantly meaningless world. In contrast with Keats and the French symbolists, who achieved timelessness semantically through emblematic objects or emotions (e.g., the Grecian Urn), "Yeats tries for a passionate fusion of the time-bound and the timeless. In him it takes the form of a time-bound content expressed with a detemporalizing technique" (Epstein 176).

In doing this, Yeats is fighting the inherent syntactic tendency of most Indo-European languages to express a sense of time sequence almost automatically. The parallelism through which he achieves this is the sort that opens "Sailing to Byzantium," in which numerous nouns express a sense of the poem's overall subject without the verb-generated sense of movement that would tie them down to time sequence. Epstein cites numerous similar instances, all from poems written after 1921, including "In Memory of Eva Gore-Booth and Con Markievicz," whose principal theme is the relationship of time to timelessness:

---

7. E. L. Epstein, "Yeats's Experiments with Syntax in the Treatment of Time," *Modern Irish Literature: Essays in Honor of William York Tindall,* ed. Raymond J. Proter and James D. Brophy (New York: Iona College Press/Twayne, 1972), 178. Hereafter cited in the text as Epstein.

> The innocent and the beautiful
> Have no enemy but time;
> Arise and bid me strike a match
> And strike another till time catch. . . .

(P 233)

A related technique cited by Epstein is the deemphasis of finite verb forms in favor of infinitives and participles. Epstein singles out "Leda and the Swan" to demonstrate the effect of the verb forms in achieving a timeless, emblematic tone:

> A sudden blow: the great wings beating still
> Above the staggering girl, her thighs caressed
> By the dark webs, her nape caught in his bill,
> He holds her helpless breast upon his breast.

(P 214)

In this quatrain describing the rape, the first four verb forms are participles, and the progression from present to past imparts a quality of eternally happening / eternally just-happened. Epstein also comments on the contrast between the *sudden* that opens the poem and the syntactically ambiguous *still* that ends the first line: the time sequence implied by the first is dampened by the dual—and timeless—implications of the second (Epstein 183). This observation underscores the necessity to view Yeats's syntactic strategies in context—this is a device that would work in no other context except precisely the one in which it occurs.

Another critic who has commented extensively on Yeatsian syntax is Richard Ellmann. Rather than focusing on phrase structure, he approaches syntax from the direction of stylistic effect. He opens his discussion with a device that might seem more semantic than syntactic, but has strong syntactic implications: "Writing English as a learned language, [Yeats] called up usages long out of fashion" (Ellmann 135). In other words, Yeats often achieves syntactic ambiguity by using common words in archaic or otherwise unusual syntactic positions. For example, we have seen *but* used to signify *except* in "Ancestral Houses." "She that but little patience knew" (P 183) contains a non-connective, archaic use of *but* to mean *only*. This line also contains evidence that Yeats employed *that* as an all-purpose relative pronoun. The more common usage would be she *who* but little patience knew. In this way both *but* and *that* acquire some of the "syntactic mask" qualities valued by Adams.

Ellmann attributes the speed and fluidity of Yeats's poetry to his compression of construction. One important syntactic way of achieving this is by use of the absolute—for example "The Second Coming" ends:

> The darkness drops again; but now I know
> That twenty centuries of stony sleep
> Were vexed to nightmare by a rocking cradle,
> And what rough beast, its hour come round at last,
> Slouches towards Bethlehem to be born?

(P 187)

Although the possessive pronoun *its* connects beast and hour into the same image, to say that it acts as a relative pronoun would be to violate the norms of acceptable syntax. It is easier to consider "its hour" an isolated noun phrase modified by the compressed participial phrase "come round at last;" the phrase fulfills the definition of the absolute construction and maintains syntactic decorum. To use "its hour come round at last" rather than the relative clause "whose hour has come round at last" achieves compression, while the intrusiveness of the absolute maintains dramatic suspense until the final line.

Ellmann briefly notes other ways in which Yeats compresses his language. Often he omits words that can be understood from context— "That is Heaven's part, our part / To murmur name upon name" (P 181)—or uses an archaic but economical expression—"What need have you to care / For wind or water's roar?" (P 122)—or, as in Ellmann's own example, "Being more indifferent to our solitude / Than 'twere an apparition" (P 139). Ellmann notes of the contraction in this last example: "Grammar permits itself to be treated thus arrogantly only when the rest of the poem is more decorous" (Ellmann 136).

Although Ellmann himself does not elaborate on the question of decorum, Yeats's poetry is decorous in two important ways. First, as we have seen in ottava rima poems such as "Sailing to Byzantium," passionate syntax is constrained by decorous form, and the resulting tension contributes to the poem's effect. Equally importantly, the syntax itself observes decorum. Although Yeats seems to violate "perceived norms," he almost always adheres to the letter of syntactic law, as if he wished to strike a balance between respecting the rules and creating new ones. Richard Ceci demonstrates at length that in terms of Transformational-Generative Grammar, a transformational rule always exists to account for any variation from the norm that Yeats might choose.[8] How different from Yeats's colleague Ezra Pound, who systematically fragments syntax throughout his *Cantos*.

Rather than diverging from the English tradition, Yeats operates within it, exploring and testing its capabilities.[9] In this way, Yeats keeps syntax itself in the background, directing the reader's attention instead to words, images, and ideas, so that in the words of Nowottny, readers unaware of the potential of syntax "will be at a loss to understand why a passage affects them as it does" (Nowottny 10).

One means of maintaining syntactic decorum is through transposition. Ellmann suggests this in his remark that Yeatsian word order is "stylized" to an extent that sometimes produces a heightened rhetorical effect (Ellmann 137). Such rhetorical effects are relatively frequent and seem to be the result of careful calculation rather than stylistic eccentricity or prosodic necessity. In other words, to Yeats transposition is another key syntactic strategy.

Yeats varies traditional word order in a number of ways, for example transposing the verb with other elements of the verb phrase. The following short passage contains four examples:

> She that but little patience knew,
> From childhood on, had now so much
> A grey gull lost its fear and flew
> Down to her cell and there alit,
> And there endured her fingers' touch
> And from her fingers ate its bit.
>
> (P 183)

"Nineteen Hundred and Nineteen" ends with an unusual extraposition of a dependent clause:

> The night can sweat with terror as before
> We pieced our thoughts into philosophy,
> And planned to bring the world under a rule,
> Who are but weasels fighting in a hole.
>
> (P 207)

---

8. Louis G. Ceci, "The Syntax of Vision: Grammatical Structures in the Visionary Poems of W. B. Yeats" (diss., Northwestern University, 1981), passim.

9. A notable exception is the fragmented beginning to "Leda and the Swan." However, in this case it is clear that the desirability of reinforcing meaning takes precedence: "A sudden blow" signifies syntactically what it signifies semantically; it is a sudden burst of sound, grammar, and meaning.

Transpositions create three major classes of effect: first, as Ellmann implies, they add to suspense by momentarily delaying more meaningful syntactic units until near the end of the sentence, or at other times interrupting a train of thought or action. Second, they affect the order in which the poem's ideas strike the reader. Third, they achieve a certain strangeness or memorability, by virtue of their unfamiliarity. This third effect is linguistically known as *foregrounding* (Traugott and Pratt 31). Briefly, it implies that the writer has made the language seem new or striking by bringing it to the reader's attention through systematic violation of the perceived norms. Though Ellmann does not put it in linguistic terms, this is precisely the sort of rhetorical effect he finds inherent in Yeats's manipulation of word order. By jarring the reader out of the ruts of habitual perception, Yeats can push the reader toward new ways of perception and toward a full experience of the text. This is another instance of the "passion" inherent in syntax.

The first stanza of "A Prayer for My Daughter" gives several examples of the subtle power of transposition:

> Once more the storm is howling, and half hid
> Under this cradle-hood and coverlid
> My child sleeps on. There is no obstacle
> But Gregory's wood and one bare hill
> Whereby the haystack- and roof-levelling wind,
> Bred on the Atlantic, can be stayed;
> And for an hour I have walked and prayed
> Because of the great gloom that is in my mind.
>
> (P 188)

The second main clause opens with "half hid / Under this cradle-hood and coverlid," an adjectival phrase of such length that normally it would be removed to the end of the sentence: "My child sleeps on, half hid under this cradle-hood and coverlid." However, Yeats has chosen instead to place the phrase at the beginning of the clause as a pre-appositive. Suspense is thereby achieved: exactly what is hidden is not revealed until the third line. In addition, syntax reinforces meaning because the child is hidden both syntactically and semantically, and the reader must look a little further into the poem to find her. The imagined act of looking moves the reader quickly into the world of the poem, so that paradoxically, even though the transposition delays the subject and complement of the clause, it simultaneously speeds the pacing of the poem.

The next sentence contains similar effects; its basic structure is simple: "There is no obstacle." Yet this raises the question, "obstacle to what?" In completing this simple thought, Yeats achieves a complex effect. Syntactically, "Whereby the . . . wind . . . can be stayed" is an adjective clause belonging with *obstacle*. However, Yeats sees fit to provide a couple of exceptions before mentioning the clause itself, again building suspense by delay. "Gregory's wood and one bare hill" stand as obstacles not only to the wind, but to the flow of meaning, even as they contribute meaning of their own. They are obstacles both ideationally and syntactically.

At this point the question implied by the idea of "no obstacle" is answered: there is no obstacle to a certain kind of wind. The progression from *haystack-* to *roof*-levelling amplifies the dangerous nature of the wind: it is not simply a danger to crops but to human habitation and therefore human life. The wind has been let loose by the syntax, and Yeats is willing to let it blow a while longer. Before it "can be stayed," another adjective clause is embedded within the first. "Bred on the Atlantic" is a reduced relative clause, transformed from a complete subject-complement unit in the deep structure to achieve a maximum of expression in a minimum of words. To say "wind / Bred on the Atlantic" is to maintain the most fundamental syntax; the participial phrase immediately follows the noun it modifies, with no transposition. This time Yeats has achieved his syntactic effect by hypotaxis. Even without transposition, *wind* and "can be stayed" have been further separated, adding to suspense and to the feeling of difficulty in staying the wind.

Lines seven and eight are analogous to the corresponding lines in another ottava rima poem discussed earlier, "Sailing to Byzantium." They are syntactically straightforward lines, and they counterbalance the syntactic complexity that preceded them. Line seven contains the principal subject and verbs of the sentence, followed by the prepositional phrase of which line eight consists.

Even in rounding out complexity with simplicity, the sentence contains an elaborate syntactical flourish. *Mind* is the object of a prepositional phrase serving as an adverb of place within an adjectival clause modifying the object of another prepositional phrase, which in turn stands as an adverb within the main clause. In terms of the sentence *per se,* then, *mind* is the least important noun, serving as a secondary qualifier remotely connected to the principal ideas of walking and praying. However, in the context of the poem as a whole, *mind* becomes quite important, for after the second stanza the entire poem takes place inside the poet's mind, as he comes to grips with his "great gloom." Thus there is some justification for placing a syntactically unimportant word in the prosodically important closing position. In this way the turn from exterior surroundings to meditation is foreshadowed. Yeats achieves a three-way tension between syntax, verse form, and meaning.

Finally, the syntax of the stanza achieves some of the effects of juxtaposition and association normally seen in Pound and Eliot. Pound achieves this sort of effect through a systematic disruption of syntax and idea:

> Palace in smoky light,
> Troy but a heap of smouldering boundary stones,
> ANAXIFORMINGES ! Aurunculeia!
> Hear me. Cadmus of Golden Prows!
> The silver mirrors catch the bright stones and flare,
> Dawn, to our waking, drifts in the green cool light;
> Dew-haze blurs, in the grass, pale ankles moving.
> Beat, beat, whirr, thud, in the soft turf under the apple trees,
> Choros nympharum, goat-foot, with the pale foot alternate;
> Crescent of blue-shot waters, green-gold in the shallows,
> A black cock crows in the sea-foam. . . .[10]

Donald Davie calls the syntax of *The Cantos* the syntax of ideas, not of grammar.[11] In such writing, because we apprehend words in the order in which they occur on the page, we associate contiguous ones; there is little or no syntactical complexity to encourage or discourage this process. In essence this is an approximation of the natural way in which sensory data are apprehended (say, by Pavlov's dogs). By contrast, syntax is an artifact, a man-made system that allows a greater range and flexibility in the expression of ideas. Nevertheless the mind will tend simultaneously to apprehend verbal stimuli by means of both systems. This is a point Yeats seems to be aware of: he manipulates the language of "A Prayer for My Daughter" so that syntax and association are at odds and create somewhat different readings of the poem. The tension between the two equally valid readings adds to the depth of meaning. In a sense, then, this is another syntactic mask.

---

10. Ezra Pound, "Canto IV," *The Cantos* (New York: New Directions, 1972), 13.
11. Donald Davie, *Articulate Energy: An Inquiry into the Syntax of English Poetry* (London: Routledge and Kegan Paul, 1955), 19.

In contrast to Pound's syntactical fragments, Yeats's stanza is syntactically "correct." However, there is more similarity between the two styles than at first meets the eye. A simple example is the archaic usage of *but* in Pound's second line. Whether Pound picked this up from Yeats or whether the two poets simply reinforced one another's interest in archaisms cannot be said. More significantly, Epstein comments that Yeats's principal experiments with the syntactic treatment of time came "in the last two decades of his life, after he had absorbed Pound's influence thoroughly" (Epstein 178). Indeed the passage from the *Cantos* shares several of the detemporalizing features Yeats was experimenting with at the same time.

Most importantly, the two passages share a concern with the associational movement of thought. Despite the syntactic "correctness" of "A Prayer for My Daughter," the strategic transpositions and delays render the exact relationship of ideas obscure. In fact, simply considering the proximity of ideas and images to one another, the stanza yields quite a different reading: after encountering the storm, the reader's attention is diverted from the child's environment to the child herself, then expanded through her geographical protectors to the forceful wind, to the even greater force of the wind's progenitor, the Atlantic. With the passive verb, "be stayed," the increasing intensity of imagery, wind, and syntax die down simultaneously, leaving the child's own parent, the poet, to walk and pray. Is the walking and praying of the loving individual a force more powerful than the great Atlantic? The interplay of syntax and imagery suggests it is so.

In this case, sequential unravelling of idea and image leaves a somewhat different impression than does the syntactical unravelling of idea. The pace of imagery is quick, that of syntax is slow; to understand exactly what Yeats is saying, it is necessary to read slowly, even to go back over what has been read, so that the connections obscured by transposition and syntactic delay can be clarified in the reader's mind. Thus another tension is established; imagery and surface appearance move quickly, syntax and underlying idea move more slowly.

The multiple transpositions achieve a strangeness of syntax. By stretching the distance between words whose meanings must be understood in relationship to one another, Yeats encourages the reading of the poem simultaneously by association and by syntax; association hurries the reader on, syntax slows the reader down. Compression creates a fast music to the poem, transpositions create a slow underlying structure.

The playing off of the two types of thought, logical and associative, against one another would seem to be one of the most important, and yet most subtle, ends to which the systematic manipulation of syntax can be put.

So far, it is obvious that much of Yeats's syntactic effects occur entirely within the long sentences he favors. However, the types of sentences he chooses also contribute to his syntactic effects. In particular, he achieves a wide range of effects with his pervasive use of questions, especially rhetorical questions.

There are over three hundred questions in Yeats's lyric poems alone. The brief volume *Michael Robartes and the Dancer* contains an average of almost two questions per poem. Broadly speaking, Yeats's questions fall into four categories: (1) dramatic questions spoken by characters within the poem:

> 'But where can we draw water,'
> Said Pearse to Connolly,
> 'When all the wells are parched away?
>
> (P 183)

(2) open questions asked of the poem's reader (or of the poet himself), often difficult philosophical ones:

> Did she put on his knowledge with his power
> Before the indifferent beak could let her drop?
>
> (P 215)

(3) questions to be answered within the context of the poem:

> Where got I that truth?
> Out of a medium's mouth. . . .
>
> (P 214)

and (4) traditional rhetorical questions:

> How can those terrified vague fingers push
> The feathered glory from her loosening thighs?
>
> (P 215)

To a certain extent all four types of questions are inherently rhetorical. None exist for the information-eliciting purposes of "normal" questions. Rather, they are questions preserved in a literary form. Each is designed to produce a certain type of effect on the reader. The distinction between normal questions and the simulation of normal questions presented in the context of a literary act raises issues with respect to all four of the question types.

First, the rhetorical effect of dramatic questions has more to do with the audience's full imagining of the scene than with any information conveyed. Regardless of syntax, the effect of a dramatized passage remains primarily with the dramatic context. Therefore, dramatic questions do not play a large part in the discussion of Yeats's interrogative syntax.

Type (2), the open question, appears identical in form to an open question in the spoken language. However, the effect of an open question in lyric poetry is not so much to elicit information as to raise issues impossible of resolution, at least in the context that the literary act has established. This is a clearly rhetorical purpose that to a certain extent creates ambiguity, as in the case of whether Leda "put on" the Swan/God's "knowledge with his power."

On the other hand, questions type (3) and (4) are almost never ambiguous. Type (3) displays characteristics midway between the dramatic question and the traditional rhetorical question. Its answer is delivered in context by the poem's persona. Relatively rare in Yeats, it is capable of producing some of the effects that Yeats derives from the traditional rhetorical question, but only to the extent that this is consistent with the given answer.

Type (4) presupposes that the reader, either through prior knowledge or through experiencing the poem, has sufficient information to derive the answer. Yeats concentrates on this type of question, principally because its effect in the literary act is broad, and is specifically linked to various forms of persuasion, as is its analogous form in speech, the traditional rhetorical question. Even though any question in a literary act is *ipso facto* rhetorical, I will use the term "rhetorical question" to apply only to the fourth type.

Before discussing rhetorical questions in further detail, several additional points should be noted about questions in general. Certain questions do not fall neatly into any of the four categories but can be read in two or more ways. For example, "Easter 1916," asks "And what if excess of love / Bewildered them till they died?" (P 182). "What if" is a favorite opening to Yeatsian rhetorical questions, and generally implies a

"So what?" attitude on the part of the speaker. Such an interpretation would suggest that Yeats felt it didn't matter that "excess of love" had bewildered his idealistic friends. However, another reading is also possible, focusing on the redeeming value of *love* rather than the negative connotations of *excess*. When Yeats asks "And what if," he may be saying "Consider this possibility." The question is open because we will clearly never know the hearts of the martyrs. Through an ambiguous question, Yeats is simultaneously saying "So what if they felt that an excess of love led to their bewildered sacrifice," and "Despite the seeming futility of their cause, could their motivations have been of the highest order?"

Why does Yeats resort to questions so frequently? Lee Zimmerman suggests two important reasons.[12] First, questions stress the personal element in a poem; they call attention to the presence of a speaker. Zimmerman notes that most poetry consists of declarative sentences "even in Yeats . . . , so that when a question does occur, by virtue of its relative oddity it calls attention to itself as a question and, thus, inevitably to the questioning voice that utters it" (Zimmerman 37). This property of questions is well illustrated by the ending of "Among School Children." After an autobiographical opening stanza, the poem becomes increasingly impersonal, until by the opening of the final stanza it has acquired a semblance of objectivity: "I walk through the long schoolroom questioning" (P 443) is a long call from "Labor is blossoming or dancing where / The body is not bruised to pleasure soul" (P 445). But following the assertion about labor appear two questions. They remind us that there is a questioner, and that rather than objective truth, the poem remains the meditation of a "sixty-year-old smiling public man." Remembering this, we recall the schoolroom setting and realize that the question asked about the chestnut tree—"Are you the leaf, the blossom or the bole?"—applies equally well to the human spirit in its passage from the condition of the schoolchildren toward the condition of the aging speaker. By allowing the speaker's questions to enter the final stanza, Yeats returns the poem to its starting point.

Zimmerman also points out that questions are well-suited to handle the themes of division, uncertainty, and paradox that are important not only in "Among School Children," but throughout Yeats's work. All

---

12. Lee Zimmerman, "Singing Amid Uncertainty: Yeats's Closing Questions," *Yeats Annual No. 2* (1983): 35–45. Hereafter cited in the text as Zimmerman.

three of these themes deny the power of assertion, thereby opening themselves to the rhetorical and syntactical potential of questions. As Yeats said of himself and his contemporaries, "Unlike the rhetoricians, who get a confident voice from remembering the crowd they have won or may win, we sing amid our uncertainty" (M 331).

A further important aspect of questions is that, unlike assertions, they are not specifically marked for time. The exchange of information demanded by interrogative syntax always occurs in the present moment. Whether the question is "Did you go?", "Are you going?", or "Will you go?" the answer is always a factual, atemporal "Yes" or "No." Thus, the preponderance of questions in a poem such as "Leda and the Swan" (more than seven of its fourteen lines) adds to the poem's broad historical sweep and, in concert with the parallelism and verb formation that Epstein has noted, contributes to the poem's timelessness.

Yeats is particularly fond of the rhetorical question. Of the 337 questions asked in his collected lyrical poems, 185 (or 54 percent) are rhetorical. The poem "Sixteen Dead Men" represents the extreme example of this tendency; its eighteen lines consist entirely of four rhetorical questions. The twelve-line poem "No Second Troy" also consists entirely of rhetorical questions, ending on two powerful ones:

> Why, what could she have done, being what she is?
> Was there another Troy for her to burn?
>
> (P 91)

Zimmerman's views on Yeats's closing questions also apply to his rhetorical questions—they stress the personal presence of the poem's speaker and underscore themes of division and paradox. Rhetorical questions have further effects as well. For one thing, their answers tend to be obvious and negative: "Was there another Troy for her to burn?" Of course not. But if the answer is obvious and negative, what is the point of asking? The question engages the reader still further with the poem; the syntax itself encourages participation. It is not the speaker who makes the point but rather the reader, who must mentally supply the answer. The rhetorical purpose of the sentence is to impart information, but its syntactic form—that of the question—requires the reader to actively participate. So the rhetorical question not only enforces the presence of the speaker, as Zimmerman notes, but encourages reader engagement with that speaker.

In this sense, the rhetorical questions are didactic. But these same properties make the questions persuasive (hence rhetorical). On the surface, the speaker's assertion is softened: he does not bluntly state "She could have done nothing else," but rather asks the reader "Why, what could she have done, being what she is?" The syntactic form seemingly leaves the conclusion open. While the assumed answer is obvious, it is the reader who must supply it. The reader's resistance to persuasion is lowered because the writer's argument approaches indirectly in question form, rather than head-on. At the same time, the argument is stronger in that the facts are deemed so obvious that the question needs no answer. The device operates regardless of content: the interrogative syntax itself, applied to what rightfully should be a statement, creates the persuasive effect.

Yeats often couples the rhetorical question with less familiar syntactic structures to achieve his ends. The poem "Politics" (P 348) contains perhaps the best example of this device. In the 1983 edition of *The Poems*, Finneran has fulfilled Yeats's apparent intention to place this poem at the end of his lyrical works, a position that underscores its importance within the context of the corpus. The poem's elaborate syntax has a bearing on this significance:

> How can I, that girl standing there,
> My attention fix
> On Roman or on Russian
> Or on Spanish politics,
> Yet here's a travelled man that knows
> What he talks about,
> And there's a politician
> That has both read and thought,
> And maybe what they say is true
> Of war and war's alarms,
> But O that I were young again
> And held her in my arms.

(P 348)

In all previously published collections the fourth line ended with a question mark. The comma, restored from the 1939 contemporary periodical versions, serves to link the poem's ideas into a single long sentence, while the opening *How* and the subject-verb inversion of "can I" continue to mark the first four lines syntactically as a question. The absence of the question mark underscores the degree to which the answer is obvious and negative, and also the extent to which the opening question gives way to the declarative structure of the rest of the poem.

Syntactically, then, the poem opens with an absolute construction embedded in a rhetorical question embedded in a statement. In prose the question might run, "How can I fix my attention on . . . politics when that girl is standing there?" The poetic version can be viewed as the result of three grammatical transformations. First the adverbial clause, "when that girl is standing there," has been reduced to an absolute construction, its nominal and participial elements grammatically disconnected from the rest of the sentence. Second, through an unusual placement transformation the absolute has found its way to a position between subject and verb. Third, the normal order of verb-object has been inverted to render "my attention fix," leaving the absolute construction standing between subject and object, the position where we normally expect to find the verb.

It could be argued that this third transformation is simply a way of forcing the sentence to conform to the rhyme scheme. However, Yeats was far too skillful to resort to such a strategy unless there were added benefits. One such benefit is that the noun-verb order in the predicate of the main clause is parallel to that in the absolute construction: "girl standing," "attention fix." Coupled with the intrusion of the absolute into the anticipated verb position, this parallelism serves to make the main clause less identifiable, so that while syntactically "my attention fix" is still the predicate, the intrusive fact of the girl's presence has become more important to speaker and, one hopes, to reader.

Yeats has also achieved an interesting effect with the relative positioning of his substantives. In the sentence "I can not fix my attention on politics with that girl standing there," the three substantives—*I, Girl* and *Attention*—are separated from one another by at least one major syntactic unit. In the poem itself, the use of the rhetorical question allows the subject, *I,* to slip inside the modal auxiliary, *can.* The use of the absolute allows the insertion of *that girl* unencumbered by connective words, and the transposition allows *attention* to precede the verb. In this way, the three substantives become three contiguous units in the sentence: "How can I, that girl standing there, my attention fix . . . ?" The close relationship between poet, attention, and object of attention is the main subject of the poem; it is established not through bald statement, but through the associative proximity created by unusual syntax.

By combining rhetorical question with nominative absolute, Yeats allows syntax to create a subtle level of meaning. Right at the start his attention is drawn to "that girl." But a public man of the time is expected to show more dignity. He quickly steers his attention back to the question at hand by naming the action which he has just proven himself incapable of achieving, namely of fixing his attention. Thus the rhetorical question has answered itself. Of course he can't fix his attention, and the syntax of his question proves it.

In the opening question, Yeats delays the proper goal of his attention as long as diplomatically possible. After the transposed verb, *fix,* comes a long prepositional phrase containing the goal of the verb, namely *politics.* But before reaching *politics* the poem passes through a series of parallel adjectives accompanied by an unnecessarily large number of connective words: "On Roman or on Russian / Or on Spanish politics."

Throughout the first four lines, syntax has enabled him to delay and fragment the order of ideas. The reader's attention, as well as the speaker's, is distracted from the idea of fixing attention on politics by the delays and by the necessity of sorting out the syntax, as well as by the syntactic emphasis placed on *speaker, girl,* and *attention.* Such complexity encourages the reader to forget that the sentence starts as a rhetorical question, so that by the time politics is reached, the reader may have to go back to the beginning to work the whole thing over.

In "Politics," Yeats is walking a tightrope, balancing increased reader engagement against overcomplexity, balancing a complex syntactic texture against a surface conformity to traditional rules of syntax. Likewise, in the poem as a whole, he balances attention to the sketchily mentioned girl against inattention to the much-mentioned politics. The extent to which he can maintain all these balances is a measure of his mastery over syntax.

The combination of question with interpositioned structures such as the absolute also occurs in such poems as "The Second Coming," "Among School Children," "A Prayer for My Daughter," "An Image from a Past Life," "September 1913," "The Cold Heaven," and "The Tower." There is no clear and simple pattern either to the exact form taken by this strategy or its uses, which implies that Yeats allowed the strategy and its corresponding effects to be determined by the poetic context. Like "Politics," "The Tower" opens with a rhetorical question:

> What shall I do with this absurdity—
> O heart, O troubled heart—this caricature,
> Decrepit age that has been tied to me
> As to a dog's tail?

(P 194)

The syntactic devices are similar: rhetorical question, intrusion, multiple parallel objects of a single preposition. However, the use to which they are put is entirely different. For one thing, rather than an absolute, the intrusive phrase is a vocative, the "troubled heart" to whom the question is addressed. Rather than containing ideas central to the sentence, as does the absolute phrase in "Politics," it directs the speaker's attention toward himself, so that the reader assumes a perspective of "listening in" to intimate thoughts. As a syntactic intrusion, the phrase serves to block the flow of thought, thereby making the reader pause at the end of the first clause and consider it, briefly, a completed thought: "What shall I do with this absurdity?"

The deliberate nature of the interruption is evident from a look at Yeats's initial prose draft (what he called his "subject" for the poem):

What shall I do with this absurd toy which they have given me, this grotesque rattle? O heart, O nerves, you are as vigourous as ever. You still hunger for the whole world, and they have given you this toy.[13]

The original impulse, or at least its original written record, included the rhetorical question (or perhaps at that point an open question whose answer required experiencing the thoughts and emotions recorded in the poem). However, in the "subject" the introduction of the troubled heart waited for the second principal thought, which appropriately concerns the vigor of the heart and nerves. In the final published version the two thoughts remain more or less intact but the heart has moved from one to the other. Obviously such a displacement singles out the troubled heart and draws the reader's attention to it, establishing the poem as a meditation of the poet himself rather than an address to the reader.

But there is a less obvious reason for the heart's movement, entailing not just the heart itself, but also its effect on the syntactic context. The intrusion brings the reader to the end of a syntactically complete thought—"What shall I do with this absurdity?" But what exactly is this absurdity? The question's syntactic contours have achieved a degree of irony: the question readers may find themselves asking is not what the poet should do with this absurdity, because the implied answer to this

13. Transcribed from a manuscript book begun at Oxford, April 7, 1921; cited in Curtis B. Bradford, *Yeats at Work* (Carbondale and Edwardsville: Southern Illinois University Press, 1965), 4.

rhetorical question is "Nothing." A more likely question for the reader to ask is "What is this absurdity?" The answer is delayed first by the intrusive vocative construction and then by another device, the appositive. Normally we would expect an appositive to clarify the situation and tell us what the absurdity is; here, however, the core of the appositive is a similarly abstract noun, *caricature,* which serves to intensify the speaker's own feelings of disgust without yet revealing the object of his scorn.

At this point, the second line of verse ends, putting the reader off a bit further. Yeats is again using syntax and verse form to reinforce one another. Finally at the start of the third line, we learn that the absurd caricature is the condition of old age, or more specifically the old age of the speaker himself. And the speaker doesn't simply find himself old; he finds old age tied to him "As to a dog's tail." The delay of this discovery achieves at least two results; first, it intensifies the importance of the old age, as in a crime drama the significance of a culprit's identity increases the longer its discovery is delayed. Second, by isolating the initial clause, the delay intensifies that, too. Yeats is determined to deal with this absurdity, with words since actions fail him, regardless of the absurdity's identity.

In "Politics" and "The Tower," different effects are achieved with similar syntactic strategies. This demonstrates the flexibility and versatility of Yeatsian syntax, and once again emphasizes that there is no easy way of codifying Yeatsian syntax. By emphasizing the rhetorical question, Yeats takes a tradition-honored device and uses it for specific, traditional effects. However, by combining it with other syntactic complications, he achieves, in addition to his fixed effects, a kaleidoscope of shifting ones. As in other aspects of his work, a balance between tradition and innovation is everywhere apparent.

It is not the rhetorical question *per se* that makes the difference but the overall syntactic texture for which it provides a context; in other words, as with Yeats's declarative sentences, what matters is not so much the nature of the context itself as the specific and sometimes unique strategies that interact with it and within it.

This overview of Yeatsian syntax has been structured around an enumeration of the strategies Yeats uses most habitually, with effects that, if not precisely the same in each application of the same strategy, are at least predictable. At the same time, almost every example discussed has demonstrated a certain uniqueness and unpredictability. Beyond displaying mastery over a set of fixed strategies, Yeats's experiments constantly expand the boundaries of syntactic possibility and, wherever possible, elicit passion out of the deliberate structuring of syntax.

The syntactic texture is only one parameter of Yeatsian poetic texture. Because it has so much influence over the interpretation of the subject matter it presents, Yeatsian syntax is inseparable from that subject matter, as are his other principal techniques such as form, imagery, and symbolism. Yeats has successfully elevated syntax to the highest level of his poetic practice and developed it simultaneously with his other techniques into the rich surface texture that characterizes his poetry. Perhaps his greatest contribution lies in the attitude he displays toward syntax. He recognizes its potential as a poetic technique and reveals the passion and power it can offer to poetry.

The Medium as Creator: George Yeats's Role in the Automatic Script

MARGARET MILLS HARPER

Although Yeats recalled some eleven years after the event that his wife of four days had surprised him "by attempting automatic writing" on 24 October 1917 (AV-B 8), the couple did not apparently begin preserving the Script until 5 November. On that afternoon Thomas of Dorlowicz, the most important of George Yeats's Controls, appeared, identified himself, and informed Yeats that he was "here for a purpose" and "for her only."[1] From that time until the completion of the Script and numerous notebooks which became the ideological structure of *A Vision,* George was convinced that she was divinely imbued with some creative force not formerly available to her.[2] Although her husband directed the Script by his questions, it has not been known until recently that many— perhaps most—seminal ideas of *A Vision* originated in the mind of George Yeats. She answered W. B.'s sometimes fumbling questions, insisting occasionally that he rephrase; and she ordered the cosmic psychology and the tetradic structure of the book, giving him "metaphors for poetry" (AV-B 8) which he made use of for the remainder of his life. In this brief study I can do little more than suggest the magnitude of Yeats's debt to his mediumistic wife. But I can, I hope, show something of what is proving to be one of the most important results of the ongoing

---

1. Automatic Script (hereafter abbreviated *AS*) 5 November 1917. I would like to thank Senator Michael B. Yeats for permission to quote from unpublished materials. I am also greatly indebted to George Mills Harper. His recent book *The Making of Yeats's "A Vision": A Study of the Automatic Script,* 2 vols. (London: Macmillan; Carbondale: Southern Illinois University Press, 1987), the only full-length study of the Script, is an invaluable tool for students of the Yeatses' experiment. Readers may refer to it (hereafter cited as *MYV*) for fuller details of any day's Script.

2. She later wrote Olivia Shakespear candidly that her original intention was to "make an attempt to fake automatic writing," but she soon found her hand "seized by a superior power" (letter of 9 July 1926, cited in Virginia Moore, *The Unicorn: W. B. Yeats' Search for Reality* [New York: Macmillan, 1954], 253).

study of the Script and other *Vision* manuscripts. We are having to take an extraordinary fact into far more serious consideration than we have before: much of the literary output of one of our century's major poets from the year of his marriage on was directly influenced by a unique imaginative partnership with a highly creative woman.[3]

It is fair to say that W. B. was always careful to give George credit, as he did most notably in the introduction to the 1937 edition of *A Vision*.[4] From the beginning, it was she and her Controls who instructed him to disguise her participation. As early as 25 November 1917, Thomas told Yeats that "the information is not to be betrayed as to *source* all else may be done . . . you can say it is a sequence[5] & your original thought that is to a degree true." They extracted a "pledge of secrecy" soon after (23 December 1917). In the important session on 4 March 1918, just before the couple left England for their first trip to Ireland together, all of the Guides and Controls[6] who had taught them previously gathered for a spiritual send-off. Their first item of business was to inform Willy (whom George would dub "William Tell" for his tendency to be indiscreet[7]), "We are not pleased because you talk too freely of spirits & of initiation." He would be allowed to "imply *invention* if need be," mention "dreams *yes,*" or even "say a good deal is of super-

---

3. Not much is known about Georgie Hyde-Lees. Luckily, though, Ann Saddlemyer's biography, which will remedy this lamentable state of affairs, is underway.

4. In this context, Harper cites a fascinating letter to John Quinn in which Yeats mentions that his wife has been "every evening in my study helping me at my work" but is silent about the occult nature of her help (*MYV* 2:386). Having promised not to talk about the Script, he was willing to imply that she collaborated even more directly in his literary work than she probably did.

5. According to the Script, Sequence and Allusion are loaded terms. The definitions given by the Controls do not make these ideas very clear: "Sequence is an intensity produced by association of words ideas & images" (31 August 1918); "Allusion is the impact of the objective image idea or thought upon the subjective and is an impact which has no relation to the content of that subjective" (2 September 1918). We do know that Sequence, associated with Phase 15, desire, and symbolic art, is a positive term. Allusion, its opposite, is associated with Phase 1, "cessation of desire," and allegorical or abstract art (*MYV* 1:200).

6. Guides have names of natural objects, such as Apple, Rose, or Leaf, while Controls are named for mythical people, such as Dionertes, Thomas of Dorlowicz, or Aymor. For a discussion of the difference between these classes of Communicators, consult *MYV* 1:269n16, and Robert A. Martinich, "W. B. Yeats's Sleep and Dream Notebooks," diss., Florida State University, 1982, 19–21. Hereafter cited as Martinich.

7. Richard Ellmann, *The Man and the Masks,* new edition (New York: Norton, 1978), 168.

normal & the rest invention & deduction," but he must not discuss *"guidance of spirits in your life."* They even threatened, "we warn now next time we shall not warn." George felt as strongly as they did, breaking into their plural voice to state in first-person singular, "I do not *wish* the spirit source revealed." On numerous occasions the excited poet was instructed not to allow visitors to the sessions. Mrs. Yeats's hand also penned the first mention of the fabricated author of the "Speculum Angelorum et Hominorum,"[8] the book outlining the System which Michael Robartes found in Cracow in the story Yeats invented for the introduction to the first version. Yeats wrote the story, but Thomas first suggested that the book's "supernormal origin [be] received through a person we will call Gyraldus" (*AS* 20 January 1919).[9]

As Yeats wished to acknowledge his wife's role in the Script, both of them were careful to give credit to her Controls, although it is difficult to discover from their frustratingly vague explanations just who or what they took the spiritual instructors to have been. The question of the relationship between the various parties involved in the automatic process, that thorny subject, is one that we shall have to ask again if we are to consider what part George played in receiving the "System." Luckily, the manuscripts can tell us much about the nature of the complex collaboration. From the beginning of the experiments, it was obvious that the questioner was not an independent variable: on 20 November 1917, W. B. asked and was told that he was correct in assuming that his questions were guided from the other side. He was guided by this side as well, as was apparent in sessions such as the one on 1 February 1918. He asked if the Control was "satisfied with our method of questioning."

---

8. The Latin title was problematical for Yeats. The final word is spelled *Homenorum* (possibly a typographical error) under the portrait of Giraldus which Yeats commissioned his friend Edmund Dulac to create for the first edition of *A Vision* but *Hominorum* in that book's introduction (xvii). Neither spelling is correct. Yeats used the proper spelling, *Hominum*, in a letter to Lady Gregory dated 4 January 1918 (L 644), but left blank spaces for the fictional title in two unfinished manuscript versions and filled in one of the spaces with "Speculum Angelorum et Hominis," a spelling he retained for a third manuscript and the Robartes-Aherne typescript (AV-A, Editorial Introduction xxxi, xlixn21). By 1937, he had settled on the best choice of the four spellings: *Hominum* is the only variant there (38, 39).

9. Who the historical Gyraldus (or Giraldus: the Yeatses spelled it either way) was has been a matter of critical debate. For a recent account of the possibilities see Kathleen Raine, *Yeats the Initiate: Essays on Certain Themes in the Writings of W. B. Yeats* (Mountrath, Ireland: Dolmen; London: Allen, 1986), chapter XIII (408–30).

"Yes quite," came the answer; "there may be some points you do not think of—if so I will put them in mind of medium."[10]

Nor was the medium merely a passive vessel into whose mind truths were to be poured. She does not seem to have been in a trance-like state, or at any rate not one so deep that it prevented her from interrupting the proceedings to add her own observations. She often did so, usually initialing them to distinguish her own remarks from those of the spirits. In one such remark, early in the Script, she asked Thomas how much influence he and other Controls had over her unconscious mind. "Do you only come when you are questioned," she asked, "or do you live for a time within our life or our thought. For instance do you enter into my dream when I am writing or thinking of writing?" To her first query Thomas answered that "the former" was true; "to the last question" he answered "no" (*AS* 11 November 1917). At one point Yeats recorded that she objected strenuously to a formulation by the Control: "medium finds it incredible that 2 persons who shared in same passion do not meet in P[assionate] B[ody]" (*AS* 31 January 1918). At another, Thomas rejects her interpretation of a question and announces "medium wrong" (*AS* 2 June 1918). As the experiment continued, Mrs. Yeats eventually dropped the convention of running the letters and words together when her pen was moved.[11] This unremarked change in her handwriting merely reflected what none of the participants had denied from the outset: George's mind and character were a necessary influence on the System.

Furthermore, the Controls readily admitted that they were influenced by the minds of both of their human collaborators. Marcus, a less confident Control than Thomas, excused his inability to answer a question by explaining, "I told you I cannot ask those questions." Ask of whom? W. B. wanted to know. "Those about you?" "No," Marcus replied; "I ask from your minds." "Do [you] obtain all your knowledge

---

10. Some of the answers as well as the questions came from his mind, as a notebook entry indicates: "Information last night from Dionertes or from me he confirming" (Martinich 196). Actually, Yeats provided a good deal of the information in his leading questions. He often, with the spirits' approval, asked questions which implied their own answers, so that the Communicators or the medium only needed to confirm or deny what he had already formulated.

11. She also began recording the questions as well as the answers (a happy change for anyone reading the Script, since her handwriting is much more legible than Yeats's) at this point, on 16 June 1919.

through us?" "Yes." "Does Thomas?" "I cant say." "Do you obtain through us more than we know of." "No" (*AS* 3 December 1917). Notice that the spirits are influenced by *both* human minds. Later, a Guide could not help Yeats place his old friend Florence Farr in a phase because, he or she explained, "Medium never saw her but twice & I can't place her from that" (*AS* 5 January 1918). Another Guide, Rose, gave a Star Wars–like description of what impeded placement of a date in the historical cone: "I cant get from your memory detail—until I do I cannot give you particulars—Force not good" (*AS* 7 June 1918). To a series of questions about the relationship between the automatic faculty by which the System was given and a person's Anima Mundi, Yeats was told clearly that the automatic faculty, and therefore the System, was neither universal nor unconscious: "The automatic faculty is a machinery & not a reservoir to begin with—It selects from memory in conscious waking States" (*AS* 15 January 1919). On another occasion this idea was re- peated: "The normal condition *does* produce automatic thought" (*AS* 2 September 1918). Of course, both of the Yeatses believed that the "nor- mal condition" involved not only their memories or subconscious minds but also the spirit world. Two Guides, Leaf and Fish, made it plain that spirits and humans had equal roles to play: "automatic writing is two," they explained. "[O]ne definite spirit thought—two subliminal—both are written by an automatic mechanical velocity purely nervous which is set in motion by a spirit" (*AS* 10 January 1918).[12] But Thomas, with Rose assisting, put it best: "This system is *not* preexistent—it is devel- oped & created by us & by you two or you three now [their daughter Anne, born six weeks earlier, was included by this time]—from a preex- isting psychology—all the bones are *in* the world—we only select & our selection is subordinate to *you both*—therefore we are dependent on you & you influence our ability to develop & create by every small detail of

---

12. Yeats tended to overstress the spiritual, he was told several times. On 21 November 1918, to his puzzlement that "you seem to give the supernatural a very small part in moral development," Thomas replied that "The reliance absolute reliance on the supernatural and the consequent abandonment of personal judgment is as great a tempta- tion as any other." In another interesting exchange, Yeats was annoyed that the spirits' knowledge was incomplete. When he was told that "[O]ften we leave medium to write answers quite independently of us from conscious mind or subliminal," he complained, "You understand process no better than we do! You can only affirm the fact!" The Control bristled: "You wont admit subliminal but you will have to before the philosophy is through" (*AS* 10 January 1918).

your joint life."[13] The System, in other words, depended upon relationships: it was a family affair.

As time passed, indeed, the Script, "more & more influenced by her will," would "therefore become less automatic," Thomas informed them on 11 November 1918. Near the end of their first pregnancy, upon hearing that they were making little headway "because mediums vitality low & sensitive," Willy seems to have suggested that he take over some of George's tasks. Despite her fatigue and perhaps bordeom—she tired of the experiments after the first few months and tried repeatedly to get him to quit, usually to write poetry—the Controls would not allow him to continue alone. They answered an unrecorded question, "Not in that way it all depends on the writer—writers nerves[;] No no because we cant use you alone—must have you & medium *equally*" (*AS* 25 December 1918). At the start of the first session after Anne's birth (perhaps reflecting a confidence in mutual creation inspired by the birth of a child), her mother's title was changed from *medium* to *interpreter* (*AS* 20 March 1919).

Interpreter is a far more accurate description of the role George Yeats played in the process than *medium,* implying as it does that she translated ideas into intelligible language. As we shall see, many of *A Vision*'s terms originated with her. She also tended to be an important organizing force, making sure that Willy's enthusiasm for new information did not outstrip their codifying of the material already received.[14] Perhaps the biggest reason for Yeats's later dissatisfaction with the first edition of *A Vision* was his sense that the raw material, given over the several years of daily reception of the System, overwhelmed his ability to shape it into a

---

13. *AS* 9 April 1919. Yeats considered this information important enough to copy it verbatim into the large Card File (hereafter cited *CF*) he used to organize ideas from the Script in preparation for writing *A Vision* (*MYV* 2:74; *CF* M41).

14. Typical of her impulse toward organization is an early session with Leaf, a Guide. To Yeats's opening question, "What would [you] like to begin with," Leaf replied, "I feel there is rather an arid ground to work on at present—it is perhaps because there is so much unfinished in this work and I had better perhaps finish the lists—yes" (*AS* 7 January 1918). Two days later, Thomas was more insistent that they straighten up their affairs before proceeding with new information. At the end of a long session, he refused to go on with other matters about which Yeats asked, answering instead, "I shall have to stop for a time—I want to get some psychological matters cleared up . . . Yes I will go on to that after man at [Phases] 15 and one so get out lists . . . I would rather for a few days go on with less constructive work or please make *one* list with *all* emblems descriptions phases masks genius & so on . . . Yes but I wont go on to inner circles till I have worked on outer fully" (*AS* 9 January 1918).

unified whole. He would doubtless have been far less able to do so if Mrs. Yeats's "interpretation" had been less effective. Dionertes, one of her Controls, explained it in telling phrases: "she finds the words, we send the wave & she as it were catches it in a box."[15]

By the time Yeats entered into a notebook that they had "decided to give up 'sleep' 'automatic writing' & all such means & to discourage mediumship, & to get our further thought by 'positive means,'"[16] George Yeats's "box" contained many of the central ideas, organizing principles, diagrams, and terminology of *A Vision*. As her husband's notebook entry implies, the "further thought" that the writing of the book would require was also hers as well as his. He asked for and received her corrections and suggestions for revision all during the frustrating process of working on *A Vision*.[17]

Let us now rummage through that box for some of the more important contributions which were made to *A Vision* through George. In the first two days of the Script which the couple recorded, she (and Thomas) initiated a discussion of sun and moon, warning her distinguished husband that his nature was too lunar or subjective and should be influenced by solar or objective forces. These cosmic polarities were personally and intellectually exciting to Yeats, elaborating as they did on ideas he had long entertained of antinomic impulses within the human personality, and they came to constitute the basic psychology of the book. Less than a week later, on 10 November, the discussion turned to the differences between Antithetical and Primary, the great opposites which inform the whole System.[18]

---

15. Notebook entry, 19 October 1921 (Martinich 165).

16. Notebook entry, 18 September 1922 (Martinich 178).

17. This help came despite the fact that, as Yeats recorded in a notebook, "She does not want me to write system for publication—not as exposition—but only to record & to show to a few people" (Martinich 181).

18. Although the questions are perceptive in this particular interchange, the answers clearly lead the dialogue. A sample of the Script from 10 November will illustrate who is leading whom on this day:

1. Is not the antithetical self (when the Primary is the stronger) sometimes a temptation? Is not the converse of this true?

2. The antithetical self is necessarily always the temptation because it offers a contrast to the primary If the primary had no contrast to look upon their [sic] would be consequent absorption in a morality outside itself which would be accepted as a thing against which there could be no conflict in the case where either the primary or *antithetic* is almost predominant it produces the idiot or the fool as distinct from lunacy

Two weeks later, she again developed an idea whose germ had apparently already entered their conversations. At the end of a late afternoon session on 24 November, Yeats asked, "What are the 28 stages." Thomas, the Control for the session, was perhaps reflecting Mrs. Yeats's readiness for dinner when he replied, "I will give their meanings later." True to his word, Thomas returned at 8:30 that evening. A circular diagram on which George appears to have begun to draw the four cardinal directions and the diagonal lines indicating the locations Head, Heart, Loins, and Fall (terms which first entered the discussion two days earlier, the fourth term supplied by George[19]) is interrupted by the instructions "No draw circle for me into 28." The numbers do appear over the sketched lines of the circle, and on the next pages are listed the descriptions of the Ego (later called Will) for each of the phases of the moon. This list appeared, with few changes, in the "Table of the Four Faculties" of *A Vision* (AV-A 30–33). In the next few months, Mrs.

Genius is implied in the conflict for domination where the antithetical is *much stronger* but not predominant it has the practical force of the primary self to control it—it is when the primary becomes submerged that lunacy ensues And learn this

The fool is born so—the predominant self submerges him from birth nothing changes that The lunatic is gradually predominated by *one or the other* & therefore *may be cured* The fool is predominated by the *antithetical* or dream self from birth—the lunatic may be predominated *by either*.

19. Yeats brought the first three terms into the discussion on 22 November, asking Thomas, "Do you know Blake terms Head, Heart Loins." Mrs. Yeats wrote "Yes—but thus" and answered with explanations and two diagrams, one of which dissects a circle into quarters, labeling the intersectors Head, Heart, Loins, and Fall, a new fourth term. She then wrote in answer to an unrecorded question, "No—but if I can get it from yourselves I may be able to—." Yeats's next question, predictably, was "What do you mean by fall," to which she wrote "The beginning of anger and the departure from wisdom." Yeats had fretted with the triad of terms earlier in his and Edwin Ellis's edition of Blake (*The Works of William Blake: Poetic, Symbolic, and Critical*, 3 vols. [London: Quaritch, 1893]), adding to complete a tetrad first *Womb* (1:262) and later doubling the term *Loins*. He explained then that the Loins

region is double, and implies both water and earth,—both procreation and excretion, both vegetation and death. In Blake, however, the symbol of loins is divided into desire and fruition in the world of mortality. . . . The sequence Head, Heart, Loins deserves to be noted, as every triad has appropriate relations with it, and with its connection with the Zoas.

                        Creation, Redemption, Judgement,

is the great triad; but even here the last member is double. . . . (1:347)

He was uncomfortable with sets not easily divisible into four, here and elsewhere in *A Vision*. See, for example, his note to the table entitled "General Character of Creative Mind affecting Certain Phases": "This and the following Table are divided into ten divisions because they were given me in this form, and I have not sufficient confidence in my knowledge to turn them into the more convenient twelve-fold divisions" (AV-A 34n).

Yeats's hand drew up lists of Good and Bad Masks (later called True and False masks), Evil and Creative Geniuses (changed to True and False Creative Mind), and Personas of Fate which are also reproduced without much alteration in the "Table of the Four Faculties."[20] Many, if not most, of the Examples for the 28 phases were also placed by her: her husband in effect chose *who* would be included, and she chose *where* historical personalities, literary figures, or friends such as Socrates (27), Luther (25), Blake (16), Dostoevsky (22), Flaubert (22),[21] Nietzsche (12), Synge (23), and AE (25) should appear. Her writing told him that there is "No human being at either" Phase 1 or Phase 15 and that "spirits at 15 [are] very beautiful" (AS 2 January 1918). And it was she who placed her husband at Phase 17, the most auspicious phase for artists, Maud Gonne at Phase 16 (with Helen of Troy, though Helen was later moved[22]), Iseult Gonne at 14, Lady Gregory at 24, and herself at 18.

Thus far I have mentioned contributions which George Yeats made to Book I of the 1925 version of *A Vision,* "What the Caliph Partly Learned," which sets forth the Great Wheel. But the other three books also bear the imprint of her extraordinary inventiveness. The second book, "What the Caliph Refused to Learn," is a rather confused and loosely organized presentation of ideas that underpin the Wheel: gyres, the Great Year, and the Four Principles, among others. The third and fourth books, "Dove or Swan" and "The Gates of Pluto," elaborate the System's use of gyres and history, continuing the old idea of the Great Year, and explain the application of the Principles and other matters having to do with the actions of souls after death. As we might expect, the Script shows many of the ideas in these books as well arriving through George's mind.

---

20. The Masks and Evil Geniuses were given on 3 January 1918 by Fish, a Guide. On 24 January Thomas and Fish gave a number of descriptions of Personas of Fate amid numerous questions about the ideas upon which the Faculties are based. Two days later Thomas oversaw a partial list of Personas, but the complete list of Personas of Fate (as well as Creative Geniuses) was given much later, by Ameritus on 25 October and Dionertes on 22 December 1919. By this late date, Mrs. Yeats and the Controls were apparently anxious to get the Table organized: they merely gave lists, refusing to allow Yeats to ask any potentially distracting questions during these sessions.

21. Two works of Flaubert, the *Temptation of St. Anthony* and the unfinished story "La Spirale," are important to *A Vision,* and both were first mentioned by Mrs. Yeats. The first is designated one of "the sacred books" of Phase 22 (the other is Flaubert's *Bouvard and Pécuchet*); the second is the primary example of "The Gyre" in that section of Book II (AV-A 93, 128). See *MYV* 2:148–49.

22. In *A Vision* she is placed at Phase 14 (AV-A 67).

On Christmas Day 1917 she and her Control presented her husband
with a valuable gift: the image of a "funnell" to be used "as a symbol."[23]
The explanation following a drawing of a spiraling cone introduced the
idea of "Stability at base only" and suggested that Willy "apply it to
your own meditations." The Communicators added, "This method is
only a machinery but you can use it." Use it Yeats did, of course, not
only in *A Vision* but also in such poems as "The Second Coming." Both
of the Yeatses later worked at length on the meaning of the symbol they
variously called *funnel, spindle, coil, watch spring, hourglass, spiral, cone,* or,
finally, *gyre.* Mrs. Yeats also originally supplied the image of two circles,
an outer of individual personality and an inner of human civilization, in a
diagram during the early months of the Script (*AS* 25 November 1917).
This image, of course, underlies the premise basic to *A Vision* that the
same principles regulate each human being and collective humankind.
Actually, it was some four months after the concept of the funnel first
entered the dialogue that the couple shifted from considering the symbol
in relation to the individual soul—a topic that was little used in *A Vi-
sion*—to the far more fruitful subject of the gyre and the movements of
civilization. At the beginning of one of their first sessions in the west of
Ireland, Yeats broached this subject by asking, "Can one apply funnel to
human history" (*AS* 8 April 1918). The Control's positive reply set off
months of investigation which provide the theme and many of the details
of "Dove or Swan," the third book of *A Vision.* There are numerous
notations of tentative dates for the phases, diagrams of diamonds and
hourglasses, and discussions as the Yeatses puzzled over this complicated
theory of history. Gradually the material became clear to them, so that in
late 1920 a new communicator named Carmichael could come during a
"sleep" and give "confirmation of classification of divisions of historical
cone."[24] Yeats wrote in the notebook they were keeping of sleeps and
meditations that Carmichael came "last night . . . and gave following
for history cone"—the "following" being an almost complete forerun-
ner of the diagram entitled "The Historical Cones" (*AV-A* 178) which
introduces and explains "Dove or Swan" (see figs. 1–2).

　　　In the 1937 edition of *A Vision* Yeats apologizes, "I knew nothing of

23. The term *funnel* was first mentioned on 25 November 1917, apparently in re-
sponse to Yeats's request for "symbolism in this system of diurnal motion of ⊙" (his next
question mentions the funnel, asking for clarification of the previous answer), but the
answers to this part of that evening's session are, unfortunately, lost. Luckily, the idea was
taken up again a month later.

24. Martinich 92.

the *Four Principles* when I wrote the last Book: a script had been lost through frustration,[25] or through my own carelessness" (187). Indeed, several pages of Script having to do with the Principles are missing: torn or cut out of the notebooks in which the couple recorded the sessions. Carelessness is probably less the reason for their loss than frustration, though that frustration is very possibly the Interpreter's: the Principles originally appeared as complex analogues of Yeats, Maud Gonne, Iseult Gonne, and herself, and much that was revealed about them was intensely personal. George Yeats had an amazing tolerance of her new husband's obsession with analyzing his desire for other women, but apparently some of these revelations were insufferable even though they were abstracted into cosmic proportions and, furthermore, recorded on pages clearly meant for no eyes but hers and his. The frustration is now ours as well, for the Script involving the Principles contains some of the most arresting material of the years of experimentation. Three of the four were first mentioned by Mrs. Yeats on 31 January 1918, in the course of a discussion of the soul after death. The Controls had established, in answer to a question from W. B. about visions of loved ones seen after death, that a spirit just separated from the body sees "friends kindred spirits guides" immediately after the moment of death but is then left alone "to meditate." "What is it set to meditate on?" asked W. B. The next several questions show him hearing, for the first time, of three of what would become the Four Principles. The soul meditates, George wrote, "on the dissolution of the passionate body." "You mean not the phisical body." "The passionate body." "How many bodies are there?" "3—physical passionate spiritual." Later in the evening the fourth term, Celestial Body, arose in response to a request for "a diagram of planes." With two minor alterations—the term *Husk* replacing *Physical Body* and *Spirit* replacing *Spiritual Body*—the Principles were now in place.

Notes in Yeats's hand on a separate page relate the Four Principles to the Four Elements (Earth, Water, Air, and Fire). He was making the immediate connection between the Principles and the tetradic relationship between himself, Maud, Iseult, and George which he and his

---

25. It is difficult to conceive how one might lose something through *frustration,* in the ordinary sense of the word. Yeats's use of the term here probably refers to Frustrators, the deceiving spirits which he describes in the 1937 introduction (AV-B 12–13) and who caused considerable trouble during the receiving of the Script and especially later during the period of the Sleeps. See AV-A, Notes, 75–76; Martinich 161–66; and *MYV* 2:180–84.

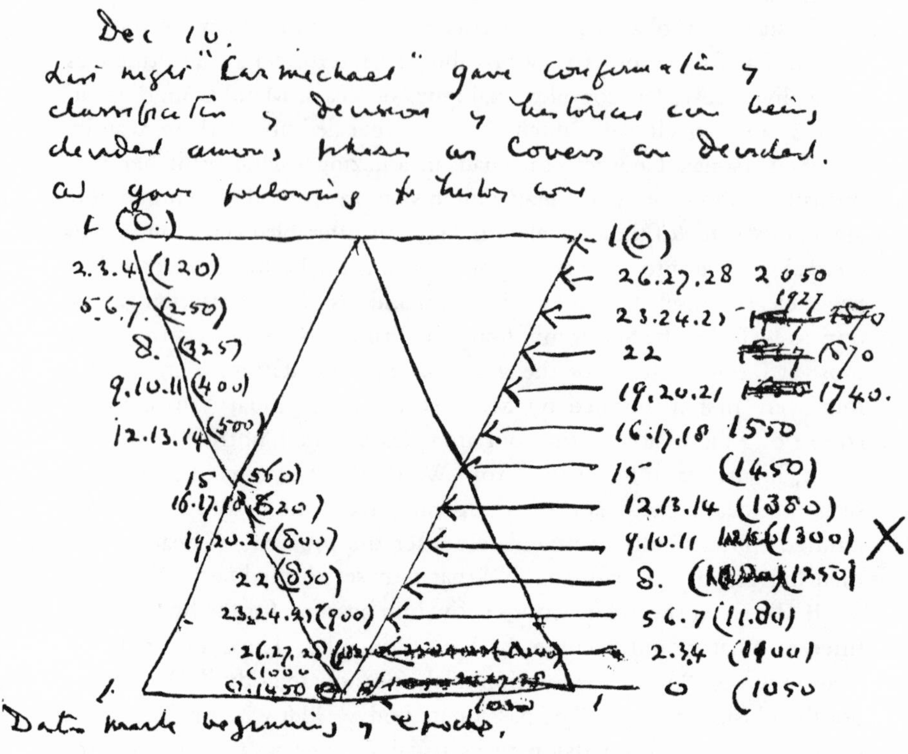

Fig. I. Notebook entry, 10 December 1920

THE HISTORICAL CONES

The numbers in brackets refer to phases, and the other numbers to dates A.D. The line cutting the cones a little below 250, 900, 1180 and 1927 shows four historical *Faculties* related to the present moment. May 1925.

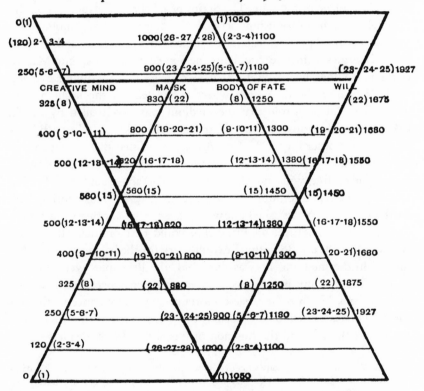

Fig. 2. Diagram of the Historical Cones from *A Vision* (1925). (Used with permission of Macmillan Publishing Company from *A Vision* by W. B. Yeats. Copyright 1937 by W. B. Yeats, renewed 1965 by Bertha Georgie Yeats and Anne Yeats. And with permission of A. P. Watt, Ltd., on behalf of Michael B. Yeats and Macmillan London Ltd.)

wife had explored in connection with *The Only Jealousy of Emer,* completed a scant two weeks earlier.[26] He asked that night several questions about the Passionate Body of George and Maud, and for the next two days continued to explore, in addition to the universal meaning of the Principles and life after death, the symbolic identification which he and the medium were developing: Willy equals Physical Body; Iseult equals Passionate Body; Maud equals Spiritual Body; George equals Celestial Body. The medium must have been gratified that her Principle was on the highest plane of the four. The Script of 1 February elaborates on the Principles and the relationships between them, establishing, among other things, that the "pb & cb cannot be joined but spirit & cb and spirit & pb"—George's Principle could not be joined to Iseult's, but Maud's could join either her daughter's or George's. The following evening W. B. reopened the discussion where it had left off the night before, when they had been told that the medium was "controlled by an old PB." "What do you mean by controlled," he asked, "when PB continues into another life?" The Control requested that they "wait for ten minutes please," then gave a complicated answer having to do with the restriction of free will and choice in her—or any—soul "by forcing images into a repetition of its former circumstances—This continues till death of old pb." Yeats asked "how . . . the ego"—another term for the Physical Body or Husk, his Principle—could best "remedy this," and was told that "It can do nothing except work for the balance of the other three." In the medium, he was then told, the Principles were not balanced: "the medium is not passionate in your sense because the old pb forces it back."[27] In these three important days many concepts that inform "The Gates of Pluto"—such as the Vision of the Blood Kindred, Dreaming Back,[28] and the function of burial ritual to the spirit—were

---

26. Yeats had written Lady Gregory, in a letter dated 14 January 1918, "To-day I finished my new Cuchulain play"—that play being *The Only Jealousy of Emer* (L 645). For an analysis of the autobiographical elements of the play, see Herbert J. Levine, *Yeats's Daimonic Renewal* (Ann Arbor: UMI Research Press, 1983), 97–100.

27. Mrs. Yeats obviously considered this information important: she quoted the last answer verbatim in a notebook, substituting G. Y. for *medium* (*MYV* 1:187).

28. Dreaming Back, an idea which fascinated Yeats, is of great significance to an understanding of the Script and the other methods by which the Yeatses received the System: the Communicators were Dreaming Back when they passed on their information through the medium. Thomas informed them on 11 November 1917 that the spirits were fulfilling this necessary stage in their journey from death back to birth as they came to their human partners: "As long as we still return we are dreaming when we cease dreaming we no longer return."

introduced and explored. At the same time, important qualities of their marriage were being defined: how the young wife and the middle-aged poet would relate sexually; how their marriage would take into account his famous, and longstanding, passions for other beautiful women. George in this instance communicated truths that are truly remarkable in how simultaneously critical they were both to the developing System and to the Yeatses' private lives.

It is beyond my purpose here to do more than mention the "personal" aspects of the Script, like these private analogues to the Four Principles. I must lament with Yeats that "I have not . . . dealt with the whole of my subject, perhaps not even with what is most important, writing nothing about the Beatific Vision, little of sexual love" (AV-A xii). Perhaps as much as 75 percent of the Script falls into this category:[29] intimate revelations about the Yeatses as individuals or as husband and wife, prophecy about their children, and private information or opinion about their friends and associates. As even a cursory reading of George Mills Harper's detailed history of the years of experimenting suggests, the purpose of the Automatic Script was, in good measure, a way of discovering symbolic meaning for Yeats's personal as well as poetic life. The Controls said as much in the early weeks of the experiment. After a lengthy exploration of the "relation to state of my life" of the four Cuchulain plays (and other private matters), Yeats asked, "Is this teaching one of the purposes for which you came." "Yes," his wife wrote[30] (AS 20 November 1917). But all this belongs to another study, even though it may well be that George's influence on her husband's ways of thinking about himself and the people and events of his life is ultimately of far more importance than her direct contributions to his literary work.

Not that she had little to do with his creative life besides A Vision. Despite the firmly negative replies which she or the Controls gave to W. B.'s several questions about the possibility of their collaboration in "practical work,"[31] images and themes for several plays and poems came

---

29. Harper estimates this percentage (MYV 1:x).

30. Her full answer was "Yes—number two." But neither she nor Willy elaborated on what the first reason was; perhaps it was clear to them.

31. After several months of Script, Yeats turned on 4 January 1918 to the question of collaboration in literary endeavors. It would be possible with several phasal combinations, he was told (notably 17—his—and 12, Ezra Pound's, or 24, Lady Gregory's), but he could not work with his wife: "you & medium could not do practical work together." "How would shoe pinch if we tried practical work?" he asked. "Different natures—neither would adapt to the other." He pressed the Control, "Could we not colaborate when ever the

directly from her. The most exciting of these works is possibly *The Only Jealousy of Emer*, for whose meaning he had been groping, unable to write until his questions about the "symbolism not apparent to me in my Cuchulain plays" (*AS* 20 November 1917) were answered. Over the course of several sittings, elaborate schemes of symbolic meaning were developed for the four principal characters of the play, who were identified by Phase, Element, planet, astrological sign, cardinal direction, and part of the human body, among other correspondences. The significance of the lack of "contact" between Cuchulain and Fand, of Bricriu as Cuchulain's opposite, and of Emer's loss of Cuchulain, among other elements of the play, all came from the interpreter's answers to Yeats's questions about his work-in-progress.[32] Yeats also explored numerous aspects of another play, *Calvary*, in the Script. He discussed with the Controls and the Interpreter such matters as the Phases of Judas and Christ (8 and 22 respectively), their Tinctures (Christ is Primary; Judas Antithetical), or the Principles represented by Judas and Peter (Judas is Creative Genius; Peter, who was dropped from the play, was to be Evil Genius).[33] The Script also contains numerous dialogues about betrayal and temptation, despair and pity, the roles of Victim and Teacher, and fate and destiny, the unusual terms for predestination and free will, or chance and choice, the great opposites whose struggle is the central ideological conflict of the play.

We should remember, too, that seminal ideas for several poems came directly out of the Script. Over the course of several sittings in January 1919 both Yeatses explored the notion of complementary dreaming and the images that inform "Towards Break of Day" and "Another Song of a Fool." As George Harper and Sandra Sprayberry have discovered, a drawing and notes made by George probably provided the image patterns for both poems and the basic organization of

---

creative power came in?" But the answer was insistent: "Yes but *not* over practical." She could—or would—not lend a hand with business at the Abbey Theatre either, he learned two weeks later. He hesitated with good reason to request her help: "I think of asking medium to help with plays etc. If so should I postpone it?" The response was decidedly negative: "Not good—not enough constructive ability." Again, he pressed, "Do you mean she cannot design costumes Etc.?" "Not well done," he was told. The work on the System was all she could manage: "She cant do anything till this is done—no good trying—plenty of activity but we use it all" (*AS* 18 January 1918).

    32. See *MYV* 1:25–28, 76–90, 119–28, 147–53 and for accounts of the more important discussions of *The Only Jealousy*.

    33. See *MYV* 1:166–69.

"Towards Break of Day."[34] The little poem "The Four Ages of Man" restates an idea from the Script with very little change, although it was written some seventeen years after Thomas and Fish told W. B. that "in every cycle—first 1/4 circle fighting body—2nd 1/4 fighting mind—3rd 1/4 fighting heart—4th 1/4 fighting soul."[35]

In addition to these poems, which are unusually collaborative, many other symbols or concepts (or even turns of phrase) we have come to think of as specifically Yeatsian are in fact not the product of his brain alone. Among these are the idea of "hunchback . . . saint . . . [and] idiot"[36] for the last three phases of the moon, used in "The Phases of the Moon" and "The Saint and the Hunchback." The butterfly, symbol of wisdom, as well as the tower, symbolizing "abundant flowing life" (AS 20 March 1918), were both originally associated with George by her Controls.[37]

34. George Mills Harper and Sandra L. Sprayberry, "Complementary Creation: Notes on 'Another Song of a Fool' and 'Towards Break of Day,'" *Yeats* 4 (1984): 69–85. The same evening's Script alludes to Cormac and his time; the strong injunction that Yeats "go to the past—A historical & spiritual past—the church the castle on the hill . . go to the hill Castle" since he was "drained dry—the true moment for vision" gave urgency and direction to the writing of "The Double Vision of Michael Robartes" (AS 7 January 1919).

35. AS 28 January 1918. This idea had considerable, and continuing, appeal to Yeats. After George recorded it, he made notes in the *CF* and in a notebook and used it in "The Four Contests of the antithetical within itself" in *A Vision* (AV-A 35). He altered the order of mind and heart (identifying the Second Quarter with heart and the Third with mind) in galley proofs of AV-A and kept the new order for the poem. For further details see *MYV* 1:172–73.

36. AS 25 November 1917; see also *MYV* 1:55.

37. The butterfly, "symbol of innocence of emotion" and of "wisdom overcoming anger" or simply of "wisdom why not," was associated both with the medium and with Iseult Gonne in the Script of 22 November 1917. Although the poet asserts in "Blood and the Moon," "I declare this tower is my symbol" (P 237), Thomas had earlier told Yeats to use it to "make a protective symbol round medium . . . a sheltering symbol," and that "the tower is for the medium *alone*" (AS 28 October 1918). According to Barbara J. Frieling, the tower "became central to the Yeatses' search for the symbolic truth of the journey of the soul in the 1918 AS, culminating in three symbolic sittings at Thoor Ballylee on 21–23 September" ("A Critical Edition of W. B. Yeats's Automatic Script, 11 March–30 December 1918," diss., Florida State University, 1987). Indeed, in the spring of that year, while they were at Glendalough with its round tower, they were told that it symbolized the Passionate Body as well as "life—abundant flowing life," most notably their life together as husband and wife. Yeats learned that the symbol "is not you alone but both"; its meaning was that "you must have a full yet simple life . . . loving normal life" (AS 24 March 1918). See *MYV* 1:243–45 for an analysis of Yeats's use of the tower as a symbol of conjugal union in "Under the Round Tower" and its connection with the spiraling movement of the historical cones. Yeats mentioned the latter in *A Vision* as "that continual oscillation which I have symbolised elsewhere as a King and Queen, who are Sun and Moon also, and whirl round and round as they mount up through a Round Tower" (AV-A 182).

Yeats appropriated them for himself and for his poetry in "Tom O'Roughley," in which he asserts that "wisdom is a butterfly / And not a gloomy bird of prey" (P 141), and in the many uses he found for towers, especially Thoor Ballylee, the Yeatses' summer residence near Gort. That tower was habitable by mid-September 1918, although Thomas complained that it was "very *cold*" on the last of the three days the Yeatses stayed there that year (*AS* 23 September 1918). The idea of Dreaming Back, that the soul after death undergoes "as it were a smoothing out or an unwinding" (AV-A 227) by reliving important events from its life in reverse order, is of course central to *Purgatory* and *The Dreaming of the Bones*. It also has a part in such poems as "Shepherd and Goatherd," in which the spirit of Robert Gregory "grows younger every second":

> Jaunting, journeying
> To his own dayspring,
> He unpacks the loaded pern
> Of all 'twas pain or joy to learn,
> Of all that he had made

> (P 144–45)

and "The Hero, the Girl, and the Fool," in which "all works that have / From cradle run to grave / From grave to cradle run instead" (P 561) once the first movement is completed. It was George, or Thomas, who first mentioned that spirits "dream backwards remember. . . . When they reach the prenatal they have returned to the condition of being able to go forward" early in the course of the Script (*AS* 11 November 1917).[38] Finally, her hand first wrote that the "soul of world [is] in centre" of the historical gyres and that the modern age is in chaos because "the worlds civilization is apart from these centres" (*AS* 12, 16 April 1918). In doing so, she introduced the apocalyptic image Yeats was to use so forcefully in the opening lines of "The Second Coming," in which "the centre cannot hold" in "the widening gyre" (P 187).

Like the Controls, then, who could only "think & elaborate our thought in as far as it is possible for us to find that necessary help from the medium" (*AS* 11 November 1917), Yeats too required her help to elaborate the System and the many other works which it informed or influenced. With the publication of the Script and the other *Vision* papers,

---

38. Yeats had touched on a similar idea earlier in "Swedenborg, Mediums, and the Desolate Places," noting that country people believe that "after death every man grows upward or downward to the likeness of thirty years . . . 'for to grow old in heaven is to grow young'" (Ex 39).

we can at last begin to recognize the extent of that help and assess its tremendous impact upon his creative life. As part of this assessment, the changes that George Yeats set in motion for her poet husband should draw our attention to several areas to be explored in future studies. First (and foremost) is the question of what new qualities his art begins to have as a result of this tremendous, and sudden, infusion of the feminine into his daily work as an occultist and writer—and the two were inseparable from the time George's Instructors came to give him "metaphors for poetry" (AV-B 8). Subtle changes can be seen in his representations of women, relationships between women and men, and male or female images or impulses, even though his work before 1917 certainly cannot be said to lack depictions which do considerable justice to a feminine point of view. In one of the important early discussions about his personal struggles, clothed in the language of *The Only Jealousy of Emer,* Yeats received answers to several questions about the changes Cuchulain would undergo after "sexual contact"—a veiled reference to the change in W. B.'s relationship to Maud and Iseult Gonne after his marriage. "After contact how will C be different?" he asked. "Man loses desire & seeks love," he was told. Love of whom? he had asked several questions earlier. "I cannot tell you till you know yourself," Mrs. Yeats wrote, "and you do know I think but perhaps unconsciously" (AS 7 January 1918). "Perhaps unconsciously" he did know already, even though *The Only Jealousy* records the process of his learning, that his relationship with his wife would enliven him—and thus his work—as Cuchulain is revived by Emer. A change occurred in Mrs. Yeats, too, as Thomas admitted some months later. Her part in their work, the automatic writing, begun in the painful first days of her married life, came like her husband's to depend on the replacement of "desire" by "love" for its success. In mirror writing, ostensibly so that she could not read it, Thomas advised Yeats, "The more you keep this medium emotionally and intellectually happy the more will script be possible now—at first it was better when she was emotionally unhappy but now the passivity is as small the opposite" (AS 10 November 1918). Satisfying a woman, not merely desiring one, became necessary to Yeats's spiritual search. Both he and George believed that her role, as it developed, had to be active for the work to proceed.[39] As Ameritus informed Willy, again in mirror

---

39. The spirits at one point warned that George's temperament was too active, however, as they continually instructed W. B. that his was not active enough. We can only speculate about exactly what was meant when, on 2 April 1918, Rose informed him, "You

writing, "Script depends on the love of medium for you—all intensity comes from that" (*AS* 30 June 1919). Wisdom would come by way of the heart, he was told, through George's Phase: "the wisdom of heart comes at 18" (*AS* 27 October 1918). A new kind of emotional and intellectual dialogue between man and woman underlies much of his later work, and we need to reevaluate that work as we learn more about the extraordinary woman who altered profoundly Yeats's conceptions of himself and his art.

The dialogue deserves close attention particularly in light of the decentralizing force it exerted to great effect on Yeats's thinking. For this sexual, spiritual, and mental partnership involved a delicate balance of harmony and tension between two opposite parties. Not only "love" but also *"discord"* was requisite, according to the Communicators. "Is this work made possible by a certain harmony of nature," asked the new husband on New Year's Day 1918. He was told that "harmony or rather *discord* [is] necessary." "What kind of discord makes such work possible?" "Similar interests—diversity of opinion," Mrs. Yeats wrote, "sex must be alike—mind different—Emotion alike—soul different but unlike—I mean in tendency not necessarily in quantity but in quality or nature" (*AS* 1 January 1918).[40] Whatever Yeats learned from this highly abstract statement, it is clear that the young English bride of the middle-aged Irish poet was certainly his opposite in many ways. Her "different" and "unlike" soul was the necessary "other" to his, they were told time and again.[41] Like Solomon and Sheba in Yeats's poems about that symbolic couple, the wisdom he and George sought was revealed only as they went "round and round" (P 138). The man and the other (whose motto in the Order of the Golden Dawn, significantly, was Nemo, "no man"[42]) strove both with and against each other through the questions and answers of their method. One reason why the Script makes fascinat-

---

must be as active & primary the medium passive & anti as you both can—You are too passive—I do not mean in communications only—."

40. They continued this important line of questioning many months later, Mrs. Yeats noting that they had done so at the top of the page for 1 January 1918: "question 50 contd Feb 16 1919."

41. Her Phase complemented his, as did the Faculties of those Phases, according to the Script of 1 January 1918. On that day, Fish explained the "wisdom from 2 people as in their communication, two souls at 17 and 18 respectively" in terms of Phase as well as Mask, Creative Mind, and Body of Fate.

42. See appendix X, "Order Names and Mottoes," in George Mills Harper, *Yeats's Golden Dawn* (London: Macmillan, 1974), 316.

ing reading, in fact, is the complex mixture of antagonism and alliance that its format encouraged, where answers were stimulated by questions and questions had to continue the topic of previous answers.[43] Although "not a man or woman / Born under the skies / Dare match in learning" (P 138) with the two experimenters, they labored long and energetically to understand the System, "a single light, / When oil and wick are burned in one" (P 177), through the contraries out of which it came. Like Blake, the couple believed that contraries "are necessary to Human existence"; when Yeats asked "Is life then opposition & contrast," Mrs. Yeats wrote "Yes it is the contact of contrasts" (AS 31 March 1918).

This is not to underemphasize the considerable similarities in their personalities and intellects. Any reader of the Script will be struck forcibly by the quality of mind that enabled George to fuse personal observations with philosophical ideas and express philosophy through occult cosmology—the same kind of mental habit that characterizes much of her husband's work (it is, of course, A Vision's most prominent feature). Throughout the thousands of pages of Script, their use of symbols meshes with uncanny precision, as do the connections they make between ideas that to an outside reader are only tangentially related, if related at all. Thomas was, perhaps, referring to the System's dependence on their related patterns of thinking when he told Yeats that "the closer the link the closer the reading by us of your thought & the easier it is" (AS 2 May 1918). Another Guide assured him that he was correct in assuming that a fortuitous "coincidence of signs" was responsible for their successful experiments and was "of supreme importance to a soul" (AS 4 January 1918).

Ultimately, the availability of the Script shows us that we need to find new ways of discussing literary creation when faced with the unique collaboration between Willy and George Yeats. They did not engage in joint authorship (the fact that George gave the name of one of her Controls as Ameritus, or "unworthy," may point to one reason for her hesitation to help with Yeats's "practical work"), but neither was she merely a passive "inspiration" for her husband's art. We may wonder, in fact, if her determined resistance to publishing the System, or even talking about it, might not have come in part from a realization that it would

---

43. We recall Yeats's description of the Communicators' method in AV-B: "Except at the start of a new topic, when they would speak or write a dozen sentences unquestioned, I had always to question, and every question to rise out of a previous answer and to deal with their chosen topic" (10–11).

be very difficult to explain just what part she was playing in the poet's work.

The poet may have articulated it best in the symbolic analogues through which he represented their artistic and conjugal partnership, Emer and Cuchulain, Solomon and Sheba, Kusta Ben Luka and his nameless bride in "The Gift of Harun Al-Rashid," and others. These likenesses tend to adjust the male myth of solitary action or creation: the hero's strength or the scholar's wisdom. They stress female agency, even though the woman's part is usually private or hidden and often renunciatory, as is Emer's saving act in *The Only Jealousy* or Sheba's denial of her knowledge in "Solomon to Sheba."[44] (We might recall in this context that George and Michael Robartes, that most shadowy bearer of mysterious knowledge, shared the same Phase, 18, according to one of the notebooks.[45]) The creation, in turn, tends to be more intimate than before, more inclusive of human as well as universal truth: life or love are added to the product, like "That dolphin-torn, that gong-tormented sea" (P 249) surrounding the changeless pavements of Byzantium. Thus Cuchulain lives again; Solomon and Sheba "make / The world a narrow pound" (P 138) by their love and fool the cockerel into thinking that they have overcome the mortal effects of the Fall; and Kusta Ben Luka confesses how he has learned from his young wife all of the wisdom attributed to him alone:

> All those abstractions that you fancied were
> From the great Treatise of Parmenides;
> All, all those gyres and cubes and midnight things
> Are but a new expression of her body. . . .
>
> (P 450)

It is not surprising, perhaps, that metaphors of childbearing and childrearing accompany this last symbolizing of creativity and wisdom as a secret "expression" of a woman's body. Parenthood, not only marriage, is evoked by Kusta Ben Luka, who can only describe his "incredi-

---

44. A soul can choose to react to the "coincidence of signs" between itself and another by "sacrifice of all & self for an idea or perhaps an ideal," Yeats was told on 4 January 1918. When he asked if the medium did this in response to the "coincidence of signs" between the two of them he was told, "Yes—there is a reason but I cant quite work it out—no you cant—I can later." We might well wonder if she, or he, did "work out" the reasons for her sacrifices.

45. *MYV* 1:276n38.

ble experience"[46] in phrases that overturn accepted familial roles—recalling that "Truths without father came" while for "A livelong hour / She seemed the learned man and I the child" (P 449). The Yeatses' daily experimenting went on during both of Mrs. Yeats's pregnancies, and the Script bears ample witness to how important their children were to both Willy and George. There are fascinating exchanges about their daughter Anne's spiritual ancestor, Anne Hyde (for whom she was named), their son Michael's prophesied future as the Avatar for the coming age, and their perfect tetradic unity as a family, among other topics.

On 12 February 1918, Yeats interrupted a line of questioning about the creation and transferral of images to ask "What special quality is given to communicati[on] by my touching medium." Physical contact "is necessary," the Guide, Rose, replied, "to establish an interchange of a psychical nature for one thing—to enable certain future work to be done." Pursuing the idea of "interchange," he wondered, "Do I then recieve [sic] as well as give?" "Yes[,] more than you give," he was told, "& also it enables me to write more quickly because I then have a double force." The response in the first person may hint that the medium, whose hand did the actual writing, has answered instead of Rose. But whoever replied knew that Yeats received much from his psychical and physical partner and that the work which resulted from their partnership had "a double force." We may understand that force no better than they did, but we may be as certain as Yeats that "a blessed moon last night / Gave Sheba to her Solomon" (P 177).

---

46. The term is that which Yeats used to describe his own (AV-B 8).

Lampedusa on Yeats:
A Newly Discovered Essay

Jeffrey Meyers

In the course of my research on *Il Gattopardo* (*The Leopard,* 1958), I found a virtually unknown essay on W. B. Yeats by one of the greatest Italian novelists of the century, Giuseppe Tomasi di Lampedusa. The eleven-page article was first published in an obscure Italian periodical in 1926, three years after Yeats had won the Nobel Prize for Literature. This journal is not owned by a British or American library; is not listed in the standard bibliographies of Yeats criticism by John Stoll (1971), K. G. W. Cross and R. T. Dunlop (1971), and K. P. S. Jochum (1978); and has never been translated into English.[1]

Lampedusa's extremely florid, highly wrought, and metaphoric essay was intended to introduce Italian readers to Yeats, whose poems had been translated by Carlo Linati and published in Milan in 1914. The critical appreciation is less interesting for its content than for its place in the history of Yeats scholarship (then in a rudimentary stage) and for the response to Yeats's work by an exquisite and sympathetic sensibility—well acquainted with the British Isles, learned in its language and literature.

Giuseppe Tomasi, Prince of Lampedusa, was born in Palermo in 1896 and brought up in decaying but aristocratic palaces in that provincial capital and in the country estate which inspired the descriptions of Donnafugata in his novel. (The traditions of the ancient country house are significant in the works of both Yeats and Lampedusa.) The novelist studied in the Faculty of Jurisprudence at the universities of Genoa and Turin during 1914–15; and spent his early manhood as a regular artillery officer in the Great War, serving on the Austrian front in northeast Italy.

---

1. The essay was first discovered by Andrea Vitello in 1965 and cited by Giuseppe Quatriglio, "Le radici del *Gattopardo,*" *Giornale di Sicilia* (Palermo), 2 April 1970, p. 3.

He was captured in battle, escaped from a prisoner of war camp in Hungary, and did not leave the service until 1921.

Lampedusa intended to follow a career as a diplomat, but suffered a nervous breakdown in the 1920s. During that decade, he and his mother traveled throughout Europe and lived in grand hotels in Rome, Turin, Paris, and London.

The essay on Yeats was published in a Genoese monthly, *Le Opere e i Giorni* ("Works and Days," after Hesiod) in November 1926 under the thinly disguised pseudonym "Giuseppe Tomasi di Palma." (Palma di Montechiaro is a town near Agrigento, founded by his ancestors in 1637.) After this early venture (and two other pieces on Paul Morand and on a "Story about the Fame of Caesar" that appeared in the same journal during 1926–27) Lampedusa lapsed into a long, thoughtful silence which was broken only by the appearance of his spectacularly successful novel, the year after his death, in 1958.

"Yeats and the Irish Renaissance" was written by a young man who had been influenced by the aestheticism of the 1890s and was recovering from the effects of the war. The essay is eccentric but illuminating, and its purple patches resemble the descriptions of Sicily in "Luoghi di mia infanzia" in *Racconti*. It becomes increasingly interesting—after a prelude on the transience of poetic fame, the difficulty of translating lyric poetry, the Celtic soul, and Ireland's tragic history—when he directs his attention to Yeats's works.

Lampedusa notes, with considerable irony, that the white-haired old men in the Nordic conclave have usually given the Nobel Prize to nonentities and second-raters ever since Sully-Prudhomme won the first award in 1901. (Kipling was the only English-language writer and the only first-rate author to win the prize before Yeats.) But he commends the hermetic judges for finally managing to make an intelligent choice in Yeats, who won the award the year after Ireland became independent and he became a senator of the Irish Free State. The prize was given not only to the poet, but also to his country and his race.

Lampedusa comments on the perfect interpenetration of the Celtic soul with the misty, barren landscape; and discusses the Celtic heroes— King Arthur, Macbeth, and Wallace—in legend, literature, and history. He notes that during the Renaissance the Gaelic chieftains lived the same patriarchal life as the kings of ancient Greece and that "the Celts are the only people who have remained until relatively modern times suffi-

ciently unknown and hidden to allow their myths to be reborn."[2] In this
tribal society, "poets always occupied a prominent rank: they sat at the
king's table, they were judges, inspirers, and with an unprecedented care
took charge of the spiritual patrimony of the race."

The oppressive rule of the English deprived the Irish of their lan-
guage and forced them to adopt the tongue of their conquerors. The
Gaelic League, founded in the 1840s, revived and saved the language
which is now taught in Irish schools. Lampedusa sees Yeats as the em-
bodiment of the Celtic spirit, as the poet who "has placed the pure crown
of his artistic glory on the degraded head of his race."

Lampedusa considers Yeats's early autobiography and childhood in
Sligo; his founding of the Abbey Theatre; and the technique of his inex-
haustibly beautiful lyrics, rooted in the earth and inspired by the Eliz-
abethans rather than the French Symbolists. Yeats and the great Eliz-
abethans have "the same intense love for the humble aspects of life, the
same capacity to transform popular themes into high art" and the same
"irremediable nostalgia for the past." (In passing, Lampedusa presciently
notes that Hardy was and is "the great unappreciated master.")

In discussing Yeats's esoteric symbolism, Lampedusa calls the mys-
tic rose "the ancient Celtic symbol in the human soul" that "represents
Ireland, beauty or the lady-love," and observes: "There is a deep conflict
in the soul of the poet, between his love of life and disdain for actual life
as opposed to dream-life."

Lampedusa examines the political meaning and the innovative stag-
ing in Yeats's plays, whose dominant theme is "the perpetual struggle of
the natural with the spiritual order, the impassioned search for this higher
order through nature itself." The patriotic and dream plays, which com-
bine pagan and Christian feeling, would have been a perfect vehicle for the
great Italian actress, Eleonora Duse.

In Yeats's finest play, *Deirdre,* "the tragedy of the two lovers striv-
ing for a perfect union they can achieve only in death is treated with
magnificent lyric fervor." The stories that portray the "heroic times in
Ireland . . . all have an atmosphere of disconsolate melancholy, and con-
cern the destruction of the hero, who seeks to establish a spiritual order
in face of the materialistic chaos of the world."

Lampedusa concludes by mentioning Yeats's great contemporaries

---

2. Valerie Meyers has translated this essay, but the Lampedusa Estate refused permis-
sion to reprint it.

in literature and painting and by justly asserting: "the arts of the new Ireland are assuming a worthy place in the traditions of a people who, in all the tragic hours of their history, have always found a poet to point them to their guiding star."

This self-reflective essay, like so many valuable critical works, is as much about the author as about the subject, as much about politics as about literature. Lampedusa sees in Yeats's relation to Ireland, an ancient island civilization exploited by and dependent upon Great Britain, his own relation to Sicily, an ancient island civilization exploited by and dependent upon Italy. Both subject peoples have their own patriarchal traditions and their own pagan gods. Both writers long for the heroic past. Lampedusa sees Yeats as an intensely patriotic poet who incarnates his race, who portrays the melancholy soul of his people and their enchanted but impoverished landscape. Yeats took part in the Irish cultural Renaissance that led to political independence in 1922; Lampedusa portrayed the Italian *Risorgimento* that led to the unification of a free Italy in 1861. "Before putting a gun in the hands of the Irish [or Sicilians]," Lampedusa observes, "it was necessary to prove that they existed."

The most extraordinary aspect of the essay is the way in which it foreshadows, in Lampedusa's perception of Yeats, the themes—meditated throughout his lifetime—that emerged thirty years later in *The Leopard:* the conflict between actual and imaginative life, the contrast between material chaos and spiritual order, the aristocratic disdain for the mob, the nostalgia for the past, and the longing "for all the withered beauty which is now only eloquent ashes."

Yeats's Sources for the Matter of Ireland: I. Edain and Aengus

Brendan O Hehir

According to his own testimony, William Butler Yeats first began the self-conscious use of Irish subject-matter in his poetry around 1885–86.[1] By *Irish subject-matter* he meant, *inter alia*, material that he understood to be derived from what he regarded as ancient Gaelic tradition and legend. Certainly such material is very evident in his poetry throughout the decade of the 1890s and thereafter: The "Wanderings of Oisin" and "The Madness of King Goll" may be instanced among the poems, with plays like *The Countess Kathleen* (1892) and *The Land of Heart's Desire* (1894). Much of what Yeats took to be early Gaelic legend in these works is actually more or less spurious—a fact not at all surprising in view of Yeats's incorrigible ignorance of the Irish language in any of its historical phases, and his concomitant need to rely upon translations and adaptations whose accuracy he was in no position to evaluate.

Within Yeats's work of this period appears the outline of a marvelous myth that seems for a time to have deeply excited him. Unfortunately that myth has virtually no substance outside of Yeats's imagination, prompted by the mistaken conjectures of certain overconfident scholars who misled the poet as well as themselves. That Yeats nevertheless created an appealing myth out of the misinformation is a tribute to

---

1. In *Early Poems and Stories* (London: Macmillan, 1925), Yeats attached this note to the section "Crossways":

> Many of the poems in *Crossways*, certainly those upon Indian subjects or upon shepherds and fauns, must have been written before I was twenty [i.e., in 1885–86], for from the moment I began *The Wanderings of Oisin*, which I did at that age, I believe, my subject-matter became Irish. (P 589)

This essay—a portion of a book I am writing on "Yeats and the Matter of Ireland"— is an expanded version of a paper titled *"Foinse Bréagach Miotais a bhí ag Yeats"* presented in the Irish language at the North American Celtic Congress held at the University of Ottawa in 1986. A condensed version in English, under the present title, was presented at the South Atlantic Modern Language Association Convention in 1987.

his mythopoetic imagination rather than to their learning. The pseudo-myth I have in mind is that of the supernatural lovers, Aengus and Edain.[2] These persons are first united by Yeats in the 1899 revision of *The Wanderings of Oisin,* wherein the otherworldly woman, Niamh, informs Oisin that:

> My father and my mother are
> Aengus and Adene [sic]. . . .[3]

(VP 5)

Yeats's pairing of Aengus and Edain as parents of Niamh has no authentication in any genuine Irish mythological text. Of course, I cannot guarantee that it did not occur in some obscure late fabrication I have not found. Not only are Aengus and Edain not Niamh's parents (Niamh herself is but a nonce-creation by the eighteenth-century Gaelic poet Mícheál Coimín, the proximate source for the "Wanderings of Oisin"), they do not constitute a mythical couple, married or unmarried. Yeats, however, came to believe they were famous mythological lovers, and that misconception colors a number of his poems from around the turn of the century. Apart from the 1899 revised *The Wanderings of Oisin,* most notable of these are three narrative poems, "Baile and Aillinn," "The Shadowy Waters," and "The Two Kings," and the shorter "The Harp of Aengus," ultimately prefixed to "The Shadowy Waters."

In "The Shadowy Waters" Aengus and Edain are invoked as wandering passionate lovers, and one speaker recounts that Aengus "carried Edain off from a king's house" (P 411). In "Baile and Aillinn" Edain is referred to as "Midhir's wife" (P 401), and "The Harp of Aengus" alludes to what Yeats thought of as an episode in the love affair: "Edain came out of Midhir's hill, and lay / Beside young Aengus" (P 407). The story Yeats envisions is clearly that of adulterous runaways, Midhir being the cuckolded king, so Yeats's impulse to make this errant pair the regal parents of Niamh must not have been fully considered—unless he also imagined a period of post-divorce domesticity, Parnell with Kitty O'Shea. Yet this detail is not consonant with the allusions in "The Shad-

---

2. Yeats's final spelling for both names; the Old Irish spellings were Oengus and Étaín; Lady Gregory used the spellings Angus and Etain.

3. The unique spelling *Adene* is a clue that Yeats had some sense of the pronunciation of *Étaín*—viz., "aid-een." The name today is usually anglicized *Aideen.* Yeats's usual spelling *Edain* against Lady Gregory's *Etain* shows also that he had grasped the phonetic value of old Irish *-t-* as /d/.

owy Waters" or "The Harp of Aengus," which seem to picture the
lovers in a perpetual whirlwind, like Paolo and Francesca in Hell.

Yeats later dated the rise of this myth in his mind to about the year
1897, a date very plausible in view of the 1899 "Wanderings of Oisin"
and the probable dates of composition of the other poems mentioned.
Very likely the Aengus who also functions in Yeats's poetry apart from
any association with Edain (as in "The Song of Wandering Aengus,"
first published in 1897 but not ascribed to Aengus until *The Wind Among
the Reeds* [1899]) took shape in his mind about the same time and out of
the same materials. In 1908 Yeats instanced "the various Aengus stories"
as among his sources.[4] In fact, although a tally of Aengus's appearances
in Irish Gaelic literature would undoubtedly reach a very high number,
he is central to only two extant stories. Both of these, as it happens, are
associated—in quite different ways—with separate and distinct parts of
the main saga of Étaín.

It is somehow from the story of Étaín that Yeats derived his concept
of Aengus and Edain as immortal lovers. How he did so is not easy to
deduce, though clues abound, nor is it easy to make clear the exact
relationship between the canonical Étaín texts and the transmutation of
Étaín's stories in Yeats's poems. At the heart of the difficulty is the fact
that the full Étaín saga had been lost before Yeats's lifetime; and the full
missing text was not rediscovered until 1930. The new text was not,
however, published until 1938, the year preceding Yeats's death, and
Yeats very likely never learned of its existence. The modern critic there-
fore has an advantage over Yeats: we can know the full story, with
events in their proper sequence, whereas he could not.

There are two different states of affairs to be considered. The first is
that of scholarship: in the 1890s, when Yeats began his version of the
myths, how much was actually known, and how much was inferred,
about Étaín? The second is, how much of this was accessible to the non-
scholar Yeats?

Two specific sequences of the complete Étaín-saga are identifiable

---

4. In a note in the *Collected Works in Verse and Prose:*
I took the Aengus and Edain of *The Shadowy Waters* from poor translations of the
various Aengus stories, which, new translated by Lady Gregory, make up so much of
what is most beautiful in both her books. They had, however, so completely become
a part of my own thought that in 1897, when I was still working on an early version
of *The Shadowy Waters,* I saw one night with my bodily eyes, as it seemed, two
beautiful persons, who would, I believe, have answered to their names. (P 687).

among Yeats's turn-of-the-century poems to point us towards what he had grasped of the canonical story. The first is contained in the fourteen lines of "The Harp of Aengus" which narrate Yeats's fiction about that harp:

> Edain, having come to live with Aengus, wove harp-strings out of his hair. Then she was turned into a fly and blown away by the wind, whereupon Aengus made a harp strung with the strings she had made.

The second sequence forms the basic plot of the poem "The Two Kings," which I must discuss in another place. The notion that Edain and Aengus were lovers is a misconception derived by older scholars from the fragments that then were known of the First Tale of Étaín. The harp is Yeats's personal invention, permitted by the scholarly misconception.

A possible partial source for Yeats's knowledge of the contents of the fragment that underlies his poem is a summary by John Rhys, which, further synopsized, goes like this:

> Aengus's foster-father was Midir, whose wife was Étaín, but a rival of Étaín's by her wiles and magic arts severed her from Midir. When her husband lost her, she was found in great misery by Aengus, who had her clad in purple and placed in a glass sun-bower. Once more Étaín's rival succeeded in separating her from her protector and in reducing her to a condition of great wretchedness.[5]

This summary is short on details—most notably the detail that Étaín's rival was Midir's wife, a detail also lacking in Yeats's first published version of "The Harp of Aengus," though later supplied. But Midir in Rhys is clearly a person, and Étaín his wife, whereas in the first version of Yeats's poem "Midher" seems perhaps to be only the name of a hill. Obviously Yeats later learned otherwise, but does not become explicit about the relationship between Midir and "Edain." Thus Rhys and Yeats uphold monogamy: Rhys by suppressing that Étaín's rival was also Midir's wife, and Yeats by suppressing that Edain was also Midir's wife.

But Rhys offers no suggestion of a love affair between Aengus and

---

5. My summary from John Rhys, *Lectures on the Origin and Growth of Religion as Illustrated by Celtic Heathendom* (London: Williams and Norgate, 1888), 145–46.

Étaín, unless calling Aengus "her protector" is a Victorian innuendo. But there is no need to attribute to Rhys's Aengus any motives beyond charity and compassion. Another detail lacking in Rhys is that Étaín's "condition of great wretchedness" entailed her having been turned into a fly. Rhys was probably unaware of this canonical detail, and so did not deliberately suppress it.

While Rhys, therefore, writing in English and so accessible to Yeats, and having been in print since 1888, could have supplied Yeats with the setting in which he placed the invention of Aengus's harp, he is unlikely as the source of the assumption that Edain and Aengus were lovers, and impossible as the source of the information that Midir's wife changed Edain to a fly. With one detail, however, he very likely did supply Yeats. Rhys's Aengus placed Étaín in a glass *bower;* Yeats's Edain lies beside Aengus in a glass *tower.* It looks very much as if a transcription error somewhere has converted *bower* into *tower.* The original Irish word involved—*grianán*—translates better as *bower* than *tower.*

The Étaín saga is known in Irish as *Tochmarc Étaíne,* "The Wooing of Étaín," and consists of three separate but sequential stories. The full tale is extant in only one manuscript, contained in ten leaves of The Yellow Book of Lecan (*YBL*)—a miscellany compiled in the fourteenth century, now in the Library of Trinity College, Dublin. Those ten leaves had gone missing from the book, perhaps in the eighteenth century, and surfaced again only about 1930.[6] In that full *YBL* text each of the three successive stories has a separate title—viz. (in translation) "Here begins the Wooing of Étaín," "The Wooing of Étaín this again," and "The Wooing of Étaín again"[7]—and a distinctive new beginning. Moreover, the First and Third are each composed of several distinguishable parts, and those parts are further subdivisible into separate sequential episodes.

The 1938 editors of the full text print the First Story as twenty-six sections or paragraphs. That story divides into three main parts, of somewhat uneven lengths. Part I occupies paragraphs 1–11, Part II paragraphs 12–15, and Part III paragraphs 16–26. The long Part III itself divides into six separate sequences. The Second Story is shorter and more unified, and is printed as nine paragraph-sections. The Third Story

---

6. The recovered pages are now not in Trinity, but in the National Library of Ireland.

7. The text was published by R. I. Best and Osborn Bergin in *Eriu* 12.2 (1938): 137–96. The part-titles are "Incipit do Thochmarc Edaine," "Tochmarc Edaine and seo beos," and "Tochmarc Etaine beos."

once more is long and complex. It is printed as twenty-three paragraph-sections, and divides naturally into two main parts and a coda.

Prior to recovery of the lost leaves of *YBL*, the best representation of the whole saga was—we can now be sure—that preserved in the Book of the Dun Cow (*LU*—initials of the Irish title of the manuscript, *Lebor na hUidre*), a manuscript compiled about the year 1100. In that manuscript the surviving text of "The Wooing of Étaín" so closely resembles that in *YBL* that it is evident both were copied from a lost common source. Yet very large portions of the complete saga are lacking in *LU*. Only the short Second Story is intact. Of the long First Story nothing is retained in *LU* prior to paragraph 20 (the text begins within the second sentence of that section). This means that all of parts I and II are missing, and the first two of the six sequences of Part III—in all more than nineteen of the story's twenty-six paragraphs. The Third Story is also seriously defective, ending on the first word of paragraph 16. Not only are paragraphs 16–23—the entire close of the story—missing, but a mutilated leaf in the surviving pages costs a gap from the middle of paragraph 3 to the end of paragraph 7. That is, overall, of fifty-eight paragraphs in the complete sequence of three stories, upwards of thirty—more than half the number—were missing before 1930, during the time Yeats was trying to absorb the myth of Étaín into his poetry.

Outside *LU* a few other sources were available for details of the sequence. For long the most frequently invoked of these was a manuscript in the British Museum styled Egerton 1732. This late-fifteenth-century compilation contains, in language close to the time it was made, a much inflated version of the Second Story, and a synopsis of the Third. Another version of the Second tale was, therefore, not badly needed, inasmuch as a close parallel to the intact *LU* Second Story also survived in the unlost portion of *YBL* (which means that *YBL* had once contained two almost identical texts of the same story). But the Egerton version for a time enjoyed undeserved prestige, arising probably out of its association with what was a full synopsis of the mutilated Third Story. The Egerton version of the Second Étaín Story was in fact the first text out of the whole saga ever to be fully published—by Eduard Müller in his "Two Irish Tales" of 1878.[8] Early scholars of the text, including Müller, even regarded the inflated Egerton text as canonical, and described the

---

8. *Revue Celtique* 3 (1878): 342–60.

more authentic earlier *LU* Second Story as a "condensation" of the content of Egerton 1732.

Although the Egerton synopsis differs in details from the remnant of the Third Story in *LU*, it had the advantage of providing an ending for the tale. On the assumption that the ending of the synopsis at least approximated the lost ending of the *LU* version, it took on almost canonical authority, and was freely drawn on to round out outline retellings of the saga. The first publication of the *LU* text was two years after Müller's edition of the Egerton Second Story. This was in Ernst Windisch's *Irische Texte* (Leipzig, 1880), wherein under the title "Das Freien um Etain" the full Egerton text, including the synopsis of the Third Story, was printed. The *LU* Second Story and fragmentary Third Story were appended as variants. Since apparatus and translation of this edition are in German, and Yeats in 1899 wrote that he was "ignorant of German,"[9] it is unlikely that Windisch could have been a source for Yeats, other than at second hand.

By the end of the nineteenth century—precisely at the time Yeats was first evincing interest in Edain and Aengus—scholarly attention, grown more cautious, began to turn back to the *LU* texts. Another source of information was noticed, to facilitate guesswork as to the contents of the lost segments of the saga. This was a manuscript, still in Trinity College Library, Dublin, designated H.3.18. This manuscript (we shall call it *H*) contains a collection of Middle Irish grammatical glosses. A sequence of literary quotations as lemmas for the glosses was recognized as derived from a lost text of "The Wooing of Étaín." Quotations toward the end of the sequence were virtually identical to passages in the surviving part of the *LU* text, from which the reasonable, and correct, inference was that the earlier quotations were from a lost text which must closely resemble the lost beginning of *LU*.

The first published collocation of the excerpts in *H* with the *LU* close of the First Story was by Ludwig Christian Stern, "Das Märchen von Etain."[10] This was of course in German, but in 1906 an elaboration of Stern's work was published in English by Yeats's acquaintance Alfred Nutt.[11] Nutt, essentially agreeing with Stern, offered a synopsis of what he deduced was the plot of the lost portion of the story that sounds very

---

9. In a note on "The Pronunciation of the Irish Words" added to the 1899 edition of the 1895 *Poems* (VP 841).

10. *Zeitschrift für celtische Philologie* 5 (1905): 522–34.

11. "Tochmarc Étaine," *Revue Celtique* 27 (1906): 325–39.

much like the notion of Aengus and Edain reflected in Yeats's poems. Nutt even ventures the conjecture that "Aengus is the original hero of the entire Étaín cycle," and takes an attitude toward the personality of Aengus not far from that implicit in Yeats. The difficulty, however, with Nutt's article as a source for Yeats's notions about Aengus and Edain is its date. Yeats had conceived of the couple as immortal passionate lovers as early as 1897, and certainly had published his first version of "The Shadowy Waters" in May 1900 in the *North American Review*. That edition contained, as a speech by the hero, Forgael, the lines that Yeats later removed to print separately as the poem "The Harp of Aengus." All this was several years before Nutt published his seeming retrospective justification of Yeats's mythologizing.

To make comprehensible the argument I am pursuing, I here synopsize the first story of Étaín as found complete only in the recovered *YBL* pages. Part I of the First Story narrates the conception and birth of Aengus. He was begotten by the Dagda, the father-god of the Irish pantheon, on Eithne, goddess of the River Boyne, wife of Elcmar, occupant of the Brugh on the Boyne (the traditional Irish name for the megalithic tumulus nowadays called Newgrange). Aengus, born unknown to Elcmar, is raised in fosterage by Midir. With the aid of Midir and the Dagda, Aengus tricks Elcmar out of the Brugh, and takes possession. (In all other literary references to Aengus he is always possessor of the Brugh. This story explains how he became so, while detailing his parentage and his relationship to Midir.)

After Aengus sets up in the Brugh he is visited by Midir, who is accidentally injured while trying to mediate in a brawl among boys. As compensation Aengus agrees to provide Midir with various valuables, including the most beautiful woman in Ireland, whose name is Étaín. This woman must be termed Étaín I. Thus ends Part I.

Part II narrates Aengus's wooing of Étaín on behalf of Midir. Her father, reluctant to part with her, imposes onerous tasks which Aengus must perform. Midir marries Étaín and the couple honeymoons at Aengus's home. This is the end of Part II. Parts I and II together constitute fifteen of the twenty-six paragraph-sections of the First Story.

Part III has several episodes. It begins with Midir bringing Étaín home to his first wife, Fuamnach, who by occult art turns Étaín into a purple fly. Midir continues to live lovingly with Étaín, casting off Fuamnach. Fuamnach stirs up a wind that blows the fly away for seven years, until at last it lands at Aengus's house. Aengus recognizes the fly as Étaín and builds a glass bower for her to live in. Fuamnach learns of her whereabouts, and of Aengus's care for her, and tricks Midir and Aengus into meeting together. Meanwhile she comes to Aengus's house and blows Étaín away again. This time Étaín is blown about for 1,012 years, at the end of which she falls into a cup from which a woman is drinking. The woman—wife of a warrior named Edar—conceives and gives birth to a reincarnated Étaín—Étaín II. While this Étaín is still a girl she is approached by a mysterious horseman, who sings to her and disappears.

Meanwhile Aengus pursues Fuamnach and cuts off her head. This is the end of the First Story of "The Wooing of Étaín." Of this tale only fragments were available to Yeats's contemporaries. The *LU* fragment, for instance, begins at the point in Part III where Étaín, in the form of a fly, is taken in by Aengus who builds her a glass bower. In the preceding text the fact of her metamorphosis had been explicit, but no wording in the surviving fragment specifically says she was a fly. It is evident that she is not in the best of health, but the actual words do not reveal precisely how bad a shape she is in.

Attempted interpretations of the story from its fragments therefore began from the crucially wrong inference that when Étaín appeared at Aengus's house there was little amiss with her that rest and care would not cure. This inference was even bolstered by a fragment of Aengus's welcoming speech that is quoted in *H:*

> Welcome, Étaín,
> wandering afflicted,
> who have entered great stress
> through Fuamnach's cunning.[12]

The subsequent *LU* text, then, going on to report that Fuamnach had learned of the "great love" that was given to Étaín by Aengus, was understood to refer to the love of a man for a woman, rather than as the compassion of a man for a weary fly. And here arises Yeats's notion that Edain had eloped from her husband, Midir, to join her lover, Aengus. And Fuamnach was perhaps seen as a loyal Number One Wife seeking to regain for her husband his missing property, Wife Number Two. Another sentence in the text led to even profounder misinterpretation. Fuamnach tells Midir to invite Aengus to meet him, so there may be

---

12. *Fo chen Edain imthechtach imnedhach adrualaidh mórgaibthiu la gaithi Fuaimnighi.* Translation mine.

goodwill between them, while she herself promises to look for Étaín. With the complete text available this translation of the relevant words is straightforward. But without the full text Fuamnach's words were invariably translated as meaning that she proposed to make peace between the two males. Peace cannot be made without prior strife, so scholarly dogma held that hostility subsisted between Aengus and Midir. The fact that Étaín was living with Aengus identified the bone of contention, and this assumption colored interpretation of the fragmentary quotations in *H*.

One fragment, for instance, mentions the brawl among the boys at Aengus's house: "A fight flared up among the boys in the Brug." Alfred Nutt translated this sentence: "A quarrel blazed up between the lads in the mansion." He translates *Brug* as "mansion"—which is acceptable— but does so because he insists that Aengus's Brugh on the Boyne *cannot* be meant, asserting that "We can only conjecture that this quarrel was about Étaín." At this point in the real story Étaín has not in fact even been mentioned yet. The next following excerpt is taken from Aengus's negotiations with Étaín's father, in which the father is raising objections to the match. This was naturally assumed to mean that Aengus had gone courting on his own behalf, and had been rebuffed. That excerpt is from paragraph-section 12, but the next quotation in *H* comes from paragraph 19. There was no way to guess that the compiler of *H* had skipped so much of his source. That quotation is the one earlier translated, Aengus's welcome to the wind-tossed fly who is Étaín.

The Nutt school of interpretation (including Lucius Gwynn)[13] deduced from the foregoing this outline story: Aengus and Midir quarreled since both desired Étaín. Aengus went to Étaín's father to seek her hand, but was refused. Thereafter Étaín was married to Midir, but unhappily, especially because of her mistreatment by Midir's senior wife, Fuamnach. So she fled in distress to Aengus, who ensconced her in a glass bower. Fuamnach, learning of this adulterous behavior, informed Midir of Étaín's whereabouts (this misreads the *LU* text)[14] and proposed a reconciliation between Midir and Aengus. Meanwhile she got rid of the cause of strife by blowing her away on a wind, but the thwarted lover, Aengus, killed Fuamnach in anger. This fable is based on inferences from genuine texts and fragments, but is quite wrong.

---

13. "The Two Versions of *Tochmarc Étaine*," *Zeitschrift für celtische Philologie* 9 (1913): 353–56. This is a comparison of the *LU* and Egerton versions.

14. On the contrary, Fuamnach tells Midir that she herself will go to seek out Étaín: *co ndechas for iarair Édaine.*

Neither Stern nor Nutt shows more awareness than had Rhys that Étaín had been turned into a fly. The fact is not explicit either in the *LU* fragment or in *H*, although something of the sort might have been inferred from the text's later statement that Étaín was swallowed in a woman's drink. Yet Yeats was aware that Edain became a fly, although he has her the wrong color, and places the metamorphosis subsequent to Edain's taking up residence with Aengus. Somehow, knowledge of that transformation reached Yeats by 1900 at the latest.[15]

In 1905 A. H. Leahy published in two volumes his *Heroic Romances of Ireland*, containing translations of a number of older Irish tales, including the *LU* fragment of the First Story of "The Wooing of Étaín." Leahy's translation makes no use of the excerpts preserved in *H*, but begins the story with a synopsis of the situation and the characters at the point where the *LU* fragment begins. In this he shows some dim awareness of the true lost details of the text. That is, he knows that Étaín has been metamorphosised by Fuamnach—but into a butterfly rather than a purple fly—and he also knows that it was in that shape Étaín arrived at Aengus's house. Unfortunately, Leahy has neither note nor hint of the source of his synopsis. Although Alfred Nutt in 1906 quotes part of Leahy's synopsis, he shows no reaction to the information that Étaín had been turned into an insect, and reveals no knowledge of Leahy's source.

Leahy's 1905 book cannot have been the source of Yeats's knowledge before 1900 that Edain was changed to a fly. Chronologically, Yeats's source must either have been the same as, or parallel to, Leahy's source. Yet it could not have been identical, for Leahy is fully aware that when Étaín came to Aengus it was under duress, and not on elopement, and that while she lived in Aengus's glass bower she was in no shape for lovemaking with him. Yeats, on the other hand, seems to think that Edain's transformation was subsequent to her stay with Aengus, for during her sojourn he has her weave strings of Aengus's hair "because her hands had been made wild by love." Neither purple flies nor butterflies have hands.

At the end I tentatively conclude that Alfred Nutt was Yeats's source, or at least its instrument. The basis of this conclusion is that only

15. The 1900 periodical text refers to "a silver fly" (see appendix). In the separate printing later that year, this was revised to "a golden fly" (VP 757).

Nutt, of all the scholars of the period, harbored the obsessed conviction that Aengus and Étaín were lovers. It is striking to read Nutt's quotations, not only of Leahy's preamble, but of his text, and to notice how details are ignored. Nutt believed that Aengus and Étaín were lovers; acknowledging an intimation that Étaín was not in a womanly body when she sojourned with Aengus would admit a doubt that she and Aengus were active lovers at the time. Aware of the intact text of the Second Story of Étaín, in which the reincarnate Étaín II, married to a mortal king, is pursued by the immortal Midir, who informs her that she was his wife in a former existence and ultimately wins her back, Nutt conjectures that Midir in the Second Story is a scribal replacement of Aengus, and that Midir throughout is merely a doublet of Aengus, who is the true original hero of *Tochmarc Étaíne*. Nutt's precursor, Ludwig Stern, had not been so obsessed, and although seeming unaware that Étaín had been a fly when she arrived under Aengus's protection, had interpreted Aengus's sheltering of Étaín as a taking of her into fosterage. Nutt explicitly rejects this suggestion. Nutt is, in a word, blinkered by his obsessions—rejecting Stern's conjecture, ignoring Leahy's hints.

Since Yeats at least for a time shared something of Nutt's *idée fixe* that Aengus and Edain were passionate mythological lovers, and is unlikely to have developed this notion independently of some supposed authority, the inference is that Nutt was his authority. Yet patently Nutt's essay of 1906 could not have influenced Yeats's imagination in 1897. The notion therefore must have been transmitted outside of print.

The year 1897, to which Yeats attributes his first formulation of his notion about Edain and Aengus, was also the year of his first friendship with Augusta Gregory. It must have been about that time that, as he later wrote, "I told her that Alfred Nutt had offered to supply me with translations of the Irish heroic cycles if I would pick the best versions and put my English upon them, attempting what Malory had done . . ." (Au 306). Thus Nutt is credited with begetting Lady Gregory's Cuchulain, but the intimation of discussion of Irish heroic tales between Nutt and Yeats implies the occasion for Nutt to infect Yeats with his own romantic theory of the role of Aengus in Old Irish mythology. Material conveyed by Nutt to Yeats could also have included information that Étaín had been turned into a fly. Such a hypothetical source, like the one that Leahy obviously had, might have had the metamorphosis at the correct point in the story, but Nutt could well have tampered with it to encourage Yeats's Malorean creativity. Enough to know that Leahy's source, whatever it was, had a nugget of truth in it, and that Alfred Nutt, if not Yeats's actual source, is its equivalent.

Although Yeats never formally repudiated the notion most clearly expressed in "The Harp of Aengus" that Aengus and Edain were famous supernatural lovers in Irish myth, his retreat from that position can be traced outside his 1908 note attributing that notion to "poor translations." In the *North American Review* initial publication of "The Shadowy Waters" in 1900, the lines that later were isolated as "The Harp of Aengus" were a speech within the closet-drama. Forgael, romantic hero of the story, is the owner of the harp, whose origin he recounts in those lines. The harp, strung with Aengus's hair woven by Edain—and thus embodying their love—magically determines the action of the play. Further text of the speech elaborates a Yeatsian myth about the nature of mortal sexual love:

> Aengus has seen
> His well-beloved through a mortal's eyes,
> And she, no longer blown among the winds,
> Is laughing through a mortal's eyes.
>
> (VP 763)

By the 1906 publication of "The Shadowy Waters"—the basic text that Yeats allowed to remain canonical among his poems—the speech describing the origin of the harp has been deleted from the body of the text and printed as a separate poem. The lines describing mortal love as incarnating Aengus reunited with an Edain rescued from her fate as a windblown fly have been completely cancelled, and the harp in the plot has been redefined as "that old harp of the nine spells" (VP 237).[16] Motivation of the action is now ascribed to phantasmal visitations from Aengus and Edain, which can be interpreted as delusions. Finally, in the stage version of "The Shadowy Waters" that Yeats first published in 1907, visitations from Aengus and Edain have been completely eliminated; and Edain is neither named nor alluded to. Even Aengus has receded to a passing allusion to "islands where the children of Aengus wind / In happy dances" (VPl 334).[17] Alfred Nutt died in 1910, but

---

16. The final version first appears in *Later Poems* (London: Macmillan, 1922): "my old harp / That is more mighty than the sun and moon" (P 421).

17. This reference is carried over from the 1906 revision of the poetic version (VP 245).

before then so had Yeats's dream of Aengus and Edain as lovers, except for its ghostly survival in the texts.

Appendix

"The Harp of Aengus"

The North American Review 11 (May 1900): 296–309

> Edain came out of Midher's hill, and lay
> Beside young Aengus in his tower of glass,
> Where time is drowned in odour-laden winds
> And druid moons, and murmuring of boughs,
> And sleepy boughs, and boughs where apples made
> Of opal and ruby and pale chrysolite
> Awake unsleeping fires; and wove seven strings,
> Sweet with all music, out of his long hair,
> Because her hands had been made wild by love;
> When Midher's wife had changed her to a fly,
> He made a harp with druid apple wood
> That she among her winds might know he wept;
> And from that hour he has watched over none
> But faithful lovers.
>
> (VP 762–63)

Poems 1899–1905 (London: A. H. Bullen; Dublin: Maunsel, 1906)

> Edain came out of Midher's hill, and lay
> Beside young Aengus in his tower of glass,
> Where time is drowned in odour-laden winds
> And druid moons, and murmuring of boughs,
> And sleepy boughs, and boughs where apples made
> Of opal and ruby and pale chrysolite
> Awake unsleeping fires; and wove seven strings,
> Sweet with all music, out of his long hair,
> Because her hands had been made wild by love;
> When Midher's wife had changed her to a fly,
> He made a harp with druid apple wood
> That she among her winds might know he wept;
> And from that hour he has watched over none
> But faithful lovers.
>
> (VP 219–20)

Yeats and Von Hügel:
A Study of "Vacillation"

David Rogers

> But is there any comfort to be found?
> Man is in love and loves what vanishes,
> What more is there to say?
> —"Nineteen Hundred and Nineteen"
>
> (P 208)

> Words, words, words & all the while the heart is bleeding & crying out for love. . . .
> —W. T. Horton to Yeats, 30 March 1917[1]

Yeats does not need admirers, and I am sure Yeats criticism does not need Yeats admirers. His reputation is not in danger of sinking. The criticism of Yeats's poetry has suffered from critics who have a way of taking on the colors, chameleon-like, of the poetic rock upon which they have settled. Curtis Bradford despised what he called "the nullity of virginity."[2] We do not have to look very far for the source of that opinion. And George Mills Harper has written "In a very real sense Yeats's most impressive creation was himself."[3] AE did not agree. Writing to George Moore on 6 April 1916, he had the following to say about Yeats:

> He began about the time of *The Wind Among the Reeds* to do two things consciously, one to create a "style" in literature, the second to create or rather to re-create W. B. Yeats in a style which would

---

1. George Mills Harper, *W. B. Yeats and W. T. Horton: The Record of an Occult Friendship* (Atlantic Highlands, N.J.: Humanities Press, 1981), 133. Hereafter cited in the text as *Y&H*.

2. Curtis Bradford, *Yeats at Work* (Carbondale and Edwardsville: Southern Illinois University Press, 1965), 127. Hereafter cited in the text as YW.

3. George Mills Harper, *'Go Back to Where You Belong': Yeats's Return from Exile,* New Yeats Papers 6 (Dublin: Dolmen Press, 1973), 12.

harmonise with the literary style. People call this posing. It is really putting on a mask, like his actors, Greek or Japanese, a mask over life. . . . The present W. B. Y. is the result. The error in his psychology is, that life creates the form, but he seems to think that the form creates life. If you have style, he argued once with me, you will have something to say. He seems to have also thought, though he never said so, that if you make a picturesque or majestic personality of yourself in appearance, you will become as wonderful inside as outside. He has created the mask and he finds himself obliged to speak in harmony with the fixed expression of the mask. . . . He bores me terribly now, and he was once so interesting.[4]

It may be that a biography of Yeats could be written considering him as the chief actor in a drama titled *Yeats*. That he was the actor of himself should be carefully considered before discussing what he thought about anything.

Mrs. Yeats, in a comment to her husband about AE, made a distinction that should help us keep a sense of balance in examining Yeats's life and work. After the death of AE, Yeats wrote to Dorothy Wellesley:

All is well with AE. His ghost will not walk. He had no passionate human relationships to call him back. My wife said the other night "AE was the nearest to a saint you or I will ever meet. You are a better poet but no saint. I suppose one has to choose." (L 838)

"You are a better poet but no saint." I would add no prophet either. If we accept unguardedly Yeats's conclusions about history and culture, we cannot learn from them, but risk being drowned in the backwash of his considerable wave. The power of his language is such that to grant him authority in areas where he has none is all too easy.

Both Yeats and Lady Gregory often spoke with an imperial tone. At first it is impressive, at length wearisome. But the point at issue is more serious than that of a literary tone which may or may not be appealing. Martin Green's criticism of Yeats is just:

Yeats invited us to quarrel with him. He wanted to seem a foolish passionate man. My objection is only that he also wanted his foolish

---

4. *Letters from AE*, ed. Alan Denson (London: Abelard Schuman, 1961), 109–10.

passionate utterances to have the dignity of prophetic truths; and the
utterer thus to have a prophetic dignity superior to the criticisms of
common sense, or morality, or exact learning, or any of the other
voices that combine in culture. And my objection is much more that
in literary circles he is effectively granted that superiority.[5]

Lady Gregory is not exempt from the same criticism. Yeats reports her
to have said, "Tragedy *must* be a joy to the man who dies" (E&I 522;
emphasis added). Both Yeats and Lady Gregory often use the word *must*,
and the word *only*. It is one occupational hazard of literary royalty. I
would like to examine briefly her statement regarding tragedy and joy,
one to which Yeats subscribed. Their notion of joy is central to "Vacilla-
tion," and the extent to which their definition flies in the face of both
literary and historical reality is an indication of why distance is necessary
between the poet and the critic.

For them the joy of the tragic figure is the joy of a person who has
seen through the folly and illusion of life and approaches the end superior
to anything outside himself because he is indifferent both to life and to its
suffering. And, of course, he is also sustained by pride, that staple of
Yeatsian moral necessity. This is the stance of the Irish airman who does
not hate his enemies or love his own people, but is driven by "A lonely
impulse of delight" to his "tumult in the clouds" (P 135). In his later
years the indifference of the tragic hero as Yeats conceived it yielded to
anger and lust: "What else have I to spur me into song?" (P 312).

But the effect is strangely the same. The gyres run on, Crazy Jane
rants about her lovers, and all things still remain in God. The poet
observes it all, but is not really engaged by any of it. How could he be
since, as Warwick Gould reports, he thought "Civilization is a dream, a
series of illusions."[6] There is an element in Yeats of skepticism in the
ancient Greek sense. Since the nature of things cannot be known, no
judgments can be made. It is pertinent to note here that according to
Ursula Bridge, T. Sturge Moore thought "Yeats was essentially scien-
tific in spirit, with a desire to be convinced intellectually of the truth of
mysticism that was never fulfilled, so that . . . he remained at heart a
sceptic" (LTSM xviii).

The gaiety that Yeats ascribes to tragic heroes in "Lapis Lazuli" is

---

5. Martin Green, *Yeats's Blessings on Von Hügel* (London: Longmans, 1967), 2. Here-
after cited in the text as *YBVH*.

6. Warwick Gould, "Yeats's great vellum notebook," *Times Literary Supplement* 26
July 1985: 824. Hereafter cited in the text as *YGVN*.

rooted in skepticism: "Hamlet and Lear are gay." Civilizations rise and crumble, "All things fall and are built again / And those that build them again are gay" (P 294–95). With the recognition that the Absolute either does not exist or is so distant that only living forms matter, the Yeatsian hero is filled with delight, for he is freed from all sense of obligation. I would like to observe, however, that Shakespeare's Hamlet and Lear are not gay in any Yeatsian sense.

They do not stand apart from the death of fathers and the fall of kingdoms. Civilization is not an illusion in Shakespeare, but magnificently real. Gloucester is not gay when he says to Edgar, "Men must endure / Their going hence, even as their coming hither; / Ripeness is all" (King Lear V.ii.9). Nor is Hamlet gay when he echoes both Gloucester's language and thought:

Not a whit, we defy augury: there is a special providence in the fall of a sparrow. If it be now, 'tis not to come; if it be not to come, it will be now; if it be not now, yet it will come—the readiness is all. (Hamlet V.ii.211)

The providence that shapes our ends is much in evidence in both plays, and Hamlet's echoing of the Bible is important for this discussion, for ripeness implies inwardness, preparation, meaning. One is ripe for something, and surely the thing that one is ripe for is more than an illusion, otherwise why bother, for ripeness is not simply had. It requires effort. There is a certitude about reality in Shakespeare that we do not find in Yeats, and which makes Yeatsian gaiety not simply inappropriate, but impossible.

Nor is there joy in Lady Gregory's and Yeats's sense in historical figures we know to have led lives in the fullest sense tragic. Abraham Lincoln was a melancholy man. He had good reason to be melancholy. If there was joy in Lincoln, it was Christian joy-in-suffering, for he had shaped his life upon the Gospels. It is a matter of some consequence for literature, and for the idea of the tragic life in the West, that in the Agony in the Garden Christ asked that the cup be taken from him. He did not embrace the cross with gaiety, in any sense, and tragedy in the West owes more to the pattern of the Christian life than to anything else. It is not necessary to conform Yeats to any tradition to love his poetry, but neither is it necessary to believe his imperial statements as if they were revelations.

Yeats saw no consolation for loving what is passing and must pass,

except perhaps art itself, or a life framed to art. Words were not enough
for W. T. Horton, who sought and found love in Christianity. What
kept Yeats from Horton's consolation and gave him the nexus of his art
will form the major discussion of this paper.

Early Experience of Religion

So get you gone, Von Hügel, though with
blessings on your head. (P 253)

With this often quoted line Yeats laid the ghost of Christianity for good
and prepared himself for the writing of his last poems. It had been a more
active ghost than most critics are willing to admit. Evidence suggests
that in the early 1930s the poet was seriously moved by the claims of
Christianity, particularly through the work and personal example of Von
Hügel. Yeats had been raised more or less Christian until the age of his
first rebellion, and of course had been surrounded by Christianity and
Christians all his life. He was certainly aware that sensitive and learned
men and women could be Christian without putting their minds to sleep.
Yeats had met Hopkins as a young man in his father's studio. Both
Lionel Johnson and Maud Gonne became Catholic. Since he had been
raised Protestant but had many Catholic friends, he was aware from his
earliest interest in poetry of the full range of the Christian tradition. He
could scarcely help but have been, since he lived in a culture at least
nominally Christian, though he came to believe it was a culture that had
largely lived through its inspiration.

Yeats had worked out a response to Christianity long before he
knew of Von Hügel, obviously avoiding it as a faith, though using
Christian material in his work. But to speak of either his religion or his
poetry in such terms is misleading, since both were the center of his life.
He was a poet and lived to write; he pursued knowledge of spiritual
reality and did not rest until he thought he possessed it, if he can be said
to have rested from that quest at all. In the early 1930s a number of
influences turned him again toward Christianity, the most powerful
being Von Hügel's massive study, *The Mystical Element of Religion*. Von
Hügel's erudition, intense honesty, and entire commitment to his faith,
as well as a broad humanity unlike anything in English theological writ-
ing since Coleridge, inform every page of the book. *The Mystical Element*
suggested Christian faith as a serious possibility to Yeats.

I do not think, with Virginia Moore, that Yeats was a Christian, though her admirable study is still the best general treatment of the subject.[7] But it is clear that the references to Von Hügel in "Vacillation" are a good deal more than Yeats's "polite" bow to orthodoxy, as Ellmann has it in The Identity of Yeats.[8] Whatever crisis of faith The Mystical Element precipitated or aided, Yeats solved it by rejecting Christianity. I would like to discuss the commitments that made such a rejection necessary.

The basic facts of the poet's early life are well known. I would like to focus briefly on some details, however, as they make his later attitudes more understandable. The family was Protestant on both sides, both his paternal grandfather and great-grandfather serving in the Church of Ireland. His mother's people were merchants and shipowners, and belonged to the middle class he often heard his father inveigh against, but these were not, as the elder Yeats would have it, shopkeepers thinking only of profit, but fiery and memorable people. "I think I confused my grandfather [Pollexfen] with God," Yeats wrote. "Even to-day when I read King Lear his image is always before me" (Au 8, 9). These people were Protestant, but lived in a Catholic land. A. G. Stock, writing about Yeats's background, has an important but misleading reflection on the differences between Catholic and Protestant culture as far as art is concerned:

> But the country is Catholic, and the difference between Catholic and Protestant culture goes beyond theology or politics. When Protestantism broke with the past it broke with ritual and imagery and all the concrete visible forms in which humanity expressed its sense of the unseen long before it had mastered abstract language. In its hatred of idolatry it broke, more completely than Catholicism ever had, with a thousand ancient ways of feeling which are not expressible in terms of Protestant thought.
>
> For making a separate identity to its regions and inhabitants, the language of imagery is an instrument far more subtle than abstract words can ever be. Its very imprecisions are capable of expressing shades and links of meaning not to be reasoned out. It is the poet's

---

7. Virginia Moore, The Unicorn: William Butler Yeats' Search for Reality (New York: Macmillan, 1954). Hereafter cited in the text as TU.

8. Richard Ellmann, The Identity of Yeats, 2d ed. (London: Faber, 1964), 274. Hereafter cited in the text as IY.

indispensable language, and if he is not born to a system of imagery
he needs to adopt or invent one before he can find full freedom of
utterance.[9]

If such a statement were accurate, we would have neither Milton nor
Rembrandt, and, if we accept such a statement, we will not understand
Yeats's debt to his father, and the extent to which he himself had an
abstract, and therefore "Protestant" mind, according to Stock. Rem-
brandt, a friend of Mennonite preachers, and obviously Protestant in
faith and culture, had no difficulty "making a felt world visible," yet he
did not do so in terms of traditional symbolism or ancient imagery. He
had his faith and his pencil, and that seems to have been enough. I think
that Stock does what Emil Brunner warned against in the 1947 Gifford
Lectures:

> The Reformation and the Puritan movements must not, however,
> be identified. Neither is the intensity of a Christian culture to be
> measured by the extent of art employed in the service of the organ-
> ised Church. We should never forget that it was within the realm of
> the early Lutheran Church that one of the greatest cultural creations
> took place in the shape of German church music, from Martin
> Luther to Johann Sebastian Bach, and that it was on the soil of
> Calvinistic Holland that a development of painting took place, equal
> to that of the Italian Renaissance. . . . Furthermore, it should not be
> forgotten that Rembrandt is a painter who increasingly made the
> interpretation of Biblical history his main artistic endeavor, just as
> Bach throughout his life had put his incomparable musical genius in
> the service of the divine Word . . . and often expressed his concep-
> tion of music as being nothing but an attempt of man to glorify
> God.[10]

We have not had a good study of Protestantism and the poetic image, or
the artistic image, for that matter. There would be no place in such a
study for easy generalizations.

Yeats, of course, inveighed all his life against the abstract, as did

---

9. A. G. Stock, *W. B. Yeats: His Poetry and Thought* (Cambridge: Cambridge Univer-
sity Press, 1961), 5.

10. Emil Brunner, *Christianity and Civilisation,* 2 vols. (London: Nisbet, 1947) 1:146–
47.

Wordsworth before him, but in neither case can we take the protest to define the mind of the poet. No one capable of writing *A Vision* could have found abstraction all that unusual. What is important in Stock's account is the idea that because Ireland had been Catholic from the earliest days of Christianity in Europe, and because Catholicism in general exists on easier terms with paganism than Protestantism, Yeats found all about him the visible signs of a long pagan past in everything from Norman towers to tales of the Sidhe, and these "images," because they rose naturally in human culture before the advent of abstract thought, carried with them the richness of the creative unconscious.

Yeats no doubt would have taken a different stance toward religion in general if his father had been a believer, but John Butler Yeats, like so many educated men of his generation, was an agnostic and could not inspire respect for a religion he did not believe. As a young boy the poet was naturally religious, enjoying "the sermon and passages of the Apocalypse" (Au 24), but the family made his life miserable on Sunday by badgering him about inessentials, even the way he walked! (Au 24). At the age of eight Yeats refused to go to church, perceiving his father did not go. This precipitated a family row that never ended until Yeats left home.

There can be no doubt that from 1873 on Yeats felt a spiritual vacuum, wanting to believe but finding nothing to believe in beyond stories and monuments that testified to the reality of the supernatural. John Butler Yeats believed that "the doctrines of the atonement, the resurrection of the dead, the Trinity, the holy spirit, the judgment to come, are all so many folk tales meant to impose only on those who wish to be imposed on, as we all do when listening to ghost stories, and as peasants do when talking about the 'gentry' in the dusk on the hill side or sitting round the turf fire and listening to the howling of the wind."[11] His son instinctively believed that there was more truth in the ghost stories than in the theories of the rationalists his father had accepted. Like Wordsworth, Yeats listened to "the ghostly language of the ancient earth" (*The Prelude* [1850] 2:309), and his chief delight was association with people who believed that there were mysteries the modern mind could not explain. By his own proclamation one of "the last romantics"

---

11. Quoted by William M. Murphy in *Prodigal Father: The Life of John Butler Yeats (1839–1922)* (Ithaca and London: Cornell University Press, 1978), 312. Hereafter cited in the text as *PF*.

(P 245), Yeats and the friends he was to make fought against the nine-
teenth century enlightenment as Wordsworth and his friends had fought
against the eighteenth.

During the London years Yeats was doubly an outcast, longing for
Ireland when he was not there, and striving to formulate a belief as yet
inevitably sketchy. His father's agnosticism troubled him: "My father's
unbelief had set me thinking about the evidences of religion and I
weighed the matter perpetually with great anxiety, for I did not think I
could live without religion" (Au 25–26). He described in *Autobiographies*
his attempt to construct a religion he could believe.

> I am very religious, and deprived by Huxley and Tyndall, whom I
> detested, of the simple-minded religion of my childhood, I had
> made a new religion, almost an infallible Church of poetic tradition,
> of a fardel of stories, and of personages, and of emotions, insepara-
> ble from their first expression, passed on from generation to genera-
> tion by poets and painters with some help from philosophers and
> theologians. I wished for a world where I could discover this tradi-
> tion perpetually, and not in pictures and poems only, but in tiles
> round the chimney-piece and in the hangings that kept out the
> draught. (Au 115–16)

That attempt was directly contrary to the spirit of the times, and fulfilled
only in his art.

In an age in which the *I Ching* can be purchased only a few feet from
the toothpaste rack in a metropolitan drug store, and more things are
believed than either Hamlet or Horatio dreamt of, it is difficult to appre-
ciate the extent to which unbelief defined the period of Yeats's youth.
G. K. Chesterton wrote:

> We might almost say that agnosticism was an established church.
> There was a uniformity of unbelief . . . not among eccentric peo-
> ple, but simply among educated people. . . . Men believed in the
> British Empire precisely because they had nothing else to believe
> in.[12]

---

12. G. K. Chesterton, *Autobiography* (London: Hutchinson, 1936), 143–45. Hereafter
cited in the text as *A*.

Yet in the best people of the day there was more of Christianity than they themselves acknowledged. Von Hügel made this point in a letter to his niece:

A friend of mine, whom I have known for 45 years, died some days back, at 76—without any traceable shred of religion (at least in the ordinary sense of the word). He was a man of finely clean life, full of philanthropy, genuine and costly, a cultivated man, a scholar, also a man of naturally religious temper. It is certainly impossible to know the depths of any soul: yet certain points are once more clear to me, over this further case—that the agnostic tempest which roared between say 1855 and 1875 was so violent, that no wonder quick-witted lads went under, many, many of them. That even so, the finer ones managed to retain much that was high and right—even that was touchingly Christian—but that they owed this, not to Agnosticism, but to the Christian faith, the tradition from which they had broken away less than they themselves thought.[13]

But in spite of "much that was high and right," no social atmosphere could have been more repellent to the young poet. As Chesterton put it, "Now against this drab background of dreary modern materialism, Willie Yeats was calmly walking about as the Man Who Knew the Fairies" (*A* 146).

There was clearly, though, more pain and upset in the young poet's life than Chesterton suggests. He read Ruskin and argued with his father. One night JBY broke a picture with the back of his son's head and volunteered to box with him, so intense was their disagreement over mysticism (Mem 19). Such scenes are more amusing in retrospect than when lived through. According to William M. Murphy, "JBY apparently thought that by sparing his son the follies of Christian belief he could move him in a single step to his own broad acres of cheerful agnosticism" (*PF* 137). But Yeats saw his father and his father's generation as unalterably opposed to *any* recognition of the spiritual world, and he set his mind against them both. In 1884 his aunt Isabella Pollexfen sent Yeats a copy of A. P. Sinnett's *Esoteric Buddhism* and the following year

---

13. Baron Friedrich Von Hügel, *Selected Letters, 1896–1924,* ed. Bernard Holland (London: J. M. Dent & Sons, 1927), 308. Hereafter cited in the text as *SL.*

he collaborated in the founding of the Dublin Hermetic Society. From
that point on pursuit of spiritual knowledge and its expression in poetry
became the overriding concerns of his life.

Catholics and Catholicism

A brief survey of Yeats's relationship with Christians and with the in-
stitutional Church will be useful, to see whether or not personal likes and
dislikes, or the social face shown by the Church would have attracted or
repelled him from the core of Christian faith. There is, of course, some-
thing artificial in such a procedure, since he did not make friends by
belief, and the Church was simply *there,* a fact of history and certainly a
potent if often misguided force in Irish society, but a scrutiny of what the
poet had to take for granted will tell us something about him.

Of course in this discussion the Church always means the Roman
Catholic Church. While Yeats admired the independence and imagina-
tion of his forebears, their Christianity did not impress him. He was
groping, even as a young man, toward unity of being as a personal ideal,
and its reflection in a unified society. Like so many others in the late
nineteenth century, including Ruskin and Morris, he felt as a personal
burden the breakup of what little was left of the late medieval European
community, and wanted to replace it with a new, integrated world based
on pre-Christian myths and symbolism. The Christianity taught by the
Church of Ireland simply could not satisfy the spiritual and intellectual
hunger of young people at mid-century. It had not been shaken into
awareness of modern problems of faith by the Oxford Movement as had
its English counterpart. There were, of course, many Irish evangelicals,
but according to John Butler Yeats,

> when Wesleyism affected the Irish leisured class, gentlemen before,
> they remained gentlemen, only with more refinement of heart and a
> more subtle sympathy. The wild men, described by Charles Lever,
> who cared for nothing except romance and courage and personal
> glory, now walked in the footsteps of their Lord and Master.[14]

If that were entirely true, Ireland would have experienced a religious
revival in the nineteenth century, and it did not. In the end nothing short

---

14. John Butler Yeats, *Early Memories: Some Chapters of Autobiography* (Churchtown,
Dundrum: Cuala Press, 1923), 48.

of dramatic involvement with the spiritual world would have claimed the young poet's attention.

Hone tells us that Yeats's paternal great-grandfather, " 'Parson Yeats' of Drumcliff . . . mixed on genial terms with the Roman Catholics."[15] Yeats's poems appeared in such journals as *Irish Monthly* and *Irish Fireside*. Father Matthew Russell, editor of the *Irish Monthly*, was liberal in his praise of the young poet, referring to Yeats as a "a new singer of Erin" (*WBY* 55). Yeats was not always attracted to what he saw of Catholic life, but thought there was a possibility that the two segments of Irish society might be fused into a unity that then would be stronger against the English.

> I began to plot and scheme how one might seal with the right image the soft wax before it began to harden. I had noticed that Irish Catholics among whom had been born so many political martyrs had not the good taste, the household courtesy and decency of the Protestant Ireland I had known, yet Protestant Ireland seemed to think of nothing but getting on in the world. I thought we might bring the two halves together if we had a national literature that made Ireland beautiful in the memory . . . freed from provincialism by an exacting criticism, a European pose. (Au 101–2)

I cannot help but point out in passing that Yeats took over completely his father's attitude toward Protestant Ireland.

Forty-one years later, in June of 1925, when he delivered his speech on divorce before the Irish Senate, Yeats was more inclined to see value in the sturdy independence of his Protestant forebears, citing, obviously with pride, "rights . . . won by the labours of John Milton and other great men, and won after strife, which is a famous part of the history of the Protestant people" (SS 92). Such a reference is not simply a case of his finding value in a tradition when it supported him and ignoring it when it didn't. As an older man, I hope to show, he more and more derived his notions of artistic and social excellence from "the foul rag and bone shop" (P 348) of the intransigent human heart, a position closer to Protestant than Catholic thought.

In 1885 Yeats met Katharine Tynan. He was twenty, she twenty-

---

15. Joseph Hone, *W. B. Yeats, 1865–1939*, 2d ed. (London: Macmillan, 1965), 55. Hereafter cited in the text as *WBY*.

four. Her family was Catholic, but staunch supporters of Parnell, both before and after the Kitty O'Shea affair, which endeared them to Yeats. Katharine's father was a farmer, and Yeats was made welcome at the farmhouse to which he often walked, though it was five miles outside Dublin. Katharine valued Yeats's opinion, and certainly his poetry. They corresponded regularly when Yeats was back in London in the late nineties, and he seems to have made her, for that time, the chief protector of his Irish associations.

If Yeats received nothing but admiration and encouragement from Father Russell and Katharine Tynan, the response of the Church was somewhat less open-armed. Yeats had his first major brush with the Church Militant in 1899 over the opening of *The Countess Cathleen*. A dreamy young poet writing lyrics evocative of the Celtic twilight is one thing, and a confident, at times arrogant, young man staging a public play in which souls are sold for bread quite something else. Rumors about the unorthodoxy of the play made Edward Martyn, who was financing its production, uncomfortable enough to threaten withdrawing his support, and in an effort to save the situation Yeats submitted the play to both an English and an Irish priest for their approval (Mem 119). The play was eventually performed without incident.

Well before the major work of his life, then, a pattern had evolved in his relationship with Christianity. Protestantism was not taken seriously as a faith because it did not seem to provide any real point of contact between man and God, and to him no ritual worthy of attention. He was well received as a poet by individual Catholics, and had many Catholic friends throughout his life, but the Church in Ireland suspected him of being un-Christian, possibly even anti-Christian. His early experiences with the Church do not seem to have embittered him toward Christianity, but he quickly came to the conclusion that the Church had too much power in Ireland and often did not use it wisely.

Yeats had joined with Edward Martyn and George Moore to found the Irish Literary Theatre. Martyn's Catholicism was naive and antiquated in ways that were unfortunately common in the late nineteenth century. For him, as for Lionel Johnson, the Church was a doorway to hieratic being, to the unchanging world of Spirit. The Gnostic-Jansenist element in their faith is obvious, and Martyn was superstitious. In 1896 Yeats stayed with Martyn and Arthur Symons at Tullyra Castle. Yeats decided "to evoke the lunar power, which was, I believed, the chief source of my inspiration." On the tenth night of invocation, while going to sleep, Yeats saw first a centaur, "then a marvellous naked woman shooting an arrow at a star." Symons came down to breakfast with a poem he had written to a woman of great beauty who had visited him in dream. Yeats wrote in his *Memoirs:*

> Martyn was really angry, for some of my invocations, I admitted, I had made in the waste room in the old tower of the castle where he lived, and this waste room was directly over the chapel. I had not known that a room over a chapel must be left empty, and that an action such as mine might be considered to obstruct the passage of prayer. I was forbidden even to speak of invocation, and I was sorry, for I knew I must have much in common with Martyn, who spent hours after we all had gone to bed reading St Chrysostom. (Mem 100–101)

Martyn's concern reveals a tendency to materialize spiritual reality to the point where it is unrecognizable. His metaphysically prissy fussing reveals a mind obsessed with triviality, not reality. No young man doing anything in a tower can obstruct the passage of someone else's prayer.

Martyn continued to play a part in Yeats's relationship with Catholicism. In 1912 *The Countess Cathleen* was revived in Dublin, with several new scenes. Yeats called on Martyn to see if some rapprochement were possible with the Church. He wanted to know what reaction he would get if the second Abbey company continued to specialize in religious drama. Nugent Monck had staged an annunciation, and Yeats thought there might be a thaw.

> "No," said Martyn, "they are too suspicious. They think that you are not only anti-Catholic but Anti-Christian."
> "We are neither of these things," Yeats replied, "and it is the interest of your Church to encourage a distinguished intellectual life in Ireland, for the alternative will be atheism in a few years." (*WBY* 257)

Martyn had withdrawn his support of Lady Gregory and Yeats because he thought Irish literature could be built upon other themes than those of peasant life. And he found their celebration of the peasant to be patronizing, since it was his experience that the peasants were far more Christian than Celtic. It is to Martyn's credit that his Oxford training did not blunt his sympathies for his own people. He eventually threw his energies into a group dedicated to performing plays in Irish.

Another Oxford graduate, Lionel Johnson, with whom Yeats was closely associated in the nineties, also became Catholic. Against the wishes of his Tory parents he became both Catholic and a supporter of Irish Nationalism. Yeats met Johnson in 1891 through the Rhymers' Club, and he was Yeats's closest friend until 1902 when he died at only thirty-five. Although he was a small man physically and two years younger than Yeats, Johnson had an imposing personality and clearly dominated the friendship. "He was the first disciple of Walter Pater whom I had met," Yeats wrote in his *Memoirs,* "and he had taken from Walter Pater certain favourite words which came to mean much for me: 'Life should be a ritual', and we should value it for 'magnificence', for all that is 'hieratic' " (Mem 35). Much that proved to be permanent in Yeats came from Johnson, his taste for elegance in clothes, his admiration for ceremony, for the formal in art.

Johnson was at this point only a few months from his conversion to Catholicism. And the life of Johnson's poetry was his new faith. T. W. Rolleston wrote of him in a *A Treasury of Irish Poetry in the English Tongue:*

> He has renounced the world and built up a twilight world instead, where all the colours are like the colours in the rainbow that is cast by the moon, and all the people as far from modern tumults as the people upon faded and dropping tapestries. . . . He has chosen to live . . . between two memories—the religious tradition of the Church of Rome and the political tradition of Ireland. . . . He has made a world all of altar lights and golden vestures, and murmured Latin and incense clouds, and autumn winds and dead leaves, where one wanders remembering martyrdoms and courtesies that the world has forgotten.[16]

Yeats wrote:

> Johnson read little but the classics. He had the sympathetic intelligence of a woman and was the best listener I have ever met. . . . (Mem 36)

---

16. *A Treasury of Irish Poetry in the English Tongue,* ed. Stopford A. Brooke and T. W. Rolleston (1900; Great Neck, N.Y.: Granger Book Co., 1979), 466–67.

But there was more to Johnson than either Yeats or the editors of *A Treasury of Irish Poetry* were aware of. He was one of the first to appreciate Thomas Hardy's genius. In 1894 he published *The Art of Thomas Hardy*, the first major study of Hardy's work, and still a classic. Hardy's characters are not "people upon faded and dropping tapestries" yet Johnson was quick to appreciate their often ironic situations. He was a brilliant critic, but one of those men for whom the twentieth century was not good news. He saw too much of the tragedy that was to come. His early loss to alcoholism and ill health was a great misfortune.

In Martyn and Johnson Yeats had eccentric friends with taste and talent, and in Johnson, certainly, a superior literary mind. And he had every reason to believe them models of Catholic orthodoxy, if not sanctity. But this was a century in which the Church valued purity more than charity, and their Christianity was weakened by a lugubrious Gnosticism. It was also a century in which the materialism of the new middle class seriously weakened the idea of the spiritual life, let alone its practice. And of course the sciences had largely stolen cosmology and philosophy from the theological fold. Faced with a difficult situation, the churches did the worst possible thing. As Owen Chadwick has written:

> Defenders of Christian orthodoxy looked to their gates, lowered the portcullis, raised the drawbridge and boiled the oil. They had too little consciousness that part of the assault rose out of some of their own principles. And this devotional siege, most powerful in the Ultramontane movement within the Roman Catholic Church, but powerful among Protestants, repelled intelligent men and widened the sense of breach.[17]

As a young man Yeats was exposed to an escapist Catholicism forcefully presented by men who could write and were interested in ideas, and an institutional church whose chief concern seemed to be that none of its elaborate belief was challenged in a socially acceptable way. After such an introduction, the wonder is that Yeats retained any interest in Catholicism at all, but in some ways the failure of the Church to recognize the world was attractive to Yeats, since the Church had been the strongest institutional guardian of the dimensions of being to which he was most

---

17. Owen Chadwick, *The Secularization of the European Mind in the Nineteenth Century* (London: Cambridge University Press, 1975), 250.

attracted. But as we shall see, his understanding of Christianity was weakened by the Church's refusal to come to grips with the world.

The same escapist attitude was largely reponsible for the pedantic rote schooling Yeats saw destroying the highest achievement of Christianity.

> The education given by the Catholic schools seems to me to be in all matters of general culture a substituting of pedantry for taste. Men learn the dates of writers, the external facts of masterpieces, and not sense of style and feeling for life. I have never met a young man from an Irish Catholic school who did not seem to me injured by the literature and the literary history he had learned at it. The arts have nothing to give but that joy of theirs which is perhaps the other side of sorrow. They are always an exhausting contemplation, and we are very ready in our youth, before habits have been formed, to turn from it to pedantry, which offers to the mind a kind of sensual ease. The young men and women who have not been through the Secondary Schools seem to me upon the other hand much more imaginative than Protestant boys and girls and to have better taste. My sisters have the same experience. Catholic education seems to destroy the qualities which they get from their religion. Provincialism destroys the nobility of the Middle Ages. (Mem 187)

But the nineteenth century in general had trouble handling facts, for if the Church insisted upon facts of a certain kind as one defense against the world, the world insisted on others as a sign that young people were prepared to enter the maze of modern life, and the latter tyranny was equally destructive of poetry, as Cissy Jupe found in *Hard Times*.

Yeats had a continuing interest in education, and the extent to which he was actively interested in improving Catholic as well as Protestant education is a measure of his open-mindedness. In a speech made to the Irish Literary Society on 30 November 1925, he made a series of broad-based suggestions for the reform of education. The first of these was that the physical condition both of schools and students must be such to make education possible. "If the children are going to be forced to school you must not only see that those schools are warm and clean and sanitary, but you must do as other countries are doing more and more, and see that children during school hours are neither half-naked nor starved" (SS 169). But that was only the beginning. Yeats had heard reports that it was common for children to have no sense of duty toward community and neighbor. To remedy the situation he suggested a four-point program that Gentile was using in Italy: the learning and saying of simple prayers, the learning and singing of famous religious songs, the narration of stories out of the Bible, and contemplation. It is a pity the children so educated could not have prevented the invasion of Ethiopia a few years later, but I do not advance that as a serious objection to Yeats's valid concern about education, or to Gentile's, for that matter. Yeats wanted "each religion, Catholic or Protestant, so taught that it permeate the whole school life" (SS 173). The attractiveness of authority was an unfortunate inheritance from a generation which felt itself "Wandering between two worlds, one dead, / The other powerless to be born" (Matthew Arnold, "Stanzas from the Grand Chartreuse," ll. 85–86). Unfortunately, Yeats did not see the human terrors implicit in Fascism before they became apparent.

In other ways, however, Yeats was very much aware of the dangers of authority, particularly the authority of the Church. A few days after he retired from the senate that body debated the Censorship of Publications Bill (1928). Unable to take part in the debate, Yeats attacked the bill in *The Spectator* for 29 September 1928. The background of the bill involves, yet again, what Yeats considered the provincialism of Irish Catholic education. In 1926 an agitated Christian Brother had burned in public an English magazine that was found to contain "a horrible insult to God." This insult was the lovely medieval Advent ballad, the "Cherry Tree Carol," in which some unflattering remarks are made about Joseph. According to Yeats, the Brother, "scandalised by its naivete . . . believed it to be the work of some irreligious modern poet." "Confident in the support of an ignorance even greater than his own," this man appealed for and eventually did get support which eventuated in the bill, which Yeats opposed. The legislation provided for the minister of justice to appoint a committee to judge books or periodicals complained about by "recognised associations" (SS 176), and here Yeats has interpolated the Catholic Truth Society! The committee would then decide if the matter were indecent or contrary to public morality.

The superb irony of the whole situation was that the ballad is a completely natural and unaffected response of people in an "Age of Faith," precisely the response and the society, one would think, that the Church would look upon with favor. Had the Brother known a little more, he might have known there were hundreds of irreverent comments about Joseph in the popular literature of the Middle Ages, and that, far from indicating sarcasm or lack of faith, they are a testimony to how deeply Christianity had taken possession of the people. In his speech Yeats rails beautifully at the Church's "holy gunmen," and goes on to make a point that will be important for this discussion later on.

> Twenty years ago illegitimacy was almost unknown, infanticide unknown, and now both are common and increasing, and they think that if they could exclude English newspapers, with their police-court cases which excite the imagination, their occasional allusions to H. G. Wells which excite the intellect, their advertisements of books upon birth control which imply safety for illicit love, innocence would return. They do not understand that you cannot unscramble eggs, that every country passing out of automatism passes through demoralization, and that it has no choice but to go on into intelligence. (SS 177)

As we shall see, it was precisely going on into intelligence that Von Hügel most desired for the Church.

Surely the strangest example of Yeats's concern for the Irish Catholic mind is that recounted by Frank Tuohy, in which Yeats tried to convince Iseult Gonne that she should civilize Dublin Catholics by introducing them to the writing of Claudel, Peguy, and Jammes![18] There is a certain Shelleyan unconcern for the practical in such a gesture that Yeats, even with all his experience in politics and the theater, had never outgrown. Though the idea is impractical, his concern is not, and it is the concern of a reformer, not an institution-hater. He clearly wanted the Church called to what he conceived of as its highest reality.

Yeats's personal association with Christians obviously did not stop with Edward Martyn and Lionel Johnson, and, though I do not intend to trace the complete history of such relationships, his friendship with W. T. Horton should be noted before I proceed directly to Von Hügel and "Vacillation."

Horton was a visionary artist and member of the Order of the Golden Dawn. Yeats first met him in 1894, and it was through Yeats's intervention with Arthur Symons that Horton's drawings first appeared in *The Savoy*. In 1898, Horton published *A Book of Images* for which

---

18. Frank Tuohy, *Yeats* (London: Macmillan, 1976), 185.

Yeats wrote the preface, and in 1910 he wrote *The Way of the Soul* with symbolic illustrations. Horton left the Order of the Golden Dawn because "as a follower of Jesus Christ" he could not accept its teaching (*Y&H* 95). Yeats insisted the Order was not anti-Christian, and urged Horton to follow the Christ within. Horton replied that it was precisely "in faithfulness to the Christ within" that he had left the Order (*Y&H* 97). Horton advised Yeats to end his experiments in spiritualism and in one of his last letters to Yeats urged both him and his wife to follow Christ "as an ordinary individual" (*Y&H* 138). Horton was temporarily a member of a group called the Brotherhood of the New Life, but that was clearly only a stopping point along the way. He became a Catholic on the feast of the Epiphany in 1919, shortly before his death.

Horton became impatient with Yeats and Ezra Pound over the constant elaboration of their opinions. In 1916, he wrote to Yeats:

> I believe in Jesus-Christ & all that this NAME means on all planes.
>
> What you or Ezra or anyone else believes or says matters not one tittle to me but I do know we are all in the hands of the Living God & sudden & quick & drastic will be the Event. (*Y&H* 129)

At this point Horton was living with Audrey Amy Locke, an Oxford graduate and historian of Hampshire, in a purely platonic relationship Yeats referred to in "All Souls' Night" and which put him in some awe of Horton. Miss Locke died in May of 1917 from a mastoid infection. Three months before, Horton had written an important letter to Yeats in which he cried out at the intellectual coldness of spiritualism.

> I am sick of all these Theosophies, Steinerisms etc. etc.; all purely intellectual & no real warm brotherliness & fellowship. I know—for 9 months I have been alone & have attended many meetings & met many people interested in Occultism & yet not one single one has troubled to shew real fellowship or interest beyond their intellectual interest. I want to have nothing more to do with the whole galoot, away with them—I just turn to the simplicity of Christ in Jesus & the common humanity of man as found in the street. Now I understand thoroughly why Jesus lived among the so-called outcasts, drunkards etc. I have found more in Brother Lawrence than in all Theosophy & Steiner etc., more real love in Walt Whitman than in

any ism, more real brotherliness in a Pugilist I know than in any
Intellectual. Words, words, words & all the while the heart is bleed-
ing & crying out for love & kindness & fellowship. (Y&H 133)

George Yeats had joined Steiner's Anthroposophical Society, and Hor-
ton was genuinely concerned both for her welfare and that of Yeats.
Horton's life reads like that of a character in a Russian novel, and he can
easily be imagined sitting down with Sonia and Lizavetta to read the
New Testament. Two years later he was dead. Yeats wrote that had
Horton lived he would have dedicated A Vision to him, though he ex-
pected Horton would not have agreed with his philosophy.

On the whole Yeats was fortunate in his Catholic friends. Katharine
Tynan, although a far simpler and less driven person, was a faithful
correspondent, an enormously productive writer in her own right, and a
life-long admirer of his work. Her untroubled faith made Catholicism
seem humanly admirable. Limited and Jansenist as the religion of Martyn
and Johnson must seem to a modern thinker, their repudiation of "the
world" earned Yeats's interest and respect. Horton's commitment to the
Christ within brought Yeats face to face with a Gospel Christianity of
psychological subtlety which did not reject the historical continuity of an
institutional Church. And, of course, he knew many other Catholics he
both admired and respected, Maud Gonne and Mabel Beardsley to name
only two. These people saved his respect for a Church which often in its
official acts and judgments, particularly in Ireland, seemed less than
Christian.

Von Hügel

Writing of Claudel, Jammes, and Peguy in 1917, Yeats concluded *Per
Amica Silentia Lunae* with a comment that suggests he had permanently
distanced himself from Catholicism.

Nothing remained the same but the preoccupation with religion, for
these poets submitted everything to the Pope, and all, even Claudel,
a proud oratorical man, affirmed that they saw the world with the
eyes of vine-dressers and charcoal-burners. It was no longer the
soul, self-moving and self-teaching—the magical soul—but Mother
France and Mother Church. Have not my thoughts run through a
like round, though I have not found my tradition in the Catholic

Church, which was not the Church of my childhood, but where tradition is, as I believe, more universal and more ancient? (Myth 368–69)

Yet fifteen years later he wrote "*Must* we part, Von Hügel, though much alike, for we / Accept the miracles of the saints and honor sanctity?" (emphasis added). Of course that was not the original first line of section VII of "Vacillation" (P 249–53), which Bradford gives as follows:

> My teacher is not Von Hügel though I scarce
>   less than he although both he and I
> Accept the miracles of the saints, honour
>   their sanctity
>
> (*YW* 128)

"Vacillation" was one of Yeats's most revised poems, occupying twenty-two pages in the vellum-bound folio manuscript book in which his most important poems were written from November 1930 to the summer of 1933. I think he had trouble getting it the way he wanted it because for a while he did not know how he wanted it. The final "Must we part" that he comes to is infinitely better poetry than "My teacher is not," and it is better because it is more acute as well as more condensed, communicating more of anguish than simple regret. The fact that he gave himself time to think about that word in a much worked-over poem makes his final choice of it even more interesting. Clearly the case had not been closed in 1917, and his reluctance to dismiss the great theologian suggests that Christianity was more and not less appealing to him as he grew older.

Who was Von Hügel, and what did Yeats know of him and his work? These questions must be answered before discussing "Vacillation." The need for some clarification is obvious when even so distinguished a scholar as Richard Ellmann can refer to Von Hügel as a "Catholic mystic" (*IY* 274), for Catholic mystic he was not. There is a vast difference between a scholar of Christian mysticism and a mystic, particularly in Von Hügel's case, since he was far from accepting mysticism as of unqualified value for religion, and indeed he was far more interested in Christianity than in mysticism as such. Baron Friedrich Von Hügel was certainly the most important English theologian of his day, many would say of the twentieth century. His father, Carl Von Hügel, was Austrian Minister at the Court of Tuscany, and later at Brussels. His mother was Scottish and had been raised Presbyterian, but became Catholic after her marriage. Before marrying, his father had taken a world tour remarkable for the day, visiting Egypt, Ceylon, India, the Himalayas, and Cashmere, bringing back an extensive collection of curiosities. Von Hügel picked up from his father a permanent interest in natural history and science.

Friedrich was born in Florence in 1852. He and his brother never attended school, first being taught by a Protestant lady, then a Lutheran pastor. Baron Carol retired from diplomatic service in 1867 and lived at Torquay, where Friedrich studied geology with William Pengelly, a self-taught Quaker stone mason. Already obvious in his background is a cosmopolitan religious and intellectual heritage that strongly influenced his work. It was impossible for Von Hügel to be small, cramped, or parochial in his ideas. He took for granted the full range of human knowledge.[19]

In 1873 Von Hügel married Lady Mary Herbert, and they settled in Hampstead. In 1903 they moved to 13 Vicarage Gate, near Kensington Gardens, where he spent the rest of his life. By personal association and an enormous correspondence in four languages with the most important theologians and philosophers of the day, Von Hügel's early interest in religion became a major quest to reinterpret Christianity for the turn-of-the-century world. He was in favor of the scientific study of Biblical texts, feeling that Christianity had nothing to fear from the truth. Ecumenical before ecumenism, he read and admired the new German Protestant thinkers, particularly Troeltsch and Eucken, and did all he could to make them known in England. He lectured at colleges and before societies, addressed students as well as learned men, attempting to explain to his contemporaries the fullness of the Christian life as he understood it. Known as the Pope of Modernism, he stuck by Tyrrell and Loisy throughout the Modernist crisis and did not alter any of his ideas, though under a sword of excommunication, which never fell.

The book that made his reputation as a scholar was *The Mystical Element of Religion,* a study of St. Catherine of Genoa published in 1908. He followed it with *Eternal Life* (1912), *The German Soul* (1916), and posthumously, *The Reality of God* (1931). His *Essays and Addresses on the Philosophy of Religion,* First Series, appeared in 1921, and the Second Series in 1926. Bernard Holland edited his letters in 1927, and in the

---

19. The details in this paragraph come from Bernard Holland's memoir of Von Hügel in *SL.*

following year *Letters of Baron Von Hügel to a Niece* appeared. In 1920 he was made a Doctor of Divinity by Oxford, the first Catholic to be so honored since the Reformation. Spiritual director and tutor of Evelyn Underhill, at his death in 1925 Von Hügel simply knew more than anyone else about Christian mysticism.

It would be a great mistake, however, to suggest that Von Hügel is remembered only for his books and ideas. He was one of those rare men who united great knowledge with great sanctity, and people loved him because he obviously loved them. He was at his best when speaking in such groups as the London Society for the Study of Religion. Edwyn Bevan remembered him in the following account:

> Those who heard the Baron speak at one of these meetings will never forget it—the grey hair standing up from his forehead, the large dark eyes in a face as of fine ivory, the divine fire which seemed to fill him, the passionate sense of the reality of God, which broke forth in volcanic utterance, strange bits of slang and collo-quialisms mingling with magnificent phrases, and left him, when he ended, exhausted and trembling. (*SL* 35)

The Rector of Freiburg University said of him after his death:

> He was one of the most remarkable of men, and, in consequence, not to be understood by such as knew him not intimately. I have seen him, after the sharpest critical argument, or after slashing away at some abuse or faultiness in clerical or Church questions, go into the nearest Church and pray, rapt and absorbed like a saint—or a child. (*SL* 48–49)

He had three daughters and buried one of them. He was deaf throughout his life owing to an attack of typhoid fever as a young man. In short, as Claude Montefiore wrote in the *Jewish Guardian:*

> He knew a lot about religion and God from endless books and much thinking, but he also knew a lot about them from experience and from life. When he talked about God, one felt, somehow, that he had a triple right to do so, because he had studied and thought so much, because he had felt and experienced so much, and, above all, because he was good and pure and devout. (*SL* 35)

What Yeats knew of Von Hügel and his work is a complicated question to which we must now turn.

Yeats lived at Woburn Buildings in London from 1896 to 1919. Of course he was often away, but, particularly in the first decade of his lease, the poet's life was organized around his London residence. From 1873 to 1903 Von Hügel lived in Hampstead, but was in and out of central London regularly. From 1903 until he died Von Hügel lived within easy walking distance of the British Museum, where Yeats often worked. I have found no record that they ever met, but it is tempting to think they might have passed each other on the street. Even that is unlikely, however, since Yeats's life was circumscribed by a self-imposed order that did not often include walking by daylight.

> Unless he was working at the British Museum, he would be indoors writing until four, when he dressed, and either received visitors or went out to seek literary friends or his "mystics". When he had no evening engagements he would take long solitary walks, because his eyesight discouraged reading or writing by candlelight; and his tall cloaked figure, seemingly oblivious of its surroundings, was very familiar to the late home-comers of Bloomsbury. (*WBY* 177)

Von Hügel was more likely to get out during the day, and Kensington Gardens was his usual place to walk, because there he could be among children, whom he loved: "Here he could often be seen, a singular contrast to the thought-free faces of nursemaids and children round him, with his soft, wide-brimmed black hat and cape-cloak, and with his . . . dog, Puck, for a companion" (*SL* 45). Both men were often away in the summer. Chesterton, who knew Yeats, met Von Hügel; and Dowden, whose chair at Trinity College Dublin Yeats came close to filling, dined with him, but as far as I know, neither man so much as saw the other. Dowden's impression is particularly interesting, as his was an academic and stuffy personality.

> I have thoughts of going to my priest at Donnybrook and saying to him: 'I have faith only as a grain of mustard seed, but I can give obedience, and I want to try if through obedience I can grow as beautiful of soul as Fried von Hügel. Will you receive?'. . . . It would be a curious experience which a nineteenth-century Jacques ought to undergo, and you know I have enough of Proteus in me to

turn into water next day and slip out of my Catholic manacles and gyves.[20]

That he should have responded so warmly to Von Hügel is a testimony to the Baron's humility-in-knowledge, and his luminous candor. The only contact that I know took place between Yeats and Von Hügel came, appropriately enough for a poet and a theologian, through a book, Von Hügel's *The Mystical Element of Religion As Studied in Saint Catherine of Genoa and Her Friends,* published in two ponderous volumes by J. M. Dent in December 1908, and reprinted in March 1909. O'Shea lists no other volume of Von Hügel's in his catalogue of Yeats's library. The product of thirty years' work, it was published when Von Hügel was fifty-six. It was his first book. The mark of the text is its absolute honesty, monumental scholarship, and a treatment of background material as elaborate and detailed as the treatment of the main subject. The main forces in western civilization are discussed, St. Catherine's physical and emotional states elaborately analyzed with the intention of eliminating all fanciful stories and coming at last to the truth of the saint's experience. All major texts are examined for authenticity, and the comments of friends and associates assessed for their truth and usefulness. A great admirer of Darwin, Von Hügel's method in *The Mystical Element* is close to Darwin's in *The Origin of Species.* An enormous body of data is carefully sifted for meaningful patterns of development. Of course the book is absolutely suffused with his deep love of God, his great sense of the mystery of being. His point was not to prove anything in regard to the existence of God, but rather to probe a particular response to that existence, that of the mystic, and to judge in what measure the mystic response is capable of teaching humanity at large a way to holy life.

The year after *The Mystical Element* was published, Bishop Talbot, the Anglican Bishop of Winchester, carried both volumes to India with him, read them en route, and wrote his enthusiastic approbation to Von Hügel from the Persian Gulf (*SL* 176). By far the most dramatic response to the book came, however, from a Mrs. Lillie, an American from Chicago, an M.D. with five children. She corresponded with him, eventually traveled to England to meet him, and became a convert to Catholicism. Von Hügel wrote to his niece, "She told us she had been

---

20. Quoted in Michael de la Bedoyere's *The Life of Baron Von Hügel* (London: J. M. Dent & Sons, 1951), 60. Hereafter cited in the text as *LBVH.*

brought into the Church—as far as human, traceable means went—by my *Mystical Element.*" He went on to say, in regard to the same affair, "neither in that book nor in my life did I, or do I aim at making Roman Catholics."[21] Yeats did not read *The Mystical Element* until much later, though possibly as early as 1929.[22]

I would like to summarize briefly what is unmistakably Von Hügelian in his treatment of mysticism and religion, what a careful reader would take away as the main thrust of the book. I shall pay particular attention to two matters which were critical to Yeats, the life of the body and the nature of history. I shall quote from works other than *The Mystical Element* to give the discussion breadth. After that one massive study Von Hügel's ideas did not change, only ripened. The world view of *Eternal Life* and the letters is unchanged from *The Mystical Element.*

Early in volume two of *The Mystical Element* Von Hügel makes a powerful statement about the necessity for Christianity's giving full dignity to the body.

It [final dualism] is directly contradictory of the central truth and temper of Christianity, since these require a full acceptance of the substantial goodness and the thorough sanctifiableness of man's body; of God's condescension to man's whole physico-spiritual organism; and of the persistence of reanimation of all that is essential to man's true personality across and after death. And it is, at bottom, profoundly un-Catholic; the whole Sacramental system, the entire deep and noble conception of the normal relations between the Invisible and the Visible being through the Incarnational type,—an action of the one in the other, which develops the agent and subject at the same time that it spiritualizes the patient, the object, is in direct conflict with it. Neo-Platonism came more and more to treat the body and the entire visible creation as an intrinsic obstacle to spirit, to be eliminated by the latter as completely as possible. . . . But Christianity has ever to come back to its central pre-supposi-

21. *Letters from Baron Friedrich Von Hügel To a Niece,* ed. Gwendolen Greene (London: J. M. Dent & Sons, 1928), 102.

22. In the 1929 *A Packet for Ezra Pound* Yeats referred to Christ, Oedipus, Saint Catherine of Genoa, and Michael Angelo in the same sentence (AV-B 28–29). Since Catherine of Genoa is a little known saint, even to believers—so little known, indeed, that Tyrrell wondered why Von Hügel had written about her—I think we can assume Yeats was reading *The Mystical Element* as early as 1929, or at least knew of the book.

tion—the substantial goodness and spiritual utility and trans-
figurableness of body and matter; and to its final end,—the actual
transformation expressions of abiding ethical and religious values
and realities.[23]

And man was created not for celibacy, but marriage, and not only mar-
riage, but the full enjoyment of sensory life in time. The need for as-
ceticism, self-discipline—and it *is* a need in Von Hügel's view—arose
only with man's inability to organize his life in keeping with the love of
God.

An exclusive commitment only to spiritual things is contrary to
God's love for creation.

> For Christianity is thus obliged to be, more than ever, busy with the
> Temporal and Spatial, the Physical and Psychical, since now it has
> to be all this according to sciences, and in the midst of circum-
> stances, and on a scale, unknown even a century ago; so that, more
> than ever, any exclusive Other-Worldliness, all quietistic suffering
> and listless waiting, would be treason against both man and God.
> Thus less than ever is the Immanentism and the Incarnational Doc-
> trine of Christianity an empty theory; indeed, its insistence that
> spirit shall penetrate and transform matter, and shall thus awaken
> and develop its own self, has never in the history of the world had so
> gigantic a field, and such immense difficulties, in which to show and
> to develop its power, as it possesses now.[24]

Since people are, in the Christian view, complexes of body and soul, in
fact *bodied*, to be brought to perfection they must have what they need to
endure in time. "The sense, then, of Eternal Life requires, for its normal,
general, and deepest development, *Duration*, history; *Space*, institutions;
Material Stimulation, and symbols, something sacramental; and *Transcen-
dence*, a movement away from all and every culture and civilization, to the
Cross, to asceticism, to interior nakedness and the Beyond" (*EL* 392–93).

---

23. Baron Friedrich Von Hügel, *The Mystical Element of Religion As Studied in Saint
Catherine of Genoa and Her Friends*, 2 vols. (London: J. M. Dent & Sons, 1908) 2:126–27.
Hereafter cited in the text as *ME*.
24. Baron Von Hügel, *Eternal Life: A Study of Its Implications and Applications* (Edin-
burgh: T. & T. Clark, 1912), 315–16. Hereafter cited in the text as *EL*.

In the life of time, religion cannot afford to remain empty of cultural values: "At the peril of emptiness and sterility, it has to move out into, to learn from, to criticize, and to teach, all these other apprehensions [philosophy, economics, art] and activities" (*EL* 330). Von Hügel felt that the Church in the nineteenth century had an almost fatal tendency to remove itself from the field of active human endeavor, in politics and in culture. "I believe this tendency to self-starvation to be the one ultimate difficulty of the Church and to remain as grave an antinomy for the practical life, as truly only capable of limitation, not of sheer removal, as are the antinomies for intellect of God and Evil and of Christ and the *Parousia.*"[25] To overcome this limitation, "We religious men will have to develop, *as part of our religion,* the ceaseless sense of its requiring the *nidus,* materials, stimulant, discipline, of the other God-given, non-religious activities, duties, ideals of man, from his physical and psychical necessities up to his aesthetic, political and philosophical aspirations" (*E&A* 62). Von Hügel invokes the then most recent observations of psychological science as authority for his position. "Such celebrated cases as the deaf-mute-blind girls, Laura Bridgeman and Rose Kellerman, indicate, plainly enough, that man's soul, whilst united to the body, remains, in the first instance, unawake even to God and to itself, until the psychic life is aroused by sense stimulation, by the effective impact of the sensible and visible upon man's mind and soul" (*E&A* 231). His argument destroys the possibility of Christian Gnosticism.

His position on history is implied in all that has been already noted. If man is bodied and requires duration and institutions to express fully what he is and is meant to be, his human nature is obscured and frustrated by notions of cyclical time—certainly his capacity for full flowering is stunted. Of course Christian eschatology did not have to wait for Von Hügel to create a sense of history, which is implicit and explicit in the Gospel. Without the notion of final judgment and last things there is no Christianity. As one would expect, for Von Hügel the finite world does have an end.

The historical development which succeeded in rendering the fundamental ethical convictions of Christianity fruitful for the work of the world, and which created a civilisation inspired by Christian ideals,

<hr/>

25. Baron Von Hügel, *Essays and Addresses on the Philosophy of Religion,* First Series (London: J. M. Dent & Sons Ltds, 1921), xii. Hereafter cited in the text as *E&A.*

has not misunderstood the Gospel, even though that development itself, in its great complexity, has not always been properly understood. It is precisely the specifically Christian element, the personalistic conception of God, and the optimism in the estimate of the world . . . from which springs the perception that the divine action has an end which comprises and fashions the world, and which assigns to human labour the task of constituting a community of personalities devoted to the sanctification of the ends of this world and to making these ends subserve the full and final end. For the teaching of Jesus to yield this result it is only necessary that the religious end lose the vehemence springing from the expectation of its immediate realisation, and, consequently, its power simply to dissolve all other pre-occupations. (*E&A* 160)

But the movement of which he speaks here has a time-scale that includes the entire historical process, and Von Hügel would be the first to say that that process, involving as it does the spiritualization of all creation, does not have an end in any ordinary sense. Since its end rests in God, its end rests in mystery. We are not able to judge this movement, for what is progress to us may be regress from a different point of view, and what seems utter failure to us may be progress toward an end that is for the Christian the mystery of being itself.

Against the background of this remarkable interpretation of Christian eschatology, Von Hügel's picture of the life and growth of an individual soul has many points of similarity with that of Yeats. Yeats, in his later years, through perfecting the revelations that came from his wife's automatic writing, became obsessed with the notion of human life and human history running through a course of near-endless cycles of contradiction, a perpetual battle between self and anti-self on the level of the person and the level of civilization. He allowed room for escape from the wheel of appearance in the much-discussed thirteenth phase of his cosmological wheel, but his main image for history is that of the oscillating cone to express virtually endless cycles, and about that I shall have more to say later. Von Hügel believed there was a double movement in the soul that was necessary for its growth.

As the body can live only by inhalation and exhalation . . . and as the mind can only flourish by looking out for sensible material and then elaborating and spiritualising it: so the soul can live, to be fully normal in normal circumstances, only by a double process: occupation with the concrete and then abstraction from it, and this alternately, on and on. If it has not the former it will grow empty and hazy, if it has not the latter, it will grow earthly and heavy. Humanity at large is under the strict obligation . . . because of its spiritual perfection . . . to practice both these activities; but at different periods excesses . . . require counterbalancing, rectifying excesses of the opposite kind. . . . Still . . . the ideal would be the plunging into the concrete and coming back enriched to the abstract, and then returning, purified and simplified, from the abstract to transform and elevate the concrete. (*SL* 72–73)

This conception is not the same as Yeats's self and anti-self, but it is close enough to warrant noting, and suggests a pattern that both men found fulfilled in the Antaeus myth to which they turned, as we shall see, for important summary statements. Such alternation, of course, is the mark of the temporal world. In the case of the individual life it will end in death when there is no more concrete world for the soul to plunge into, and the fluctuations of civilization will end with history and the subsuming of all people into the fuller life of God.

And as to what God is, Von Hügel uses all the traditional Christian designations, but with a different vocabulary and perspective appropriate to his understanding of mysticism. God is the eternal now, the perpetually present Being from whom we could not distance ourselves if we wanted to, except by a final determination not to love. He reaches out to us in love, a Person, not an abstraction.

For God is an immense *concretion,* not an abstraction. He is a *multiciplicity* (for our apprehension) in *unity.* He has "gone *out of Himself*" by love, and shows His nature supremely in His *attention and care for every sparrow;* He has come down to man, He has given Himself no doubt everywhere, yet in *different* degrees and ways. . . . He has made my body and its senses, He has made my love of the historical, social, institutional, even the legal; I am to *incarnate,* in my turn, the *incarnate* God, I am not only to express spirit in and through matter, I am also to awaken, and cause to grow, and to purify (by the painful contraction and friction involved) by my contacts with, by my give and take, this my spirit from and to matter. No floating, no drifting, no dreaming above the body, the family, society, history, institutions, but a penetrating into them, and a retiring out from them, again to return *Antaeus-like,* to earth. (Letter to Miss Fogelkou, quoted in *LBVH 254*)

One could add to his sentence "no escaping and no abandoning." In such a statement the Baron threw down the gauntlet before late Victorian Church and society alike, but of course neither picked it up. Yeats agreed that life could only be renewed through contact with elemental things. In "The Municipal Gallery Re-visited" he wrote:

> John Synge, I and Augusta Gregory, thought
> All that we did, all that we said or sang
> Must come from contact with the soil, from that
> Contact everything Antaeus-like grew strong.
> We three alone in modern times had brought
> Everything down to that sole test again,
> Dream of the noble and the beggarman.
>
> (P321)

It was characteristic of Yeats that he should claim to have cornered insight. He did not know to what extent he had an ally at 13 Vicarage Gate, Kensington. In the tidal flow of consciousness out to the world and back into itself both saw the source of human creativity and enrichment. In the end they only differed widely on the nature of the God that governed both ebb and flow.

At the end of *The Mystical Element,* after demonstrating to his own satisfaction the truth of St. Catherine's remarkable life with God and the incorruptibility of her body after eighteen months, Von Hügel is hesitant to affirm the way of the mystic as a life to be emulated by humanity at large. There is no question but that he believed, without qualification, that the great mystics had entered into the life of God and revealed in their lives and writing depths and heights of human nature otherwise hidden. Mysticism demonstrates for him the reality of God, but insomuch as it is a wholesale catapulting of the soul out of space and time, Von Hügel does not find it appropriate to humankind in general, which needs, as we have seen, institutions, history, and symbols in order to be itself. It remains to be seen how his ideas are echoed or denied by Yeats, particularly in the pivotal poem "Vacillation."

"Vacillation": *Intellectual and Spiritual Background*

In 1927, Yeats was seriously ill, suffering from influenza that led to a lung infection, and he seems to have suffered some sort of nervous collapse as well, possibly brought on by overwork and the knowledge that he could die. While recovering he read Wyndham Lewis's *Time and Western Man*, Browning's "Paracelsus," and St. Teresa's autobiography. Mrs. Yeats took him south to Spain, Cannes, and Rapallo. This was the beginning of a transitional period in Yeats's career and thinking which lasted for several years. Two years later he was again in Rapallo, sick with Malta fever. On 29 December 1929 he made a brief will which was witnessed by Ezra Pound and Basil Bunting. His doctors tried to forbid him intellectual labor, knowing that would excite him and hinder his recovery, but he continued to read, write, and of course think, though pacified by westerns with which his wife kept him in good supply.

He did not die, but his life and work changed direction. John Unterecker wrote about his new departure:

> *The Tower* had been a distortion, half the picture, its emphasis on a man making his soul; flesh, too, demanded its due. Life, the silken sheath, a woman young and old, the immortality of generation, body surviving through body, all these needed to be sung.[26]

He had expended great energy in elaborating a vision of a hieratic world of spirit lit by "Flames that no faggot feeds" (P 248), but his soul did not "clap its hands and sing" (P 193) when his own mortal dress began to unravel. That is perhaps the only paradox he did not notice. "Sailing to Byzantium" had been written in the autumn of 1926, "Byzantium" in 1930. The first Crazy Jane poem, "Crazy Jane and the Bishop," was written in early March 1929. In this sequence we are clearly moving from abstract purity to animal vitality, one might almost say frenzy. He had not, however, given up "monuments of unageing intellect" (P 193). Yeats had to clarify the relationship between flesh and spirit before he would be free to begin the frenzy of poetic activity that ended his life. He made no such decision consciously, but it was implicit in his careful and lengthy changes in *A Vision*, in his rethinking of the claims of Chris-

---

26. John Unterecker, *A Reader's Guide to William Butler Yeats* (New York: Noonday Press, 1959), 201.

tianity, and in his intensified interest in sex that led to the Steinach operation in 1934. He was not satisfied with what he had made of life and knew he did not have much time to explore new paths.

In 1927 Yeats had begun to revise *A Vision*. Originally published in January of 1926, the first edition had many errors. He set about to correct them, and to clarify the text. The source of the book in Mrs. Yeats's automatic writing was not to be made known until *A Packet for Ezra Pound* was published in 1929, and the final version of *A Vision* was not published until 1937, two years before Yeats's death, although he had had the final proofs since the autumn of 1934.

A Vision attempts to make sense of history as well as personal life through the "twenty-eight incarnations" into which Yeats divides experience, his symbol for which is a wheel that constitutes "every completed movement of thought or life" (AV-A 81). He had read the work of most of the great modern thinkers who had attempted to see some overall pattern in history—Giambattista Vico, Henry Adams, Oswald Spengler, Sir William Matthew Flinders Petrie, Wyndam Lewis, Arnold Toynbee (Russian writers such as Nicholas Berdyaev and Lev Shestov are curiously absent from the list)—and claimed to see in them nothing but corroboration of his own ideas. But he was uneasy about his judgments, and I think we can see in one of the final statements in the book, the one regarding the thirteenth cone, an escape from his own system should he be embarrassed by its claims.

> I have already said all that can be said. The particulars are the work of the Thirteenth Cone or cycle which is in every man and called by every man his freedom. Doubtless, for it can do all things and knows all things, it knows what it will do with its own freedom but it has kept the secret. (AV-A 302)

By building human freedom into his system, and making that freedom a mystery, he escapes from the confines of the system while at least in part retaining it.

The freedom in every man, which in Yeats's account almost seems to possess consciousness, sounds rather like a slightly depersonalized version of Horton's Christ within us. It was to Horton, of course, that he would have dedicated *A Vision* if Horton had lived. *A Vision* provided Yeats with an intellectual structure without limiting him to it, and structure without commitment seems to have been exactly what his muse

required. There is nothing in the overall pattern of life and history delin-
eated by *A Vision*, particularly with the thirteenth cone considered, that is
anti-Christian. And it is relevant here to note that divinatory wheels
were subsumed into active Christian faith in the Middle Ages. One such
is in the Rawlinson collection of the Bodleian library (D. 939). It is a
divinatory calendar with an accompanying chart in the shape of a wheel,
and certainly strongly reminiscent of Yeats's Great Wheel. The crucified
Christ is pictured in the center, and Matthew, Mark, Luke, and John are
pictured at the corners, working clockwise from right to left in that
order. The chart was clearly used for astrological predictions, possibly
related to agriculture, as there are certain symbols on it which may
represent farm implements. The chart is important because it demon-
strates that there is nothing in either astrology or a largely cyclical view
of practical life, if not of history, to keep one from a devotion to Christ
and the Apostles. Christ, of course, is not at the center of Yeats's Great
Wheel, but neither does Yeats say he is not there. Again, the poet en-
joyed playing with possibilities.

If we can see in the thirteenth cone an unwillingness to impose
airtight categories upon history, this view is also suggested by a sentence
he wrote in a manuscript book in 1930: "History seems to me a human
drama, keeping the classical unities by the clear division of its epochs,
turning one way or the other because this man hates or that man loves"
(Ex 290). The reduction of all things to hate and love is typical of Yeats's
judgments in his last decade. It is not at all typical of the largely deter-
minist and mechanical conception of life and history afforded by *A Vi-
sion*, although a defender of the system can always argue that who and
what is hated or loved is determined by position on the wheel. He is not
moving toward determination in his last years, however, but away from
it toward the freedom, such as it is, of "the foul rag and bone shop of the
heart" (P 348).

History as human drama is more appealing than the overworked
complexities of *A Vision*, though I do not mean to suggest that Yeats had
cooled toward the source of so many of his figures. I do want to suggest,
however, that during this time, possibly owing to his illness, he was
unsure what mask to put on for the final period of his life. Certainly
ambiguity is suggested in this statement from *A Packet for Ezra Pound*,
dated March and October 1928:

> At Oxford I went constantly to All Souls' Chapel, though never at
> service time, and parts of *A Vision* were thought out there. In Dublin I

went to St. Patrick's and sat there, but it was far off; and once I remember saying to a friend as we came out of Sant' Ambrogio at Milan, "That is my tradition and I will let no priest rob me". I have sometimes wondered if it was but a timidity come from long disuse that keeps me from the service. . . . I am too anaemic for so British a faith; I shall haunt empty churches and be satisfied with Ezra Pound's society and that of his travelling Americans. (AV-A 6–7)

The implication that in some obscure way he is more Christian than the priests, or more religious, and that real Christianity is something priests want to hide, goes back to the Gnostic notion that the Church hid on purpose the true nature of Christ lest it lose power with the people. The idea is echoed in some Protestant writers, but that he should couple it, in the same passage, with an impulse to High Church Anglicanism is a marriage, however temporary, that we cannot be expected to take seriously, no matter how seriously he may have taken it. There is a self-denigration in the passage, obviously to attract attention to himself, which helps him to avoid commitment, and which is reminiscent of an early letter to Katharine Tynan:

My life has been in poems. To make them I have broken my life in a morter, as it were. . . . I have seen others enjoying while I stood alone with myself—commenting, commenting—a mere dead mirror on which things reflect themselves. I have buried my youth and raised over it a cairn—of clouds. (CL1 92–93)

There is a tendency in Yeats toward the Shelleyan self-pity of "Lines Written in Dejection Near Naples," mastered always, certainly verbally mastered, but resurfacing, often in gestures toward religion, and manipulated to justify his refusal to commit himself. But he had more direct confrontations with the possibility of orthodoxy.

A letter Yeats received from William Force Stead early in 1931, which preceded the beginning of his work on "Vacillation" by about a year, suggested Catholicism as a solution to the problem of traditionless modern man attempting to preserve his humanity and cultural values in a reductionist era. Stead had baptized T. S. Eliot in 1927, and had been a frequent caller at the Yeatses' in Oxford.

There seems only one hope, and that is to join the Church of Rome—With its two thousand years of continuous history, it is the

one great institution that has come down unbroken from the days of
Greece and Rome. That is enough to make it sacred and mysterious
in my eyes. But is is even older than that, because all the religions of
the world poured into Imperial Rome, they were melted down and
welded together and live forever in the august institution which still
rises before us, and like a colossus doth bestride the world.
(LTWBY 514)

The idea of historical continuity through Christianity would only have
been reinforced by Yeats's reading of Von Hügel, who as we have seen
thought that history and the historical sense were necessary for humanity
to fulfill itself. The letter, of course, suggests an understanding of history
as linear development, and not the cyclical re-enactment that is required
by Yeats's system in *A Vision*. I shall have more to say about this conflict
of philosophies of history when I discuss his rejection of Von Hügel.
Stead ends his letter by saying, "Let's you and Mrs. Yeats and I all go to
Rome and be received at Easter," then adds as an afterthought, "I am not
jesting I would not jest about the Holy" (LTWBY 515).

Three years later Stead gave up his fellowship at Worcester College
to become a Catholic. He announced his decision to Yeats in a letter of 29
September 1934, and in the same note said he had great admiration for
Von Hügel, whom Yeats referred to in *Wheels and Butterflies,* published
in the same year, as "the sincere and noble Von Hügel" (VPl 934).

To refer to the Baron as "sincere" and "noble" in 1934 was some-
thing of an afterthought, as by that time Yeats had already ruled out
Christianity for himself, but in December of 1931 he had written to
Olivia Shakespear, "I have begun a longish poem called 'Wisdom' [i.e.,
"Vacillation"] in the attempt to shake off 'Crazy Jane' and I begin to
think I shall take to religion unless you save me from it" (L 788). She
wrote back to the effect that if he got religion he would be a bore. She did
not have anything to worry about. Yeats wrote the poem between De-
cember of 1931 and March of 1932. We know that Yeats was reading *The
Mystical Element* while he wrote "Vacillation." In June he was correcting
proofs for the Edition de Luxe volume of his poems, and wrote to Olivia
Shakespear about the book.

As it is all speech rather than writing, I keep saying what man is this
who in the course of two or three weeks—the improvisation sug-
gests the tune—says the same thing in so many different ways. My

first denunciation of old age I made in *The Wanderings of Usheen* (end of part I) before I was twenty and the same denunciation comes in the last pages of the book. The swordsman throughout repudiates the saint, but not without vacillation. Is that perhaps the sole theme—Usheen and Patrick—'so get you gone Von Hügel though with blessings on your head'? (L 798)

Lady Gregory died on May 22. Yeats was in good health, and in spite of the loss of Coole, optimistic. He would live to rant against bodily decrepitude and anything else that sapped full human vigor.

Yeats's rejection of Von Hügel and Christianity must be handled with care, as his opinions well after the composition of "Vacillation" suggested Catholicism to at least one friend. In the last four years of his life Yeats saw a good deal of Dorothy Wellesley at her home, Penns in the Rocks, and they carried on an active correspondence. Knowing perfectly well that virtually anything he said about what he thought would be important, she attempted to draw him out. She asked him what happens to the soul after death, and reports him to have said that at first the dead person does not realize he is dead, but rather exists in a half-conscious state which is followed by a period of purgatory, the length of which is determined by the sins of the person while on earth.

And then again I asked: 'And after that?' I do not remember his actual words, but he spoke of the return of the soul to God. I said: 'Well, it seems to me that you are hurrying us back to the great arms of the Roman Catholic Church.' He was of course an Irish Protestant. I was bold to ask him, but his only retort was his splendid laugh. (LDW 195)

The passage obviously suggests a view very close to Catholicism, at least in regard to the life of the dead. His ideas seemed "Catholic" to Dorothy Wellesley, yet he skirted Catholicism, skirted Christianity for that matter. Yeats rather enjoyed keeping himself an enigma. In that way he could toy with the world without committing himself to anything.

In April of 1934 Yeats had the Steinach operation, important for this study because it reveals an attitude of mind that was in its formative period while he wrote "Vacillation." The operation was a simple vasectomy. As Ellmann notes, Steinach's theory was "that the production of the male hormone would thereby be increased and vitalize the whole body's functioning."[27] Yeats had told his London doctor "that for about three years . . . he had lost all inspiration and been unable to write anything new," and as Ellmann has noted:

> Versemaking and lovemaking had always made connections in his mind. Not to be able to do the one meant not to be able to do the other. (WBYSP 7)

We have already seen that in the late twenties and early thirties Yeats was moving from the delineation of hieratic being in the Byzantium poems to the sensual monologues of Crazy Jane, from which, as he wrote to Olivia Shakespear in December of 1931, the composition of "Wisdom" ("Vacillation") was supposed to save him. Although his comment to her is tongue-in-cheek, it revealed, as such comments often do, a serious problem. The problem was, as we have seen, to reconcile the seemingly opposing claims, the claims seen as opposing by Yeats, of body and spirit. In part "Vacillation" was written to solve that problem. If "Versemaking and lovemaking had always made connections in his mind," it is small wonder he felt obliged to reject Von Hügel, for from Yeats's earliest contact with Catholicism as a young man he associated it with rejection of the flesh. Johnson, Martyn, and Horton, all of whom he respected, and all of whom influenced him, practiced a radically dualistic Christianity, and we know that Horton's Joseph-and-Mary relationship with Audrey Locke, "that sweet extremity of pride / That's called platonic love" (P 228), impressed him thoroughly. It would obviously be a mistake to suggest that Yeats's understanding had not matured since his early youth, but I see no sign that his understanding of Christianity had. He does not seem to have picked up Von Hügel's unequivocal rejection of Jansenism in The Mystical Element.

There were, of course, more philosophical reasons for his dismissal of Von Hügel. On 9 October 1938 Yeats told Ethel Mannin that the 1937 edition of A Vision had expressed his "public philosophy," but that his "private philosophy" was incomplete (L 916). That statement could mean almost anything, but clearly Yeats did not feel he had come to the end of his spiritual and philosophic quest in the last years of his life. And

---

27. Richard Ellmann, W. B. Yeats's Second Puberty (Washington: Library of Congress, 1985), 7. Hereafter cited in the text as WBYSP. For the fullest account of the operation, see Virginia Pruitt and Raymond Pruitt, "Yeats and the Steinach Operation," Yeats 1 (1983): 104–24.

we have seen that in *A Vision* he left himself an escape from commitment in his retention of radical human freedom. As Graham Hough has written:

The Thirteenth Cone is Yeats's joker. What it is and where it fits into the system is impossible to say; but it is there as a charm or talisman to enhance the obscurer assertions of man's freedom.[28]

Within the limits imposed by the considerable ambiguity of the thirteenth cone—a cultivated ambiguity, by the way—and taking that ambiguity as a warning not to expect consistency in any logical sense, I think it is important to see what ideas kept him from Von Hügel, both in order to understand "Vacillation" as well as the driving mood that produced his last poems.

When Yeats had gone to church as a boy, he had heard the following creed recited:

I believe in one God the Father Almighty, Maker of heaven and earth, And of all things visible and invisible:
And in one Lord Jesus Christ, the only-begotten son, Son of God, Begotten of his Father before all worlds, God of God, Light of Light, Very God of very God, Begotten, not made. Being of one substance with the Father; By whom all things were made, Who for us men, and for our salvation came down from heaven, and was incarnate by the Holy Ghost of the Virgin Mary, And was made man, And was crucified also for us under Pontius Pilate. He suffered and was buried, and the third day he rose again according to the Scriptures, And ascended into heaven, And sitteth on the right hand of the Father, And he shall come again with glory to judge both the quick and the dead: Whose kingdom shall have no end.
And I believe in the Holy Ghost, The Lord and Giver of life, Who proceedeth from the Father and the Son together, is worshipped and glorified, Who spake by the Prophets. And I believe in one Catholick and Apostolick Church. I acknowledge one Baptism for the remission of sins, And the life of the world to come.
Amen

---

28. Graham Hough, *The Mystery Religion of W. B. Yeats* (Sussex: Harvester Press, 1984), 117. Hereafter cited in the text as *MR*.

I would like to make a few very basic observations about this creed. Between 1662 and 1928 the creed was unchanged. The 1928 revision affected only minor matters of wording. Today the Anglican Church uses a small c in catholic to distinguish itself from the Roman Catholic Church. If you leave out the statement about the Virgin and the word Catholic, whether capitalized or not, the creed would be accepted by the great bulk of the Protestant denominations. Virginia Moore, in an attempt to save Yeats from the charge of heresy, emphasized the difference between Christians so Yeats's peculiarities would seem less glaring. I emphasize the very broad area of agreement among Christians to make Yeats's peculiarities more apparent. The creed places Christians in a historical process. Christ has died, Christ is risen, Christ will come again. These changes of tense created the western sense of history. God is the God of the Old Testament, a Creator and Begetter. He is also a God of love who has reached out to all people through Christ. History began with Him, and history will end with Him. He is triune not in definition, but in experience. The Prophets knew Him as the Creator. In Christ we see Him as the Son who sent the Holy Spirit to be the comforter and guide of all Christians. The original Apostles as well as the apostles of all ages could not, in their own understanding, have led the lives they did in the absence of the Spirit.

We have already seen that in Von Hügel's summation of Christianity, life in time, through history, with institutions and symbols, is necessary because we are bodied and do perceive ourselves as existing in time. Von Hügel, several generations ahead of his time in theological thinking, would now be accepted as a sober, middle-of-the-road Christian. I would like to point out that Blake, upon whom Yeats cut his intellectual eyeteeth, had an abhorrence of institutional Christianity. In his view ultimately all Christian institutions would die out, leaving only the religion of the heart. Von Hügel would reply that until we as people are no more than heart that will not happen. The mystic and visionary is inevitably drawn to the purity of what he has experienced, what he has in some sense "seen," and anything less will seem small beer indeed. In the Catholic Christian tradition, however, the insights of the mystic are submitted to the historical Church for confirmation. St. Teresa of Avila told her nuns never to alter their pattern of life because of a vision. Moore wrote that Yeats "connected esoteric Christianity with the pre-Patrick Celtic Church, and the latter with the high spirituality of India and Christian Egypt" (TU 401). The essence of this high spirituality is otherworldly, pure, unconnected with things of the earth. But in the 1937 *A Vision* Yeats quotes "a fourth century philosopher," who referred to the Church as "that fabulous formless darkness," blotting out "every beautiful thing" (AV-B 278).[29] And this Church "will make man also featureless as clay or dust. Night will fall upon man's wisdom now that man had been taught that he is nothing" (AV-B 274). In short, Yeats first maintains that the Church is not sufficiently spiritual, following the lead of Blake, then that it is too spiritual, teaching man he is nothing. How could the Church be teaching man that he is nothing if it is also teaching man that God so loved the world he gave his only Son for its redemption, and not only gave, but incarnated in human flesh?

Another major twentieth century poet. Boris Pasternak, saw Christianity as really inaugurating human personality. In *Doctor Zhivago* Pasternak puts his theory of Christian history into the mouth of Nikolai Nikolaievich:

Rome was a flea market of borrowed gods and conquered peoples, a bargain basement on two floors, earth and heaven, a mass of filth convoluted in a triple knot as in an intestinal obstruction. Dacians, Herulians, Scythians, Sarmatians, Hyperboreans, heavy wheels without spokes, eyes sunk in fat, sodomy, double chins, illiterate emperors, fish fed on the flesh of learned slaves. There were more people in the world than there have ever been since, all crammed into the passages of the Coliseum, and all wretched. . . . And then into this tasteless heap of gold and marble, He came, light and clothed in an aura, emphatically human, deliberately Galilean, and at that moment gods and nations ceased to be and man came into being—man the carpenter, man the ploughman, man the shepherd with his flock of sheep at sunset, man who does not sound in the least proud, man thankfully celebrated in all the cradle songs of mothers and in all the picture galleries the world over.[30]

At this point Yeats would be crying out for the purity of Byzantium, having largely given himself over to the logic of opposites. But for Pasternak both purity and humanity are centered in Christ, purity be-

<hr />

29. See P 651–52 for the identification of the philosopher as Antoninus, son of Eusthatius.

30. Boris Pasternak, *Doctor Zhivago,* trans. Max Hayward and Manya Harari (New York: Pantheon, 1958), 43–44.

cause He raised men out of convoluted beastliness and gave them a vision of God; humanity because never again could men lightly dismiss the needs of others, since all are created in the image of God and are equally important in His sight. The notion of an incarnate God who dies once to redeem creation rather than a perpetually returning god, a god who returns only to be sacrificed and return again, ripped humankind out of the ancient world, and in Pasternak's analysis created history in the modern sense. Lacking such a God metaphysics is perpetually swinging between the abstract and the particular with nothing to keep it in balance, and not metaphysics only but at times poetry as well.

Yeats, of course, was fascinated with the idea of cyclical rather than linear time. In *A Packet for Ezra Pound* (1929) he wrote:

> What if Christ and Oedipus or, to shift the names, Saint Catherine of Genoa and Michael Angelo, are the two scales of a balance, the two butt-ends of a seesaw? What if every two thousand and odd years something happens in the world to make one sacred, the other secular; one wise, the other foolish; one fair, the other foul; one divine, the other devilish? What if there is an arithmetic or geometry that can exactly measure the slope of a balance, the dip of a scale, and so date the coming of that something? (AV-B 28–29)

Expecting Pound's irritation, he added, "You will hate these generalities, Ezra" (AV-B 29). Cyclical time is not the only problem here. From a Christian point of view there is no strict division between the sacred and secular. All creation is certainly sacred because it comes from God. Nature proclaims in its own way the glory of God. Man can render sacred nature more sacred by specific acts and creations. He can build a shrine for sacrifice, a temple for prayer. He can also turn against God and by acts of barbarity in a sense desacralize nature, and certainly himself. Though the earth did not offend, we are not likely ever to think of Treblinka as a holy place. By making that which is sacred and that which is secular depend upon forces exterior to man himself, Yeats reduces humanity to spiritual slavery in a mechanistic universe.

Virginia Moore, attempting to show that Yeats was not heretical, points out that in the 1937 *A Vision* Yeats quotes with approval Nemesius, Bishop Emessa: "Certain Christians would have us consider the Resurrection linked to the restoration of the world, but they deceive themselves strangely, for it is proved by the words of Christ that the Resurrection could not happen more than once, that it came not from a periodical revolution but from the Will of God" (AV-A 249–50). This is a crucial point. A. P. Sinnett, whose *Esoteric Buddhism* had started Yeats on his serious pursuit of spiritual truth, had made of Christ only one of many great teachers of hidden knowledge. Unless Moore can show Yeats clearly departing from such a belief she cannot show him to be Christian. To do so she focuses on certain changes that Yeats made in the revised version of *A Vision:*

> For now Yeats was very sure that Christ was not just one among many world-reformers. What changes the whole complexion of the . . . statement is his conviction that "the Birth of Christ took place at about the symbolic centre of the first Solar Month of the Great Year," hence because of the Sun's relation to the Moon, on "the First Day of the Lunar Great Year." This means that Christ has a special relation to the entire Wheel . . . in a unique way He represents the whole. (*TU* 391)

What is remarkable about Yeats's approach to the problem is that he thinks Christ unique not because he says with Thomas, "My Lord and my God" (John XX.28), or with Pascal, "This is life eternal. . . . And Jesus Christ Whom Thou Hast Sent,"[31] but because he, Yeats, is convinced that Christ was born at a certain conjunction of the stars, as if all conjunctions were not under the determination of God, as if there was something mechanical about the salvation of the human race. Of course to repeat the words of Thomas or Pascal would be to make an act of faith, and that Yeats is not about to do, which is precisely my point. One does not require faith of him, but rather would like to formulate accurately what he accepted as real.

But the spiritual slavery in a mechanistic universe does not suggest the Yeats of the great poems, and anyone to whom the Yeats material is familiar knows there is more to be considered, and there is. In the 1937 *A Vision*, for example, he writes of love:

> Fragment delights in fragment and seeks possession, not service; whereas the Good Samaritan discovers himself in the likeness of

---

31. Quoted in Ernest Mortimer, *Blaise Pascal: The Life and Work of A Realist* (New York: Harper, 1959), 124.

another . . . and in that other serves himself. The opposites are gone; he does not need his Lazarus; they do *not* each die the other's life, live the other's death. (AV-B 275; emphasis added)

If the opposites are unified through love, that is not so much escape from the wheel of appearance as triumph over it. Such love is only possible through freedom, so Yeats's thirteenth cone saves him from determinism. The evidence, however, is contradictory and incomplete. In one passage he takes delight in the cycles, in another he takes delight in escape from them. Certainly the passage about the Good Samaritan I have just quoted suggests that the *complete person* may escape from the wheel through love. There is much discussion in Yeats criticism of "unity of being" both on the personal and cultural level, since both he and Lady Gregory made much of that notion. Here, however, the idea is more fullness of being, maturity. The fragment is driven to possess because it is a fragment. In Christian terms the way to wholeness is self-abandonment. Yeats keeps the self, and sees in disinterested love a superior self concern, which it is. The difference in emphasis is small, but it is there, and it is a difference one must learn to expect from Yeats.

If some statements in *A Vision* (1937) suggest a growing rapport with Christianity, that is not what the text suggested to F. P. Sturm:

Personally I think your philosophy smells of the fagot.

Some dead & damned Chaldean *mathematekoi* have got hold of your wife and are trying to revive a dead system.

All these gyres & cones & wheels are part of a machine that was thrown on the scrap-heap when Ptolemy died. It won't go.

. . . the Primum Mobile no longer moves, the seven planetary spheres of crystal are dull as a steamy cookshop window—so they are trying to speak through your wife & are using much that she has read in the past.

. . . .My new book . . . is to be called *Seven Fagots for the Burning of the Great Heretic Yeats*—or *The Wheel Dismantled*— . . . to be purchased at the Sign of the Screaming Seraph in Byzantium.[32]

Whether or not he agreed with Yeats, Sturm was parodying a style that Yeats worked very hard to create both in his life and in his poetry, one he

___

32. *Frank Pearce Sturm: His Life, Letters, and Collected Work*, ed. Richard Taylor (Urbana: University of Illinois Press, 1969), 99–100.

grew beyond in *Last Poems*, but which certainly pervaded his work throughout most of his life. Stefan Zweig noted it in an early reading. Zweig was present at a reading by Yeats in 1904. He had translated part of *The Shadowy Waters* into German, and through Arthur Symons secured an invitation to the reading. The great man entered wearing a robe and read his work by candlelight:

> . . . we sat fairly crowded in a hot very large room and some even had to sit on folding chairs and on the floor. Finally Yeats began, after two huge altar candles had been lighted next to the black or black-covered reading desk. All the other lights in the room had been extinguished so that the energetic head with its black locks appeared plastically in the candlelight. Yeats read slowly with a melodious sombre voice, without becoming declamatory, and every verse received its full value. It was lovely. It was truly cere-monious. The only thing that disturbed me was the preciousness of the presentation, the black monkish garb which made Yeats look quite priestly, the smouldering of the thick wax candles which, I believe, were slightly scented.[33]

Yeats's priest-like appearance projected something of the inner reality he was attempting to cultivate. The cult atmosphere of the reading suggests that flowering of late classical spirituality we refer to as the mystery religions—and of course we know Yeats had read Plotinus—but in his later years he cast off this influence as decisively as that of Von Hügel to throw himself into the life and thought that produced *Last Poems*. "Vac-illation" stands at the dividing of the ways. Before examining that poem in detail I would like to look at two of his plays which deal with the central Christian mysteries, *Calvary* and *The Resurrection*.

Calvary (1920) is a short play in which cyclical time plays the tune the actors dance to. The play opens with three musicians with faces made up to resemble masks, unfolding a cloth which covers the stage so the actors can take their places unseen. The cloth is then folded up again. As the cloth is folded and unfolded they chant lines of poetry about a white heron staring in a stream and ignoring the fish which jump about him. Each stanza has for refrain "God has not died for the white heron" (VPl 780–81). Narcissus-like, the heron is absorbed in its own image. Lazarus enters and complains that he wanted to die, not to be raised from the

---

33. Stefan Zweig, *The World of Yesterday* (London: Cassell, 1944), 157–58.

dead. Christ, leaning upon his cross, defends himself by saying that he did his father's will, but Lazarus goes off longing for oblivion that now cannot be found anywhere because through Christ's death all are to be raised from the dead. Judas enters and says he betrayed Christ because all men have been put into His hands and "that was the very thought that drove me wild" (VPl 784). So Christ is betrayed not through human blindness and greed, but through insight and knowledge. Judas says that Christ cannot save him. Three Roman soldiers throw dice and one says, "They say you're good and that you made the world, / But it's no matter." Again the three musicians fold the cloth and chant poetry. This time the refrain is "God has not appeared to the birds" (VPl 786–88).

The play projects an atmosphere of frozen hopelessness that cannot even mount to despair, because "it's no matter." Where nothing matters, there is not enough energy for despair. The play was published in *Four Plays for Dancers* (1921), and Yeats added this commentary:

> I have used my bird-symbolism in these songs to increase the objective loneliness of Christ by contrasting it with a loneliness, opposite in kind, that unlike His can be, whether joyous or sorrowful, sufficient to itself. I have surrounded Him with the images of those He cannot save, not only with the birds, who have served neither God nor Caesar, and await for none or for a different saviour, but with Lazarus and Judas and the Roman soldiers for whom He has died in vain. (VPl 790)

The 1937 *A Vision* echoes the passage: "because His sacrifice was voluntary . . . He was love itself, and yet that part of Him which made Christendom was not love but pity, and not pity for intellectual despair" (AV-B 275). Neither of the prose commentaries, of course, can make sense of the play for a Christian reader, because for such a reader Christ's sacrifice was not limited, and extends even to the birds whose life is not lost in self-absorption, but lost in God. There is no one Christ has not saved, including Lazarus, Judas, and the Roman soldiers. Therefore, when Yeats says Christ cannot save them, he is putting such a private understanding upon a totally public event that I do not understand him. If you were to judge from such a text alone, you would have to conclude that his understanding of Christianity was seriously flawed. Jeffares remarks about the final dance in the play, "visually the tableau of Christ crucified on the cross supported by Judas and soldiers dancing round it suggests the inescapability of the cycles."[34] Again, the notion that Christ, the Word, is not above any cycle, is absurd to a Christian, though the final scene is effective dramatically.

The Resurrection (1931) is an even more revealing document, and more important for "Vacillation." Warwick Gould tells us that "Vacillation" was revised "alongside the redrafting of his Frazerian play The Resurrection" (YGVN 824). Yeats began the play in 1925 or 1926. It was printed originally in 1927 and not reprinted again until Stories of Michael Robartes and His Friends (1932), after having been reworked in the vellum book.

At the very beginning it is obvious that although better than a decade later than Calvary in final execution, we have not escaped from the cyclical world-view.

> Another Troy must rise and set,
> Another lineage feed the crow,
> Another Argo's painted prow
> Drive to a flashier bauble yet.
>
> (VPl 902–3)

From the beginning Dionysus is paired with Christ, virgins attendant upon both, and the atmosphere is that of barely controlled mania. In the words of the Greek, "The followers of Dionysus have been out among the fields tearing a goat to pieces and drinking its blood" (VPl 905). Not much happens in the play, which opens just after the crucifixion. The Greek observes worshipers of Dionysus cavorting in the street, but the Hebrew will not look upon "such madmen" (VPl 915). Eventually a Syrian comes in with first-hand news of the resurrection, and the "figure of Christ wearing a recognisable but stylistic mask" passes through the room toward an inner chamber where the apostles are (VPl 929).

The Hebrew, the Greek, and the Syrian sum up just about every attitude toward Christ other than the Christian. For the Jew, "He was nothing more than a man, the best man who ever lived." Then he echoes A Vision: "Nobody before him had so pitied human misery" (VPl 909). For the Greek, Jesus never had human materiality: "I am certain that Jesus never had human body; that he is a phantom and can pass through

---

34. A. Norman Jeffares, A New Commentary on the Poems of W. B. Yeats (Stanford: Stanford University Press, 1984), 171. Hereafter cited in the text as NCP.

that wall" (VPl 923). The Syrian is alive to the mystery of the returning and perpetually sacrificed god. He speaks for Yeats:

> What if there is always something that lies outside knowledge, outside order? What if at the moment when knowledge and order seem complete that something appears. . . . What if the irrational return? What if the circle begin again? (VPl 925)

The Syrian echoes Yeats's own words in the 1929 *A Packet for Ezra Pound* which I have quoted earlier: "What if Christ and Oedipus . . . are the two scales of a balance. . . . What if every two thousand and odd years something happens . . . to make one sacred, the other secular. . . . What if there is an arithmetic or geometry that can exactly measure the slope of a balance . . . and so date the coming of that something?" (AV-B 28–29) The Syrian is wildly excited and bursts into laughter although nothing is funny. For him, clearly, the irrational has returned. There is no sense whatsoever in the play of the joy of Easter, the triumph of life over death, holiness over sin. There could not be because these concepts are simply not alive in the world of the play. The sacrifice of the goat by the followers of Dionysus is meant to parallel Christ's sacrifice. Yeats is looking at the crucifixion as though it were a rite he discovered in *The Golden Bough*.

The Greek is given the final line in the play: "God and man die each other's life, live each other's death" (VPl 931). As we have seen, in the passage on the Good Samaritan in the 1937 *A Vision* Yeats specifically denies this statement. Through love the Samaritan sees himself in another: "The opposites are gone; he does not need his Lazarus; they do *not* each die the other's life, live the other's death" (AV-B 275; emphasis added). It would be satisfying to prove that the 1937 statement represented a change from the 1925 text of *A Vision,* but it was not one of the revised passages and is the same in both editions. It would also be satisfying to see the Samaritan passage echoed either in other prose passages or in poems, for there would then be some evidence for a movement on Yeats's part toward Christian love as a reconciler of the self and anti-self, and the Christian eschatology as a reconciler of historical cycles, but I have found no such echoes and no such movement. I think we must view the Samaritan's love, from Yeats's point of view, as a development of the human psyche appropriate to the Christian period in history, but lacking the absolute value a Christian would find in it.

It was not my intention in this essay to describe Yeats's "beliefs" exhaustively, but rather to provide an adequate background for understanding his final dismissal of Von Hügel and Christianity. It is difficult, however, to discuss his rejection of orthodox Christianity without delineating something of his own ideas, which I have done. A brief summary statement is now necessary.

The age into which Yeats was born, as we have seen, was irreligious. The great effort of the poet's early years was to establish to his own satisfaction the reality of spiritual life, and then to explore its different manifestations. Although his ideas were continually changing, he had a basic commitment in both religion and philosophy that remained constant. In an essay of 1901 titled "Magic" Yeats sets down three principles that he never contradicted:

(1) That the borders of our mind are ever shifting, and that many minds can flow into one another, as it were, and create or reveal a single mind, a single energy.
(2) That the borders of our memories are as shifting, and that our memories are a part of one great memory, the memory of Nature herself.
(3) That this great mind and great memory can be evoked by symbols. (E&I 28)

God exists, but He is distant.

As Graham Hough has written:

. . . although the religious tradition to which Yeats belongs posits as the ultimate goal a condition of union with the divine in which the accidents of human individuality are simply burnt away, this goal is for him so infinitely remote that he does not often turn to it, even in contemplation. It is the lower slopes of the holy mountain that allure his footsteps—just as in popular Neoplatonism it is the daimons, the subordinate powers, that attract most attention, rather than the imageless, passionless, unconditioned One. (MR 74)

There was a good reason for Yeats's not turning even in contemplation to union with the divine. He thought it would cripple his art. Yeats wrote:

If it be true that God is a circle whose centre is everywhere, the saint goes to the centre, the poet and artist to the ring where everything comes round again. The poet must not seek for what is still and fixed, for that has no life for him; and if he did his style would become cold and monotonous. (E&I 287)

It was unfortunate that many Christians, accepting too readily conclusions about the nature of God arrived at under the influence of ancient philosophy, agreed that God was still and fixed, and not a ceaseless flame of love, but they did believe God to be still and Yeats did as well. So he focused his attention on contact between people that proved the validity of the soul's powers, or contact between soul and departed soul, for that proved immortality. History and personal life he believed to be governed by a pattern of ceaseless alternation of opposites described in *A Vision*. When the soul achieved fullness of being it would escape the wheel of appearance through the thirteenth cone, and begin another life.

In formal philosophy Yeats's position is far closer to that of Wordsworth and Coleridge than he would have us think. L. A. G. Strong has written of his position:

The tangible world is a dream, a representation, in terms prescribed by the level and quality of human perceptions, of an eternal reality. Everything in nature is a symbol, in the sense that it is an interpretation put by our senses upon a reality we cannot otherwise know. Belief therefore ceases to be a literary acceptance of the evidence of the senses, or a criticism of experience for apparent failure to conform to that evidence. It becomes an intuition of harmony within a system.[35]

Belief in this passage does not mean religious belief, but belief in reality. Wordsworth believed the world to be half perceived and half created. The day to day reality we live in is a collaboration of the "something" whose dwelling is "the light of setting suns" ("Tintern Abbey," l.97) and our own perceptions. We never know absolute reality, but that is not a severely felt loss for either poet. Yeats occasionally refers to the world as an illusion, but he never lived as though it were, and in terms of absolutes the world is no more illusory for Yeats than for Wordsworth. Wordsworth, after the depredations of Enlightenment philosophy, made

---

35. L. A. G. Strong, "William Butler Yeats," in *Scattering Branches: Tributes to the Memory of W. B. Yeats,* ed. Stephen Gwynn (London: Macmillan, 1940), 209.

man one of the double cornerstones of the world. Yeats found a similar place of honor for "Man's own resinous heart" (P 214). It was the one thing he could be sure of. Hough tells us, "Yeats opens himself freely to his vision, but there is always a substratum of scepticism and reserve" (MR 90).

"Vacillation": A Reading of the Poem

For M. L. Rosenthal and Sally Gall " 'Vacillation' as a whole seems mainly a preliminary structuring on its way to *Last Poems*."[36] That I think is a superficial judgment, though they are certainly right in finding the poem leans towards his last work. J. R. Mulryne is more helpful when he writes "among the poems of *The Winding Stair* 'Vacillation' asks the question ["What is joy?"] which precipitates the concern and commitment of *Last Poems*."[37] That question is asked in so many words in the first section of "Vacillation," and it is to the poem we must now turn.

It is typical of Yeats that a stanza which will end with the question "What is joy?" should begin with an examination of the nature of human life in time. The "extremities" between which "Man runs his course," derive in part, as Jeffares has noted, from Blake and Boehme (*NCP* 300). It should be pointed out, however, that the idea of life as a revolving sequence of opposites is inherent in human experience and does not depend on visionaries, mystics, and poets. All early cultures took notice of the more obvious dichotomies of experience: male–female, day–night, sky–earth, sea–land, up–down, inner–outer, spirit–matter. That is why primitive, and I do not use the word in a pejorative sense, religion is virtually always dualistic. That is also why it was difficult for early man to find real worth in temporal life. True being was elsewhere, removed by an all but impassable gulf from the world of appearance and time. Radical dualism is so universally the case with ancient man that it is the Judeo-Christian tradition with its insistence on the goodness of creation that seems strange by comparison.

Section one tells us that life is like running a gauntlet between extremes. "A brand, or flaming breath / Comes to destroy" all opposites.

---

36. M. L. Rosenthal and Sally Gall, *The Modern Poetic Sequence: The Genius of Modern Poetry* (New York: Oxford University Press, 1983), 132–33.

37. J. R. Mulryne, "Last Poems," in *An Honored Guest: New Essays on W. B. Yeats,* ed. Denis Donoghue and J. R. Mulryne (London: Edward Arnold, 1965), 133.

For the body this is death, for the heart remorse. The reduction of duality to singleness is obviously accomplished by death, which removes one pole of the tension. For B. L. Reid "what is especially significant in this poem is that he refuses a crudely absolute separation and accepts a marked cross-fertilization of values; the Swordsman triumphs [over the saint], but not without concessions."[38] Death is remorse to the heart because it means the end of passion, or "original sin" in the seventh stanza. Yeats frequently remarked, as after AE's death, that passionate commitment to life kept ghosts walking, and he was more interested in ghosts than in God, I think, because he felt forced to conceive of God as static rather than dynamic. We have seen he did not think poets should be overly interested in absorption into the infinite, lest they lose the images and themes that are their stock in trade. In nothing does Yeats so reveal his a-Christian attitude as in this. God *is,* but *is remote.* There is no notion whatsoever of Christ as revealing the nature of God. It is revealing to contrast Rembrandt's last work with that of Yeats. Rembrandt did not have any qualms about losing his images in an approach to the infinite, because he believed Christ to be the supreme revelation of the infinite. He could therefore explore the life of Christ in his remarkable drawings and know he was dealing with God. Rembrandt's meditation on God was through Christ, and it gave him images, did not take them away. I am not making a value judgment here, but pointing out a difference that will help us to understand the problems Yeats had to solve in "Vacillation."

Yeats ends the first stanza with a question. If body and heart are right about the end of the antinomies, "What is joy?" His question is philosophic, not existential. He wants to know what joy is, not how to possess it and to live under its influence. The experience he recounts in section four of the poem I think explains in part this question. That he continued to have such experiences tells us he was alive and open to joy, possessing it, if you will, at an age when Wordsworth could only look back on it. It is a wonder, if he was so open to the source of his poetic power, that he bothered to ask the question at all. But there is in Yeats a fractiousness of intellect, a delight in questioning and opposition for opposition's sake that I think helped to keep him poetically alive to the last. Wordsworth, very much concerned with joy, was not the least

---

38. B. L. Reid, *William Butler Yeats: The Lyric of Tragedy* (Norman: University of Oklahoma Press, 1961), 193.

interested in *what it was*. He was happy in its possession, destitute without it, but not concerned with its nature. Joy for C. S. Lewis had an element of mystery in it. It is "an unsatisfied desire which is itself more desireable than any other satisfaction."[39] And such a desire is not associated with any particular image:

> . . . all images and sensations, if idolatrously mistaken for Joy itself, soon honestly confessed themselves inadequate. All said, in the last resort, "It is not I. I am only a reminder. Look! Look! What do I remind you of?" (SBJ 207)

Joy for Yeats is more complicated. He begins its delineation in stanza two. The burning sacred tree, the image of which begins section two of the poem, is a representation of the perpetual motion of being, the essential energies of the world flowing back and forth in a sequence of embodiments one would be tempted to call endless were it not for the thirteenth cone. Half the tree is "in flames," says Yeats, half is "green and in full leaf" (E&I 176).

> And he that Attis' image hangs between
> That staring fury and the blind lush leaf
> May know not what he knows, but knows not grief.

Ellmann tells us "that Yeats identified the poet with the priest, himself castrated in honour of his god, because . . . he conceived of the artist as forced to sacrifice his life for the sake of his art" (IY 172). When the image of the god is hung in the exact center of the world between energy in dissolution and energy resolved in form, the devotee sees into the life of things. Yeats knew Frazer's *Attis, Adonis and Osiris* as well as *The Golden Bough*. In 1937 he wrote in his preface to *The Ten Principal Upanishads* that "*The Golden Bough* has made Christianity look modern and fragmentary. . . ."[40] Frazer's recapitulation of ancient religion, emphasizing ritual yearly sacrifice to ensure the fertility of the earth and the beginning again of the perpetual Great Year, entirely corroborated Yeats's inclination to see history in terms of endlessly repeating cycles.

---

39. C. S. Lewis, *Surprised By Joy: The Shape of My Early Life* (London: Geoffrey Bles, 1955), 23. Hereafter cited in the text as *SBJ*.

40. *The Ten Principal Upanishads*, trans. Shree Purohit Swami and W. B. Yeats (London: Faber, 1937), 10.

These ideas, as we have seen, lay behind his play *The Resurrection,* and it is no surprise to see them restated here. To be in the middle of the forces, between the burning fury and the leaf, is symbolic of a state in which the forces are experienced within the self, and in such a state one rises above them. It is akin to the love of the Good Samaritan in its effect, though not in recognition of God in the other. At the eye of the whirlwind of spirit and matter, however, consciousness is frozen. He may not know what he knows. On the question of consciousness, C. S. Lewis seems to depart from Yeats:

> We do not love, fear, or think without knowing it. Instead of the twofold division into Conscious and Unconscious, we need a threefold division: The Unconscious, the Enjoyed, and the Contemplated. (*SBJ* 207)

I say seems, because there is not so great a rift between them as the comment might suggest. Yeats certainly left room for the contemplation of joy, and for the remembering in joy of his friends, and moments they had shared, let alone ecstatic experiences unshared. And that arch memorializer of ecstatic moments, Wordsworth, wrote of one such moment, "Thought was not; in enjoyment it expired" (*The Excursion,* 1:213). There is room here, then, for rapprochement, important to point out, I think, because in the end they do differ. They differ because of what they make of their experience. Yeats has an ideology to satisfy, a long-standing commitment to view life in terms of perpetual conflict between opposites. For Wordsworth and Lewis the sense of opposition is likely to come in terms of human finiteness and limitation contrasted with the infinity and love of God.

Yeats's answer to the question "What is joy?" continues in the third section, which appeared as part of section two in the first printed version of the poem. In the third stanza Yeats gathers strength. For him the opening is not brilliant. The second section concludes very powerfully though, with the much quoted "blind lush leaf" and the surface paradox of not knowing what he knows. The third stanza divides itself into two contrasting meditations on life and human nature. The first begins with an unequivocal directive to the reader:

> Get all the gold and silver that you can,
> Satisfy ambition, or animate
> The trivial days and ram them with the sun.

Yeats is never happier than when telling someone what to do or think. It always raises his spirits, as does presenting the reader with what appears to be a home truth drawn from some fund of common wisdom of which he is the keeper. So while ramming our days we are to meditate upon two maxims:

> All women dote upon an idle man
> Although their children need a rich estate;
> No man has ever lived that had enough
> Of children's gratitude or woman's love.

The first of these maxims is certainly debatable, and certainly dated in terms of its attitude toward women who are seen as doters and not doers, but the verbal certainty and imperial tone of the lines compels belief even from those who do not believe, at least for the purpose of the poem. We do cease to disbelieve in tribute to music and diction. The second of these maxims is no more flattering to men than the first to women. It presents men as weak, kept alive by an insatiable need for love. Yeats seems to delight in these pictures of men and women caught in the trap of their own obsessions. He likes their obsessions, I think, because they are dramatic.

The second part of the third stanza is even more forceful and presents a picture of those who have outlived obsession and must now prepare for death. Having lived through the forgetfulness of Lethean foliage, we are now urged from our "fortieth winter" to test all things, "every work of intellect or faith," to see if they are fit for one journeying "Proud, open-eyed and laughing to the tomb." Jeffares implies that the reference to the fortieth year has something to do with Maud Gonne, because in 1905 when Yeats was forty Maud Gonne and MacBride separated, bringing to a head all his former desires and hopes (*NCP* 302).[41] I think this is a case of the scholar knowing too much. It is likely Yeats is referring to the fairly common observation that life does break itself in two at mid-point, and that at forty one is facing in another direction. But this *is* a home truth and one does not have to invoke scholarly sources to see its pertinence. Lincoln said that every man over forty was responsible for his own face, which is another way, and a poetic one, of saying the same thing.

Yeats says "Begin the preparation for your death." It should be

---

41. See P 657 for the view that "fortieth winter" refers to the winter of 1904–05.

pointed out that there is a very old tradition in the West of viewing life as a preparation for death. It is in Plato's account of the death of Socrates, it is in the letters of St. Paul, Augustine's *Confessions,* and Thomas à Kempis's *Imitation of Christ.* The idea in each case is similar. Since life on earth is a transient thing, prepare for the life that will never end by cultivating that which is not subject to space and time. There is, of course, a great difference between pride and laughter as virtues of those facing death, and attitudes more commonly expected of Christians, final repentance and confidence in God's grace and the promises of Christ. As I have noted in the introduction, history is not illusory in Christianity, nor is life, nor suffering, which was given a positive value by Christ. It would be better not to have to drink the cup, but if one has to, there is a way of doing so that turns defeat into triumph. Yeats and Lady Gregory created a myth in which proud aristocrats approach death indifferent to their fate, with the glory of their disdain all about them rather than halos. It is important to note, especially in the light of Yeats's commitment to Homer in section eight of "Vacillation," that pride, arrogance, and strength are pagan virtues, and that Christianity turned upside down the values of the ancient world by substituting for them humility, understanding, and love. But Yeats's code of aristocratic manners owed a very great deal to Christianity, especially as it was transposed into books of conduct such as Castiglione's *The Courtier,* or he never would have been commended for his bearing by the King of Sweden. In the end the swordsman never unsheathed his sword, except verbally. It is hardly necessary to observe that although love and self-abnegation are absolute values in Christianity, such values did not produce a mealy-mouthed religion. It would be hard to find a group of men who faced more difficult deaths than the Apostles, and it was not recorded that they died badly. But the values are a corollary of belief, and Yeats was committed to another belief and other values. In effect he dismisses Von Hügel implicitly long before reaching section eight.

From Yeatsian, aristocratic joy in stanza three, we move in the fourth section to an account of an actual experience at least implicitly democratic. With the announcement that "My fiftieth year had come and gone" the poem assumes a new imaginative freedom. The poet will range over his entire life, over all he knows of history and human nature, to find experiences and images that allow him to speak. Sitting "In a crowded London shop" over "an open book and empty cup" he is suddenly overcome with happiness:

While on the shop and street I gazed
My body of a sudden blazed;
And twenty minutes more or less
It seemed, so great my happiness,
That I was blessèd and could bless.

Although he does not point it out in so many words, to be able to bless is
to be able to love. At this point the barriers of the solitary self have been
dropped and the love of the Good Samaritan triumphs over the anti-
nomies. We have a prose gloss on this experience in Yeats's "Anima
Mundi."

At certain moments, always unforeseen, I become happy, most
commonly when at hazard I have opened some book of verse.
Sometimes it is my own verse when, instead of discovering new
technical flaws, I read with all the excitement of the first writing.
Perhaps I am sitting in some crowded restaurant, the open book
beside me, or closed, my excitement having overbrimmed the page.
I look at the strangers near as if I had known them all my life, and it
seems strange that I cannot speak to them: everything fills me with
affection, I have no longer any fears or any needs; I do not even
remember that this happy mood must come to an end. It seems as if
the vehicle had suddenly grown pure and far extended and so lumi-
nous that the images from *Anima Mundi,* embodied there and drunk
with that sweetness, would, like a country drunkard who has
thrown a wisp into his own thatch, burn up time.

It may be an hour before the mood passes, but latterly I seem to
understand that I enter upon it the moment I cease to hate. I think
the common condition of our life is hatred—I know that this is so
with me—irritation with public or private events or persons. (Myth
364–65)

The statement is reminiscent of "A Prayer for My Daughter": "all
hatred driven hence, / The soul recovers radical innocence" (P 189). One
could easily argue that the whole point of Christianity is the abolition of
hatred. No Christian theologian could want a more down to earth or
accurate assessment of "the common condition." This is not the life of
depravity, but rather the day-to-day, selfish niggling that blinds us to
plenitude of being and which must be conquered in any attempt to live a

more ample, let alone a holy life. The wonder is, Yeats's analysis of
innate selfishness being so in keeping with the Christian view of human
nature, and his experience of love overcoming that selfishness so recon-
cilable with Christian psychology, that Yeats was not drawn, against his
cosmological ideas, to some form of Christianity. It is a measure of the
strength of those ideas in him that he was not.

Thomas Merton had an experience so similar to Yeats's that it is
worth noting here:

> In Louisville, at the corner of Fourth and Walnut, in the center of the
> shopping district, I was suddenly overwhelmed with the realization
> that I loved all those people, that they were mine and I theirs, that
> we could not be alien to one another even though we were total
> strangers. It was like waking from a dream of separateness, of spu-
> rious self-isolation in a special world, the world of renunciation and
> supposed holiness. The whole illusion of a separate holy existence is
> a dream. Not that I question the reality of my vocation, or of my
> monastic life: but the conception of "separation from the world"
> that we have in a monastery too easily presents itself as a complete
> illusion: the illusion that by making vows we become a different
> species of being, pseudo-angels, "spiritual men," men of interior
> life, what have you.[42]

The dropping of the barriers to love in Merton's case results in a serious
examination of the foundation of his moral judgments. There is a similar
self-examination in the fifth stanza of "Vacillation" which we will come
to shortly. I think Merton's comment about vows not making "a differ-
ent species of being" has some application to Yeats's character. AE
thought that by believing form creates content Yeats had inverted the
natural order of things whereby life creates form, and not form, life.
Yeats at least in part created Yeats, the kind of man necessary to write the
poetry he wanted to write. He cast, in short, life in the image of art. This
is implicit in his many posturings, his entrances into crowded rooms
delayed for effect, in his increasing attention to his dress and manners as
he grew older. Pride was part of the aristocratic mask he chose to wear.

---

42. Thomas Merton, *Conjectures of a Guilty Bystander* (Garden City, N.Y.: Double-
day, 1966), 140–41. Hereafter cited in the text as *CGB*.

All of these things, the total of his partly assumed or created character, cut him off from all those people he felt suddenly close to in his "happy mood." I think that to become Christian he would have had to take off the mask, and it had been the creation of a lifetime.

There is in the fifth section of "Vacillation" the psychological if not the theological reality of *mea culpa*. He looks over his past life and is burdened by a sense of responsibility.

> Things said or done long years ago,
> Or things I did not do or say
> But thought that I might say or do,
> Weigh me down, and not a day
> But something is recalled,
> My conscience or my vanity appalled.

The poem begins with a question, and moves through the definition of a spiritual center in stanza two, to imperious directives about the reformation of life. The fourth and fifth sections are like the slow movement in a symphony. He reasserts his common humanity in the fourth, and in a sense confesses sins against his fellow man in the fifth. Part of the preparation for death is certainly self-knowledge. Conscience suggests his failure to come up to an objective standard of behavior; vanity suggests he has not realized his idea of himself. It is difficult to imagine Yeats not satisfied with Yeats, but that seems to have been the case, at least for one stanza of "Vacillation." At this point the poem is pausing and gathering strength for its final assertion.

The sixth section invokes "the great lord of Chou" who intones "Let all things pass away" as the refrain for each of the three stanzas. Before he can make any final assertion in a poem which is groping toward a credo, Yeats must reduce reality, both historical and personal, to its common source. Lords and conquerors cry "Let all things pass away." It is a joyful cry, joyful in the specifically Yeatsian sense of joy, the joy of men who are beyond commitment, or who know and accept the fact that what they are committed to cannot be kept, and so throw it all to the wind. The source of all reality is discovered to be the human heart:

> From man's blood-sodden heart are sprung
> Those branches of the night and day
> Where the gaudy moon is hung.

This discovery is not entirely new. It was certainly implicit in the Ruskin's cat correspondence with T. Sturge Moore, but did not receive definitive poetic statement until much later. These lines look forward to "Egypt and Greece, good-bye, and good-bye, Rome!" (P 289), and to "the foul rag and bone shop of the heart" (P 348). They signify the end of the domination of the poet's imagination by gyres, cones, and cycles, or perhaps more accurately their reduction to man who created them in the first place.

The little dialogue-drama of section seven is a kind of intellectual sparring between two metaphysical possibilities, truth as the Absolute and truth as the multiplicity of earth where opposites are paired and there is the possibility for growth. The attitude of the Soul is exactly what one would expect of the Gnostic dualist. Here below nothing *is,* but all things *seem.* This is precisely the ontological situation in Shelley's "The Sensitive Plant," a poem that Yeats knew. Reality provides no theme for the Heart because in the dialogue reality means the spiritual being of the undifferentiated One. Instead of the fulfillment of life, this notion of the afterlife is for Yeats its opposite, death, and he naturally enough shies away from it. Because he had not really studied the Christian idea of God he did not know what it was. His idea of God was more that of the mystery religions, and did not offer much to look forward to for a man who delighted in image, drama, transformation. No wonder he thought the poet must not follow the mystic to the absolute core of reality, but remain in the mouth of the serpent multiplicity, for there are the life and the images without which the poet simply has nothing to do. Soul resolutely maintains that salvation lies in the fire, echoing the image of Isaiah's coal. Heart, really talking past Soul in the last line of the dialogue, replies "What theme had Homer but original sin?" Soul is not looking for a theme, but for salvation, so these lines cannot really be paired. They are speaking in opposite directions, and neither recognizes the other. Heart is really the poet, and Soul the mystic. Here there is no communication between them. I commented earlier in regard to the thirteenth cone of Yeats's Great Wheel that it might be seen as an escape route from temporality through human freedom which is grounded in God, but that the way is never really made clear. Another approach to the problem is to see that Yeats did not really want to escape from the wheel. In near perpetual transformation through death and re-embodiment the wheel was more attractive than the One, though he retains in principle the idea of eventual "escape" to bodiless eternity.

The eighth section is carefully organized for dramatic effect. By asking the question "Must we part" in the very first line and not answering it until the last, Yeats wrings a sweetness from the situation, almost like a lover who raises the question of parting to enjoy the emotion without the loss. I mentioned earlier that I detect a note of real personal regret in Yeats's "*Must* we part, Von Hügel." I do not want to overstate the case, but I would like to reiterate that Yeats gave himself a long time with this poem, one that did not come easily. To write *must* for an artist as self-conscious as Yeats means that he wanted the word, and what the word implies, at the least, real regret. Certainly reading *The Mystical Element* would have told Yeats that in Von Hügel he could find, if not quite a soul-mate, nevertheless a man of great learning who assumed man's spiritual nature and the constitution of the universe by God, and certainly a worthy adversary for the modern rationalists Yeats saw as enemies. And it is more than a little likely Yeats knew something of Von Hügel's constant efforts to make known the reality of God to a generation that had largely abandoned spiritual values. The Baron was a frequent speaker at universities and before groups dedicated to the discussion of religious phenomena during the years Yeats was in London. He was known to many thinkers, and it is inconceivable Yeats had not heard of him, even before publication of *The Mystical Element* in 1908.

Yeats assumes friendship with Von Hügel. Without such an assumption "Must we part" loses its force. The assumed friendship is based on acceptance of the miracles of the saints and honoring sanctity. Yeats was more interested in miracles than in sanctity, and devotes the next five lines to the miraculous preservation of St. Teresa's body, but none at all to the quality of her holiness. Martin Green thinks Yeats may have confused St. Teresa with St. Catherine of Genoa in this stanza, as Von Hügel had studied St. Catherine, not St. Teresa (*YBVH* 2).

Yeats was writing a poem, however, not a scholarly text, and St. Teresa's incorruptibility was more dramatic than St. Catherine's! Yeats had read in Alice, Lady Lovat's biography of Saint Teresa, that when her tomb had been opened in July of 1583, nine months after she had been buried,

the wood of the coffin was found to be split and decayed, and the coffin was filled with earth and water, but the body of the saint was intact, her flesh white and soft, as flexible as when she was buried, and still emitted the same delicious and penetrating smell. More-

over, her limbs exuded a miraculous oil which bore a similar per-
fume, and embalmed the air and everything with which it came in
contact.[43]

Yeats may have forgotten, or simply written off as uninteresting Von
Hügel's account of the exhuming of St. Catherine's body after eighteen
months so that it could be reinterred. The body of the saint had not
decayed, and the coffin was kept open for several days for believers to
witness.

In 1928 Yeats had referred to the miracle of St. Teresa's incorrup-
tibility in a letter to T. Sturge Moore:

> By the bye, please don't quote him [Moore's brother, G. E., the
> philosopher] again till you have asked him this question: 'How do
> you account for the fact that when the Tomb of St. Teresa was
> opened her body exuded miraculous oil and smelt of violets?' If he
> cannot account for such primary facts he knows nothing. (LTSM
> 121–22)

Yeats accepts the miracle, but cannot believe it requires anything of him.
In a letter to Olivia Shakespear from Coole on 3 January 1932, he spoke
of St. Teresa yet again:

> I feel that this is the choice of the saint (St. Theresa's ecstasy,
> Gandhi's smiling face): comedy; and the heroic choice: Tragedy
> (Dante, Don Quixote). Live Tragically but be not deceived (not the
> fool's Tragedy). Yet I accept all the miracles. Why should not the
> old embalmers come back as ghosts and bestow upon the saint all
> the care once bestowed upon Rameses? Why should I doubt the tale
> that when St. Theresa's tomb was opened in the middle of the
> nineteenth century the still undecayed body dripped with fragrant
> oil? I shall be a sinful man to the end, and think upon my death-bed
> of all the nights I wasted my youth. (L 790)

The letter echoes the poem.

---

43. Alice Lady Lovat, *The Life of Saint Teresa* (London: Simpkin, Marshall, Hamil-
ton, Kent & Co., 1920), 606.

The body of Saint Teresa lies undecayed in tomb,
Bathed in miraculous oil, sweet odours from it come,
Healing from its lettered slab. Those self-same hands perchance
Eternalised the body of a modern saint that once
Had scooped out Pharaoh's mummy.

The miracle was something of a problem for him. He believed it, and he had to account for it by invoking the "spiritual" paraphernalia of his Golden Dawn days. What Yeats proposes as an "explanation" of the miracle, that the ghosts of the embalmers of Rameses may have come back to embalm the saint, is a far more outrageous insult to reason than the miracle the explanation is invoked to explain. It is doubly outrageous since Rameses' body did not survive and St. Teresa's did. The ghosts are needed, of course, because here there is no God, at least not the God of David, Abraham, Moses, and John the Baptist who could manage the preservation of a saint's body quite nicely without the intervention of Egyptian ghosts.

It is important to note that Yeats feels obliged to accept sinfulness because he refuses to give up the life of the body. The beginnings of such a judgment go all the way back to the extreme Jansenism of Lionel Johnson and W. T. Horton, and the Jansenism of the late Victorian Church in general. It was against their extraordinary dismissal of matter, the body, and history that Von Hügel fought all his life. In short, Yeats understood Christianity to measure sanctity by rejection of the body, which is another way of saying he didn't understand it at all, but his misunderstanding was ably assisted by the Church itself and by many who considered themselves to be following in the footsteps of the saints.

In the light of the tilting between Heart and Soul in section seven, the preparation for Yeats's final declaration requires some comment.

> I—though heart might find relief
> Did I become a Christian man and choose for my belief
> What seems most welcome in the tomb—play a predestined part.

What would seem most welcome in the tomb I think has to be spiritual life, the life of the soul, for after death what else could there be? But what would the heart require relief from, relief that "might" be found in Christianity. In section seven Heart rejects "the simplicity of fire," salvation, because there is nothing in salvation for the poet to write about.

Perhaps agitation about the authenticity of feeling, or the continuance of feeling, drives Yeats to think for a moment he might find relief in Christianity, or perhaps a moment's weariness with uncertainty. But juggling possibilities was one source of Yeats's poetic power, and he knew it. He could not seriously give in to any such weariness for long. I think *heart* is used here in a more general sense than in section seven, representing more the whole human condition in the poet's present, than the focused drive toward the thematics of poetry. But in any case Yeats denies himself the possibility of choice. He plays a predestined part, again avoiding commitment.

Harold Bloom concludes that the predestined part is the poet's.[44] That is doubly true since in the next line Yeats announces, "Homer is my example and his unchristened heart." Yeats is predestined both by natural proclivity and inevitable alliance. Bloom shrewdly observes that in choosing Homer and "a belief in action and the poetry celebrating action," Yeats returns to the faith of his iconoclast father (*Y* 397). Jeffares suggests that "this poem's contrast between Homeric and Christian ideas probably came from a passage in Von Hügel," and then quotes a key passage from the Baron:

> For the survival after the body's death indubitably attributed to the Psyche in the Homeric poems, is conceived there, throughout, as miserably shrunken consciousness, and one which is dependent for its continuance upon the good offices bestowed by the survivors upon the corpse and grave. (*NCP* 304)

It would be ironic indeed if Von Hügel's upsettingly bleak picture of the Homeric afterlife influenced Yeats to choose action over contemplation. But then his choice was a lifetime commitment and not a choice at all in any ordinary sense, and he did not understand the dynamics of Christian contemplation.

In the last line but one Yeats invokes the Old Testament: "The lion and the honeycomb, what has Scripture said?" For Bloom the Biblical "Out of the eater came forth meat, and out of the strong came forth sweetness" suggests that "One strength both slays the lion, and then feasts upon its sweetness" (*Y* 397). The dichotomy is perfect for Yeats,

---

44. Harold Bloom, *Yeats* (New York: Oxford University Press, 1970), 397. Hereafter cited in the text as *Y*.

who had a talent for finding just what he needed in a text and ignoring the rest. He will join Homer in slaying the lion of reality with words in order to draw from it the sweetness of verse. The last line is as inevitable as any line in any poem: "So get you gone, Von Hügel, though with blessings on your head." Although he allowed for a way to leave the Great Wheel of the world, he could not take it. He blesses Von Hügel for making a commitment he did not make, and turns once again to the source of his poetry in the elemental situations of life.

Epilogue

In a brilliant but unfair letter of 14 December 1916, John Butler Yeats wrote to his son:

> There is some mysterious and perfectly inexplicable connection in the mind between the apprehension of a truth and the music of verse. To put it in a metaphor, the moment truth enters the mind by some fairy magic it releases the notes of a musical expression. Therefore it is that Protestantism favours poetry, in spite of its most stern disapproval of such "frivolity." For it is the very essence of Protestantism to command that its votaries think hard, and refuse to be satisfied with anything short of the *ultimate truth*. Roman Catholicism, on the other hand, inculcates the *teaching* of doctrine and cares little as to whether the doctrines be the ultimate truth, being only anxious that it should be the *politic* truth. For that reason Roman Catholic countries are rich in oratory and poor in poetry, all their so-called poetry being a species of melodious orations. (LTWBY 329)

There is a "truth" behind the music of Yeats's later work which he toyed with before the composition of "Vacillation" and finally committed himself to in that pivotal poem. And that truth is that man needs nothing beyond himself to create, sustain, and find value in the universe. This "truth" is the result of a lifelong intellectual labor in which the poet was sustained and urged on by a spirit of questioning inherited from his iconoclast father and the Protestant tradition from which he came.

As early as 1919 Yeats had written in "A Prayer for My Daughter":

> Considering that, all hatred driven hence,
> The soul recovers radical innocence

And learns at last that it is self-delighting,
Self-appeasing, self-affrighting,
And that its own sweet will is Heaven's will.

(P 189–90)

I have quoted these lines before and pointed out their inherent Chris-
tianity, but it should be further pointed out that innocence is achieved
here by an act of the independent will which casts out hatred. Innocence
casting out darkness by decision of the sovereign will is a notion at the
Protestant end of the Christian spectrum. Of course it is no ordinary
will, but one dedicated to a spiritual quest. In "The Tower" his ideas
were shaped enough for him to speak of his "faith":

And I declare my faith:
I mock Plotinus' thought
And cry in Plato's teeth,
Death and life were not
Till man made up the whole,
Made lock, stock and barrel
Out of his bitter soul.

(P 198)

It is too bad Yeats apparently did not know the work of Nicolai Berdy-
aev, as he would have found in him something of an ally. Berdyaev's *The
Meaning of the Creative Act* was published in London in 1914. In it he
wrote, "Creativeness is not only a struggle with sin and evil—it wills
another world, it continues the work of creation."[45] Sin and evil for
Berdyaev are largely the natural inclination toward sloth and self which
the poet must overcome to accomplish anything. Yeats goes beyond
Berdyaev in his claims for man, but there is in the Russian an early and a
very sophisticated appreciation of the extent to which great art creates a
world, not *ex nihilo,* but out of the personal chaos of images in all of us.

Self-determination is a note sounded again in"A Dialogue of Self
and Soul" (1927):

I am content to follow to its source
Every event in action or in thought;
Measure the lot; forgive myself the lot!

---

45. Nicholas Berdyaev, *The Meaning of the Creative Act,* trans. Donald A. Lowrie
(New York: Collier Books, 1962), 95.

When such as I cast out remorse
So great a sweetness flows into the breast
We must laugh and we must sing,
We are blest by everything,
Everything we look upon is blest.

(P 236)

It should be pointed out that in these passages Yeats is performing for himself spiritual offices which in the Catholic tradition would be performed by a priest or by God. He finds in his own act of casting out hatred a source of grace, making Heaven the creation of man himself. He does recognize the need to be forgiven, but forgives himself rather than going to the Church. In Bryon's *Manfred* there is a remarkable foreshadowing of Yeats's idea. At the very end of the drama Manfred concludes his soliloquy with the following words:

The mind which is immortal makes itself
Requital for its good or evil thoughts,—
Is its own origin of ill and end—
And its own place and time; its innate sense
When stripp'd of this mortality, derives
No colour from the fleeting things without,
But is absorb'd in sufferance or in joy,
Born from the knowledge of its own desert.

(II.iv.129–36)

Manfred leaves the Abbot much as Yeats leaves Von Hügel, with respect and affection, but without commitment. Yeats was, of course, a lifelong student of Blake, and for Blake the church of the heart was the only church. In refusing to recognize the need for any historical institution Yeats takes up his stand with Blake, Boehme, and other visionaries, needless to say a valley apart from Von Hügel who would view them with interest from an opposite height.

Written in 1930–31, along with the revisions for *The Resurrection,* and at the same time his work was proceeding on "Vacillation," "Two Songs from a Play" echoes the notion of a universe upheld by the self.

Everything that man esteems
Endures a moment or a day.
Love's pleasure drives his love away,
The painter's brush consumes his dreams;
The herald's cry, the soldier's tread

Exhaust his glory and his might:
Whatever flames upon the night
Man's own resinous heart has fed.

(P 213–14)

The building of the self's constructions exhausts the need to build, and
transiency becomes a virtue, for if things did not pass away, there would
be no need for man to exercise his creativity in building them up again.
And in "Stream and Sun at Glendalough," written on 23 June 1932, a
little more than six months after the completion of "Vacillation," he
wonders at his own spiritual rebirth, here tied to nature.

What motion of the sun or stream
Or eyelid shot the gleam
That pierced my body through?
What made me live like these that seem
Self-born, born anew?

(P 255)

"Man's own resinous heart" is called upon to part-perform, part-receive
from nature, new life in a poetic rite that resembles baptism. Salvation
consists in renewed life, the responsibility for which here lies on the
individual's shoulders. Yeats's own testimony—"Myself must I re-
make"—is a seal on this identification of poetry with spiritual self-cre-
ation (P 301). Yeats was always challenging himself to new life. That is
what made him such a difficulty for the theological establishment, and
such a joy for the poetic and social world, as his acts of re-creation gave
him a fascinating tension other men did not have. Having finally dis-
missed Von Hügel, and a conception of God I think he mistakenly sup-
posed to presume a deity external to man, he seems to have opened his
"unchristened heart" in new life.

From 1926 to 1931, just before he began to work on "Vacillation,"
Yeats carried on a remarkable correspondence with T. Sturge Moore
about the nature of reality. He had been writing to Moore since the turn
of the century, but during this five years the correspondence took a
philosophical turn, prompted by the appearance of Ruskin's cat. Yeats
wrote to Moore on 16 January 1926:

John Ruskin, while talking with Frank Harris, ran suddenly to the
other end of the room, picked up, or seemed to pick up, some object
which he threw out of the window. He then explained that it was a

tempting demon in the form of a cat. Now if the house cat had come in both cats would have looked alike to Ruskin. (I know this for I once saw a phantom picture and real picture side by side.) Neither your brother [G. E. Moore] nor Russell gives any criterion by which Ruskin could have told one cat from the other. No doubt if pressed they would have said that if Ruskin's cat was real Harris would have seen it. But that argument amounts to nothing. (LTSM 63)

For the next five years the two poets carried on an intense debate over the reality of Ruskin's cat, complete with references to Eddington, Einstein, and numerous spiritualists of the day. They referred each other to recent articles in *TLS* and to relevant books they had read. It is the most delightful exchange of letters I know of in modern literature.

Yeats stoutly defended the reality of Ruskin's cat against the cool observations of Moore, who wrote:

Do you deny that there are such things as hallucinations? Do you think that there are black snakes wriggling on the counterpane of a man who has D.T.? . . . If you suppose there is a separate reality it is putting a new meaning to the word. . . . Do you deny that our senses can be deranged and make mistakes, just as our reasoning faculty may, as in Othello's case, make a mistake? If you bang your head against a door you see stars that are not there but swim around you as though they were. The blow has deranged your sense of sight, just as a disease may, or a hypnotic trance, or even a conviction may. (LTSM 64–65)

Yeats wrote back in closely consecutive letters:

As to the empiric argument, the 'reality' of Ruskin's cat grows with the number who hear it mew, according to the idealist position, yet reality may be what Napoleon said of history 'a lie that we have agreed on'. . . . Russell and his school cannot escape from the belief that each man is a sealed bottle. Every man who has studied psychical science by watching his own life knows that we share emotion, thought and image. (LTSM 67–68)

Inevitably they never came to any agreement. The importance of the correspondence for the present discussion is that in it Yeats was forced to consolidate and sum up his philosophical ideas at a period when he was in

need of redirection. He clearly believed that we do not know ultimate
reality. The world we live in is in part created by us, but not solely by us
as individuals. Intense subjective experiences are real whether or not they
are shared, and produce images or symbols which may be used in art. In
the end our world is an imaginative construct and is as much within as
without. These conclusions distanced him yet farther from the transcen-
dent God of the Hebraic-Christian tradition, or shall we say that in these
conclusions transcendence is so redefined as to bear little resemblance to
anything comparable in the main tradition of European spirituality. And
of course they helped him to reject Von Hügel in "Vacillation."

The poems that issued from the denial of transcendence are rather
more negative than a self-projected, self-graced universe might sug-
gest—brilliant, of course, but in many ways negative. In "Under Ben
Bulben" Yeats tells us the poet should "Bring the soul of man to God"
(P 326), but God is not much in evidence in Last Poems. It is the poet who
is in evidence, for there is no other principle of order. In fact in both New
Poems (1938) and Last Poems (1939) we have a riot of skepticism. Yeats
takes delight in reporting that all things which formally constituted a
center of life have completely failed.

In "The Curse of Cromwell" the fall of a whole society is chron-
icled.

> All neighbourly content and easy talk are gone,
> But there's no good complaining, for money's rant is on.
> He that's mounting up must on his neighbour mount
> And we and all the Muses are things of no account.
>
> (P 305)

Culture, the easy spread of mind in "easy talk," goes out with aristocracy.
In its place we have democracy, or what passes for it, men on the make, to
whom the arts are nothing. He is quite explicit in "A Statesman's
Holiday":

> Riches drove out rank,
> Base drove out the better blood,
> And mind and body shrank.
>
> (P 583)

Yeats only saves himself by a hair from an *obnoxious* elitism. He does
save himself, through great simplicity and power of language, and an
innate humanity that never deserted him. He was faced with obvious

cultural decay and explained it by a revolution in taste and values, not simply by a redistribution of wealth. Desire for power rather than knowledge has destroyed a world.

The religious quest fares no better in *Last Poems*. There is a spirit of hilarity-in-despair in "The Pilgrim" who goes to Lough Derg to pray:

> Round Lough Derg's holy island I went upon the stones,
> I prayed at all the Stations upon my marrow bones,
> And there I found an old man and though I prayed all day
> And that old man beside me, nothing would he say
> But fol de rol de rolly O.
>
> (P 313)

The poet questions the shapes of the holy dead who cluster about the place, but they also reply "fol de rol de rolly O," nonsense for a nonsensical world.

Love between man and woman still exists, but has serious problems. In *Yeats's Quest for Eden* George Mills Harper speaks of Yeatsian radical innocence as "the perfect union of mind and body,"[46] but there is rampant disunion in *Last Poems,* and radical dualism, not radical innocence. Mind and body seem isolated though mortally linked, like Siamese twins perpetually cut off from each other psychically, though sharing the same flesh. In "Crazy Jane on the Day of Judgment" Yeats wrote:

> 'Love is all
> Unsatisfied
> That cannot take the whole
> Body and soul';
> And that is what Jane said.
>
> (P 257)

But in *Last Poems* that is impossible. In "The Three Bushes" the lady cannot endure the loss of her chastity, but neither can she endure the loss of her lover, so the chambermaid sleeps with him, and all are happy. They are all buried together by a rose-tree:

> And now none living can
> When they have plucked a rose there
> Know where its roots began.
>
> (P 298)

---

46. George Mills Harper, *Yeats's Quest for Eden,* Yeats Centenary Papers 4 (Dublin: Dolmen Press, 1973), 324.

The twisting of the roots around the graves is symbolic of complexity without unity. In "The Lady's First Song" she is obviously tormented by a love that is not at all ennobling which makes her "No better than a beast / Upon all fours" (P 299). Her soul adores what hurts her; humankind is divided against itself and even consciousness of the plight—and she is conscious—does nothing to mitigate it. In "The Lady's Second Song" an even stranger division is apparent:

> He shall love my soul as though
> Body were not at all,
> He shall love your body
> Untroubled by the soul. . . .
>
> (P 299)

In a way reminiscent of "The Three Bushes," the lady seems to be talking to another woman, and one is to be loved for soul, one for body. In "The Lady's Third Song" there is again a split between the daylight lady and the evening lady, one representing carnal love and one spiritual. In his later years Yeats was several times heard to remark that the tragedy of sex was that the soul always remained virginal. In Yeats's later work body and soul are rather like man and God in the Leibnitzian universe, parallel but untouching.

What the soul of man is really brought to in his later work is the poet's sovereign power to shape chaos to his own form, for nothing much of value survives except his art. The wheel has come full course, and we are brought back to "Words alone are certain good" from "The Song of the Happy Shepherd" (P 7), though of course on an infinitely more sophisticated level, for now his "masterful images" are known to come from

> A mound of refuse or the sweepings of a street,
> Old kettles, old bottles, and a broken can,
> Old iron, old bones, old rags, that raving slut
> Who keeps the till.
>
> (P 347)

With these elementals, whose source is not really outside the poet at all, but the "Foul rag and bone shop of the heart" (P 348), is created the personal and collective dream of art that makes civilization possible. As in "Meru":

Civilisation is hooped together, brought
Under a rule, under the semblance of peace
By manifold illusion.

(P 289)

The artist's is not the only, but is one of the chief illusions holding it together. But art is self-conscious, and if the world falls apart, as in "The Gyres," it can be built up again.

Conduct and work grow coarse, and coarse the soul,
What matter! Those that Rocky Face holds dear,
Lovers of horses and of women, shall
From marble of a broken sepulchre
Or dark betwixt the polecat and the owl,
Or any rich, dark nothing disinter
The workman, noble and saint, and all things run
On that unfashionable gyre again.

(P 293)

The rich, dark nothing is the dark of the creative unconscious out of which come new images to reconstitute civilization. For men return, and with them images, as in "Under Ben Bulben":

Though grave-diggers' toil is long,
Sharp their spades, their muscle strong,
They but thrust their buried men
Back in the human mind again.

(P 325)

So the final word Yeats leaves us is that of "Lapis Lazuli": "All things fall and are built again / And those that build them again are gay" (P 295). Yeats deeds us the gaiety of the maker, not the holiness of the saint. Thomas Merton thought that in unusual circumstances "It might be the will of God—as it certainly was in the case of the Old Testament Prophets and in that of St. John of the Cross—that a man should remain *at the same time a mystic and a poet* and ascend to the greatest heights of poetic creation and of mystical prayer without any evident contradiction between them" (*CGB* 414). But as we have seen, Yeats was jealous of his images and held an idea of God that made him think their abandonment was necessary for life with God. He did believe, however, that we bring God the work of our hands, and it is a great tragedy if we have nothing to bring:

To seek God too soon is not less sinful than to seek God too late; we must love, man, woman, or child, we must exhaust ambition, intellect, desire, dedicating all things as they pass, or we come to God with empty hands. (E&I 483)

The formulation is typical of him, activity dedicated to the enlargement of being. That defined his life.

The Dialogical Combat in *The Wanderings of Oisin:* The Shape of Things to Come

ANCA VLASOPOLOS

Narrative theories have bloomed, occasionally come to fruition, and disseminated at a tremendous rate in this latter half of the twentieth century. Since it has generated such an outpouring of critical attention, the novel or long narrative fiction has clearly established itself as a domi-nant literary genre, not as a poor, or sometimes synonymously, a female, relation. The question that concerns those of us who are still attracted by the less popular genres of poetry and drama is whether narrative theories apply at all to narrative poetry and, more importantly, whether narrative theory itself has not learned from poetry and from drama the insights that it brings to prose fiction. Conversely, we Romanticists, who have been severely chided for having bought and perpetuated the ideology of Romanticism in our critical vocabulary and evaluations, can profit from theories that arise from the contemplation of the middle-class, nouveau-riche genre of narrative prose.

Rereading *The Wanderings of Oisin* and the criticism surrounding it in the context of narrative theory can become a salutary experience. Despite the occasional bows to *Oisin* as an anagogical prefiguration of the really great Yeats, most critics regard *Oisin* as a phase that Yeats had to go through, like the terrible twos or painful adolescence.[1] They fault Yeats for his Nineties allegiance, that is, for a style that expresses a dreamy sensuousness. Bloom blames Yeats for not having written *Al-astor,* for not having Oisin seek "an object that itself shatters nature's value as well as context," namely, a product of the imagination instead of

---

1. Thomas L. Byrd, Jr., in *The Early Poetry of W. B. Yeats: The Poetic Quest* (Port Washington, N.Y.: Kennikat, 1978) comes closest to finding in *Oisin* the roots of Yeats's lifelong artistic concerns (65); while regarding the Oedipal complex as an impetus for much of Yeats's work, Brenda Webster reads *Oisin* as a more transparent, less mature representa-tion of Yeats's psychic problems (*Yeats: A Psychoanalytic Study* [Stanford: Stanford Univer-sity Press, 1973], 18–24).

the "super-nature" to which he travels.[2] Albright criticizes the whole Romantic-Quest genre when he accuses Oisin of having abandoned the genuine mode of existence of the Fenians for "a life in fantasy."[3]

Critics agree that Yeats needed to move toward a unified vision and a tougher diction, and paradoxically they discover such a direction in Yeats's concept of the mask, of the anti-self, which, there seems to be universal agreement, Yeats found right around the turn of the century, about ten to twelve years after he had written *Oisin*. Curiously, what had seemed escapist or divisive in *Oisin* is revaluated as unifying and humanizing in the later Yeats. Bloom insists on Yeats's vacillation between determinism and freedom throughout *A Vision* as evidence of the poet at his greatest;[4] Christ writes that "the mask as an element in a systematic model of personality . . . offers both unity and multiplicity of being."[5] Herbert Levine insists that "Ego Dominus Tuus" at the moment of composition was a vacillating poem which only time and contextualization have made into an exemplum of "unity of being."[6] Even Rajan, in his cogent examination of Yeats's dialogue poems, declares that Yeats did not begin writing these poems until he had laid the theoretical foundations for them, circa 1919. He dismisses *The Wanderings of Oisin* as true dialogue because "steady attention is needed to perceive that [it] is a dialogue poem." He notes the inequality of line distribution between St. Patrick, with his less than twenty lines, and Oisin, with his 870, and concludes, "it is not even clear that we even have an exchange of views."[7] Yet Rajan's analysis of the function of dialogue in the later Yeats is strikingly similar, as we shall see, to Bakhtin's dialogics, which in turn proves illuminating when applied to *Oisin*.

The common thread that connects these critics' opinions about Yeats's early versus later poetry comes from an overvaluation of unity. Even the praises that Yeats's vacillation earns appear only when the

---

2. Harold Bloom, *Yeats* (London: Oxford University Press, 1970), 99.

3. Daniel Albright, *The Myth Against Myth: A Study of Yeats's Imagination in Old Age* (London: Oxford University Press, 1972), 64.

4. Harold Bloom, "*A Vision:* The Dead and History," *William Butler Yeats: Modern Critical Views,* ed. Harold Bloom (New York: Chelsea House, 1986), 129–53.

5. Carol T. Christ, *Victorian and Modern Poetics* (Chicago: University of Chicago Press, 1984), 34–35.

6. Herbert J. Levine, *Yeats's Daimonic Renewal* (Ann Arbor: UMI Research Press, 1983), 22.

7. Balachandra Rajan, "The Poetry of Confrontation: Yeats and the Dialogue Poem," *Myth and Reality in Irish Literature,* ed. Joseph Ronsley (Waterloo, Ontario: Wilfrid Laurier University Press, 1977), 117–28; see 118. Hereafter cited in the text as Rajan.

antagonism and division are internalized, even when by such superficial devices as giving the two voices of "A Dialogue of Self and Soul" the names of My Soul and My Self. My own contention, to which I came through an admittedly filtered reading of Mikhail Bakhtin's theories of the utterance and dialogism, is that Yeats had learned the use of the anti-self and the mask before the turn of the century, as he was writing *The Wanderings of Oisin*. Nietzsche's writings, therefore, represent less of a revelation than an authentication of Yeats's own discoveries.[8] What I shall argue, then, is that poets learn more from themselves, from their imaginative and historical experiences, particularly when they develop critical or mystical theories, than they do from any one figure, precursor or contemporary.

In his "Dialogic as an Art of Discourse in Literary Criticism," Bialostosky provides a useful if somewhat reductive summary of Bakhtin's dialogics: existing in opposition, or in completion as Bakhtin might say, to dialectics and rhetoric, "dialogics concerns the relations among persons articulating their ideas in response to one another, discovering their mutual affinities and oppositions, their provocations to reply, their desires to hear more, or their wishes to change the subject."[9] Thus, unlike the Hegelian dialectic that has informed much Romanticist criticism, dialogism recognizes the impossibility of synthesis or of resolution in most dialogues and separates that open-endedness from the completion and coherence imposed upon what Bakhtin calls "the material of identification," the material used for artistic production. Bakhtin provides us with a clarification that seems admirably applicable to the dialogical structure of *Oisin:*

> Presuppose two consciousnesses that do not fuse; they are events whose essential and constitutive element is the relation of a consciousness to another consciousness, precisely because it is other. All the characteristics and definitions of present being that launch this being into dramatic movement, from . . . naive anthropocentrism . . . to the devices of contemporary art . . . burn from the borrowed light of *alterity*.[10]

---

8. Richard Ellmann, *The Identity of Yeats*, 2d ed. (1964; New York: Oxford University Press, 1975), 92–96.

9. Don H. Bialostosky, "Dialogic as an Art of Discourse in Literary Criticism," *PMLA* 101 (1986), 788–97; see 789.

10. Tzvetan Todorov, *Mikhail Bakhtin: The Dialogical Principle*, trans. Wlad Godzich (Minneapolis: University of Minnesota Press, 1984), 100. Hereafter cited in the text as Todorov.

This infusion without fusion of *other* into individual utterance makes Yeats's *Oisin* a complex and exciting experiment, in some ways more complex, more *novel* in its attachment to history and in Yeats's awakened consideration of historiography than the more famous later dialogues of his poetry.

In discussing Bakhtin, Martin uncovers the two layers of dialogism, the one that takes place within the text and the added dimension of the reader's "linguistic knowledge" interacting "with the words on a page." About the former, he writes:

> This jostling of disparate languages is what Bakhtin calls *hetero-glossia*. . . . Its essential quality emerges most clearly in disagreements, when the way in which things are said becomes as visible an object of contention as the subject of dispute. The words of the other cut deep, penetrate our own language, and we return them as taunt or retort.[11]

In addition to this contest for meaning that occupies the text, readings—or as Martin puts it, "Those who talk or write about narratives"—further expand the boundaries of dialogue by contributing "to the total dialogic context of literature, where the production of words entails the creation of value, through the work and pleasure of understanding" (Martin 152). Within Martin's laudable embrace both of Marxist preoccupations—work—and aesthetic goals—pleasure—we should proceed to an understanding of *The Wanderings of Oisin*.

As he does in the later dialogues, only more extravagantly here, Yeats bestows the authority of lengthy speech on the more favored persona of the dialogue, on Oisin and not on St. Patrick. Like My Self, Ille, Crazy Jane and others, Oisin runs away with the story, and there is general agreement that Patrick, like the Bishop, is a paltry antagonist to the Yeatsian self-projection, who overwhelms by sheer volume of speech as well as by command of more varied poetic language. Yet the authority of these better or more long-winded speakers comes into question precisely because of its combative nature. Why fight so hard for dominance, for having your own version of history accepted as the appropriate one, if the position of the antagonist is not already so secure that s/he need not voice it?

---

11. Wallace Martin, *Recent Theories of Narrative* (Ithaca: Cornell University Press, 1986), 149. Hereafter cited in the text as Martin.

Reading Bakhtin, Todorov touches on the voice of the *other* as we internalize it, in the fashion legitimized by Romanticists: "It is a question of the role played by the second voice when we talk to ourselves. In most instances, this second voice is that of a typical representative of the social group to which we belong, and the conflict between the two is that lived by the individual confronting his or her own norm" (Todorov 70). I am not suggesting that Patrick represents such a second voice for Oisin; in fact, that is where the energy of the poem lies, in Oisin's efforts not to internalize Patrick as a norm. However, Yeats throughout his life struggled with a much greater belatedness in relation to Christianity than that of Oisin; despite his protests against it, Christianity remained the evaluative norm of his age, and Yeats's poetry, with all of its phantasmagorical machinery, defines itself in opposition to Patrick's takeover.

The poem about Oisin, not his wanderings, takes place at the moment in Ireland's history when in Yeats's view the scales had just tipped in favor of Christianity, when perhaps there is still the remotest chance of mounting a successful resistance. Both Patrick and Oisin are men decrepit with mythic old age, and Oisin expresses his disgust at not being able to resolve the conflict by physical contest:

> If I were as I once was, the strong hoofs crushing the sand and the
>   shells,
> Coming out of the sea as the dawn comes, a chaunt of love on my
>   lips,
> Not coughing, my head on my knees, and praying, and wroth with
>   the bells,
> I would leave no saint's head on his body from Rachlin to Bera of
>   ships.
>
>   (P 383)

To these conditional threats Patrick does not bother to reply. His intervention in the poem occurs whenever Oisin's narrative breaks out of the mold of fiction and threatens to become, once more, Irish history.

Patrick, in fact, prompts Oisin into song by presenting a version of his adventures and of Oisin himself that the hero is bound to contradict. Apart from the bodily, emotional, and mental decrepitude with which Patrick endows him ("bent, and bald, and blind, / With a heavy heart and a wandering mind"), Oisin has lived a life of delusion that in Patrick's Christian terms has betrayed his soul: "You . . . / Have known three centuries . . . / Of dalliance with a demon thing" (P 355). Patrick recasts the supernatural of Irish legend into the mold of Christian dichotomy, the either/or of holy/unholy. Patrick's description of Oisin makes it clear that what he expects is perhaps not conversion, but unwitting accusation of self from this man whose presence challenges Christian historic interpretation and whose story has entered a rival discourse, that of which "poets sing."

Oisin begins by accepting Patrick's version of him, not without ambiguity, given the floating modifier "Sad to remember, sick with years" that seems to refer to a self that is not named in the stanzaic sentence. However, six lines into the reply, Oisin asserts the primacy of his story on a cosmic, not Christian, plane: "But the tale, though words be lighter than air, / Must live to be old like the wandering moon" (P 355).

The combative nature of this dialogic poem appears most unmistakably in Patrick's interruptions of Oisin and in Oisin's apostrophes and direct replies to Patrick, although the entire narrative defines itself through the opposition of the respective versions of history represented by hero and saint. Patrick is moved to speech not in response to Oisin's direct taunts and challenges to Christian historical interpretation, but by the need to reiterate the victory of his faction over Oisin's and to proclaim Christian triumph. Thus, whenever Oisin laments the loss of his companions, the Fenians he left behind in order to follow Niamh into the supernatural, Patrick intervenes with an admonition that attempts to wipe out the historical memory of Ireland's heroic age. When Oisin speculates, "In what far kingdom do you go, / Ah, Fenians, . . . / Or are you phantoms," Patrick chides, "Boast not, nor mourn with drooping head / Companions long accursd and dead, / And hounds for centuries dust and air" (P 358). As Oisin recalls his deeds on the Isle of Many Fears, he resurrects a paean that implicitly glorifies the heroic age, "We sang the loves and angers without sleep, / And all the exultant labours of the strong," and openly mocks the present: "But now the lying clerics murder song / With barren words and flatteries of the weak" (P 372). That irony turns bitter since Oisin now counts himself among those weak and sees them and himself as defenseless against "the beak / Of ravening Sorrow, or the hand of Wrath" (P 372).

Despite or rather because of Patrick's office—the crozier—the weak are now hopeless. Patrick attempts to silence Oisin with so powerful an image of a wrathful god that he himself weeps, while Oisin chooses to hear not god's "angry mind" but "amid the thunder / The Fenian horses" (P 372–73). This combat in Book Two is replayed in the conclusion of the poem, in which Patrick threatens Oisin with the images of the orthodox hell that burns the Fenians, and Oisin attempts to rewrite a heroic, national version of immortality, in which the Christian hierarchy can be overthrown by determined fighters so that hell will be made "clean as a broom cleans," or at the very least, and last, a version of immortality that glorifies friendship and loyalty among heroes and that casts a final doubt upon Patrick's truth: "I will . . . / dwell in the house of the Fenians, be they in flames or at feast" (P 386).

Were *The Wanderings of Oisin* confined to the mere opposition of Oisin and Patrick, its complexity, its connections with Romanticism, and its position as prefiguration of the later Yeatsian dialogues would be much diminished. Instead, what happens in the combat is that through Patrick's and Oisin's utterances pierce the voice, the presence, and the authority of that *other* which the Romantics strove to encompass without silencing. Despite his dismissal of *Oisin* as true dialogue, Rajan's remarks about the later poetry resemble Bakhtin's concept of alterity and reach back to illuminate Yeats's first major experiment with dialogue. Rajan characterizes Yeats's work as "a poetry in which the energy of rejection is shaped to some degree by what it rejects," and he identifies the dialogical in "Ego Dominus Tuus" as "each position not only defined by reference to the other, but stating itself partially in the other's language" (Rajan 118, 125). Yet already in *Oisin* saint and hero question each other's interpretation of quests, of self, of the world of experience and suffering, and of immortality, whether on the human or cosmic scale, and each utters a truth thoroughly suffused with the other's view. Patrick accepts the reality of Oisin's experience among the immortals and his three-hundred-plus age. He attempts to deconstruct the meaning of that experience as "heathen dreams," demonic delusions that have just about wrecked Oisin's chances for Christian immortality (P 356), but he never dismisses Oisin's account as lies or hallucinations. In fact, he must regard it as supremely authoritative since the events that Oisin narrates necessitate his recantation and life of penance. Even his repeated dismissal of the Fenians as mere mortals subject to nature's law, "For centuries dust and air" (P 358), turns into an acquiescence of their power over the living, a power Patrick would like to erase, as he incorporates their beings into his vision of immortality: "the demons whip them with wires on the burning stones of wide Hell / . . . Between them a gateway of brass, and the howl of the angels who fell" (P 385). The energy of this hell matches the energy of Oisin's description of his companions as "exultant" (P 385), and "equal to good or grievous chance" (P 365), so that the Fenians in hell prove indeed to be not Patrick's cowed sinners but Oisin's Irish heroes, who need to be kept back from returning to Ireland and to history by an army of demons and a heavy gate.

In a parallel movement, Oisin organizes his supernatural experience along the Christian paradigm of the journey, only in reverse, from paradise through purgatory to hell. From within each recollection he addresses Patrick with visions of immortal satisfactions, relivings, and paralysis unavailable to Patrick's blessed or damned but defined from within that ruling paradigm. From the passionate "O Patrick, by your brazen bell, / There was no limb of mine but fell / Into a desperate gulph of love" to the understated "O Patrick! For a hundred years / The gentle Niamh was my wife" (P 357, 364–65), Oisin projects for the saint a paradise of unexhausted sensual happiness deriving from the antithesis between the eternally youthful and the "slaves of God," the dwellers in a cosmos ruled by God's law (P 365). When Patrick urges him into story-telling again, Oisin reflects, "these [fasting and prayer] were ancient Oisin's fate / Loosed long ago from Heaven's gate, / For his last days to lie in wait" (P 365). The heaven of youth and love is threatened not by a pagan apocalypse when "the stars drop down from the sky" but by Oisin's own desire for mortality's risk, "good or grievous chance" (P 366, 365).

Oisin's purgatory, his one-hundred-year encounter with the protean demon whom he defeats and fights again, resembles the obsessive reliving of Dante's purgatorial characters and the obsessive retellings of other Romantic Quests. Yet Oisin exults in "the labours of the strong," which in the Island of Victories play the same role as pleasure in the Island of Dancing and seem inexhaustible: "an endless feast, an endless war" (P 372–73). Like the protean demon, his desire for mortality overtakes him, and he moves on to the supernatural hell characterized not by Christian demonology but by Tennysonian paralysis. From within that narrative of sleep Oisin calls to Patrick, "the man of the many white croziers," in order to represent to him a different kind of hell, a hell of the forget-fulness of earthly things, "How the fetlock drip blood in the battle," "That the spear-shaft is made out of ashwood, the shield out of osier and hide" (P 378–79). Oisin's tale of his travels through immortality is filled with mortal longings for a dynamism that Christian dogma denies more emphatically than the supernature of old Ireland. If this easy hell, this unremorseful purgatory, and sensuous paradise have no power to appease Oisin, how can their Christian counterparts fulfill his desire?

Yet, just as Patrick's utterance voices Oisin's legendary authority, so Oisin's choice as he utters it at the end represents, in its defiance, an acceptance of historiographic defeat; henceforth his immortal life with the Fenians, "be they in flames or at feast," will be known as a descent into the Christian hell and will no longer contain that element of mortal chance for the sake of which he abandoned Niamh and her worlds (P 386). Oisin's opting for what amounts to an "anywhere out of this world," "Enfer ou ciel, qu'importe" as Baudelaire would have it,[12] rises out of the recognition that his mortal condition, the chance he took on returning, gives him no power to challenge the newly established Christian hegemony. What Oisin has found on earth is not what he desired, not the mortal imperfections of his Fenian companions, which he would have gladly accepted ("Ah, sweet to me now were even bald Conan's slanderous tongue!" P 380), but the true existential hell of extravagant old age: "A creeping old man, full of sleep, with the spittle on his beard never dry" (P 385). His anachronism in an Ireland that has turned Christian, a development for Yeats always synonymous with creative weakness and physical degeneracy, proves to be a greater weight to bear than his bodily decay. Oisin notices the problem of being trapped in a paltry age as soon as he lands, but he does not yet know how to account for it:

. . . a small and a feeble populace stooping with mattock and spade,

Or weeding or ploughing with faces a-shining with much-toil wet;
While in this place and that place, with bodies unglorious, their
      chieftains stood,
Awaiting in patience the straw-death, croziered one, caught in your
      net. . . .

(P 383)

Oisin realizes that old Ireland is dead and gone when he hears another old man (there seem to be no other representatives of Christian Ireland on hand in the poem) say, "the gods a long time are dead" (P 384).

In perhaps the most brilliant articulation of the conflict over history captured in *The Wanderings of Oisin,* Yeats has Oisin learn through expe-

---

12. Charles Baudelaire, *Oeuvres Completes,* ed. Claude Pichois (Paris: Bibliothèque de la Pléïade, 1975), 1:134.

rience a lesson to which he himself ought to have returned in his more obnoxious moments of historiographic combat. Oisin attempts to intervene in history, to remedy the present by means of physical force, only to be defeated by the very weakness he despises. From his "gem-studded saddle" on the wondrous horse, he watches the men of Christian Ireland stagger and fall under the burden of a sand-filled sack, and "With a sob for men waxing so weakly, a sob for the Fenians' old strength," he leans over and flings the sack "five yards with my hand" (P 384). But the touch of earthly things, the contamination of an age that has established another history, reduces him to an unwilling, caught participant who partakes of the impotence of mortal achievement within a Christian theogony.

Yeats replayed the combat between age and individual being throughout his career, whether by openly designating his personae as the Self or by adopting the numerous masks of his poems and plays. The open-endedness of *The Wanderings of Oisin,* the interpenetrating utterances of its dialogic form, the recognition that the age, however recast by creative spirits as puny and contemptible, takes its toll, not merely prefigure but inform Yeats's lifelong, though not constant, refusal of the either/or of any dogma, including his own. In his most objectionable moments Yeats trembled in pleased anticipation at the violent inscription of a new heroic age on the pale pages of what he saw as the waning Christian era. But, as he had envisioned in his very early poetry, the heroes who are also writers and singers keep a divided, thus a weaker but a subtler, strength than that needed for violent action. In immortal paradise, Oisin's wanderings need no voicing, and he and his instrument are silenced, as they would be in Christian afterlife. Only in the hell of existence in which the self is at odds with its age does the story acquire the power that moves the saint to cry out "Be still" (P 372) and to threaten the revolutionary artist with all the resources of his orthodox imagination.

A Yeats Bibliography for 1986–87

K. P. S. JOCHUM

Most items in this bibliography were published in 1986 and 1987; there are some from 1981–85. The appendix lists additions to previous entries. As usual, items marked ° could not be inspected personally; J refers to my 1978 bibliography; and 81-, 82-, etc. identify entries in previous compilations in this annual. I do not include items that I cannot read, unless they have a summary in English. I therefore omit two items listed in the 1985 MLA Bibliography and published in a periodical entitled *Foreign Literature Studies,* because they turned out to be, not in English, but entirely in Chinese. Thank you this time to Brian Arkins, George Bornstein, Alan M. Cohn, Karin Dolling, Eleonore Engelhardt, Richard J. Finneran, John Kelly, Gerd Schmidt, Patrick Hugh Sheerin, Dee Ella Spears of the Modern Language Association, Hugh Witemeyer, the Yeats Society of Japan, and again to Susanne Heindel.

86-1. *The Abbey Reads.* Dublin: National Theatre Society / Paycock Publications, 1986.

A collection of cassette recordings. The following include selections from Yeats, read by various readers: ABB 004, four poems; ABB 006, one poem; ABB 007, 22 poems; ABB 012, two poems.

86-2. ABSE, DANNIE, and JOAN ABSE, eds.: *Voices in the Gallery: Poems and Pictures Chosen by Dannie & Joan Abse.* London: Tate Gallery, 1986. 212 pp.

Prints "The Municipal Gallery Revisited" together with the Mancini portrait of Lady Gregory and "Leda and the Swan" together with the British Museum marble relief, 139–41, 186–87, 204.

86-3. *Actas do II Congresso internacional de estudos Pessoanos (Nashville, 31 de Março / 2 de Abril, 1983).* Oporto: Centro de Estudos Pessoanos, 1985. 687 pp.

Sol Biderman: "Arcane Imagery in Yeats and Fernando Pessoa," 79–90; special reference to Rosicrucianism and the image of Mount Abiegnos.

175

86-4. ALBRIGHT, DANIEL: "Pound, Yeats, and the Noh Theater," *Iowa Review*, 15:2 (Spring–Summer 1985), 34–50.

Includes a discussion of Pound's references to Yeats in his *Cantos*.

86-5. ALBU, RODICA: "The Poetry of Yeats and Blaga: Suggestions for a Comparative Analysis," *Synthesis*, 12 (1985), 15–22.

86-6. ———: "Reading a Poem by Yeats," *Analele stiintifice ale Universității "Al. I. Cuza" din Iasi. Sectiuna III e: Lingvistică*, 31 (1985), 43–45.

"The Mother of God."

86-7. ALDERSON SMITH, PETER: "Nugent the Magician," *Notes and Queries*, os 227 / ns 29:4 (August 1982), 352.

Request for the source of a story which in turn is the source of "Red Hanrahan."

86-8. ———: *W. B. Yeats and the Tribes of Danu: Three Views of Ireland's Fairies*. Gerrards Cross: Colin Smythe, / Totowa, N.J.: Barnes & Noble, 1987. 350 pp. (Irish Literary Studies, 27.)

Incorporates "'Grown to Heaven like a Tree': The Scenery of *The Countess Cathleen*," *Éire-Ireland*, 14:3 (Fall 1979), 65–82; and 82–174. Discusses the early mythological cycles, the collections of Irish fairy tales and folklore, and fairy lore in Yeats's early works, especially *The Countess Cathleen, The Land of Heart's Desire, The Shadowy Waters, Stories of Red Hanrahan*, and the poems in *The Wind among the Reeds*.

86-9. ANON.: "Seventy-Five Years On," *TLS*, 26 December 1986, 1449.

An extract from J4468; the author is not identified.

86-10. ĀRĀR: *Cimpalisam*. Tirupputtur: Arivarankam, 1982. 232 pp.

In Tamil. On p. 2 the book's title is given as *Symbolism: An Introduction to the Critical Idiom. With a Comparative Study of Symbolism in Yeats and Bharati*.

86-11. ARKINS, BRIAN: "Yeats's Version of Colonus' Praise," *Classical and Modern Literature*, 7:1 (Fall 1986), 39–42.

The poem "Colonus' Praise" radically alters the meaning of the original Sophoclean choral ode.

86-12. ———: "Yeats and Bishop Xenaias," *Notes and Queries*, os 232 / ns 34:1 (March 1987), 56–57.

The identity of this bishop, referred to in section IV of "Dove or Swan" in *A Vision*.

86-13. ARONSON, ALEX: "Yeats and Balzac," *Visvabharati Quarterly*, 47:1&2 (May–October 1981), 107–23.

86-14. ASOCIACIÓN ESPAÑOLA DE ESTUDIOS ANGLO-NORTEAMERICANOS: *Homenaje a Esteban Pujals Fontrodona*. Oviedo: Servicio de Publicaciones, Universidad de Oviedo, 1981. Unpaged.

Ramón Sainero Sánchez: "Ibsen y el movimiento literario irlandés," no. 20; contains some notes on Yeats.

86-15. AYTON, WILLIAM ALEXANDER: *The Alchemist of the Golden Dawn: The Letters of the Revd W. A. Ayton to F. L. Gardner and Others 1886–1905*. Edited with an introduction by Ellic Howe. Wellingborough: Aquarian Press, 1985. 112 pp.

See index for a few references to Yeats.

86-16. BALLIET, CONRAD A.: "Yeats Material Needed," *Library Journal*, 111:10 (1 June 1986), 14.

Material needed for a projected guide to the manuscripts.

86-17. BARKER, VARA SUE TAMMINGA: "W. B. Yeats: Poetry as Meditation," °Ph.D. thesis, University of Texas at Austin, 1984. 318 pp. (*DAI*, 47:6 [Dec. 1986], 2165A).

86-18. BARNES, GEORGE: "George Barnes's 'W. B. Yeats and Broadcasting' 1940." Introductory note by Jeremy Silver, *Yeats Annual*, 5 (1987), 189–94.

86-19. BAROLSKY, PAUL: *Walter Pater's Renaissance*. University Park: Pennsylvania State University Press, 1987. xiv, 214 pp.

See index for a few notes on Yeats and Pater.

86-20. BARON, MICHAEL: "Yeats, Wordsworth and the Communal Sense: The Case of 'If I Were Four-and-Twenty,'" *Yeats Annual*, 5 (1987), 62–82.

The relevance of the Wordsworth references to Yeats's own writings.

86-21. BARRY, SEBASTIAN, ed.: *The Inherited Boundaries: Younger Poets of the Republic of Ireland*. Edited with an introduction by Sebastian Barry. Mountrath, Portlaoise: Dolmen Press, 1986. 192 pp.

"Introduction," 13–29; contains some references to Yeats.

86-22. BAWER, BRUCE: *The Middle Generation: The Lives and Poetry of Delmore Schwartz, Randall Jarrell, John Berryman, and Robert Lowell*. Hamden, Conn.: Archon Books, 1986. ix, 216 pp.

"Berryman and the Influence of Yeats," 90–103; see index for some other Yeats references.

86-23. BEACHAM, WALTON, ed.: *Research Guide to Biography and Criticism*. Washington, D.C.: Research Publishing, 1985. 2 vols.

See 2:1315–19; a short chronology and bibliography and overviews

178 K. P. S. Jochum

of biographical, autobiographical, and critical sources, compiled by
Joseph M. Hassett.
86-24. BECKSON, KARL: *Arthur Symons: A Life*. Oxford: Clarendon
Press, 1987. xi, 402 pp.
Numerous references to Yeats (see index), including quotations
from letters from and to Yeats.
86-25. BEJA, MORRIS, PHILLIP HERRING, MAURICE HAR-
MON, and DAVID NORRIS, eds.: *James Joyce: The Centennial Sym-
posium*. Urbana: University of Illinois Press, 1986. xvii, 234 pp.
Ellen Carol Jones, ed.: "Yeats and Joyce," 21–30; transcription of a
panel discussion between A. Walton Litz, Giorgio Melchiori (who
comments on the tower image of both writers), and Richard
Ellmann.
86-26. BELL, IAN F. A.: "Oblique Contexts in Yeats: The Homer of
'The Nineteenth Century and After,'" *Philological Quarterly*, 65:3 (Sum-
mer 1986), 335–44.
The Homeric imagery of this poem was suggested by Pound's
"Hugh Selwyn Mauberley."
86-27. BENCE-JONES, MARK: *Twilight of the Ascendancy*. London:
Constable, 1987. xvii, 327 pp.
See index for some references to Yeats as an Ascendancy figure.
86-28. BERMAN, DAVID, ed.: *George Berkeley: Essays and Replies*.
Blackrock, Co. Dublin: Irish Academic Press, 1986. i, 171 pp.
D. Berman: "George Berkeley: Pictures by Goldsmith, Yeats and
Luce," 9–23; reprint of 85-24.
86-29. BERTHA, CSILLA: "The Natural and the Supernatural in the
Plays of W. B. Yeats," *Studies in English and American*, 6 (1986), 14–22.
86-30. BERTHOFF, WARNER: *Literature and the Continuances of Virtue*.
Princeton: Princeton University Press, 1986. xi, 294 pp.
"The Analogies of Lyric: Shelley, Yeats, Frank O'Hara," 223–73.
86-31. BERTIN, MICHAEL, ed.: *The Play and Its Critic: Essays for Eric
Bentley*. Lanham, Md.: University Press of America, 1986. xxvii, 349 pp.
Herbert Blau: "The Myth of Ritual in the Marketplace of Signs,"
305–39; contains some remarks on Yeats.
86-32. BILLIGHEIMER, RACHEL V.: "The Dance as Vision in Blake
and Yeats," *Unisa English Studies*, 24:2 (September 1986), 11–16.
86-33. ———: "The Female in Blake and Yeats," *CEA Critic*, 48:4/49:1
(Summer–Fall 1986), 137–44.

Mainly on *The King of the Great Clock Tower* and *A Full Moon in March*.

86-34. ———: "Self and Soul in W. B. Yeats," *Éire-Ireland*, 21:4 (Winter 1986), 52–65.

86-35. BLACKMUR, RICHARD PALMER: *Selected Essays*. Edited and with an introduction by Denis Donoghue. New York: Ecco Press, 1986. v, 372 pp.

"The Later Poetry of W. B. Yeats," 145–69; reprint of J2460.

86-36. BLOCK, ED: "Walter Pater, Arthur Symons, W. B. Yeats, and the Fortunes of the Literary Portrait," *Studies in English Literature 1500–1900*, 26:4 (Autumn 1986), 759–76.

Pater's portrait essays provided structural models for both Symons and Yeats. Discusses "The Happiest of the Poets" and "Discoveries" as indebted to Pater's deductive principle.

86-37. BLOOM, HAROLD, ed.: *James Merrill*. New York: Chelsea House, 1985. viii, 214 pp. (Modern Critical Views.)

Leslie Brisman: "Merrill's Yeats," 189–98. Allusions to Yeats (particularly to "Lapis Lazuli") in Merrill's poetry. Further short references to Yeats in some of the other contributions.

86-38. ———, ed.: *Twentieth-Century British Literature*. New York: Chelsea House, 1985–87. 5 vols.

"W. B. Yeats," 5:3153–3212; short introduction and 12 extracts from previously published criticism.

86-39. ———, ed.: *William Butler Yeats*. New York: Chelsea House, 1986. viii, 232 pp. (Modern Critical Views.)

"This book gathers together what in its editor's judgment is the most useful criticism yet published on the writings of William Butler Yeats" (vii). Bloom's introduction is a reprint of "Yeats, Gnosticism, and the Sacred Void" from *Poetry and Repression* (1976); it is followed by 11 reprints of previously published articles or parts of books, all of them shorn of their footnotes, and an altogether insufficient bibliography.

86-40. BÖHM, RUDOLF, and HENNING WODE, eds.: *Anglistentag 1986 Kiel: Vorträge*. Giessen: Hoffmann, 1987. 535 pp. (Tagungsberichte des Anglistentags Verbands deutscher Anglisten, 8.)

Axel Goodbody: "Wilhelm Lehmann and English Literature," 63–86; on Lehmann's preoccupation with Yeats.

86-41. BORGES, JORGE-LUIS: *Textos cautivos: Ensayos y reseñas en "El hogar."* Edited by Enrique Sacerio-Garí and Emir Rodrígues Monegal. Barcelona: Tusquets Editores, 1986. 345 pp. (Marginales, 92.)

See pp. 135–36 for a short review of the *Oxford Book of Modern Verse,* reprinted from *El hogar* [Buenos Aires], 28 May 1937.

86-42. BRAMANN, JORN K.: *Wittgenstein's Tractatus and the Modern Arts.* Rochester, N.Y.: Adler, 1985. xv, 204 pp.

"Yeats: 'An Irish Airman Foresees His Death,' " 127–29. The connection between this poem and Wittgenstein's *Tractatus* is not explained.

86-43. BRATER, ENOCH, ed.: *Beckett at 80 / Beckett in Context.* New York: Oxford University Press, 1986. x, 238 pp.

Katharine Worth: "Beckett's Auditors: *Not I* to *Ohio Impromptu,*" 168–92; notes Yeats's influence.

86-44. BRENNAN, GENEVIEVE: " 'The Binding of the Hair' and Yeats's Reading of Eugene O'Curry," *Yeats Annual,* 5 (1987), 214–23.

Discusses the source of the story in O'Curry's *On the Manners and Customs of the Ancient Irish* and the singing head motif.

86-45. *British Writers.* Edited under the auspices of the British Council. General editor Ian Scott-Kilvert. Volume VI: Thomas Hardy to Wilfred Owen. New York: Scribner's, 1983. xxxv, 460 pp.

G. S. Fraser: "William Butler Yeats (1865–1939)," 207–34; a revised version of J1085.

86-46. BROOKER, JEWEL SPEARS: " 'The Second Coming' and 'The Waste Land': Capstones of the Western Civilization Course," *College Literature,* 13:3 (Autumn 1986), 240–53.

86-47. BROOKS, CLEANTH: *The Language of the American South.* Athens: University of Georgia Press, 1986. xi, 58 pp. (Mercer University Lamar Memorial Lectures, 28.)

Concludes with a note on Yeats's view of the oral tradition, pp. 53–54.

86-48. BRUNNER, LARRY: *Tragic Victory: The Doctrine of Subjective Salvation in the Poetry of W. B. Yeats.* Troy, N.Y.: Whitston, 1987. viii, 184 pp.

Based on "The Doctrine of Subjective Salvation in the Poetry of W. B. Yeats," Ph.D. thesis, Duke University, 1973. vii, 288 pp. (*DAI,* 34:11 [May 1974], 7222A). "The aim of this study is to investigate the nature of the Yeatsian answer to tragic despair, to analyse its appearance in his poetry, to determine the reasons for its failure and consequent rejection by the poet, and to recognize possible alternatives available to him after this rejection" (p. 3). Does not consider any Yeats criticism published after 1971.

86-49. BURZYŃSKA, JOANNA: "Evocation of the Creative Consciousness: W. B. Yeats's *Purgatory*," *Uniwersytet Gdański. Zeszyty Naukowe Wydziału Humanisticznego. Filologia Angielska*, 4 (1984), 95–109.

86-50. BYARS, JOHN A.: "W. B. Yeats and *Wise Blood*," *Flannery O'Connor Bulletin*, 14 (1985), 88–93.

Two episodes in Flannery O'Connor's novel seem to be indebted to "The Last Gleeman" in *The Celtic Twilight*.

86-51. CAVE, LAWRENCE HAROLD: "Purgatory: A Chamber Opera in One Act after Yeats," °Ph.D. thesis, Harvard University, 1986. 135 pp. (*DAI*, 47:7 [January 1987], 2359A).

86-52. CAVE, RODERICK. *The Private Press*. Second edition, revised and enlarged. New York: Bowker, 1983. xvi, 389 pp.

Revised version of J7461; see pp. 183–84.

86-53. CHADWICK, JOSEPH: "Family Reunion as National Allegory in Yeats's *Cathleen ni Houlihan* and *The Dreaming of the Bones*," *Twentieth Century Literature*, 32:2 (Summer 1986), 155–68.

86-54. CLARK, DAVID R., and ROSALIND E. CLARK: "Sailing from Avalon: Yeats's First Play, *Vivien and Time*," *Yeats*, 5 (1987), 1–86.

Yeats's earliest poetic work, an early version of *Time and the Witch Vivien*. The Clarks print the MS. text and discuss the play's place in Yeats's poetic development as well as his use of the Arthurian tradition and of pictorial sources.

86-55. CLAUSEN, CHRISTOPHER: *The Moral Imagination: Essays on Literature and Ethics*. Iowa City: University of Iowa Press, 1986. xii, 195 pp.

"Padraic Pearse: The Revolutionary as Artist," 125–38; contains some remarks on Yeats.

86-56. °CNUDDE-KNOWLAND, A.: "Maurice Maeterlinck and English and Anglo-Irish Literature: A Study of Parallels and Influences," D. Phil. thesis, Oxford University, 1984.

86-57. COBB, ANN VALENTINE: "Seamus Heaney: Poet in a Destitute Time," °Ph.D. thesis, Tufts University, 1986. 107 pp. (*DAI*, 47:10 [April 1987], 3761A).

Discusses the influence of Yeats, according to abstract.

86-58. CORCORAN, NEIL: *Seamus Heaney*. London: Faber & Faber, 1986. 192 pp.

See index for several references to Yeats.

86-59. COTHRAN, DIANNE ALLBRITTON: "Myth and Eudora Welty's Mississippi: An Analysis of *The Golden Apples*," °Ph.D. thesis, Florida State University, 1982. 134 pp. (*DAI*, 46:1 [July 1985], 151A). Discusses the influence of Yeats.

86-60. CROFT, BARBARA LEA: *"Stylistic Arrangements": A Study of William Butler Yeats's "A Vision."* Lewisburg, Pa.: Bucknell University Press, 1987. 196 pp.

Based on "'Stylistic Arrangements': A Comparative Study of the Two Versions of W. B. Yeats's *A Vision*," Ph.D. thesis, University of Toronto, 1977. x, 269 pp. (*DAI*, 39:3 [September 1978], 1545A–46A). Includes discussions of the early occult writings, of the stories contained in *A Vision*, and of its prose style, also a comparison of the two versions.

86-61. D'ARCH SMITH, TIMOTHY: *The Books of the Beast* [. . .]. [Wellingborough?]: Crucible, 1987. 128 pp.

"'Pregnant with Mandrakes': Florence Farr," 98–103; originally published as a foreword to a reprint of her *Egyptian Magic*. Wellingborough: Aquarian Press, 1982. xvii, 85 pp. (pp. ix–xv). Contains some references to Yeats.

86-62. DARUWALA, MANECK HOMI: "Good Intentions: The Romantic Aesthetics of Oscar Wilde's Criticism," *Victorians Institute Journal*, 12 (1984), 105–32.

Discusses Wilde's influence on Yeats's poetry and criticism.

86-63. DAVIE, DONALD: "Attending to Landor," *Ironwood*, 12:2 (Fall 1984), 103–11.

On Yeats and Landor; comments on "Men Improve with the Years" and "Easter 1916."

86-64. DEANE, SEAMUS: *Irish Writers 1886–1986*. Dublin: Eason, 1986. [24 pp.] (Irish Heritage Series, 57.)

86-65. DE MAURIAC, GWENN, comp.: "Dissertation Abstracts, 1986," *Yeats*, 5 (1987), 199–208.

The abstracts of Gramm (85-110), Ponnuswamy (85-239), Opitz (85-226), Rhee (85-254), Fleming (85-88), Giannotti (85-100), Earle (85-78), Goggin (86-94), Barker (86-17), and Ravindran (86-215).

86-66. DE MAURO, LISA: "The Rugged, Quicksilver Beauty of Yeats's Sligo," *New York Times*, 4 October 1981, section 10, pp. XXI, 15.

86-67. DOBSON, ROGER: "Yeats and the Golden Dawn," *Antiquarian Book Monthly Review*, 14:4 (April 1987), 136–39.

86-68. DODD, PHILIP, ed.: *Modern Selves: Essays on Modern British and American Autobiography*. London: Cass, 1986. vii, 192 pp.

Shirley Neuman: "Autobiography, Epistemology and the Irish Tradition: The Example of Denis Johnston," 118–38; contains some references to Yeats.

86-69. DONOGHUE, DENIS: *We Irish: Essays on Irish Literature and Society*. New York: Knopf, 1986. ix, 276 pp.

On Yeats see especially: "We Irish," 3–18.

"Romantic Ireland," 21–33; first published in Jeffares: *Yeats, Sligo, and Ireland* (1980).

"Yeats: The Question of Symbolism," 34–51; from Ronsley: *Myth and Reality* (1977).

"Yeats, Ancestral Houses, and Anglo-Ireland," 52–66; see 86–103.

"On *The Winding Stair*," 67–88; from J1078.

"Maud Gonne," 218–25.

Reviews:

Patrick Keane: "A Balanced Stance," *Salmagundi*, 73 (Winter 1987), 177–86.

David Krause: "On Irish Poetics and Politics," *Irish Literary Supplement*, 6:1 (Spring 1987), 5–6.

Edna Longley: "Hauteur, Hauteur," *TLS*, 5 June 1987, 612.

86-70. DOWLING, LINDA C.: *Language and Decadence in the Victorian Fin de Siècle*. Princeton: Princeton University Press, 1986. xvi, 295 pp.

"Yeats and the Book of the People," 244–83, and passim (see index); on Yeats's changing attitude and unending adherence to "Victorian literary Decadence," particularly in the stories of *The Secret Rose*.

86-71. EAGLETON, TERRY: "The Ballad of Willie Yeats," *Irish Literary Supplement*, 6:1 (Spring 1987), 3.

Extract from a nine-verse affair, printed under the heading "Poets at Sligo." The same issue contains a pastiche of Yeats phrases in an untitled poem, presented by Ruth H. Bauerle (p. 24).

86-72. EGAN, DESMOND: *Collected Poems*. Orono, Maine: National Poetry Foundation, 1983. 224 pp.

See "In Francis Ledwidge's Cottage," 210–12, and "Non Symbolist," 216–17, where Egan declares his aversion to Yeats.

86-73. ELLMANN, RICHARD: *Wilde, Yeats, Joyce, and Beckett: Four Dubliners*. London: Hamilton, 1987. xii, 106 pp.

"W. B. Yeats's Second Puberty," 27–51; "Samuel Beckett: Nay-

man of Noland," 79–104; revised versions of 85–81 and 85–82.
Reviews:
Francis Doherty: "Dubliners All," *PN Review*, 58 (14:2) (1987), 75–76.
Declan Kiberd: "Ellmann and the Big Four," *Irish Times*, 13 June 1987, Weekend, 5.
Claude Rawson: "A Question of Potency," *TLS*, 24 July 1987, 783–85.

86-74. ———: *Oscar Wilde.* London: Hamilton, 1987. xiv, 632 pp.
Numerous references to Yeats (see index).

86-75. ERZGRÄBER, WILLI, and PAUL GOETSCH, eds.: *Mündliches Erzählen im Alltag, fingiertes mündliches Erzählen in der Literatur.* Tübingen: Narr, 1987. 206 pp. (ScriptOralia, 1.)
K. P. S. Jochum: "W. B. Yeats und die mündliche irische Überlieferung," 136–53; discusses Yeats's preoccupation with the oral Irish tradition in theory and practice, especially in *The Celtic Twilight.*

86-76. ESPMARK, KJELL: *Det litterära Nobelpriset: Principer och värderingar bakom besluten.* Stockholm: Norstedts, 1986. 202 pp.
See pp. 60–64 and passim.

86-77. FALDET, DAVID STEVEN: "Visual Art and the Poetics of Rossetti, Morris, and Yeats," °Ph.D. thesis, University of Iowa, 1986. 327 pp. (*DAI*, 47:9 [March 1987], 3433A).

86-78. FALLETTI, CLELIA: "Yeats e l'attore di cultura poetica," *Quaderni di teatro*, 4:16 (May 1982), 92–101.
Yeats's dramatic theories and his ideas on actors and acting.

86-79. FINNERAN, RICHARD J.: "The Manuscript of W. B. Yeats's 'Reprisals,'" *Text: Transactions of the Society for Textual Scholarship*, 2 (1985), 269–77.
The version usually accepted as definitive is only a working draft. The best text is the original typescript in the National Library of Ireland (MS. 13,583). The various texts (here reprinted) "help us to understand the complex and ambivalent attitudes which Yeats had towards Robert Gregory" (p. 273).

86-80. ———, ed.: *Critical Essays on W. B. Yeats.* Boston: Hall, 1986. viii, 258 pp.
The selection of the essays was made by the critics themselves; they were asked "to choose their own most appropriate essays for inclu-

sion in this volume" (p. v). Contains "Introduction," 1–8 (a short survey of Yeats criticism), and 14 previously printed pieces.

86-81. FITZGIBBON, MAJORIE: Sculpture of Yeats (photograph), *Irish Literary Supplement*, 6:1 (Spring 1987), 14.

86-82. FLETCHER, IAN: *W. B. Yeats and His Contemporaries*. Brighton: Harvester Press, 1987. x, 350 pp.

Revised and expanded versions of previous publications. On Yeats see especially: "Bedford Park: Aesthete's Elysium?" 43–82 (J1350); "Rhythm and Pattern in Yeats's *Autobiographies*," 127–52 (J1078); "Yeats's Quest for Self-Transparency," 153–65 (J5523b); "Poet and Designer: W. B. Yeats and Althea Gyles," 166–96 (J651); "Yeats and Lissadell," 197–219 (J1112); "Yeats's 'Leda and the Swan' as Iconic Poem," 220–51 (82–65); "Symons, Yeats and the Demonic Dance," 252–66 (J2686).

86-83. FOSTER, JOHN WILSON: *Fictions of the Irish Literary Revival: A Changeling Art*. Syracuse: Syracuse University Press / Dublin: Gill & Macmillan, 1987. xxi, 409 pp. (Irish Studies.)

See especially "The Path of the Chameleon: The Symbolist Strategy—W. B. Yeats," 73–93; "Visions and Vanities: Yeats, Lady Gregory, and Folklore," 203–18; "The Mount of Transfiguration: The Writer as Fabulist—W. B. Yeats, James Stephens," 236–72.

86-84. FOX, F. S.: "Nationalism in the Lives and Works of W. B. Yeats and Alexander Blok: A Comparative Study," °Ph.D. thesis, University of Manchester, 1982. (Abstract in *Index to Theses*, 35:1 [1986], 41).

86-85. FOX, PETER, ed.: *Treasures of the Library: Trinity College Dublin*. Dublin: Royal Irish Academy for the Library of Trinity College Dublin, 1986. xiii, 258 pp.

Nicholas Grene: "Modern Irish Literary Manuscripts," 230–38; contains a note on the Yeats MSS.

86-86. FRANK, ELIZABETH: *Louise Bogan: A Portrait*. New York: Columbia University Press, 1986, xvi, 462 pp.

See index for some notes on Yeats's influence on Louise Bogan's poetry.

86-87. FRAZIER, ADRIAN: "The Making of Meaning: Yeats and *The Countess Cathleen*," *Sewanee Review*, 95:3 (Summer 1987), 451–69.

The play, although insignificant as a piece of drama, is a "fundamentally significant document in the coming to consciousness of the Irish nation."

86-88. GALLATIN, MICHAEL: *Shakespearean Alchemy: Theme and Variations in Literary Criticism*. Ann Arbor: Q.E.D. Press, 1985. xvii, 83 pp.

"Ode to Tragic Joy," 53–59; on "Lapis Lazuli" and "Sailing to Byzantium."

86-89. GARRATT, ROBERT F.: *Modern Irish Poetry: Tradition and Continuity from Yeats to Heaney*. Berkeley: University of California Press, 1986. xii, 322 pp.

"Tradition and Isolation: W. B. Yeats," 16–43, and passim (see index). On Yeats's place in Anglo-Irish poetry and his influence on other writers, particularly Austin Clarke, Brian Coffey, Padraic Fallon, Seamus Heaney, F. R. Higgins, Patrick Kavanagh, Thomas Kinsella, and John Montague.

86-90. GARRETT, JOHN: *British Poetry since the Sixteenth Century: A Students' Guide*. London: Macmillan, 1986. viii, 248 pp.

"The Last Romantic: W. B. Yeats," 200–12; particularly on "The Lake Isle of Innisfree" and "Sailing to Byzantium."

86-91. GILBERT, R. A.: "Magical Manuscripts: An Introduction to the Archives of the Hermetic Order of the Golden Dawn," *Yeats Annual, 5* (1987), 163–77.

Descriptions of the various collections and of the material referring to or written by Yeats; reprints of some of the material, including letters by Yeats.

86-92. GLASSIE, HENRY, ed.: *Irish Folktales*. New York: Pantheon, 1985. xvii, 357 pp.

The introduction, 3–29, includes a discussion of Yeats's interest in Irish folktales. Further references to Yeats in the notes, 337–53.

86-93. GLENDINNING, VICTORIA: *Vita: The Life of V. Sackville-West*. London: Weidenfeld & Nicolson, 1983. xviii, 430 pp.

See pp. 80, 220, 278–79, 299 for a few Yeats references.

86-94. GOGGIN, EDWARD WILLIAM: "Blest: Cohesion and Ironic Deflation in Six Short Poem Sequences of W. B. Yeats," °Ph.D. thesis, Fordham University, 1985. 305 pp. (*DAI*, 47:3 [September 1986], 910A).

The sequences are "Upon a Dying Lady," "A Man Young and Old," "Meditations in Time of Civil War," "A Woman Young and Old," "Supernatural Songs," and "The Three Bushes."

86-95. GOLDSTEIN, LAURENCE: *The Flying Machine and Modern Literature*. London: Macmillan, 1986. xv, 253 pp.

On the Robert Gregory poems, pp. 89–93.

86-96. GOOD, MAEVE: *W. B. Yeats and the Creation of a Tragic Universe*. London: Macmillan, 1987. ix, 176 pp.

Based on 84-64. Contains chapters on Cuchulain as an archetypal hero, three dance plays (*At the Hawk's Well, The Only Jealousy of Emer,* and *The Dreaming of the Bones*), *A Vision,* four later plays (*Calvary, The Resurrection, The Words upon the Window-Pane, Purgatory*), and *The Death of Cuchulain.*

86-97. GORDON, ANDREW: "Shakespeare's *The Tempest* and Yeats's 'Sailing to Bysantium [sic]' in *Seize the Day,*" *Saul Bellow Journal,* 4:1 (Fall–Winter 1985), 45–51.

86-98. GOULD, WARWICK: "The 'Myth [in] . . . Reply to a Myth': Yeats, Balzac, and Joachim of Fiore," *Yeats Annual,* 5 (1987), 238–51.

Explanations of a textual puzzle in Yeats's introduction to *The Resurrection* with reference to "The Adoration of the Magi," "The Tables of the Law," "Rosa Alchemica," and Yeats's cyclical view of history.

86-99. ———: " 'What Is the Explanation of It All?': Yeats's 'Little Poem about Nothing,' " *Yeats Annual,* 5 (1987), 212–13.

A poem written by Yeats for Edith Shackleton Heald in 1938.

86-100. ———: "A Recent Yeats Bibliography, 1984–85," *Yeats Annual,* 5 (1979), 320–40.

86-101. GRIFFIN, JON NELSON: "Profane Perfection: Yeats' *Last Poems,*" °Ph.D. thesis, University of Rochester, 1986. 171 pp. (*DAI,* 47:4 [October 1986], 1318A).

86-102. GRIFFIN, WILLIAM: *Clive Staples Lewis: A Dramatic Life.* San Francisco: Harper & Row, 1986. xxv, 507 pp.

See pp. 24–25 for a short Yeats reminiscence.

86-103. GUINNESS, DESMOND, and DENIS DONOGHUE: *Ascendancy Ireland.* Papers read at a Clark Library Seminar, 28 September 1985. Los Angeles: William Andrews Clark Memorial Library, University of California, 1986. ix, 54 pp.

Denis Donoghue: "Yeats, Ancestral Houses, and Anglo-Ireland," 31–52; see also 86–69.

86-104. HAGAN, EDWARD A.: *"High Nonsensical Words": A Study of the Works of Standish James O'Grady.* Troy, N.Y.: Whitston, 1986. viii, 229 pp.

See index for references to Yeats.

188 K. P. S. Jochum

86-105. HARBISON, JOHN: *Full Moon in March*. Opera in one act, libretto adapted from W. B. Yeats's play by the composer. Composers Recordings CRI SD454H, 1983. 12″ long-play record.

Performed by the Boston Musica Viva; jacket notes by an anonymous author. For the printed score see 84-75.

86-106. HARDY, THOMAS: *The Collected Letters of Thomas Hardy*. Edited by Richard Purdy and Michael Millgate. Oxford: Clarendon Press, 1978–. In progress.

For references to Yeats see vol. 4 (letters of 1909–13), 1984, pp. 37, 113; vol. 5 (letters of 1914–19), 1985, p. 151.

86-107. HARPER, GEORGE MILLS: *The Making of Yeats's "A Vision"*: *A Study of the Automatic Script*. London: Macmillan, 1986. 2 vols. (xvi, 301, xvii, 463 pp.)

A chronological study with copious quotations from the script, made by Yeats and Mrs. Yeats between 5 November 1917 and 22 April 1925. Includes references to various poems and plays indebted to *A Vision*, especially *Calvary*, *The Only Jealousy of Emer*, and *The Player Queen*.

Reviews:

Steven Helmling: "Yeats Early and Late," *Sewanee Review*, 95:3 (Summer 1987), 490–94.

Claude Rawson: "A Question of Potency," *TLS*, 24 July 1987, 783–85.

86-108. HART, HENRY: *The Poetry of Geoffrey Hill*. Carbondale: Southern Illinois University Press, 1986. xiv, 306 pp.

See index for numerous remarks on Yeats and Hill.

86-109. °HASKELL, DENNIS: "The Poetic Theory and Practice of W. B. Yeats," Ph.D. thesis, University of Sydney (Australia), 1982.

86-110. HASSETT, JOSEPH M.: " 'The Crazed Moon' and the Myth of Dionysus," *Yeats Annual*, 5 (1987), 232–37.

The myth in the Neoplatonic interpretation by Thomas Taylor.

86-111. HATCHER, JOHN: *From the Auroral Darkness: The Life and Poetry of Robert Hayden*. Oxford: Ronald, 1984. xii, 342 pp.

See index for some references to Yeats's influence.

86-112. HATFIELD, LEONARD L.: "Speaking with Authority: Credibility and Authenticity in Browning's *Men and Women* and Yeats' *The Wild Swans at Coole*," °Ph.D. thesis, Indiana University, 1986. 232 pp. (*DAI*, 47:8 [February 1987], 3047A).

86-113. HAWKINS, HUNT: "W. B. Yeats: A Profile," *Florida State*

University Bulletin: Research in Review, 81:2 (Spring 1987), 16.
86-114. HAYLEY, BARBARA: "Artifex and Artifact: 'Ingenious Lovely Things' in the Poetry of W. B. Yeats," *Gaéliana,* 7 (1985), 35–43.
86-115. HESSENBERGER, ERNST: *Metapoesie und Metasprache in der Lyrik von W. B. Yeats und T. S. Eliot.* Passau: Haller, 1986. xiv, 395 pp.
   Originally a Dr. phil. thesis, University of Passau, 1986. Discusses "poetic statements on poetry and linguistic reflexions on language" (p. 1) in the poems of both writers and of Ezra Pound in order to connect them with their poetic theories. No index.
86-116. HIRSCH, EDWARD: "Wisdom and Power: Yeats and the Commonwealth of Faery," *Yeats Eliot Review,* 8:1&2 (1986), 22–40.
86-117. HOFFMAN, HERBERT H., and RITA LUDWIG HOFFMAN, comps.: *International Index to Recorded Poetry.* New York: Wilson, 1983. xlvi, 529 pp.
   See pp. 257–59.
86-118. HOFFMAN, HERBERT H., comp.: *Recorded Plays: Indexes to Dramatists, Plays, and Actors.* Chicago: American Library Association, 1985. ix, 141 pp.
   See pp. 87–88.
86-119. HOPE, ALEC: "Daytime Thoughts about the Night Shift: Alec Hope Talks to Peter Kuch and Paul Kavanagh," *Southerly,* 46:2 (1986), 221–31.
   Hope comments on Yeats's influence.
86-120. HOUGHTON LIBRARY. HARVARD UNIVERSITY: *Catalogue of Manuscripts in the Houghton Library, Harvard University.* Cambridge: Chadwyck-Healey, 1986. 8 vols.
   See 8:436–38 for a list of MSS. and letters by and referring to Yeats, also items relating to the Yeats family.
86-121. HUNTER, CHARLES: "A Tale of Two Theatres," *Irish Times,* 28 March 1987, Weekend, 1–2.
   The Abbey and the Gate, with occasional references to Yeats.
86-122. HYDE, H. MONTGOMERY: "Yeats and Gogarty," *Yeats Annual,* 5 (1987), 154–60.
   Reminiscences.
86-123. JAFFE, GRACE M.: "Vignettes," *Yeats Annual,* 5 (1987), 139–53.
   Memories of George Yeats and, marginally, of WBY; an amplification of the author's reminiscences in *Years of Grace* (1979).
86-124. JANOUŠEK, MIROSLAV: "Na okraj literárních jubileí 1985

(Anglická e americká literatura)," *Cizí jazyky ve škole,* 28:5 (1984/85), 168–78.

Contains a phonological analysis of "Down by the Salley Gardens."

86-125. JEFFARES, A. NORMAN: "Foreword," *Hermathena,* 141 (Winter 1986), 7–9.

To a special Samuel Beckett edition, comments on Yeats's influence.

86-126. ———: *Parameters of Irish Literature in English: A Lecture Given at the Princess Grace Irish Library on Friday 25 April 1986 at 8.00 P.M.* Gerrards Cross: Colin Smythe, 1986. 44 pp.

Several references to Yeats.

86-127. ———: *W. B. Yeats: Selected Poems. Notes by A. N. Jeffares.* London: Longman / York Press, 1986. 112 pp. (York Notes.)

Notes on some 90 poems, nine pages of commentary, hints for study, etc.

86-128. JENNRICH, PETER: *Die Okkupation des Willens: Macht und Methoden der neuen Kultbewegungen.* Hamburg: Hoffmann & Campe, 1985. 254 pp.

See pp. 156–66 for some rather perfunctory notes on Yeats's occult interests.

86-129. JONES, JAMES T.: *Wayward Skeptic: The Theories of R. P. Blackmur.* Urbana: University of Illinois Press, 1986. ix, 217 pp.

"The Outsider at the Heart of Things: Blackmur on Stevens, Eliot, and Yeats," 139–47.

86-130. JONES, R. T.: *Studying Poetry: An Introduction.* London: Arnold, 1986. vi, 74 pp.

Note on "Easter 1916," pp. 16–21.

86-131. JORDAN, CARMEL: "The Harlot in Yeats' *The Death of Cuchulain,*" *English Language Notes,* 24:4 (June 1987), 61–65.

The harlot represents "the tendency of modern Ireland to prostitute herself."

86-132. KARL, FREDERICK ROBERT: *Modern and Modernism: The Sovereignty of the Artist 1885–1925.* New York: Atheneum, 1985. xviii, 459 pp.

On Yeats, pp. 220–31; mainly on his occult interests, his early plays, particularly *Deirdre,* and "The Indian to His Love."

86-133. KEANE, PATRICK J.: "Faithful in His Fashion: Yeats and the Eros Chorus from Sophocles' *Antigone,*" *Yeats Eliot Review,* 8:1&2 (1986), 3–21.

A study of the working MSS. and the finished version of "From the

Antigone," including a discussion of the poem's place as a coda to "A Woman Young and Old." N.B.: Note 12 refers to reproductions of the MSS.; these reproductions have been omitted.

86-134. KEARNEY, RICHARD: "Berkeley and the Irish Mind," *Études irlandaises*, 11 (1986), supplement "Berkeley et l'Irlande," 27–43.

Contains notes on Yeats's view of Berkeley.

86-135. KELLIHER, HILTON, and SALLY BROWN: *English Literary Manuscripts*. London: British Library, 1986. 80 pp.

Includes a reproduction of a corrected and annotated proof version of "The Mother of God," p. 67.

86-136. KENNER, HUGH: "The Three Deaths of Yeats," *Yeats*, 5 (1987), 87–94.

Yeats's various poetical summings-up in the course of his career.

86-137. KING, JAMES: *Interior Landscapes: A Life of Paul Nash*. London: Weidenfeld & Nicolson, 1987. xiv, 258 pp.

See pp. 60–61 for a short Yeats reminiscence.

86-138. KISSELGOFF, ANNA: "Dance: 'Lunar Parables' by Pearson Company," *New York Times*, 1 June 1985, 31.

Review of a performance of a work "keyed to fragments of text by W. B. Yeats" by the Pearson Dance company.

86-139. KLEIN, LEONARD S., ed.: *Encyclopedia of World Literature in the 20th Century*. Revised edition. New York: Ungar, 1981–84. 4 vols.

Based on J1347. David Castronovo: "Irish Literature," 2:458–63; Edward Hirsch: "Yeats, William Butler," 4:673–79.

86-140. KOMESU, OKIFUMI: "*At the Hawk's Well* and *Taka No Izumi* in a 'Creative Circle,'" *Yeats Annual*, 5 (1987), 103–13.

Taka No Izumi is Yeats's play, retranslated into a Japanese Nō play by Mario Yokomichi.

86-141. KUCH, PETER: "'Laying the Ghosts'?—W. B. Yeats's Lecture on Ghosts and Dreams," *Yeats Annual*, 5 (1987), 114–35.

The lecture "Ghosts and Dreams," delivered to the London Spiritualist Alliance on 28 April 1914, published in *Light*, 2 May 1914, 211–14, and 9 May 1914, 223–24 (here reprinted).

86-142. KULLMAN, COLBY H., and WILLIAM C. YOUNG, eds.: *Theatre Companies of the World*. Westport, Conn.: Greenwood Press, 1986. 2 vols.

Laura H. Weaver: "Abbey Theatre Company," 2:664–71.

86-143. LAITY, CASSANDRA: "Yeats's Changing Image of Maud Gonne," *Éire-Ireland*, 22:2 (Summer 1987), 56–69.

The image of Maud Gonne in the plays, poems, and *A Vision*.
86-144. LAWRENCE, KAREN, BETSY SEIFTER, and LOIS RAT-
NER: *The McGraw-Hill Guide to English Literature*. New York:
McGraw-Hill, 1985. 2 vols.

> K. L.: "W. B. Yeats," 2:303–16; notes on the following poems: "To
> the Rose upon the Rood of Time," "Leda and the Swan," "Sailing
> to Byzantium," "Among School Children," and "The Circus Ani-
> mals' Desertion."

86-145. LEAVIS, FRANK RAYMOND: *Valuation in Criticism and Other
Essays*. Collected and edited by G. Singh. Cambridge: Cambridge Uni-
versity Press, 1986. vii, 305 pp.

> "Yeats: The Problem and the Challenge," 88–102; reprinted from
> J2567.

86-146. LE BROCQUY, LOUIS: *Louis Le Brocquy and the Celtic Head
Image*. An exhibition: September 26 through November 29, 1981. Intro-
duction by Kevin M. Cahill. Essays by Proinsias MacCana and Anne
Crookshank. Albany, N.Y.: New York State Museum, 1981. 64 pp.

> See pp. 28–32, 49, 57–58 for some Yeats heads and comments.

86-147. LENSE, EDWARD: "Sailing the Seas to Nowhere: Inversions of
Yeats's Symbolism in 'Sailing to Byzantium,'" *Yeats*, 5 (1987), 95–106.

> An "analysis of the poem's context," i.e., its images and ideas as
> reflected in some of Yeats's other poetical works.

86-148. LEONARD, JENNIFER L.: "Wise and Crazy Jane," *Chrysalis*,
1:2 (Summer 1986), 131–35.

86-149. °LEPPARD, D. G.: "An Investigation into the Theory and
Structure of Metaphor, with Special Reference to Wordsworth and
Yeats," D. Phil. thesis, Oxford University, 1984.

86-150. LOEFFLER, CHARLES MARTIN: *La Mort de Tintagiles: Five
Irish Fantasies*. New World Records, NW 332, 1985. 12″ long-play
record.

> Includes recordings of the poems in J5681 by Neil Rosenshein, tenor,
> and the Indianapolis Symphony Orchestra, conducted by John Nel-
> son. Sleeve notes by Ellen Knight.

86-151. LOGES, MARY KAISER: "The Poetry of Walter de la Mare: A
Re-Evaluation," Ph.D. thesis, University of Denver, 1985. iii, 276 pp.
(*DAI*, 46:11 [May 1986], 3349A).

> "De la Mare and W. B. Yeats: The Symbolist Mode," 50–58, and
> passim.

86-152. LOIZEAUX, ELIZABETH BERGMANN: *Yeats and the Visual*

Arts. New Brunswick, N.J.: Rutgers University Press, 1986. xix, 238 pp. (Illustrated).

Based on 81-9, incorporates 83-129 and 84-115. Contains chapters on Yeats and the Pre-Raphaelites, "Poems and Pictures: Yeats's Early Poetic Theory," the early poems, "From Painted Stage to Sculpted Image: The Theater Years," *A Vision* and the visual arts, the visual arts in the later poetry, and the influence of the Nō. Discusses Yeats's views of various painters and artists.

Reviews:

Terence Diggory, *Yeats,* 5 (1987), 246–52.

Ian Fletcher: "Yeats: Letters and the Visual Arts," *English Literature in Transition,* 30:4 (1987), 475–81.

Claude Rawson: "A Question of Potency," *TLS,* 24 July 1987, 783–85.

86-153. LONGENBACH, JAMES: *Modernist Poetics of History: Pound, Eliot, and the Sense of the Past.* Princeton: Princeton University Press, 1987. xviii, 280 pp.

Based on 85-180. See "Pater and Yeats: The Dicta of the Great Critics," 29–44, and passim. Discusses Yeats's influence on Pound and Eliot.

86-154. LONGLEY, EDNA: *Poetry in the Wars.* Newcastle: Bloodaxe, 1986. 264 pp.

Incorporates 85-181. Many references to Yeats (see index), particularly to "Nineteen Hundred and Nineteen" (pp. 14–21), and in discussions of Edward Thomas, Louis MacNeice, Philip Larkin, Derek Mahon, and the poets of Northern Ireland.

86-155. LUCAS, JOHN: *Modern English Poetry: From Hardy to Hughes. A Critical Survey.* London: Batsford, 1986. 218 pp.

"W. B. Yeats: The Responsibilities of the Poet," 103–29.

86-156. MCCORMACK, WILLIAM JOHN: *The Battle of the Books: Two Decades of Irish Cultural Debate.* Gigginstown, Mullingar: Lilliput Press, 1986. 94 pp.

Numerous references to Yeats (see index).

86-157. MCDOWELL, EDWIN: "A New Yorker's Link with Literary Figures," *New York Times,* 3 September 1984, 12.

Jeanne Robert Foster, whose collection of letters, diaries, and manuscripts is now in the Rare Books and Manuscripts Division of the New York Public Library. The collection includes correspondence with Yeats.

194 K. P. S. Jochum

86-158. MCFARLAND, RONALD E.: "'The Finney Prey': Some Observations on Fish in Poetry," *Centennial Review*, 31:2 (Spring 1987), 167–82.

Contains a note on "The Fish," pp. 173–75.

86-159. MACGLOIN, T. P.: "Yeats's Faltering World," *Sewanee Review*, 95:3 (Summer 1987), 470–84.

The faltering world is that of the Anglo-Irish, "devastated, doomed, and unredeemable."

86-160. MCGRATH, FRANCIS CHARLES: *The Sensible Spirit: Walter Pater and the Modernist Paradigm*. Tampa: University of South Florida Press, 1986. xi, 299 pp.

Numerous references to Yeats (see index).

86-161. MACHIN, RICHARD, and CHRISTOPHER NORRIS, eds.: *Post-Structuralist Readings of English Poetry*. Cambridge: Cambridge University Press, 1987. x, 406 pp.

Daniel O'Hara: "Yeats in Theory," 349–68. The reception of Yeats by various schools of literary criticism, notably by R. P. Blackmur, Northrop Frye, Harold Bloom, and Paul de Man. Includes a short analysis of "Her Vision in the Wood."

86-162. MCNALLY, JAMES: "Cast a Cold Eye on Yeats and Arnold," *Victorian Poetry*, 25:2 (Summer 1987), 173–80.

Arnold's influence on Yeats's poetry.

86-163. MACNEICE, LOUIS: *Selected Literary Criticism of Louis MacNeice*. Edited by Alan Heuser. Oxford: Clarendon Press, 1987. xxiii, 279 pp.

See pp. 44–45, 116–19, 171–73, 180–92, 190–94, 216–20, 239–41 for reprints of J4867, 5023, 5055, 5080, 5143, 5193, and review of 2439.

86-164. MAGILL, FRANK N., ed.: *Critical Survey of Drama: English Language Series*. Englewood Cliffs, N.J.: Salem Press, 1985. 6 vols.

Cóilín D. Owens: "William Butler Yeats," 5:2115–22.

86-165. MALLARMÉ, STÉPHANE: *Correspondance*. Edited by Henri Mondor and Lloyd James Austin. Paris: Gallimard, 1959–85. 11 vols.

See vol. 6 (1981), pp. 223, 225, 230, 237, 238 for Yeats's letter to Mallarmé and some notes.

86-166. MANNING, MARY: "I Remember It Well: Some Bits of Autobiography," *Journal of Irish Literature*, 15:3 (September 1986), 17–41.

See pp. 32–33 for a short Yeats reminiscence.

86-167. MARCUS, PHILLIP L.: *Yeats and the Beginning of the Irish Re-*

naissance. Second edition. Syracuse, N.Y.: Syracuse University Press, 1987. xliii, 298 pp. (Irish Studies.)

Second edition of J1110; contains a long "Preface to the New Edition," xi–xxxvi.

86-168. ———: "Yeats's 'Last Poems': A Reconsideration," *Yeats Annual,* 5 (1987), 3–14.

Reopens the question of the contents and order of this group of poems.

86-169. MARTIN, HEATHER CARMEN: *W. B. Yeats: Metaphysician as Dramatist.* Gerrards Cross: Colin Smythe, 1986. xiv, 153 pp.

Based on 81-89, incorporates 81-90, 83-143. Argues that Yeats's metaphysics, the result of his magical, mystical, and philosophical studies, finds its most elaborate expression in the plays.

86-170. MASON, HAROLD ANDREW: *The Tragic Plane.* Oxford: Clarendon Press, 1985. vii, 197 pp.

Note on "Sailing to Byzantium," pp. 84–85.

86-171. MATSON, LESLIE: "Conviviality and Challenge: Leslie Matson Recalls the Yeats International Summer School in Sligo," *Books Ireland,* 113 (May 1987), 87–88.

86-172. MEGGISON, LAUREN LOUISE: "Keepers of the Flame: Hermeticism in Yeats, H. D., and Borges," °Ph.D. thesis, University of California, Irvine, 1987. 281 pp. (*DAI,* 48:2 [August 1987], 386A).

Mainly on "The Two Trees" and the Crazy Jane poems, according to abstract.

86-173. MEIHUIZEN, NICHOLAS: "Yeats, Frye, and the Meeting of Saint and Poet," *Theoria,* 67 (October 1986), 53–60.

The meeting of saint and poet in "Solomon and the Witch," explained by references to Frye's essay on *A Vision* (J1078).

86-174. MENGEL, HAGAL: *Sam Thompson and Modern Drama in Ulster.* Frankfurt am Main: Lang, 1986. xxiii, 603 pp. (Bremer Beiträge zur Literatur- und Ideologiegeschichte, 3.)

See "The Origins of Modern Drama in Ulster," 1–164, for notes on Yeats's dramatic theories and theatrical activities.

86-175. MERCIER, VIVIAN: "The Morals of Deirdre," *Yeats Annual,* 5 (1987), 224-31.

The versions written by modern playwrights (including Yeats) are characterized by "puritanical habits of behaviour" and do no justice to the original.

86-176. MILLER, LIAM: *The Dolmen Book of Irish Stamps.* Preface by Feargal Quinn. Mountrath: Dolmen Press, 1986. 61 pp.

On the Yeats stamp of 1965, p. 52.

86-177. MILLER, SUSAN FISHER: "'Rooting Mythology in the Earth': W. B. Yeats at Ballylee," °Ph.D. thesis, Northwestern University, 1986. 301 pp. (*DAI*, 47:8 [February 1987], 3033A).

Discusses the importance of Thoor Ballylee for Yeats's work, especially his poetry, the influence of Milton, Morris, Martyn, and the importance of architect William Scott, Yeats's unpublished correspondence with the Irish Congested Districts Board, and provides a biographical context.

86-178. MITGANG, HERBERT: "To Begin With," *New York Times Book Review*, 4 September 1983, 23.

Yeats as a "champion modern supplier of epigraphs" for other writers' works.

86-179. MIZEJEWSKI, LINDA: "Patriarchy and the Female in Lady Gregory's *Grania*," *Éire-Ireland*, 22:1 (Spring 1987), 122–38.

Frequent references to Yeats.

86-180. MOORE, MARIANNE: *The Complete Prose of Marianne Moore*. Edited and with an introduction by Patricia C. Willis. New York: Viking, 1986. xi, 724 pp.

See pp. 39–41, 294–96, and 312–16 for reprints of J4513, 4706, and 1800. See index for further references to Yeats.

86-181. MORRIS, BRUCE: "Reassessing Arthur Symons's Relationship with Lady Gregory," *Yeats*, 5 (1987), 107–15.

The relationship as it influenced both writers' attitude towards Yeats.

86-182. ————: "Arthur Symons's Letters to W. B. Yeats: 1892–1902," *Yeats Annual*, 5 (1987), 46–61.

An annotated edition of 12 letters.

86-183. MURAWSKA, KATARZYNA: "An Image of Mysterious Wisdom Won by Toil: The Tower as Symbol of Thoughtful Isolation in English Art and Literature from Milton to Yeats," *Artibus et historiae*, 3:5 (1982), 141–62.

An extensively researched and illustrated article on the iconographical sources and predecessors of the tower image in Yeats's poetry.

86-184. MURPHY, DANIEL: *Imagination & Religion in Anglo-Irish Literature 1930–1980*. Blackrock, Co. Dublin: Irish Academic Press, 1987. 228 pp.

Contains some remarks on Yeats, especially in the chapters on Patrick Kavanagh, Sean O'Faolain, and Austin Clarke.

86-185. MURPHY, MAUREEN O'ROURKE, and JAMES MAC-
KILLOP, eds.: *Irish Literature: A Reader.* Syracuse: Syracuse University
Press, 1987. xxiii, 454 pp. (Irish Studies.)

> Several references to Yeats (see index), but does not include any
> Yeats texts.

86-186. MURPHY, RUSSELL: "A New Source for 'Veronica's Nap-
kin,'" *English Language Notes,* 23:4 (June 1986), 42–49.

> The source is Mrs. Arthur [Eugénie] Strong's *Apotheosis and After
> Life* (1915), which also influenced "Byzantium." Both poems are
> concerned with the fate of the soul after death.

86-187. ————: "Yeats's Christ Pantokrator and the Image of Edessa:
Some New Observations on the Significance of Byzantium in Yeats's
Historical System," *Yeats Eliot Review,* 8:1&2 (1986), 41–49.

> The image of Christ Pantokrator, as appropriated by Yeats from
> Byzantine art and used in the historical system of *A Vision.*

86-188. NATIONAL LIBRARY OF IRELAND: *Partial List of Manu-
scripts in the Collection of Senator Michael B. Yeats.* [Dublin: National Li-
brary of Ireland, 1981?]. 100 pp.

> Photocopied list, unpublished, "compiled June 1978 and July 1981";
> includes manuscripts, notebooks, letters to and from Yeats, collec-
> tions of newspapers, clippings, and other material.

86-189. NORMAN, DIANA: *Terrible Beauty: A Life of Constance Mar-
kievicz 1886–1927.* London: Hodder & Stoughton, 1987. 320 pp.

> Some notes on Yeats (see index); does not improve on previous
> biographies (J7026-27).

86-190. O'CONNOR, BRENDAN: "Le farfadet Mac Phellimey était
un nègre!" *Nyx: Dernières lettres avant la nuit,* 1 (First Trimester 1987),
75–79.

> "The pooka M. was a ghost writer"; discusses Yeats's contribution
> to a book entitled *James Joyce and the Pooka Mac Phellimey: A Study of
> a Literary Fabrication* (Dublin: Flaherty, 1923), in which he proves
> that Molly Bloom's monolog is actually the work of Mac Phel-
> limey, who lived in the seventh century.

86-191. O'DONNELL, WILLIAM H.: *The Poetry of William Butler
Yeats: An Introduction.* New York: Ungar, 1986. xvi, 192 pp.

> Contains a chronology, a short biography, chapters on "Back-
> grounds for Reading Yeats's Poems" and "Yeats and Modern Po-
> etry," and short interpretations of some 35 poems.

86-192. OLDFIELD, LAURIE: "Hades' Bobbin and the Mummy-

198   *K. P. S. Jochum*

Cloth: Images of Poet and Language in Yeats's 'Byzantium,' " *Yeats Eliot Review*, 8:1&2 (1986), 72–75.

86-193. O'LOUGHLIN, MICHAEL: *After Kavanagh: Patrick Kavanagh and the Discourse of Contemporary Irish Poetry.* Dublin: Raven Arts Press, 1985. 38 pp.

Contains some references to Yeats.

86-194. O'NEILL, CHARLES LEE: "Circumventing Yeats: Austin Clarke, Thomas Kinsella, Seamus Heaney," °Ph.D. thesis, New York University, 1987. 386 pp. (*DAI*, 48:3 [September 1987], 655A-56A).

86-195. OPPEL, FRANCES NESBITT: *Mask and Tragedy: Yeats and Nietzsche, 1902–10.* Charlottesville: University Press of Virginia, 1987. xi, 255 pp.

Based on 84-160. Unfortunately, the author does not consider any German-language material and is thus unaware of what is perhaps the best study of the subject, Eitel F. Timm's *William Butler Yeats und Friedrich Nietzsche* (1980).

86-196. OXBURY, HAROLD: *Great Britons: Twentieth-Century Lives.* Oxford: Oxford University Press, 1985. x, 371 pp.

See pp. 362–63.

86-197. PAREKH, PUSHPA NAIDU: "Response to Failure as Reflected in the Poetry of G. M. Hopkins, His Contemporaries (Francis Thompson and Lionel Johnson), and the Moderns," °Ph.D. thesis, Louisiana State University, 1986. 251 pp. (*DAI*, 47:9 [March 1987], 3426A-37A).

Includes a short discussion of the "anti-heroic clown persona" in Yeats, according to abstract.

86-198. PARKINSON, THOMAS: *Poets, Poems, Movements.* Ann Arbor: UMI Research Press, 1986. ix, 330 pp. (Studies in Modern Literature, 64.)

See pp. 21–30, 117–28, 131–52, and 203–12 for reprints of J1906, 3146, 1222, and 85-235. See index for further references.

86-199. PATRIDES, C. A.: "Gaiety Transfiguring Áll That Dread: The Case of Yeats," *Yeats*, 5 (1987), 117–32.

The context of Yeats's concept of tragic joy, discussed with reference to "Lapis Lazuli," his literary criticism, the Oedipus plays, the figure of the fool in *On Baile's Strand, The Hour Glass,* and *The Herne's Egg,* the influence of Shakespeare, and Crazy Jane.

86-200. PAULIN, TOM: "The Politics of English Verse," *Poetry Review*, 76:1–2 (June 1986), 34–38.

Discusses Yeats's political poetry.

86-201. PEARCE, DONALD: "Shadows Deep: Change and Continuity in Yeats," *Colby Library Quarterly*, 22:4 (December 1986), 198–204.

Comments on "When You Are Old" and "The Lake Isle of Innisfree."

86-202. PERKINS, DAVID: *A History of Modern Poetry: Modernism and After*. Cambridge, Mass.: Belknap Press of Harvard University Press, 1987. xiii, 694 pp.

Numerous references to Yeats (see index).

86-203. PETER, JOHN: *Vladimir's Carrot: Modern Drama and the Modern Imagination*. London: Deutsch, 1987. xi, 372 pp.

Some notes on Yeats's plays, particularly *At the Hawk's Well* (see index).

86-204. PHILLIPS, C. L.: "The Writing and Performance of *The Hour-Glass*," *Yeats Annual*, 5 (1987), 83–102.

86-205. PITTOCK, MURRAY: "Falcon and Falconer: 'The Second Coming' and Marvell's 'Horatian Ode,'" *Irish University Review*, 16:2 (Autumn 1986), 175–79.

Marvell's ode is taken as the "basis for an ironic reading by Yeats of Cromwell's achievement."

86-206. ———: "Thoor Ballylee," *Cumberland Poetry Review*, 6:2 (Spring 1987), 89.

A poem.

86-207. *Poeziĩa A. Bloka i fol'klorno-literaturnye traditsii: Meshvuzovskiĭ sbornik nauchnykh trudov*. Omsk: Omskiĭ gosudarstvennyĭ ordena "Znak Pocheta" pedagogicheskiĭ institut imeni A. M. Gor'kogo, 1984. 140 pp.

V. V. Khorol'skiĭ: "A. Blok i U. B. Ĭets: Puti simbolizma" [Blok and WBY: Developments of symbolism], 118–25, contains only a few notes on the rose symbol in Yeats's poetry.

86-208. PRASAD, BAIDYA NATH: *The Literary Criticism of W. B. Yeats*. New Delhi: Classical Publishing Company, 1985. xiii, 257 pp.

Includes chapters on the Romantic and Victorian background, the influence of John Butler Yeats, John O'Leary, Pater, Wilde, and Nietzsche, Yeats's idea of symbolism, and his theory of drama.

86-209. PRESLEY, JOHN W.: "Strategies for Detemporalizing Language in Modern Literature," *Language & Style*, 18:3 (Summer 1985), 293–301.

Contains a note on the stylistic means used by Yeats to express timelessness in his poetry.

86-210. *Problemy metoda i poetiki v zarubezhnykh literaturakh XIX–XX vekov: Mezhvuzovskiĭ sbornik nauchnykh trudov.* Perm': Permskiĭ ordena trudovogo krasnogo znameni gosudarstvennyĭ universitet im. A. M. Gor'kogo, 1985. 168 pp.

T. M. Poliūdova: "Svoeobrazie zhanrovoĭ struktury poeticheskoĭ dramy U. B. Ĭetsa" [The originality of the genre structures of WBY's poetic drama], 75–84; discusses Yeats's dramatic theories and *Cathleen ni Houlihan.*

86-211. PUHVEL, MARTIN: "Yeats's 'The Wild Swans at Coole,'" *Explicator,* 45:1 (Autumn 1986), 29–30.

The 59 swans, difficult to count in reality, come from the 59 silver bells in "Thomas Rhymer."

86-212. QUINN, KATHLEEN ANNE: "Mothers, Heroes, and Hearts Turned to Stone: Mythologizing and Demythologizing in Irish Drama," °Ph.D. thesis, Washington State University, 1986. 297 pp. (*DAI,* 47:10 [April 1987], 3755A).

On Irish mythological characters in Yeats's dramas.

86-213. RAMRATNAM, MALATI. *W. B. Yeats and the Craft of Verse.* Lanham, Md.: University Press of America, 1985. x, 135 pp.

Based on "Studies in the Craftsmanship of W. B. Yeats," Ph.D. thesis, Brandeis University, 1973. iv, 176 pp. (*DAI,* 34:7 [January 1974], 4281A). Includes chapters on stylistic and prosodic problems.

86-214. RAO, N. M.: "Yeats's 'Among School Children': Text and Context," *Aligarh Journal of English Studies,* 11:1 (1986), 98–108.

The context is defined by references to Mallarmé.

86-215. RAVINDRAN, SANKARAN: "William Butler Yeats and India: Indian Themes of Art, Religion, and Philosophy in Yeats' Works, 1885–1939," °Ph.D. thesis, University of Kansas, 1986. 217 pp. (*DAI,* 47:6 [December 1986], 2171A).

According to abstract, there are discussions of Yeats's early "Indian" poems, of the relationship with Tagore and Shri Purohit Swami, the Upanishadic concept of self, *The Herne's Egg,* and impersonality in poetry. Uses unpublished letters.

86-216. REEVES, MARJORIE, and WARWICK GOULD: *Joachim of Fiore and the Myth of the Eternal Evangel in the Nineteenth Century.* Oxford: Clarendon Press, 1987. x, 365 pp.

"W. B. Yeats: A Noble Antinomianism," 202–71; "A Note on James Joyce and Joachim," 271–78 (Joyce's indebtedness to "The Tables of the Law").

86-217. ROBERTS, BARBARA: "Yeats's Rhetorical Imperative," *Yeats Eliot Review*, 8:1&2 (1986), 64–71.

On the use of imperatives in the poetry.

86-218. ROBERTSON, JILLIAN: "Yeats Mystery Unearthed," *Times*, 19 August 1986, 8.

The question of whether the wrong body was disinterred in Roquebrune and interred in Drumcliffe.

86-219. ROBERTSON, LINDA K.: "Irish Ghosts: The Haunting of William Butler Yeats," *Publications of the Missouri Philological Association*, 10 (1985), 44–49.

Discusses Yeats's belief in ghosts.

86-220. ROCHE DOLAN, MARY: "La influencia de Sir Samuel Ferguson sobre el joven Yeats," *Miscelania* [University of Zaragoza], 3 (March 1984), 65–76.

86-221. ROGERS, PAT, ed.: *The Oxford Illustrated History of English Literature*. Oxford: Oxford University Press, 1987. xvi, 528 pp.

Bernard Bergonzi: "Late Victorian to Modernist, 1880–1930," 379–430; includes some passages on Yeats.

86-222. ROSE, JONATHAN: *The Edwardian Temperament 1895–1919*. Athens: Ohio University Press, 1986. xiv, 275 pp.

See index for some notes on Yeats's interest in theosophy and the doctrine of the mask.

86-223. ROSENTHAL, M. L.: "Notes on the 'Memory'-Sequence in Yeats's *The Wild Swans at Coole*," *Yeats*, 5 (1987), 133–41.

86-224. RUSSELL, JANE: *James Starkey / Seumas O'Sullivan: A Critical Biography*. Rutherford, N.J.: Fairleigh Dickinson University Press, 1987. 148 pp.

"A.E., Yeats, and the 'School' of Thought," 79–87; "Seumas O'Sullivan and Drama," 99–104; and passim on the strained Yeats-O'Sullivan relationship.

86-225. RYBOWSKI, TADEUSZ: "Niektóre problemy przekładu poetyckiego: Uwagi warsztatowe na prszykładzie utworów Williama Butlera Yeatsa," *Acta Universitatis Wratislaviensis*, 905 / *Studia Linguistica*, 10 (1986), 41–51.

On the problem of translating Yeats's poems into Polish.

86-226. SADDLEMYER, ANN, and COLIN SMYTHE, eds.: *Lady Gregory Fifty Years After*. Gerrards Cross: Colin Smythe / Totowa, N.J.: Barnes & Noble, 1987. xiv, 464 pp. (Irish Literary Studies, 13.)

Numerous references to Yeats, especially in the following: Colin Smythe: "Chronology," 1–12.

Gabriel Fallon: Extracts from an unpublished history of the Abbey Theatre, 30–34.

Elizabeth Longford: "Lady Gregory and Wilfrid Scawen Blunt," 85–97; also on the Blunt-Yeats relationship.

Gareth W. Dunleavy: "The Pattern of Three Threads: The Hyde-Gregory Friendship," 131–42.

Maureen Murphy: "Lady Gregory and the Gaelic League," 143–62.

John Kelly: " 'Friendship Is the Only House I Have': Lady Gregory and W. B. Yeats," 179–257; also on the Yeats-Robert Gregory relationship, and the Gregory and Coole Park poems.

Robert Welch: "A Language for Healing," 258–73 (the Irish language).

Colin Smythe: "Lady Gregory's Contributions to Periodicals: A Checklist," 322–45; includes the collaborations with Yeats.

Richard Allen Cave: "Robert Gregory: Artist and Stage Designer," 347–400; includes comments on Gregory's designs for Yeats's plays, i.e., *On Baile's Strand, Deirdre,* and *The Hour-Glass.*

86-227. SANDULESCU, CONSTANTIN-GEORGE, and CLIVE HART, eds.: *Assessing the 1984 "Ulysses."* Gerrards Cross: Colin Smythe / Totowa, N.J.: Barnes & Noble, 1986. xxiv, 247 pp. (Princess Grace Irish Library, 1.)

Richard M. Kain: "Dublin 1904," 92–110, 226–27. What some of the celebrities of the Irish literary revival (including Yeats) did in this year.

86-228. SCHIRMER, GREGORY A.: "Yeats's Ghost and Irish Poetry Today," *Sewanee Review,* 95:3 (Summer 1987), 485–90.

A review article on 86-89, 85-148, and 85-185.

86-229. SCHWARTZ, DELMORE: *Portrait of Delmore: Journals and Notes of Delmore Schwartz 1939–1959.* Edited and introduced by Elizabeth Pollet. New York: Farrar, Straus, Giroux, 1986. xix, 663 pp.

See index for some notes on Yeats.

86-230. SEKINE, MASARU, ed.: *Irish Writers and the Theatre.* Gerrards Cross: Colin Smythe / Totowa, N.J.: Barnes & Noble, 1986. viii, 246 pp. (Irish Literary Studies, 23. / IASAIL-Japan Series, 2.)

Richard Allen Cave: "Dramatising the Life of Swift," 17–32; on *The Words upon the Window-Pane.*

Christopher Murray: "Lennox Robinson: The Abbey's Anti-Hero," 114–34; contains some notes on Yeats.

M. Sekine: "Yeats and the Noh," 151–66.

Sumiko Sugiyama: "What's *The Player Queen* All About?" 179–207; also on the poem "The Mask."
Robert Welch: "The Emergence of Modern Anglo-Irish Drama: Yeats and Synge," 208–17; asks "What was Yeats's idea of Drama?"; analyzes *Cathleen ni Houlihan*.
Katharine Worth: "Scenic Imagery in the Plays of Yeats and Beckett," 218–32.

86-231. SHAKESPEARE, WILLIAM: *Henry V*. Edited by Gary Taylor. Oxford: Clarendon Press, 1982. ix, 330 pp. (The Oxford Shakespeare.)
Criticizes Yeats's view of Henry V, pp. 73–74.

86-232. SHAW, GEORGE BERNARD: *The Diaries 1885–1897: With Early Autobiographical Notebooks and Diaries, and an Abortive 1917 Diary*. Edited and annotated by Stanley Weintraub. University Park: Pennsylvania State University Press, 1986. 2 vols.
See index for references to Yeats in 1888 and 1892–1895.

86-233. SHERRY, VINCENT: *The Uncommon Tongue: The Poetry and Criticism of Geoffrey Hill*. Ann Arbor: University of Michigan Press, 1987. xi, 274 pp.
See index for some notes on Hill and Yeats.

86-234. SILVER, JEREMY: "W. B. Yeats and the BBC: A Reassessment," *Yeats Annual*, 5 (1987), 181–85.
Expands considerably on George Whalley's note on "Yeats and Broadcasting" (J12) and includes a list of radio and television broadcasts of Yeats material, 1926–1938.

86-235. ————: "Yeats Material in the Radio Telefis Eireann Archives," *Yeats Annual*, 5 (1987), 186–88.
A checklist, mostly of reminiscences broadcast by various of Yeats's friends and acquaintances.

86-236. SIMMONS, JAMES: *From the Irish*. Belfast: Blackstaff Press, 1985. xi, 78 pp.
Poems; on Yeats: "On Baile Strand," 29; "Beautiful Lofty Things," 31–32; "The Busker," 37–38.

86-237. SLATER, ARDIS M.: "A Vision of the Valley: Mesoamerican and Yeatsian Planes of Malcolm Lowry's *Under the Volcano*," °Ph.D. thesis, Kent State University, 1986. 309 pp. (*DAI*, 47:9 [March 1987], 3437A).
Discusses the influence of *A Vision* and "The Second Coming" on Lowry's novel.

86-238. SLOAN, BARRY: *The Pioneers of Anglo-Irish Fiction 1800–1850*.

Gerrards Cross: Colin Smythe / Totowa, N.J.: Barnes & Noble, 1986.
xxxvii, 277 pp. (Irish Literary Studies, 21.)

See index for some references to Yeats's comments on the early
Anglo-Irish novelists.

86-239. SMITH, EVANS LANSING: "The Descent to the Under-
world: Towards an Archetypal Poetics of Modernism," °Ph.D. thesis,
Claremont Graduate School, 1986. 273 pp. (DAI, 47:5 [November
1986], 1736A).

Includes "close readings of works by W. B. Yeats" (abstract).

86-240. SMITH, STAN: "Porphyry's Cup: Yeats, Forgetfulness and the
Narrative Order," Yeats Annual, 5 (1987), 15–45.

The motif of forgetfulness in the fictive stories contained in some of
the poems and its source in Neoplatonism.

86-241. °SOPHOCLES: Oedipus Rex. In a version by W. B. Yeats. A
Stratford Shakespearean Festival Foundation of Canada production, di-
rected by Tyrone Guthrie, produced by Leonid Kipnis. S.l.: Corinth
Video, [1985?]. Videocassette (VHS), 90 mins.

See J5574.

86-242. SOTHEBY'S: English Literature and History, Comprising Printed
Books, Autograph Letters and Manuscripts. Sale of 23 and 24 August 1987.
London: Sotheby's, 1987.

Item 127 is the vellum manuscript book given by Yeats to Maud Gonne.
It contains seven poems and the titles of eleven further poems, some of
them unpublished. Item 206 includes letters to A. P. Watt. See also the
anonymous note: "To Maud . . . ," Times, 2 July 1987, 2; Maurice Chit-
tenden: "For Sale: Lost Love Poems of Yeats," Sunday Times, 28 June
1987, 3 (and correspondence by Ivo Jarosy: "Accursed Verse," 5 July
1987, 31); Warwick Gould: " 'The Flame of the Spirit': A Love Tribute
from W. B. Yeats," TLS, 17 July 1987, 770; Geraldine Norman: "High
Prize for Love Poems," Times, 24 July 1987, 14.

86-243. STEPHEN, MARTIN: English Literature. London: Longman,
1986. ix, 246 pp. (Longman Exam Guides.)

See pp. 214–15 for "Examination Topics in Yeats's Poetry."

86-244. STIFFLER, RANDALL: Theodore Roethke: The Poet and His
Critics. Chicago: American Library Association, 1986. xviii, 211 pp.

"The Influence of W. B. Yeats," 139–56; a review of what the critics
said about the Roethke-Yeats relationship.

86-245. SUGIYAMA, SUMIKO: Yeats: Fatherland and Song. Kyoto:
Yamaguchi Shoten, 1985. x, 406 pp.

The treatment of the reality of Ireland in Yeats's works, i.e., its history and poetic tradition. Discusses the early poetry, the theatrical activities until 1909, *Poems Written in Discouragement*, "Coole and the Gregorys," the impact of the Easter 1916 rising, the Anglo-Irish tradition in the poetry of the thirties, and the later and last poems.

86-246. SULLIVAN, ALVIN, ed.: *British Literary Magazines: The Modern Age, 1914–1984*. Westport, Conn.: Greenwood Press, 1986. xxxi, 629 pp.

See index for some references to Yeats.

86-247. SULLIVAN, JACK, ed.: *The Penguin Encyclopedia of Horror and the Supernatural*. New York: Viking, 1986. xxx, 482 pp.

See pp. 475–77.

86-248. SUPER, R. H.: "Dining with Landor," *Yeats*, 5 (1987), 143–49.

Landor's influence on Yeats's poetry.

86-249. SUTTON, DAVID C.: "Location Register of Twentieth-Century English Literary Manuscripts and Letters: A Cumulative Yeats Listing (to Autumn, 1985)," *Yeats Annual*, 5 (1987), 289–319.

86-250. TEGTMEIER, RALPH: *Okkultismus und Erotik in der Literatur des Fin de Siècle*. Königswinter: Tegtmeier, 1983. 140 pp.

"William Butler Yeats," 68–73; a note on hermaphroditism in *A Vision*.

86-251. THIESMEYER, LYNN: "Excluded Myths: Vision and Disguise in Yeats's 'The Tower,'" *Yeats Eliot Review*, 8:1&2 (1986), 50–63.

On the poems in the volume *The Tower*, particularly the title poem.

86-252. TIEN, RENÉ: "La pensée indienne selon Yeats," *Gaéliana*, 7 (1985), 45–55.

Mainly on Yeats's views of the Upanishads.

86-253. TIMM, EITEL: *W. B. Yeats*. Darmstadt: Wissenschaftliche Buchgesellschaft, 1987. x, 178 pp. (Erträge der Forschung, 251.)

An extended review of research (in German).

86-254. TOOMEY, DEIRDRE: "Bards of the Gael and Gall: An Uncollected Review by Yeats in *The Illustrated London News*," *Yeats Annual*, 5 (1987), 203–11.

Review of a book by George Sigerson, published in the issue of 14 August 1897, here reprinted. The introduction comments on the Sigerson-Yeats relationship.

86-255. *Tragicheskoe i komicheskoe v zarubezhnoĭ literature: Mezhvuzovskiĭ sbornik nauchnykh trudov*. Perm': Permskiĭ gosudarstvennyĭ pedagogicheskiĭ institut, 1986. 111 pp.

206 K. P. S. Jochum

T. M. Poludova: "Svoeobrazie dramaticheskoĭ struktury tragedii
V. B. Ĭetsa *Deĭrdre*" [The originality of the dramatic structure of Y's
tragedy *Deirdre*], 46–59.

86-256. TYTELL, JOHN: *Ezra Pound: The Solitary Volcano*. New York:
Doubleday, 1987. xv, 368 pp.

See index for notes on the Yeats-Pound relationship.

86-257. VOLLI, UGO: "E Angelo incontrò un poeta," *Grazia* [Milano],
13 April 1986, 84–86.

On the Branduardi Yeats record (85-34).

86-258. WAGNER, LINDA WELSHIMER, ed.: *Critical Essays on Sylvia Plath*. Boston: Hall, 1984. viii, 231 pp.

Sandra M. Gilbert: "In Yeats' House: The Death and Resurrection
of Sylvia Plath," 204–22.

86-259. WALKER, KATHRINE SORLEY: "The Festival and the Abbey: Ninette de Valois' Early Choreography, 1925–1934," *Dance Chronicle*, 7:4 (1985), 379–412; 8:1–2 (1985), 51–100.

For notes on productions of various Yeats plays see pp. 389–90,
408–10; 61–62, 68, and 71–73.

86-260. WALLACE, EMILY MITCHELL: "Some Friends of Ezra
Pound: A Photographic Essay," *Yale Review*, 75:3 (June 1986), 331–56.

Including Yeats.

86-261. WALTON, JAKE, ed.: *Keltische Folksongs: Texte und Noten mit
Begleit-Akkorden*. Frankfurt am Main: Fischer, 1983. 175 pp.

Contains the following musical version: Jack Walton: "Innisfree,"
32–33; Ciaran Brennan: "Down by the Salley Gardens," 80–81;
Richard Dyer Bennet: "The Song of Wandering Aengus," 91–92.

86-262. WASSERMAN, ROSANNE: "Helen of Troy: Her Myth in
Modern Poetry," °Ph.D. thesis, City University of New York, 1986.
451 pp. (*DAI*, 47:4 [October 1986], 1340A).

Contains a chapter on Yeats.

86-263. WATKINS, STEVE: "A Yeats Man: George Harper Unlocks
the Secrets of the Great Irish Poet and His Mysterious Script," *Florida
State University Bulletin: Research in Review*, 81:2 (Spring 1987), 14–17.

On George Mills Harper and his studies in Yeats's occult writings.

86-264. WATKINS, VERNON: *The Collected Poems*. Ipswich: Golgonooza Press, 1986. xvii, 495 pp.

See pp. 13–14, 59–68, and 480–82 for reprints of J5835-37.

86-265. WEST, TREVOR: *Horace Plunkett: Co-operation and Politics: An*

Irish Biography. Gerrards Cross: Colin Smythe / Washington, D.C.: Catholic University Press, 1986. xviii, 288 pp.

On Yeats, pp. 87–93, and passim (see index).

86-266. WILCOX, JOHN CHAPMAN: *Self and Image in Juan Ramón Jiménez: Modern and Post-Modern Readings*. Urbana: University of Illinois Press, 1987. xvii, 207 pp.

See index for a few notes on Yeats.

86-267. WILLIAMS, JOHN: *Twentieth-Century British Poetry: A Critical Introduction*. London: Arnold, 1987. x, 117 pp.

On Yeats, passim (the index is unreliable).

86-268. WILLIAMS, MOELWYN I., ed.: *A Directory of Rare Books and Special Collections in the United Kingdom and the Republic of Ireland*. London: Library Association, 1985. xiii, 664 pp.

See index for a few references to Yeats.

86-269. WILLIAMS, PONTHEOLLA TAYLOR: *Robert Hayden: A Critical Analysis of His Poetry*. Urbana: University of Illinois Press, 1987. xviii, 243 pp.

See index for notes on Yeats's influence on Hayden.

86-270. WOODMAN, KIERAN: *Media Control in Ireland 1923–1983*. Carbondale: Southern Illinois University Press, 1985. viii, 248 pp.

See index for some notes on Yeats's views on censorship.

86-271. WORTHEN, WILLIAM B.: "The Discipline of the Theatrical Sense: *At the Hawk's Well* and the Rhetoric of the Stage," *Modern Drama*, 30:1 (March 1987), 90–103.

86-272. YAMAGUCHI, KIMIHO: [In Japanese] "W. B. Yeats: Two Combustions of Life Energy: A Study of *At the Hawk's Well*," *Memoirs of the Osaka Institute of Technology*, series B, 27:2 (1983), 269–83.

Includes an abstract in English.

86-273. °YEATS, W. B.: *Autobiografieen*. Translated by Sjaak Commandeur, Rien Verhoef, and Jan Eijkelboom. Amsterdam: Arbeiderspers, 1985. 2 vols.

86-274. ———: *The Early Poetry*. Volume I: *Mosada* and *The Island of Statues*. Manuscript materials by W. B. Yeats, edited by George Bornstein. Ithaca: Cornell University Press, 1987. xii, 442 pp. (The Cornell Yeats.)

See "Introduction," 3–16, on the composition of the two plays. The MSS. are printed in facsimile with transcriptions on facing pages.

86-275. ———: *Essais et introductions*. Traduction du Centre de littérature, linguistique et civilisation des pays de langue anglaise de l'Université de Caen sous la direction de Jacqueline Genet. Lille: Presses universitaires de Lille, 1985. 257 pp.

J. Genet: "Introduction," 9–28. Most of the essays are followed by explanatory notes. Reviewed by René Fréchet, *Études anglaises,* 39:4 (December 1986), 473–74.

86-276. ———: "Hablando con el salterio." Translated by Esther Elena Sananés, *Pauta: Cuadernos de teoria y critica musical,* 3:12 (October, November, December 1984), 61–66.

86-277. ———: " 'k Zat op mijn krukje bij het vuur te slapen." Translated by Jan Eijkelboom, *Nieuw wereld tijdschrift,* 1:6 (December 1984), 25.

A translation of "Two Songs of a Fool," II, together with two Yeats heads by Louis Le Brocquy.

86-278. ———: "Pesme." Translated by Aurel Covaci, *Lumina,* 38:7–8 (1984), 70–73.

86-279. ———: *A Poet to His Beloved: The Early Love Poems of W. B. Yeats.* Introduction by Richard Eberhart. New York: St. Martin's Press, 1985. xiii, 66 pp.

"Introduction," ix–xi.

86-280. ———: *Selected Poems and Three Plays of William Butler Yeats.* 3d ed. Edited and with a new foreword and revised introduction and notes by M. L. Rosenthal. New York: Collier Books, 1986. xl, 248 pp.

The first edition of 1962 (Wade 211W) was entitled *Selected Poems and Two Plays.* "Introduction: The Poetry of Yeats," xv–xl; "Notes," 219–34; "Glossary of Names and Places," 235–41; also a rather insufficient bibliography.

86-281. °———: "Smierć." Translated by Leszek Engelking, *Literatura na świecie,* 8/9 (August/September 1985), 3.

86-282. ———: "Su visión en el bosque." Translated by Ulalume González de Léon, *Vuelta,* 9:100 (March 1985), 25.

86-283. ———: "Uil'îam Batler Ĭeĭts ob iskusstve," *Voprosy literatury,* 1 (January 1987), 174–204.

"WBY on art"; a collection of extracts from Yeats's prose, selected, translated and introduced (pp. 174–80) by A. Livergant.

86-284. ———: "W. B. Yeats's Unpublished Talk on His Version of *King Oedipus* Broadcast from the BBC Belfast Studio on 8 September 1931." Introductory note by Karen Dorn, *Yeats Annual,* 5 (1987), 195–99.

N. B.: Karen Dorn seems unaware of the fact that this talk was published in the *Irish Weekly and Ulster Examiner,* 12 Sept. 1931, 9 (see J147); perhaps not quite in the same form as printed here.

86-285. ————: *Where There Is Nothing by W. B. Yeats. The Unicorn from the Stars by W. B. Yeats and Lady Gregory.* Edited with an introduction and notes by Katharine Worth. Washington, D.C.: Catholic University of America Press / Gerrards Cross: Colin Smythe, 1987. ix, 166 pp. (Irish Dramatic Texts.)

Includes a long introduction and annotations to the texts. The introduction is concerned with background, composition, and publication, sources (occultism, Blake, Spenser, Nietzsche, Tolstoy, Vedantism, Ibsen), analyses of the plays, production and critical reception, and the reworking of the one play into the other.

86-286. *Yeats: An Annual of Critical and Textual Studies: Volume V, 1987.* Edited by Richard J. Finneran. Ann Arbor: UMI Research Press, 1987. xvi, 270 pp. (Studies in Modern Literature, 76.)

Contains the following items: 86-54, 86-65, 86-136, 86-147, 86-181, 86-199, 86-223, 86-248, reviews, brief notices by Mary FitzGerald, and this compilers's 1985–86 bibliography (pp. 151–97).

86-287. *Yeats Annual No. 5.* Edited by Warwick Gould. London: Macmillan, 1987. xxi, 341 pp.

Contains the following items: 86-18, 86-20, 86-44, 86-91, 86-98, 86-99, 86-100, 86-110, 86-122, 86-123, 86-140, 86-141, 86-168, 86-175, 86-182, 86-204, 86-234, 86-235, 86-240, 86-249, 86-254, 86-285, and reviews.

86-288. *Yeats Club Review,* 1:1 (Summer 1987).

This is published in Oxford (PO Box 271, Oxford OX2 6DU). The first issue (16 unnumbered pages, including covers) contains notes on the club's activities, brief essays on "Yeats and Tagore" by Chris Morgan, and "A Turn of the Century" by Dwina Murphy-Gibb, as well as other matter not concerned with Yeats. The club plans to publish an annual, *Celtic Dawn,* and conducts poetry competitions.

86-289. *Yeats Society of Japan: Bulletin,* 17 (October 1986).

All articles, except the last two items, are in Japanese. Contains: Yoko Saito: "The Function of the Musicians in *At the Hawk's Well,*" 1–14; English abstract, 73–72.

Shiro Naito: "Yeats and Pastoral," 15–25; 72–71.

Seishi Matsuda: "A Paradoxical Vision of Life and Death in *Purgatory,*" 26–33; 71–70.

210 K. P. S. Jochum

Tadaaki Miyake: "*Purgatory* Another Cuchulain Play of W. B. Yeats," 34–41; 70–69.

Akiko Suzue: "*Purgatory*—A Mother's Dream," 42–50; 69.

An article on Yeats's "Suggestions and Corrections" (see 85-46) with extensive quotations from a Yeats letter, 68–62.

Reviews and bibliographies.

Yoko Nakano: "A Study of *Beyond the Grave: Letters on Poetry to W. B. Yeats from Dorothy Wellesley*," 86–74.

Augustine Martin: "Time and Place in *The Wild Swans at Coole*," 93–87.

86-290. YENSER, STEPHEN: *The Consuming Myth: The Work of James Merrill*. Cambridge, Mass.: Harvard University Press, 1987. xiii, 367 pp.

See index for several references to Yeats.

86-291. YOUNG, DAVID: *Troubled Mirror: A Study of Yeats's "The Tower."* Iowa City: University of Iowa Press, 1987. xiv, 153 pp.

Discusses the 1928 volume as a coherent book of poetry. It is Yeats's equivalent of the long poem and elevates him to the stature of major modern poet.

86-292. ZACH, WOLFGANG, and HEINZ KOSOK, eds.: *Literary Interrelations: Ireland, England and the World*. Tübingen: Narr, 1987. 3 vols. (SECL: Studies in English and Comparative Literature, 1–3.)

On Yeats see especially: Birgit Bramsbäck: "William Butler Yeats and Sweden," 1:51–60; expanded version of 85-33.

Ivanka Koviloska-Poposka: "The Reception of Yeats in Macedonian," 1:61–67.

Theo D'haen: "Translation, Adaptation, Inspiration: The Creative Reception of Anglo-Irish Works in Dutch Literature," 1:81–89; refers to A. Roland Holst's interest in Yeats.

Mirko Jurak: "Irish Playwrights in the Slovene Theatre," 1:159–67; contains a note on the performance of *The Countess Cathleen* in the Slovene National Theatre, Ljubljana, in February 1933.

Richard Ellmann: "The Uses of Decadence: Wilde, Yeats, and Joyce," 2:27–39: "They are not decadents but counter decadents . . . they went through decadence to come out on the other side."

Johannes Kleinstück: "Yeats and Ibsen," 2:65–74.

Mária Kurdi: "Parallels between the Poetry of W. B. Yeats and Endre Ady," 2:75–83.

Csilla Bertha: "An Irish and a Hungarian Model of Mythical Drama: W. B. Yeats and Aron Tamási," 2:85–93.

Jacqueline Genet: "W. B. Yeats and W. H. Auden," 2:95–110.

Patrick O'Neill: "Ossian's Return: The German Factor in the Irish Literary Revival," 2:207–20; contains notes on Yeats's views of Goethe, Nietzsche, and Spengler.

Suheil Badi Bushrui: "Yeats, India, Arabia, and Japan: The Search for a Spiritual Philosophy," 2:221–34.

B. N. Prasad: "The Impact of W. B. Yeats on Modern Indian Poetry," 2:235–44.

Donald T. Torchiana: "W. B. Yeats and Italian Idealism," 2:245–54; Yeats's reading of Vico, Croce, and Gentile.

Margaret E. Fogarty: "The Fiction of Iris Murdoch: Amalgam of Yeatsian and Joycean Motifs," 2:323–34.

Joseph Swann: "The Poet as Critic: Seamus Heaney's Reading of Wordsworth, Hopkins and Yeats," 2:361–70.

Aladár Sarbu: "Literary Nationalism: Ireland and Hungary," 3:19–26.

Jochen Achilles: "Transformations of the Stage Irishman in Irish Drama: 1860–1910," 3:103–14; contains some remarks on *The Unicorn from the Stars* and *The Pot of Broth*.

Robert O'Driscoll: "'A Greater Renaissance': The Revolt of the Soul against the Intellect," 3:133–44.

Maurice Riordan: "Matthew Arnold and the Irish Revival," 3:145–52.

Additions to Entries in Previous Bibliographies

81-56. GENET: *William Butler Yeats*
Reviews:
Eric Neuhoff: "Yeats: L'élégant irlandais," *Quotidien de Paris*, 25 August 1981, 28.

81-100. O'HARA: *Tragic Knowledge*
Reviews:
Lawrence Kramer, *Yeats Eliot Review*, 8:1&2 (1986), 142–44.

82-4. ALLEN: *Yeats's Epitaph*
Reviews:
Andrew Parkin, *Yeats Eliot Review*, 8:1&2 (1986), 137–39.

82-144. NEUMAN: *Some One Myth*
Reviews:
James Lovic Allen, *Yeats Eliot Review*, 8:1&2 (1986), 134–35.
82-168. SCHRICKER: *A New Species of Man*
Reviews:
Elizabeth Mackenzie, *Notes and Queries*, os 231 / ns 33:4 (December 1986), 565–66.
Samuel Rees, *Yeats Eliot Review*, 8:1&2 (1986), 133–34.
83-7. ARCHIBALD: *Yeats*
Reviews:
Elizabeth Bartlett, *National Forum*, 65:1 (Winter 1985), 45–46.
L. M., *West Coast Review of Books*, 9:6 (November/December 1983), 41.
Leslie B. Mittleman, *Magill's Literary Annual*, 1984, 988–91.
83-44. DIGGORY: *Yeats & American Poetry*
Reviews:
Peter Makin, *Yearbook of English Studies*, 17 (1987), 338–39.
Julia M. Reibetanz, *Yeats Eliot Review*, 8:1&2 (1986), 136–37.
83-55. FINNERAN: *Editing Yeats's Poems*
Reviews:
John P. Frayne, *Journal of English and Germanic Philology*, 86:1 (January 1987), 139–44.
Elizabeth Mackenzie, *Notes and Queries*, os 231 / ns 33:4 (December 1986), 565–66.
83-108. KENNER: *A Colder Eye*
Reviews:
Gary Gach, *San Francisco Review of Books*, 8:2 (July–August 1983), 11–12, 15.
Harry Goldgar: "An Eye on Irish Writers," *Times-Picayune* (New Orleans), 19 June 1983, section 3, 4.
Daniel Taylor, *Magill's Literary Annual*, 1984, 173–77.
83-117. KNOWLAND: *W. B. Yeats: Dramatist of Vision*
Reviews:
Andrew Parkin: "Drama East and West," *Canadian Journal of Irish Studies*, 12:1 (June 1986), 79–84.
83-187. SHAH: *Yeats and Eliot*
Reviews:
Sisirkumar Ghosh, *Literary Criterion*, 20:4 (1985), 118–21.

83-212. VLASOPOLOS: *The Symbolic Method of Coleridge, Baudelaire, and Yeats*
Reviews:
Hazard Adams, *Modern Language Studies*, 16:4 (Autumn 1986), 93–94.
Suzanne Nalbantian, *Yearbook of Comparative and General Literature*, 34 (1985), 142–43.
84-2. ADAMS: *Yeats and the Masks of Syntax*
Reviews:
Edmund L. Epstein, *Yeats*, 5 (1987), 209–20.
Kathleen Wales, *Yeats Annual*, 5 (1987), 260–66.
84-15. BRAMSBÄCK: *Folklore and W. B. Yeats*
Reviews:
René Fréchet, *Études anglaises*, 39:4 (October–December 1986), 473.
Maureen Murphy, *Irish Literary Supplement*, 6:1 (Spring 1987), 25.
Christopher Murray, *Comparative Drama*, 21:1 (Spring 1987), 91–93.
84-34. CULLINGFORD: *Yeats: Poems*
Reviews:
Declan Kiberd: "Taking Stock of Yeats," *TLS*, 13 February 1987, 166.
84-96. JEFFARES: *A New Commentary on the Poems of W. B. Yeats*
Reviews:
Josephine Johnson, *Literature in Performance*, 6:2 (April 1986), 103–4.
84-106. KOMESU: *The Double Perspective of Yeats's Aesthetic*
Reviews:
Edward Engelberg, *Yeats Annual*, 5 (1987), 267–70.
Jacqueline Genet, *Études irlandaises*, 11 (1986), 244.
Declan Kiberd: "Taking Stock of Yeats," *TLS*, 13 February 1987, 166.
Andrew Parkin: "Drama East and West," *Canadian Journal of Irish Studies*, 12:1 (June 1986), 79–84.
Anthony Roche, *Southern Humanities Review*, 20:3 (Summer 1986), 271–73.
84-125. MCDIARMID: *Saving Civilization*
Reviews:
David Bradshaw: "L'entre deux guerres," *Essays in Criticism*, 36:4

(October 1986), 352–55.
Andrew Gibson, *Yeats Annual,* 5 (1987), 272–76.
Sister Bernetta Quinn: "Modern Poets," *Contemporary Literature,* 28:1 (Spring 1967), 133–41.
84-132. DE MAN: *The Rhetoric of Romanticism*
Reviews:
George Bornstein, *Yeats,* 5 (1987), 222–26.
84-138. MAXWELL: *A Critical History of Modern Irish Drama*
Reviews:
Ronald Ayling: "The Irish Dramatic Movement 1891–1980: A Review Essay," *Essays in Theatre,* 5:2 (May 1987), 139–44.
Seamus Deane, *Canadian Journal of Irish Studies,* 12:1 (June 1986), 95–97.
84-222. YEATS: *Byzantium*
Reviews:
S[hyamal] B[agchee], *Yeats Eliot Review,* 8:1&2 (1986), 147–48.
84-229. YEATS: *The Poems: A New Edition*
Reviews:
John P. Frayne, *Journal of English and Germanic Philology,* 86:1 (January 1987), 139–44.
Anthony Gardner, *Harpers and Queen,* May 1984, 204.
Harry Goldgar: "The Great Yeats Event," *Times Picayune* (New Orleans), 11 December 1983, section 3, 12.
Judith L. Johnston, *Magill's Literary Annual,* 1985, 692–96.
84-230. YEATS: *Poems of W. B. Yeats*
Reviews:
John P. Frayne, *Journal of English and Germanic Philology,* 86:1 (January 1987), 139–44.
85-42. CAVANAUGH: *Love and Forgiveness in Yeats's Poetry*
Reviews:
Thomas Parkinson, *Yeats,* 5 (1987), 220–22.
85-65. DEANE: *Celtic Revivals*
Reviews:
Nicholas Murray: "To Sing the Burden of History," *New Statesman,* 6 September 1985, 26.
85-125. HASSETT: *Yeats and the Poetics of Hate*
Reviews:
Edward Engelberg, *Yeats,* 5 (1987), 226–30.

Declan Kiberd: "Taking Stock of Yeats," *TLS*, 13 February 1987, 166.

Thomas Parkinson: "Yeats and Hate," *English Literature in Transition*, 30:4 (1987), 473–75.

85-170. KOHFELDT: *Lady Gregory*

Reviews:

James F. Carens, *Yeats*, 5 (1987), 235–43.

James Pethica, *Yeats Annual*, 5 (1987), 257–60.

85-172. KUCH: *Yeats and A. E.*

Reviews:

James F. Carens, *Yeats*, 5 (1987), 243–46.

Eileen Douglas, *Studies*, 36:301 (Spring 1987), 121.

Robert Greacen: "Poet and Puritan," *Books Ireland*, 115 (July/August 1987), 135–36.

John Hanratty: "Literature," *Linen Hall Review*, 3:4 (Winter 1986), 31.

Declan Kiberd: "Taking Stock of Yeats," *TLS*, 13 February 1987, 166.

Maureen Murphy, *Irish Literary Supplement*, 6:1 (Spring 1987), 25–26.

85-185. MCCORMACK: *Ascendancy and Tradition*

Reviews:

Terence Brown, *Hermathena*, 140 (Summer 1986), 111–14.

Richard Fallis, *Clio*, 15:3 (Spring 1986), 321–23.

William H. O'Donnell, *Yeats*, 5 (1987), 253–55.

Mary Helen Thuente: "Two Books on Irish Literature," *English Literature in Transition*, 30:1 (1987), 104–9.

Robert Tracy, *Victorian Studies*, 29:4 (Summer 1986), 619–20.

85-217. NORTH: *The Final Sculpture*

Reviews:

Sister Bernetta Quinn: "Modern Poets," *Contemporary Literature*, 28:1 (Spring 1987), 133–41.

Andrew Swarbrick: "Modern Perplexity," *Critical Quarterly*, 28:3 (Autumn 1986), 109–14.

85-228. O'SHEA: *A Descriptive Catalog of W. B. Yeats's Library*

Reviews:

Sarah E. How, *American Reference Books Annual*, 17 (1986), 466–67.

216 K. P. S. Jochum

85-245. PUTZEL: *Reconstructing Yeats*
Reviews:
Carolyn Holdsworth, *Yeats*, 5 (1987), 255–63.
Declan Kiberd: "Taking Stock of Yeats," *TLS*, 13 February 1987, 166.

85-249. RAINE: *Yeats the Initiate*
Reviews:
John Hanratty: "Countries of the Mind," *Books Ireland*, 108 (November 1986), 228.
Claude Rawson: "A Question of Potency," *TLS*, 24 July 1987, 783–85.

85-255. RIÁPOLOVA: *U. B. Ĭeĭts*
Reviews:
V. Khorol'skii: "Dramaturgiĭa V. B. Ĭeĭtsa," *Voprosy literatury*, 11 (November 1986), 268–74.

85-287. STEAD: *Pound, Yeats, Eliot and the Modernist Movement*
Reviews:
George Bornstein, *Yeats*, 5 (1987), 222–26.

85-317. YEATS: *The Collected Letters*, vol. 1
Reviews:
Ronald Blythe: "Almost Instant Maturity," *Country Life*, 20 February 1986, 458.
Terence Brown: "The Music of Time," *Irish Review*, 1 (1986), 93–95.
Ian Fletcher: "Yeats: Letters and the Visual Arts," *English Literature in Transition*, 30:4 (1987), 475–81.
John P. Frayne, *Journal of English and Germanic Philology*, 86:3 (July 1987), 464–66.
René Fréchet, *Études anglaises*, 39:4 (October–December 1986), 474–75.
Roy Fuller: "Log-Rolling," *London Magazine*, 26:1&2 (April/May 1986), 145–46, 148.
Jacqueline Genet: "Yeats Revisited," *Études irlandaises*, 11 (1986), 241–44 (in French).
Rüdiger Görner: "Vom Werden eines Dichters: Über die Briefe des jungen W. B. Yeats," *Neue Zürcher Zeitung*, 8 November 1986, 70.
John Gross: "Books of the Times," *New York Times*, 22 April 1986, 23.

Steven Helmling: "Yeats Early and Late," *Sewanee Review*, 95:3 (Summer 1987), 490–94.

David Holloway: "Yeats on the Way Up," *Daily Telegraph*, 7 February 1986, 16.

Nicholas Jenkins: "Retrospective Intimacy," *Literary Review*, 97 (July 1986), 52.

Elizabeth Bergmann Loizeaux, *Yeats*, 5 (1987), 230–35.

Colin Meir: "Literature," *Linen Hall Review*, 3:3 (Summer 1986), 30–31.

Jeffrey Meyers: "Fairies and Peahens," *National Review*, 38:15 (15 August 1986), 43–44.

Robert Nye: "Early Thoughts of the Gland Old Man," *Scotsman*, 5 April 1986, Weekend Scotsman, 3.

Phoebe Pettingell: "Young Yeats," *New Leader*, 22 September 1986, 14–15.

Diane Roberts, *Western Humanities Review*, 41:1 (Spring 1987), 88–91.

Alan Robinson, *Review of English Studies*, 38:150 (May 1987), 271–72.

Noel Russell: "Revising the Batty Image," *Irish News*, 3 April 1986, 6.

Colin Smythe: "Yours, W B," *London Standard*, 26 February 1986, 19.

Frank Stack: "Lyricism and Life," *Times Higher Education Supplement*, 21 March 1986, 23.

Daniel Taylor, *Magill's Literary Annual*, 1987, 142–45.

Helen Vendler, *New Yorker*, 16 March 1987, 96, 100–104.

Auberon Waugh: "Voice from Innisfree," *Sunday Telegraph*, 2 February 1986, 12.

85-323. YEATS: *Purgatory*

Reviews:

James W. Flannery: "No Racist Apologia for Yeats," *Irish Literary Supplement*, 6:1 (Spring 1987), 24.

85-329. *Yeats Annual No. 4*

Reviews:

Edward Engelberg: "Yeats Annual," *English Literature in Transition*, 30:2 (1987), 249–51.

Alan Robinson, *Review of English Studies*, 38:151 (August 1987), 405–6.

Dissertation Abstracts, 1987

COMPILED BY GWENN DE MAURIAC

Purgatory: A Chamber Opera in One Act After Yeats.
[Original Composition]
Lawrence Harold Cave III, Ph.D. Harvard University, 1986. 135 pp. Order No. DA8620441.

Purgatory by Lawrence Cave is a chamber opera in one act based on the play of the same title by William Butler Yeats.

(*DAI* 47.7 [January 1987] 2359A)

"Rooting Mythology in the Earth": W. B. Yeats at Ballylee.
Susan Fisher Miller, Ph.D. Northwestern University, 1986. 301 pp. Order No. DA8627379.

Yeats scholarship has tended to stress the poet's debt in the Tower poems to literary precursors and occult symbolism, portraying his proprietorship of Ballylee Castle as an inconvenience ventured for the sake of a romantic pose. But Yeats called his Tower both "monument" and "symbol"; he directed that the cover of his *Tower* volume "suggest the real object . . . all my art theories depend on just this rooting of mythology in the earth." In addition to appearing in his poetry, he believed,

---

*Minor corrections have been made.

the building bore witness to his life. This study endeavors to illuminate the actual property's importance in Yeats's career, and argues that Yeats's poetic Tower is very much rooted in his experience with "the real object" and its West of Ireland surroundings. Yeats's creation in verse of a third tower, the product of archetypical and literary associations combined with the powerful realities of the place itself, is what Miller's work attempts to clarify.

The Introduction surveys previous Tower scholarship and outlines Miller's aims in treating Yeats's Tower period. The following chapter traces Yeats's increasing use of earth-bound imagery as his career matures, and looks to the medieval literary method *figura* for an analogue of Yeats's "rooted" Tower symbolism. Chapter 3 briefly surveys the poetic legacy of Milton's melancholy tower-dweller in *Il Penseroso,* and goes on to argue for contrasting influences at Ballylee: *L'Allegro,* the Irish Normans, William Morris, Yeats's fellow tower-dweller Edward Martyn, and the architect William Scott. The fourth chapter, drawing on Yeats's unpublished correspondence with Ireland's Congested Districts Board and on reminiscences by local residents and the poet's daughter, provides a biographical account of Yeats's purchase, restoration, and life at the Tower. The dissertation overall gives special attention to the nine "residential" Tower poems; Chapter 5 consists of extended readings of six of them.

Having completed the *Tower* cover, T. Sturge Moore assured Yeats, "I think that the Tower is recognisably your Tower and not anyone else's." The dissertation concludes with a look at how Thoor Ballylee, as it is today, continues to reflect that third entity, "Yeats's Tower."

(*DAI* 47.8 [February 1987] 3033A)

Speaking With Authority: Credibility and Authenticity in Browning's Men and Women *and Yeats's* The Wild Swans at Coole.
Leonard L. Hatfield, Ph.D. Indiana University, 1986. 232 pp. Order No. DA8627991.

How do the speakers in poems and books of poems seem more or less authoritative, commanding, credible, or authentic? The theories of reader-response criticism and narratology provide the foundation for this inquiry, and Hatfield explores for each volume a reader's responses to the characters, personae, and the textual presence of the author. A speaker's

status, attitude, and relation to the subject and the listener all help the
reader assess the degree and kind of authority each speaker claims. In
addition, the arrangements of poems in collections such as these, in
concert with thematic and structural repetitions and parallels, further
enhance our awareness of the author's textual presence and in turn his
own credibility and authenticity. For example, in *Men and Women*
Browning encourages the reader to make certain judgments of his fifty
dramatic and lyric speakers before demonstrating decisively his own
authenticity and credibility as a poetic speaker. Yeats's *Wild Swans,* on
the other hand, seems at first to demonstrate a simple progression among
its poetic utterances through which the textual author promotes the au-
thority of a transcendent authority system. Yet the work undercuts this
movement, allowing the reader to decide whether the system finally does
have credibility. These discussions form the main demonstrations of the
approach, and Hatfield follows them with suggestions for future research
in explorations of historical and contemporary readers' responses to
works in other genres and periods. To provide examples of the former,
Hatfield concludes with brief readings of Ezra Pound's "Canto I" and
John Barth's "Menelaiad" section in *Lost in the Funhouse.* These readings
argue that both Pound and Barth, in different ways, aim to disrupt
readers' expectations about continuity and the nature of fictive utterances
in order to teach new ways to perceive literature and, in turn, to enforce
the authenticity of their textual voices.

(DAI 47.8 [February 1987] 3047A)

*Response to Failure as Reflected in the Poetry of G. M. Hopkins, His Contem-
poraries (Francis Thompson and Lionel Johnson), and the Moderns.*
   Pushpa Naidu Parekh, Ph.D. The Louisiana State University and
   Agricultural and Mechanical College, 1986. 251 pp. Director: Re-
   becca W. Crump. Order No. DA8629188.

The study of the poetic persona's responses to the experience of
failure, as expressed in the poetry of G. M. Hopkins, his minor contem-
poraries (Francis Thompson and Lionel Johnson), and the moderns (par-
ticularly Dylan Thomas), actualizes the poet-text-reader interactions in
the reading experience.
   Chapter 1 concentrates on the Hopkins persona as he responds to his
failures in priesthood and poetry writing, the effects upon the reader, the

reader's involvement in the outcome of the poem, and the parallels and divergences between Hopkins and the persona.

Chapter 2 studies Hopkins's persona in his struggle to move from human isolation to human association. The poems of isolation emphasize the persona's dissociation from family, homeland, and humanity in general. Through the medium of human interaction, the persona establishes a bond with God.

Chapter 3 deals with the dual vision expressed in Francis Thompson's poetry—the vision of the playful child and the aged man. In examining the poems in which the persona fails or succeeds in integrating the heavens and the London streets, the central interest is Thompson's pull towards and away from Hopkins and the decadents.

Chapter 4 is concerned with Lionel Johnson and his aesthetics of failure. A combination of the "mark," "anti-mark" polarities of the self, the persona here is preoccupied with antithetical elements such as art and religion, life and death, and success and failure.

Chapter 5 examines the emergence of the anti-heroic clown persona in modern poetry. The clown figure images the central paradox in the modern world-view: a rejection of theology, yet a yearning to image the self as a kind of god. The chapter briefly analyzes the use of personae in Yeats, Pound, and Eliot, and concentrates on the variety and complexity of the clown personae as developed by Dylan Thomas.

The conclusion traces the movement from Hopkins, through Thompson and Johnson, to the moderns as that of a shift from a renewed integration of the self with God to a comic-pathetic collision of self with self and the existential reality.

(DAI 47.9 [March 1987] 3436-37A)

Visual Art and the Poetics of Rossetti, Morris, and Yeats.
David Steven Faldet, Ph.D. The University of Iowa, 1986. 327 pp. Supervisor: Florence S. Boos. Order No. DA8622765.

This dissertation examines the relationship between the visual art and the poetry of Dante Gabriel Rossetti and William Morris. Its primary purpose is to argue that Rossetti and Morris compared their poetry to their art and that their idea of the structure and function of the poem was partly shaped by the comparison. A secondary purpose of the study is to outline the ways in which the art and poetics of Rossetti and Morris proved influential on a later poet: Yeats. Another secondary purpose of the work is to examine the limitations which all three writers applied to the literary theory of mimesis, and to argue that each is firmly part of the post-Kantian tradition of idealist literary theory.

The first chapter is a study of Rossetti's use of the cloaked expression of allegory, especially as it grows out of his sense of the relationship between the signifier and the signified in painting. The second chapter deals with the idealism of Rossetti's aesthetics, focusing on his use of the image of the mirror to demonstrate his mistrust of passive description. The third chapter argues that the paradigm of artistic activity for Rossetti was embodied in the figure of the musician and that Rossetti used this figure especially in his paintings to create the effect of synesthesia. The fourth chapter examines the way in which the silence of the visual image affected Rossetti's poetic ideal.

The fifth and sixth chapters study the relation between the two arts in the work of Morris. The first of these uses the semiotic concept of the index to explain Morris's special sensitivity to the physical presence of the artist in the work of art. The second of these chapters is a study of the way in which pattern takes precedence over the referential in Morris's work.

The final chapter studies the ways in which William Butler Yeats found a prototype in the art and literature of Rossetti and Morris for dramatizing the tension between the world of fact and the world of desire.

(*DAI* 47.9 [March 1987] 3433A)

A Vision of the Valley: Mesoamerican and Yeatsian Planes of Malcolm Lowry's Under the Volcano.
Ardis M. Slater, Ph.D. Kent State University, 1986. 309 pp. Director: Bobby L. Smith. Order No. DA8628948.

Malcolm Lowry structured *Under the Volcano* on various "planes," a method which has enabled critics to systematically analyze this complex work. This dissertation examines the relatively unexplored Mesoamerican and Yeatsian planes, revealing them as important thematic and structural scaffolding. They also serve as necessary keys to author intention: Lowry realized only after publication of the novel that many readers viewed the ending as pessimistic, while he had not meant it to be even depressing. Slater illustrates that his familiarity with Mexico and with concepts of W. B. Yeats, as evidenced in *A Vision* and "The Second Coming," created the dichotomy; readers lacking Lowry's extensive knowledge in these areas miss important references and allusions which point toward a more optimistic conclusion.

Slater's work supports Lowry's claim that he had "designed, counterdesigned and interwelded" a book that "could be read an indefinite number of times and still not have yielded all its meanings." Slater maintains that the inherent, interrelated ideas embedded in the Mesoamerican and Yeatsian planes are essential to a complete understanding of the novel. The first chapter demonstrates that the wheel-like structure imposes order on Lowry's work and supports the major theme of eternal recurrence. Manifested in a seemingly endless network of associative references, symbols, and allusions, this theme is particularly reinforced through the leitmotif of "The Second Coming," and through Mesoamerican mythology. Chapter 2 is concentrated on the ancient gods of Mexico, who not only serve as archetypes for characters but also add another dimension to the overall understanding of the human condition as perceived by Lowry; furthermore, they illustrate that the characters are, as he intended, aspects of one being.

The third chapter focuses on the novel's animals and birds, revealing their thematic importance, symbolic relevance, and intrinsic relationship to the Mesoamerican and Yeatsian planes. Chapter 4 explains certain political references and allusions, providing the reader with an easily accessible guide to this level of the novel, while illustrating the significance of seemingly casual comments. The final chapter further examines aspects of Lowry's method, his conception of time and fate, and his unorthodox presentation of eternity.

(DAI 47.9 [March 1987] 3437A)

Mothers, Heroes, and Hearts Turned to Stone: Mythologizing and Demythologizing in Irish Drama.
    Kathleen Anne Quinn, Ph.D. Washington State University, 1986. 297 pp. Chair: Virginia M. Hyde. Order No. DA8702560.

This dissertation explores modern dramatic adaptations of two powerful Irish mythological motifs: the sovereignty goddess and the warrior hero. Critics who discuss the treatment of myth by such major dramatists as W. B. Yeats, J. M. Synge, and Sean O'Casey have failed to acknowledge that the archetypes used hold such authority that invoking them (mythologizing) or breaking the mythic pattern (demythologizing) allows even minor works to be relatively potent. Therefore, this study, while including major writers, also examines dramatists relatively unknown outside of Ireland—Alice Milligan, Eimar O'Duffy, Donagh MacDonagh, Bryan MacMahon, Maurice Meldon, and Dorothy Robbie. In addition, because of the close ties of myth, literature, and nationalism in Ireland, this study includes plays by such political figures as Padraic Pearse, Thomas MacDonagh, Constance Markievicz, and Terence MacSwiney.

Chapter 1 depicts Mother Ireland, a poetic image derived from the ancient sovereignty goddess and invested with strong political overtones, while chapter 2 shows the polarities between mothers' views of heroism: as a route to renown and glory for their children or as a complete waste of human life. Concentrating on the sovereignty powers of Mother Ireland, chapter 3 examines her mythological and historical prototypes—Deirdre, Maeve, and Dervorgilla. Chapter 4 discusses ancient heroic figures, Cuchulain and Finn, who served as sources for Irish drama and as models for a myth of sacrificial bloodshed. By focusing on plays concerning the 1916 Rising, chapter 5 explores dramatic tensions produced by the tradition of the hero as a political martyr. Pearse's and MacDonagh's plays, predictably, glorify the mythic hero, but other dramas stress the negative results of the tradition of sacrificial bloodshed. Chapter 6 discusses dramatizations of stone images, often suggesting "hearts o'stone," as O'Casey called those who were myth-possessed. Although stone, like myth, endures, it is static and inflexible; works in the chapter, therefore, tend to demythologize, at least in part, the myths discussed in the previous chapters. Finally, the conclusion of this study examines the need for remythologizing as reflected in many twentieth-century Irish dramas.

(*DAI* 47.10 [April 1987] 3755A)

Seamus Heaney: Poet in a Destitute Time.
Ann Valentine, Ph.D. Tufts University, 1986. 107 pp. Order No. DA8702391.

Seamus Heaney: Poet in a Destitute Time is a developmental study of the first twenty years of Heaney's poetry, 1966–86, which includes a discussion of Heaney's early, unpublished version of *Buile Suibhne*, later rewritten and published under the title *Sweeney Astray*. The poet's own critical terms, the structural dichotomies he employs in *Preoccupations* and in later interviews and essays, are used to discuss his poetry. Parts I and II of *North* reflect the feminine and masculine modes of creativity and a consciousness divided by the demands of civil war. The extent to which the poet's response to public crisis, the conflict between participation in history and artistic detachment or transcendence, influences Heaney's artistic development is analyzed. *Fieldwork* is seen as a dialectical response, and the similarities and differences of Heaney's and Yeats's reactions to war and violence are considered.

Sweeney Astray and the earlier version of *Buile Suibhne* are contrasted with each other and with a literal translation of the work by O'Keeffe which Heaney refers to. Heaney's two versions of the Sweeney legend are seen as alternative artistic responses to the poet's situation. *Sweeney Astray* addresses Ireland's need for a unifying vision of itself. Use of current place-names and language "put the present in the past and the past in the present," the limit, Heaney says, of what poetry can accomplish politically. In the earlier version of the Sweeney story and in the "Sweeney Redivivus" sequence Sweeney represents the poet as alienated anti-hero, iconoclast, and critic of the tribe rather than mediator and healer.

Patterns of attachment and detachment which emerge in the poetry are traced in *Door into the Dark, Wintering Out* and "Sweeney Redivivus." The influence of Joyce and Yeats is taken up; Heaney's development is viewed in terms of their mapping of literary evolution. The artist's relationship to his community, a central theme in Heaney's work, is analyzed. In "Station Island," old debts are settled, and the poet balances the claims of art and life. This equilibrium frees him to make a new, metaphysical connection with the past in *Hailstones* and recent uncollected poems.

(*DAI* 47.10 [April 1987] 3761A)

Keepers of the Flame; Hermeticism in Yeats, H.D., and Borges.
   Lauren Louise Meggison, Ph.D. University of California, Irvine, 1987. 281 pp. Chair: Julian Palley. Order No. DA8710250.

Hermeticism has often been relegated to a minor and arcane role in established literatures and literary criticism. Hermetic literatures have operated primarily as hidden and oral traditions and therefore have not been as readily available as more conventional written literatures. Hermetic studies are beginning to enjoy a renaissance due to the study of myth and mythic language and the incorporation of psychoanalytic theory in literary criticism with the theories of Freud, Jung, and Lacan.

Yeats, H.D., and Borges, roughly contemporaries, rely on hermetic allusions to increase symbolic potency in their writings. Hermetic imagery surpasses the richness of ordinary symbolic language by stimulating the deep structures of memory and activating what Yeats would call "The Great Mind," what Jung would term "The Collective Unconscious," and what Meggison suggests is an "archetypal language." An introductory analysis of the relationship between poetry and the sacred explores the historical genderizing of language and perception which leads to the repression of the feminine and the irrational in language and culture. These repressed elements surface in the literary privileging of lunar imagery, the biological privileging of lunar time, and the appropriation of pagan, matriarchal elements by the failed patriarchy of Christianity.

Robert Graves's studies of the ancient poetic colleges of the Druids and the tree alphabets of ancient and modern Irish contextualize Yeats's imagery. The Celtic Revival of the 1890s and Yeats's use of the kabbalistic rose are considered in his early poetry; "The Two Trees" provides a model of the Sephirotic Tree of Life and Crazy Jane and the Bishop provide Yeats's contrast of pagan and Christian elements in *Words for Music Perhaps;* H.D.'s *Trilogy, Sagesse,* and *Hermetic Definition* invoke Isis and alchemical imagery to emphasize the materiality of language and effect its transformation. Borges's "Una vindicacion de la Cabala" and "Casas Como Angeles" parody gnosticism and Ruben Dario's *modernismo.* The tiger is a central alchemical image. "The Library of Babel" is an architectural version of the kabbalistic tree. Borges's inversion of lunar and solar imagery suggest "The Divine Marriage" of the alchemist's athanor.

(*DAI* 48.2 [August 1987] 386A)

Circumventing Yeats: Austin Clarke, Thomas Kinsella, Seamus Heaney.
Charles Lee O'Neill, Ph.D. New York University, 1987. 386 pp.
Advisor: Denis Donoghue. Order No. DA8712774.

The poetry of Yeats asserts more than a poetic authority: it has also delineated and fostered several imaginative myths, two of which—that of the Celtic Twilight and that of the Anglo-Irish "intellectual tradition"—have been taken for true images of Ireland. Irish poets after Yeats, challenged by both his authoritative poetic voice and his imaginative myths of Ireland, faced a formidable task as they undertook to establish their own poetic authority and to identify or invent myths of their own.

Austin Clarke spent much of his career in the "shadow" of Yeats. He first developed a Celtic-Romanesque image of Ireland to circumvent Yeats's influence. Later, he developed a "neo-Catholic" poetry (a phrase Yeats himself offered Clarke). Clarke's "neo-Catholic" Ireland stresses social criticism and satire. His poems play with a variety of prosodic devices to accentuate their differences from those of Yeats.

Thomas Kinsella's Ireland is a place of psychic fragmentation. In his most distinctive poetry, he embraces that fragmentation, both in form and content. By calling on archetypal figures from the collective and personal unconscious, he attempts to recover the buried contents of the Irish psyche and, in so doing, begin what he regards as a necessary process of individuation, national and personal.

Seamus Heaney's Ireland is a pastoral landscape into which violence has erupted. His early poetry details that landscape, his later poetry the divisions and the violence to which it has been subjected. His myth of "North," a place of ritual sacrifice annually repeated, is a deterministic one. The tensions between Heaney's instinctive poetry parallel the pastoral landscape itself and the violence with which it must come to terms.

The work of these poets displays a "swerve" away from the poetry of Yeats. Each has manufactured his own version of the language, created distinct points of view, and experimented with poetic form. This dissertation explores those strategies of circumvention.

(*DAI* 48.3 [September 1987] 656A)

Epiphany Blazing into the Head: The Quest for Inner Truth and Transcendence in W. B. Yeats's Verse Drama.
Frank Mkalawile Chipasula, Ph.D. Brown University, 1987. 203 pp. Order No. DA8715467.

This thesis consists of four chapters which attempt to trace the evolution of an aesthetic form in Yeats's verse drama. Chipasula borrows James Joyce's term *epiphany* to identify the "new form" of Yeats's plays for dancers and to describe both thematic and structural epiphanies. This study focuses on the following middle and last plays, *At the Hawk's Well*

(1917), *The Only Jealousy of Emer* (1919), *The Dreaming of the Bones* (1919), *A Full Moon in March* (1935), *Purgatory* (1939), and *The Death of Cuchulain* (1939). Chipasula also studies Yeats's early plays, such neo-traditional dramas as the Elizabethan, double-plotted *On Baile's Strand* (1904), the Greek-based *The King's Threshold* (1904), and *Deirdre* (1907), which epiphanize theme. These plays build up to an epiphanic resolution, and they anticipate the dance plays which fuse thematic and structural epiphanies in a rigorously compressed, hence epiphanic form. To achieve that astringent form, Yeats stripped the form of all the impurities of conventional drama, fused dance, mask, ritual, and poetry into a tight, new form. Yeats experiments with a variety of epiphanic moments, dances, and music in the middle plays as an image-making strategy and, with darkening vision, he projects denied or dark epiphanies in the last plays. Having noticed subtle aesthetic echoes between Yeats's ritualistic epiphany plays and various folk traditions, especially African, Chipasula includes an appendix in which is suggested a new approach to Yeats's dance dramas.

(DAI 48.4 [October 1987] 927A)

The Bardic Style in the Poetry of Gerard Manley Hopkins, William Butler Yeats, and Dylan Thomas.
Sheila McColm Deane, Ph.D. The University of Western Ontario (Canada), 1987. Advisers: B. Rajan, F. McKay.

There have always been elements in the poetry of Gerard Manley Hopkins, William Butler Yeats, and Dylan Thomas that have been difficult to account for. Although each of these writers is generally engaged with modern poetics and sensitive to the issues of his time, certain characteristics of the work—such as Hopkins's unusual diction, Yeats's concern for traditional meters, or Thomas's elaborate rhyme schemes—seem out of keeping with a position in the mainstream of modernism. This dissertation attempts to shed some light on these puzzling characteristics by revealing them to be features of a bardic style, the consequence of these writers' involvement with the work of Welsh and Irish medieval poets. The distinctive traits of bardic poetry—its orality, formality, and purposiveness—are, in the opinion of this study, what gives rise to some of the more provocative aspects of the poetry of Hopkins, Yeats, and Thomas.

Each poet is discussed separately, but the shape of each discussion is the same. First, the poet's early influences and original conceptions of the bardic tradition are dealt with. Second, a close analysis of several important poems indicates the extent to which each poet made use of the principles of bardic prosody and versification. Third, the poet's reasons for re-animating a bardic stance in a modern world, and some of the interesting incongruities of that endeavor, are explored.

What the study discovers is that a better understanding of how the bardic style functions in the poetry of Hopkins, Yeats, and Thomas illuminates not only some of their more difficult works, but also brings a new perspective to some of their most familiar poems. And the study demonstrates that, far from being outmoded or regressive, the bardic style offers these three writers a source of linguistic refreshment and a formal challenge that enables them to take an entirely new approach to the very modern problems of poetic language, meaning, and efficacy.

(DAI 48.6 [December 1987] 1458A)

Review Essays

The Authors Were in Eternity—or Oxford: George Yeats, George Harper, and the Making of *A Vision*

George Mills Harper. *The Making of Yeats's* A Vision: *A Study of the Automatic Script.*
Carbondale and Edwardsville, Ill.: Southern Illinois University Press; London: Macmillan, 1987. Volume 1:xvi + 301 pp. Volume 2:xvii + 463 pp.

A review essay by PHILLIP L. MARCUS

Do the souls of the dead survive, and haunt the margins of our consciousness? Supernatural powers weave and unweave our destinies? We shall all find out, of course, in the fullness of time. Some achieve a fideistic confidence while still in the flesh. In others, of whom W. B. Yeats was famously one, the will to believe constantly struggles against demands for empirical evidence. Yeats himself *may* have received such evidence; but although we now have for the first time the full story of the "incredible experience" (AV-B 8) that led to *A Vision,* that story will undoubtedly leave the skeptical reader still skeptical. George Mills Harper's diligent researches enable us to know "what happened," but he himself remains (perhaps inevitably) unable to answer definitively the question of "what *really* happened."

Yeats's occult interests have generally been easiest to take seriously when they involve such respectable strands of "the tradition" as neoplatonism, the religions of the East, and even the "prophetic books" of Blake. Many readers have drawn the line firmly at ritual magic, astrology, and spiritualism, though Yeats, anticipating their criticism of *A Vision,* provokingly compared the Muses to "women who creep out at night and give themselves to unknown sailors and return to talk of Chinese porcelain— . . . except that the Muses sometimes form in those low haunts their most lasting attachments" (AV-B 24). While others, notably F. A. C. Wilson, Kathleen Raine, and James Olney, have also demonstrated convincingly Yeats's own place in the occult tradition, none of them has been as willing as Harper to pursue the relationship when it took the poet to the metaphoric waterfront where he consorted with mediums, fortune-tellers, and the magicians of the Golden Dawn. For years Harper has been laboring with difficult, obscure, and often forbidding materials. His *Yeats's Golden Dawn* uncovered the history of Yeats's involvement with that admittedly often ludicrous secret order— involvement the length and passionateness of which had seldom been suspected. The fine collection *Yeats and the Occult* and editions of the correspondence of the enigmatic, mystical W. T. Horton and of the neglected but crucial 1925 edition of *A Vision* firmly established him as the leading authority in the field. No one, then, could have been more qualified to tackle the even more daunting task of studying the voluminous unpublished materials out of which *A Vision* itself had developed. Most scholars had either ignored those documents entirely or else snatched a fragment here and there to illustrate some argument. Harper has devoted over a decade to organizing, deciphering, transcribing, and, finally, analyzing the more than 3600 pages of manuscript; *The Making of Yeats's* A Vision is the result of those heroic labors. He has done his work splendidly, and the result is a book no subsequent study of Yeats can afford to ignore.

Faced with presenting so great a mass of hitherto unknown material, Harper has wisely chosen a principally historical approach, describing session after session of the 450 sittings of "automatic writing" from the first tentative experiments in October 1917 to the substitution in early 1920 of communication through "sleeps." The Automatic Script itself is quoted at length, but the obscurity of the subjects considered and the elliptical "question and answer" form of much of the Script make it largely unintelligible without his valuable narrative and commentary.

A substantial amount of the Script bears directly upon the poems and plays Yeats was working on during the same period, especially *The Only Jealousy of Emer,* and should provide fuel for studies of the creative work. Of course much also relates to the concepts eventually presented in *A Vision* and to similar materials, such as the Initiatory and Critical Moments, that did *not* get into *A Vision* because, as Yeats himself admitted, he did not understand them. What is at first most surprising, because Yeats's own published accounts do not prepare us for it, is how much of the Script (perhaps three quarters by Professor Harper's own estimate) was devoted to *highly* personal matters: Yeats's love affairs, his and George's sex life, the children (with Michael destined to be the Avatar of a new cycle). Such things, of course, could not have gotten into *A Vision,* and were in fact obviously not intended for it. Essential to the biographer, they are also relevant to the vexing question of what was actually going on.

Although Yeats chose in the 1925 edition of *A Vision* to disguise the origins of the text in the elaborate narrative fiction of Michael Robartes, Owen Aherne, and the *Speculum Angelorum et Hominorum,* he gave a more accurate if indirect version of the "incredible experience" in the same volume in the poem "Desert Geometry or the Gift of Harun Al-Raschid," and then a "straight" account in the introduction to the revised edition. On 24 October 1917 Mrs. Yeats began doing automatic writing, serving as medium for spirit communicators who wanted to give Yeats both a philosophical system and "metaphors for poetry" (AV-B 8–9). But if such were their purposes, why did they spend so much time on philosophical concepts that came to nothing and especially on affairs so private that they could appear in the creative work only *concealed by* rather than *as* metaphors? Anyone who has studied transcripts of seances knows that the concerns of the departed are often distressingly banal, their "lifestyles" mundane, their "wisdom" trivial; and the Yeatses ostensibly had to contend also with "frustrators," hostile spirits who wished to interrupt communication and to that end often introduced bogus materials and instigated the pursuit of chimerae. Such explanations might suffice except that they beg the question of the supernormal nature of the events, and that seems (whatever our general attitude towards the subject) particularly risky to do in this case; for there is considerable reason to suspect that here, in a sense that McLuhan never intended, the Medium *was* the Message.

Harper's own view on the matter seems ambiguous. He notes several signs that the communication was *not* "automatic" (1:x–xiii). His statement that George herself "was soon caught up in her own imaginative scheme and was in fact more readily convinced than Yeats by the revelations of her Communicators" (1:x, 5) counterpoints the negative implications of "imaginative scheme" against an apparent affirmation of external forces at work. Throughout the text, credit for specific materials is usually given to "George and her Controls" but sometimes we are told that "George had dropped her mask momentarily" (1:217) or that she slipped "out of character for a moment" (2:219). These ambiguities mirror the contradictory signals given by Yeats himself. In the revised version of *A Vision* we find "My wife's interests are musical, literary, practical, she seldom comments upon what I dictate except upon the turn of a phrase; she can no more correct it than she could her automatic script at a time when a slight error brought her new fatigue" (AV-B 21); yet he was being somewhat disingenuous, for he wrote of her to John Quinn that she was "a student in all my subjects" (1:57) and in an unpublished passage he dedicated the book "To my wife who created this system which bores her" (Richard Ellmann, *Yeats: The Man and the Masks,* new edition [New York: Norton, 1978], 266). As Harper puts it, Yeats was "sceptical and . . . required proof," but did convince himself that "George was the medium, never the source of the revelations" (2:410, 413). Yeats, of course, *wanted* to accept the supernatural interpretation. Harper may be unsure, or perhaps is only politely veiling his own doubts. Although I personally am willing to credit the *possibility* of supernatural events, I feel that in the case of the Yeatses the overwhelming implication of the evidence is that it was not supernatural beings or spirits but George herself who was the source of everything in the Script not contributed by her husband.

By George's own admission, the Script *began* with deception on her part. As she told the late Richard Ellmann, she saw that her new husband was gloomy and

> understood that he felt he might have done the wrong thing in marrying her rather than Iseult, whose resistance might have weakened in time. Mrs. Yeats wondered whether to leave him. Casting about for some means of distraction, she thought of attempting automatic writing. Yeats was familiar with this procedure although it was disapproved of by the Golden Dawn. Her idea was to fake a sentence or two that would allay his anxieties over Iseult and herself, and after the session to own up to what she had done. . . . Yeats was at once captured, and relieved. His misgivings disappeared, and it did not occur to him that his wife might have divined his cause of anxiety without preternatural assistance (Ellmann xii–xiii).

In 1917, she did not need to look far for a "means of distraction." Due largely to the bereavement of countless families during the Great War, spiritualism was undergoing a boom, with the preceding year constituting a sort of annus mirabilis: Sir Oliver Lodge published his best-selling *Raymond* (twelve impressions by 1919); Conan Doyle began receiving spirit communications through automatic writing and spreading the spiritualist gospel through highly successful lecture tours; and (a particularly relevant parallel, though presumably unknown to George) Edith

Somerville and her recently deceased co-author "Martin Ross" (Violet Martin) began the collaboration through automatic script that was to produce fifteen more jointly authored books. It was, then, not so surprising that George (who had also assisted Yeats in some of his earlier investigations of spiritualist phenomena) should have thought of automatic writing.

It is true that she went on to claim that the "pencil began to write sentences she had never intended or thought, which seemed to come as from another world." George, who disapproved "with unexpected severity" of Ellmann's own skepticism, probably would not have downplayed with him the ostensibly supernatural aspects of the incident (Ellmann xvii). In any case, as the Script itself shows, Yeats's misgivings and anxieties about the women in his life by no means "disappeared": rather they dominated many of the early sessions, and even after he was able to accept that what he had done was best for all concerned, he continued regularly to ask the Controls questions about Iseult, and *many* about Iseult's famous mother. George had not *solved* the problem that first day, but she *had* discovered a valuable strategy for dealing with it. That same strategy not only promised to save and strengthen her marriage but also offered a unique outlet for her own creative impulses.

And so, I think, she continued the deception. Why else were the Controls so insistent, from the beginning of the experiments to the end, that there could be no Script before observers, "unbelievers in the house" (2:350; see also 1:73, 138–39, 160, 198)? Why else was George so opposed to his plan to tell openly of the automatic writing in the revised edition of *A Vision* that they had "the first and only serious quarrel of their marriage" (Ellmann xvii).? Yeats did sometimes press her to admit observers, but, though persistently probing and often mistrustful, he was so personally involved that he did not bring to his own experiments the same rigorous investigatory approach that had gotten him into trouble with Madame Blavatsky and characterized his ongoing participation in the Society for Psychical Research. If we are troubled by the idea that George was intentionally deceiving him, we may choose to see some or even all of the deception as *unconscious;* in either case, the source of the Script lay in her own mind, in her emotional and psychological needs. So in December 1917 Yeats was assured in the Script that he "need not have any of the old fear" about Iseult, and later that month was instructed to *"be comforted in the thought of her happiness"* (1:73, 92). Many passages in the Script were directly or indirectly strongly critical of Maud Gonne (e.g., 1:124), and however just the criticisms they seem motivated by personal dislike and jealousy; Yeats was even told that in a previous incarnation Maud "hated your wife & tried to destroy her" (2:313). On the other hand, "script depends on the love of medium for you—all intensity comes from that" (2:294), and George was also destined for a central role as mother of the "Initiate or New Messiah" (1:154).

Such efforts were paying off, but the success was bought at considerable cost to George herself. As early as 13 March 1918, Lolly Yeats reported to J. B. Yeats that George and "Willie seemed in such perfect accord. I never saw him look better, so young looking and so handsome. . . ." (1:227). But George herself was frequently brought close to exhaustion. Furthermore, Yeats often seemed so absorbed in the personal revelations that he was ignoring the philosophical ones and the development of the projected book that was to become *A Vision,* as well as his own creative work. Thus we sometimes find a careful rationing of the Script and of the personal elements in it. On 29 March 1919, "before the formal writing began," George (directly, Harper suggests) issued a stern warning: "For every public speech or lecture you give after tomorrow during the next 6 months I shall stop script one month—For every occasion you talk system in private conversation one month—Yes you must begin writing—Yes but dont fish for questions" (2:239). In March 1918, Yeats was told that "personal message[s] . . . are the most important of all our communications" (1:217). On 1 August 1919, "Ameritus," who was "weary of Yeats's preoccupation with personal experiences," ordered him to "get a new topic . . . orders are to leave that topic" (2:303). A few days later, however, the Communicators were deep in personal matters and Yeats was allowed for several sessions to pursue information about his and George's previous incarnations, but at the peak of his excitement about his discoveries he was told that the information he had been given was all bogus, that "The interpreter [George] has had too much strain," and that he should "wait five minutes & think of system—you are too full of the personal" (2:304–8).

It is in this context that deficiencies in the "spirits'" knowledge become especially suspicious. The Script reveals Yeats to have been a shrewd, often relentless questioner, and sometimes he pushed too far. "Thomas," pressed about why the Creative Genius is solar, the Ego lunar, confessed to being in a "muddle" (2:23); on another occasion Yeats was rebuked, "when you ask questions ask specifically—dont feel about or you mix me up" (2:83). Harper himself was shocked by the response to Yeats's request for a name for the state of spirits at phase 15, "you invent I cannot": "to say the least, this is a curious admission from spiritual Communicators, who are presumed to have more knowledge and power than living recipients" (2:137). Asking about the avatars of different cycles, "were they all born in Judea then?" Yeats received as answer only a brusque "goodbye" (2:76). No wonder that on another occasion, frustrated by failure to get "Thomas" to be more specific, Yeats exasperatedly broke out, "you mean that you know no more about it than I do" and was answered "exactly" (2:264). A far cry from "Where got I that truth? / Out of a medium's mouth" (P 214)!

Yet, despite the ironic flourish, I do not mean to imply condemnation. In a recent book about *A Vision,* Barbara L. Croft rejects the scenario of "a sly, womanly-wise George Yeats, aware of her new husband's lingering passion for Maud Gonne and her daughter, dup[ing] the credulous old man with the most transparent of carnival flimflam"; Croft considers it "unlikely that Mrs. Yeats could or would have deceived her husband for so long" (*"Stylistic Arrangements": A Study of William Butler Yeats's* A Vision [Lewisburg: Bucknell University Press, 1987], 16–17, 164). Of course Yeats was scarcely a "credulous old man": such faith as he achieved was won against an ongoing awareness of the potential for (self-) deception; his need and desire to believe provide much of the creative energy that informs his poems and plays; and the discoveries of *A Vision,* whatever their source, were central to the full flowering of his genius in the later work. Moreover, the Automatic Script and "sleeps" were in fact far too sophisticated to be described as "the most transparent of carnival flimflam"; but George certainly had the substantial talents required to carry out the demanding task of faking them. She had originally hoped to be an artist (Ellmann ix), she was a "student in all [Yeats's] subjects" and a member of the Golden Dawn; and she even seems to have been adept at personification, for Yeats reported that he had "heard my wife in the broken speech of some quite ordinary dream use tricks of speech characteristic of the philosophic voices" (AV-B 22). If George engaged in deception it was not, as with many professional mediums, for material gain, self-aggrandizement, or the pleasure of baffling the experts. And if the resultant Script offers no empirical evidence for the existence of the spirit realm, it contains another story, human and deeply moving.

Recent feminist theory provides a perspective from which to make sense of that story. Mary Ann Caws, exploring gender-determined differences in "self-presentation," actually used the story of the Automatic

Script, as Yeats had presented it in *A Vision,* to demonstrate that "it is not always permitted to engender one's own voice and text." As Caws saw it, "the writing wife's role . . . consisted of letting the writing pass through her transparently, of not getting in the way. The symbolists had particular designs on the transparent woman, who served up the sign, conveying it with fidelity, patience, and absolute personal silence" ("The Conception of Engendering / The Erotics of Editing," in *The Poetics of Gender,* ed. Nancy K. Miller [New York: Columbia University Press, 1986], 45). This account cannot be squared with the actual events, but the description of the underlying problem remains valid. Yeats himself, though often classed as a Symbolist, actually seems from a feminist point of view to have been rather enlightened; but there is no doubt that as a young bride who had grown up before the watershed of the Great War, George would have found it daunting to speak for herself on equal terms with one of the great modernist word-masters. The fiction of the Script enabled her both to communicate with him on even the most intimate subjects, and to share an imagined world of which they were in fact co-creators.

If, as many feminist critics have argued, ordinary language reflects phallocentric values, the burden under which women writers labor is to find a way of modifying language to fit it for their own use. The fiction of automatic writing seems, of course, to absolve the writer of responsibility for its content. Additionally, it posits a volition outside the range of normal human experience, and offers by that very feature a first step towards a women's writing, for "normal" implies the phallocentric status quo. A look at the earliest preserved page of the Script, reproduced by Harper on page 9 of his first volume, shows that George Yeats extensively modified the vehicle for those ostensibly supernatural revelations; the hand she used was not her ordinary one (present at the top of the page in the date), the words are run together without breaks or punctuation, and words themselves are supplemented by astrological symbolism— astrology being one area of the occult with which George was more deeply involved than Yeats. Not observable here, but common in the Script whenever particularly delicate matters are touched upon, is mirror writing, which, by reversing the normal order of words again symbolically suggests escape from the phallocentric, while its superficial unintelligibility promises the revelation of "occult" experience (the feminine realm, as much hidden as that of the spirits). That these features were essential to George for enabling her to find her voice both for communication and for creation is paradoxically underscored by the fact that in the later stages of the experiment she abandoned most of the distinctive features of automatic writing, using her normal hand, using regular punctuation and capitalization, and leaving breaks between words (1:xiii). Once the barriers between her and her husband were down, her place as a collaborator fully recognized, her own voice, represented by her own handwriting, could exist in a symbolic union with "his" language.

According to the Script, "the wisdom of heart comes at 18," George's own phase (2:155). Such wisdom characterized much of the advice she offered to Yeats concerning their life together: "tower renew renew—alone in it—yes through your wife" (2:163; 31 October 1918). In June 1919, with the guerilla war between Ireland and England now under way, the Script warned him "not to be drawn into anything— possible trouble in Ireland . . . you may be tempted to join in political schemes if there is trouble—& you must not . . . Some are brewing rebellion." That "some" unsurprisingly included Maud: "Nothing must be said *unless* she speaks of it—then simply say you are destroying the souls of hundreds of young men / That method is most wicked in this country wholesale slaughter because a few are cruel" (2:292). On the other hand, he was informed that "script depends on the love of medium for you—all intensity comes from that" (2:294). Consistently George urged him towards personal closeness and creativity, away from political activism and public involvement in general.

The Script allowed discussion of even the most personal matters, including sexual intercourse (2:360, 367–68) and family planning (1:217– 18, 2:224). According to Yeats's later notes, in one Script so personal that the collaborators destroyed it, he was told that "we were not to have a child at all unless I was quite sure I wanted it because (in mirror writing) 'The child would only give her happiness in being your child she does not want a child for its own sake' " (1:218). On one occasion the Yeatses were advised "not to have script when medium has Martha" (2:333). Harper speculates that "Martha" was "a maid or nurse, probably," but since there is no other evidence of a domestic of that name it seems just as likely that this was merely a euphemistic phrase for George's menstrual periods, during which she might well have found the always fatiguing sessions of automatic writing even more of a strain.

In any case, moods of tension, irritability, and loneliness did sometimes occur. As early as January 1918, the Script contained a reference to "medium being lonely," and in April of that year Yeats was accused (in mirror writing) of "boredom and coldness of heart" (1:154; 2:16). When George's patience and temper were pushed too far, she was capable of responding to Yeats's questions with such hostile replies as "you ought to know by now," "of course not," and even "nonsense" (2:169). George, it should be recalled, was pregnant during much of the time their experiments were conducted. Perhaps the most extreme and poignant outburst in the Script came on 30 January 1919, less than a month before the birth of Anne Butler Yeats:

> I dont like you
> You neglect me
> You dont give me physical symbols to use . . .
> looking at flowing water flowing life
> Any odd time.
>
> (2:219)

But it would be a mistake merely to dismiss such complaints by attributing them to the hypersensitivity of an expectant mother. As the lyric images suggest, the sense of deprivation here is at least partly *literary*. George had already come to think of herself as creator as well as medium. Earlier that very month she had sketched in the Script a symbolic drawing that had become the basis for at least three poems: "Another Song of a Fool," "The Double Vision of Michael Robartes," and "Towards Break of Day" (2:198 ff.). It depicted "Cormac's Chapel" at Cashel, surrounded by key images including hand, eye, book, butterfly, bird, circle, and cross. The associated dialogue warned Yeats that he was "empty— drained dry" (an anticipation of the later reference to "flowing water flowing life") and urged him to "go to the past—A historical & spiritual past" for a new inspiration. George went on to describe "complementary dreams" that encapsulated the central image pattern of "Towards Break of Day," so that, as Harper concludes, "George must be given credit for the basic organization if not the idea of the poem" (2:202).

    In their largest outlines, the philosophical concepts underlying both the material that found its way into *A Vision* and the philosophical (as opposed to personal) material that did not had virtually all appeared in Yeats's own work before 1917, and of course originated in the rich, complex occult tradition with which Yeats and George had both been familiar. Nevertheless, many of the specific ideas, terms, and schematic representations were contributed by her, so that she was "far more important in the making of *A Vision* than anyone has suggested . . . The book was in truth an unusual collaboration" (1:18–19).

In the Script itself, George carefully nurtured awareness that the collaborative process was essential. In January 1918, when Yeats stated "I have collaborated with Lady G (24) both intellectually & practically. So intellectual work is presumably possible with 12 & 24" he was informed that his relationship with Lady Gregory was "imbalanced—you created she transferred not real collaboration" (1:112). He then queried, "Present of M[edium] & self only condition of true collaboration?" As the long series of sessions continued, George sometimes became bored or tired and urged Yeats to stop the experiments and write, but Yeats himself pushed the questioning process relentlessly and thus seemed to be taking control (2:101). But when he suggested that they should work out a format in which he did all or most of the writing, he was told "no, . . . because we cant use you alone—must have you & medium *equally*" (2:192; 25 December 1918). The relationship was not to become one of those James had envisioned in *The Sacred Fount:* "vital one should not be vampirised by the non vital." The following July, inquiring again whether he should "take more definite control of topics taken up in script" he was rebuked with advice that reflects not only George's desire for equal involvement but also her own favored imagery and the wisdom of much of her advice: "NO but think more intimately . . . Do not see the flower without the petal / The stream without its stones / The child without its smile / The house without its windows" (2:295). In the fall of 1919 she sometimes recorded material in the Script without "even the pretence of questions" (2:338–39).

The "sleeps" that largely came to supplant the Script, although they placed George in a role apparently more passive than the automatic writing, put less physical strain on her but actually gave her greater active involvement, as they facilitated monologues as well as responses to questions. The Script had explained that daemonic communication, which occurred in circumstances "when *both* individuals are creative," arose from "sexual union"; the "sleeps," therefore, might incorporate such union: "let her sleep naturally—then when she is asleep put her into the mesmeric sleep—when she speaks you will know the sleep has changed—make love and I will see that *she suggests a sleep* to come first I want her to wake up just as it comes—a still lake" (2:369–70). Later still, Yeats recorded, "after we gave up the sleeps . . . we have worked at the system by discussion" (2:404–5). At this final stage George could, and did, participate in the process without the benefit of any of their previous enabling fictions.

As late as 1922, George apparently opposed publication of "the system" (2:405); while to Yeats *A Vision* meant "a last act of defence against the chaos of the world" that he hoped would allow him to write for ten years "out of [his] renewed security" (2:407–8). George may have found their closeness during the exploratory stage more meaningful than the fruits of their explorations. Yet a passage in the Script for 22 July 1919, in which the Initiatory and Critical Moments that loom so large in the notebooks are identified as a "deliberate work of art" by the collaborators (2:298), clearly suggests George's own creative pride and brings us back to the discarded dedication in which Yeats acknowledged her as creator. Being a modest person, she wanted, as Harper observes (1:19), no public recognition; but with the publication of the Script we can offer such recognition as her simple due.

"The Passing of the Shee": After Reading a Book about Yeats and the Tribes of Danu

Peter Alderson Smith. *W. B. Yeats and the Tribes of Danu: Three Views of Ireland's Fairies.*
Gerrards Cross, Bucks.: Colin Smythe; Totowa, N.J.: Barnes & Noble, 1987. 350 pp.

A review essay by BRENDAN O HEHIR

> Adieu, sweet Angus, Maeve and Fand,
> Ye plumed yet skinny Shee,
> That poets played with hand in hand
> To learn their ecstasy.
>
> We'll search in Red Dan Sally's ditch,
> And drink in Tubber fair,
> Or poach with Red Dan Philly's bitch
> The badger and the hare.
> —J. M. Synge, "The Passing of the Shee"

The combined title and subtitle of this book suggest an uncertainty of aim that in the realization has produced three very uneven essays yoked together into the semblance of a single work. That is, most students of Yeats will automatically equate "Tribes of Danu" with "Ireland's Fairies," yet will be curious to learn how the yoking of Yeats with the "Tribes" elicits *three* views of the "Fairies." Because for perhaps most readers the recurrent Yeatsian equation of "Tribes of Danu" with "the Fairies" may be hazy, eagerness for enlightenment will likely overcome initial quibbling and act as a powerful magnet towards this alluringly titled book.

Inside the covers a nine-and-a-half page Introduction (13–21) itself breaks into three mini-introductions: Part 1, pp. 14–17; Part 2, p. 18; Part 3, pp. 19–21. Thereafter follow the three separate parts: Part 1, "Na Tuatha Dé Danann," containing six chapters further subdivided into numbered sections; Part 2, "Na Daoine Sídhe," of five chapters; and Part 3, "The Unappeasable Host," like Part 1 of six chapters.

Part 3, occupying more than half the bulk of the text, is both the least exceptionable and the least novel portion of the book, comprising discussion, in the form of annotation and exegesis, of the major portion of Yeats's literary production in the decade of the 1890s—that is, the period during which he was most self-consciously responding to his sense of ancient Irish myth. The works covered are *The Countess Cathleen;* the poems of *The Rose; Stories of Red Hanrahan;* poems of *The Wind Among the Reeds;* and *The Shadowy Waters.* The discussions are enlightening relative to Yeats's changing and ambivalent attitudes vis-à-vis the "Fairies," but otherwise the explications are rather unexceptionable, as said before, than profound.

The novelty of this book, and the source of its possible allure, is precisely its implied promise to illuminate those pesky "Tribes of Danu," the Fairies, whom that rooted man, John Synge, called the "plumed yet skinny Shee." Unhappily to one enjoying something of relative intimacy with those Shee, a solecism in the title of Smith's first section reveals a certain insecurity with the Irish language in which the proceedings of Danu's people are recorded. Na Tuatha Dé Danann seems intended as Irish for "The Tribes of the Goddess Danu," but in fact redundantly means "Goddess Danu's the Tribes," whereas the correct formula Tuatha Dé Danann, means succinctly "Goddess Danu's Tribes" which may be reformulated in the gallicized syntax of English as "The Tribes of [the] Goddess Danu." The fact that Smith's feeble grasp of the Genitive Case is shared with the IRA (who have similarly named their boys' auxiliary *Na Fianna Éireann* ["Ireland's the Warriors"] instead of *Fianna Éireann* ["Ireland's Warriors"]), is not necessarily reassuring.

From the title, the first section proceeds to an elaborate unintended vindication of Pope's notorious dictum that a little learning is a dangerous thing. Chapter 1, "Before the Celts Left the Land of Summer," begins by quoting the first sentence of Lady Gregory's *Gods and Fighting Men,* and then asks (25) "But who are the Tuatha de Danaan . . . the ancestors of the fairies?" (The erroneous de Danaan is Lady Gregory's; within the paragraph Smith reverts to the correct Dé Danann). Lady Gregory had already provided to that question an answer that is now uncontested by any reputable Celtic scholar: by the *Gods* of her title she means precisely the Tuatha Dé Danann. Historical linguistics, archaeology, and comparative anthropology have all long ago confirmed that "the mysterious and splendid race of Ancient Ireland" are the gods of the Irish Celts, most of them readily identifiable with the gods of the continental and British Celts, seen through a mist of Irish Christian euhemerization.

Although Lady Gregory is a frail reed to lean on, in this instance Smith would have done better to trust her. Even Daniel Murphy, author of the foreword to the 1970 second edition (The Coole Edition) of *Gods and Fighting Men*, brought out by Colin Smythe, Gerrards Cross—publishers of Smith's present book—accepts and supports Lady Gregory's identification of the Tuatha Dé as the Irish gods. But relying on an *a priori* definition of the essential nature of gods, Smith has persuaded himself that whatever gods may have been worshipped among the ancient Irish, members of Tuatha Dé were not among them. His argument, largely concentrated in chapter 5, "Dei Terreni," is a mockery of scholarship. I have already commented on the weakness of Smith's grasp of Irish syntactical grammar, and the first section of this chapter, "Linguistic Evidence," shows that Mr. Smith lacks all linguistic competence in the language, in any of its historical stages. He asserts, for instance, that Tuatha Dé Danann "could alternatively mean 'the tribes of the gods of Danu' " (77). *Dé* in fact can be a nominative plural, but cannot be a genitive plural, as his proposed translation requires, because it never nasalizes the following word. Although Smith's bibliography runs to eleven closely printed pages, and his sources include two dictionaries of Modern Irish, it does not include the Royal Irish Academy *Dictionary* and *Contributions*, the chief lexicon of the older language, nor even Windisch's nineteenth-century *Wörterbuch*. In the R.I.A. *Contributions to a Dictionary of the Irish Language,* Fascicule *degra-dodelbtha* (Dublin 1959), he could profitably peruse the article on "2 dia": 53.31–54.23, with supplemental consultation of the notes on seven separate words spelled *dé* in the first Fascicule *D-degóir* of the actual *Dictionary* (Dublin, 1913). Those two fascicules represent a spread of 46 years of Irish-language scholarship, and might also shake Smith's belief (commented on below) that the element *-da* can possibly mean "hand."

The dangers of a little learning are manifest throughout this entire first part of the book, in unconscious parodies of scholarship, in travesties of scholarship, in plain fumbling incompetence, and chiefly in the uncritical choice of a notorious forgery as a prime authority. An uninformed parody of scholarship is the unblinkingly confident assertion that "there is an Ancient Ethiopian god called Medr, whose name must surely be cognate with" that of the Old Irish mythological personage Midir (59). This is a parody of philology. Must surely be cognate: who dare gainsay such manifest erudition? Of course, that Medr and Midir (Smith's preferred spelling Midhir is Modern Irish) are cognate names is in the highest degree unlikely. What is the etymology of either name, and above all, in what language does the name Medr exist? An Ethiopian god is likely to have an Ethiopic name, and Ethiopic and Indo-European are not at all cognate; Irish, even Old Irish, is a distinctively Indo-European language. The name Midir is not transparent, but in an Old Irish linguistic context suggests something like "judge" or "assayer" or "balancer." Has Mr. Smith any notion of this, and what does *Medr* mean in what language? Smith's speculation belongs to the "Tower of Babel" school of pre-nineteenth century linguistic guessing games. One wonders also what is the point of this game, since Medr is said to have been an earth-god, and Smith will not have Midir be any kind of god at all.

A literal travesty of scholarship is a statement attributed to the authority of the distinguished scholar Francis John Byrne, in whose seminar at the Yeats Sligo Summer School Smith was a student in 1980: "many Continental towns, including Lyons, bear names related to that of Lugh" (80n14). Doubtless Byrne spoke words to this effect in the form of *obiter dicta* to his seminar; they are a commonplace of Celtic scholarship. I doubt, however, that Byrne literally said "names related to that of Lugh." The fact is that the name is literally Lugh's: "the place-name [Continental Celtic] *Lugudunon,* Latin *Lugudunum,* which includes his name in its older form *Lugus* [Celtic *Lugos*] and from which derive— among other modern names—Lyon and Laon in France, Leiden in Holland and Leignitz in Silesia." So Proinsias Mac Cana iterates the same commonplace in a book Smith elsewhere cites, but which he has not apparently read very attentively.[1] The Old Irish representation of the name *Lugh* is *Lug,* and there is no doubt that its archaic form was *Lugos,* identical to that of the Continental Celtic god after whom so many settlements were named. His wording allows Smith to avoid facing the fact that the Irish Lugh is the Common Celtic Lugos, the god Caesar identifies with Mercury; in other words, that Lug is, like the rest of the Tuatha Dé, a god.

An example of simple ignorant blundering involves the name of the Dagda, the father-god of the Old Irish pantheon. There has not for a long time been any dispute about the etymology of this name. *Dag-* clearly means "good," and *-da* is a reduced enclitic form of *dia,* "god." A man named David Fitzgerald in the early 1880s asserted that the element *-da* really means "hand," relying on a seventeenth-century gloss, but

1. *Celtic Mythology,* rev. ed. (New York: P. Bedrick Books, 1985), 25.

within a year he was set right by Whitley Stokes, and except for Smith, that ghost has been unseen since until the present book. After reviewing the Fitzgerald-Stokes controversy, Smith concedes that at best "Fitzgerald's case must be considered unproven" (79), yet on an earlier page he says outright of the Dagda, "his name . . . means 'good hand' " (34). Again, his dogmatic belief that the Tuatha Dé are not gods militates against his accepting the simple fact that the name, or title, of one of them is simply "the Good God" (or "The God of the Nobles" as Eric Hamp has recently suggested).

The most serious blunder of all, however, reflects his mistaken preference of an even less reliable authority than Lady Gregory, namely *Lebor Gabála Érenn,* the so-called *Book of Invasions.* This choice occasions an astounding statement: "The mythological pre-history of Ireland bears an extraordinary resemblance . . . to her early known history" (38). What astonishes about this statement is its implicit equation of what Smith takes to be a "mythological pre-history" with the "early known history" of Ireland. His source for both is the self-same *Lebor Gabála,* a purported history of pre-Christian Ireland that treats all of the characters in Irish mythology as historical persons of the remote, but relatively datable, past. The book does not purport to be a "mythological pre-history," that is, a compendium of native beliefs about the persons and races of Irish mythology; rather it is a denial of mythology, a work of thorough-going euhemerization, that insists on treating mythology as history. The work is totally Christian, and therefore one of its functions is to destroy all sense of the pagan supernatural. The names and stories of the gods preserved in the popular memory are rigorously demythified and crammed forcibly into a chronological scheme derived from Genesis. By the same token it provides the Irish with a thoroughly fictitious history of the lost past. Therefore, Smith's "mythological pre-history" and "early known history" of Ireland are one and the same: an all but total forgery brought into final form about the twelfth century. Although no doubt it is, as Smith says, "a repository of pagan mythology" (25), it is certainly a gross distortion, and it is impossible with any security to draw out of it a clear picture of pagan mythology. Only when other surviving texts are available, that draw from sources anterior to the *Book of Invasions,* can one reasonably begin to deduce from the fragments some sense of the probable real content of Old Irish pagan myth.

The compilers of *Lebor Gabála Érenn* (literally *The Book of the Taking of Ireland* but frequently translated as *The Book of Invasions*) had several ends in mind: One was to accommodate Irish cultural self-awareness to history. Pre-Christian Ireland, tantamount to pre-literate Ireland, had a learned professional class, much as Caesar and others describe for the Gauls, whose function was to preserve the oral "documents" of law, religion, and dynastic rights and treaties. Among the mass of their preserved lore were no doubt more-or-less factual memories of significant events that really had taken place in the past, intermingled with legends of the doings of gods, and aetiological tales of "culture heroes"—e.g., King Eochaid Airem, "the Ploughman," who introduced the correct method of ploughing with oxen. But they knew nothing of what Herodotus or Thucydides would recognize as "history"—that is, a temporal sequence of recorded human events located firmly in linear time. The Old Irish seem in fact, from their records, to have had the utmost difficulty in grasping the concept of linear time: for instance, Irish Christian authorities that Smith would rely upon, in attempting to fit the career of the wholly legendary King Conchobar Mac Nessa into European linear history, are quite unembarrassed to have his birth coincide with that of Jesus Christ, and his death in old age (certainly as a grandfather) occur precisely on the day of the Crucifixion—when Christ, according to most European sources, was about 33 years old. The compilers of *Lebor Gabála* in fact had no critical tools by which to discriminate among pagan deities and legendary figures, heroes and dynastic founders, who might have had a genuine prehistorical existence. All were treated equally and placed in temporal correlation with world-historical figures such as Moses, Alexander, Julius Caesar, and Jesus Christ. There is no "early known history of Ireland" whatsoever in any way predating the first annals that began to be recorded in ecclesiastical circles no earlier than the late fifth century.

A correlative purpose of the *Book of Invasions* forgers was to censor Irish paganism out of existence. Starting perhaps about the seventh century there had been a growing corpus of written narratives of the exploits of the pagan gods and heroes, many accompanied by caveats that the events described were fabulous nonsense dating from the time "before Faith" when demons held sway among the Irish, and worthy to be believed only by fools. Such caveats can be reassuring to the modern reader, implying that the monkish scribes have not tampered much with the "idiotic rubbish" they are recording. The *Book of Invasions* authors have no such weakness; they want to be sure that none among their frailer countrymen may continue to harbor belief in the divinity of the vanquished gods, so all the gods are resolutely euhemerized into a race of one-time invaders of the country, the Tuatha Dé Danann, who are of course not gods, but merely historical predecessors of the contemporary mortal Irish. Many mortal Irish, and non-Irish, since the compilation of this deplorable book have swallowed it whole as genuine history. Peter Alderson Smith is but the latest victim of the hoax.

Another function of the *Book of Invasions* is to account for the medieval population of Ireland, which was composed of several ethnic groups that the *Book* forcibly reduces to two: Gaels [*Goidil*] and Fir Bolg [*Belgae*]. Both of these were genuine peoples, among several others, all of which were probably Celtic in race, and certainly all Celtic in speech and culture. Irish society was tribal, with certain tribes dominant and others subordinate. Most of the dominant tribes, though not all, were Gaels; the *Book of Invasions* simplified the taxonomy by reckoning all dominant tribes as Gaels, all the subordinate tribes as Fir Bolg, freely faking genealogies and tribal ancestors to "prove" the classifications. Since the Gaels' own tribal traditions, and universal consensus, held that they themselves—the ruling tribes—were later arrivals in Ireland than their subject tribes, the *Book of Invasions* had to represent the coming of the Gaels to Ireland as last in a succession of prior invasions, wherefore a preceding history of invasions, back to post-Adamic generations, had to be concocted. A particular embarrassment was another component of the current population of Ireland that could not be ignored. That was *Tuatha Dé Danann,* a race that everybody knew continued to lurk hiddenly throughout the country— inside mountains, beneath lakes, and notably within the megalithic chamber tombs the Irish called *síde,* literally "mounds." (Certain of these, such as the magnificent monument in the Boyne Valley now called Newgrange, Mr. Smith seems never to have seen, since he denigrates the *sídhe* universally as "small, dark, dirty and grim" [45]). Since the Tuatha Dé were the gods of the Gaels, dispossessed by Christianity, but also the gods of the Fir Bolg, the historicizing solution was to make the Fir Bolg, the Tuatha Dé and the Gaels of related ancestry, and to constitute successively the last three waves of invaders of the island, each wave in turn conquering and subduing the preceding. So the Tuatha Dé had enslaved the Fir Bolg, and the Gaels in turn, having defeated the Tuatha Dé and driven them into hiding, took over as masters of the Fir Bolg. All three thereafter coexisted: Fir Bolg as serfs tilling crops, hewing wood, and drawing water; Tuatha Dé animating the natural features of the countryside, controlling the weather, and regulating the succession of kingships; the Gaels, after

Christian literacy and the shocking introduction of linear Roman time, writing books to stabilize dynastic hierarchies and the new religion.

The truth in this is exemplary of the distortions of *Lebor Gabála*. The Goidil and the Belgae were both Celtic peoples, and therefore ethnically and culturally related. Tuatha Dé Danann for the most part were pan-Celtic gods, and therefore gods of both the Belgae and the Goidil, a genuine *tertium quid* between them. This truth is an ingredient of *Lebor Gabála Érenn,* but is scarcely extractable out of that book.

But even to the producers of *Lebor Gabála* it was evident that the Celts—Gaels, Belgae, Dumnonii, and others, including the Érann after whom the island is still named, together with their gods—were not the first inhabitants of Ireland. Whatever their evidence, modern archaeology, to which I shall advert shortly, confirms its truth. Wherefore they invented a whole series of previous occupiers of the land, going back prior to the Flood (since Scripture assured that the Flood was universal, it was incumbent upon the Irish to supply some record of its effect on their own country)—all of whom fortunately had perished leaving only marks on the landscape as their memorials.

A final purpose of the "Invasions" forgery was to support and validate royal dynastic ambitions, especially those of the dynasty of the Uí Néill, a major Goidelic lineage and aspirants to a fictitious suzerainty over all the other petty and provincial kings of Ireland. Since the bulk of our sources for ancient Irish literature and mythology, especially the Ulster, or Red Branch, Cycle of sagas, were written down under Uí Néill auspices, not surprisingly most of them echo to a greater or lesser extent the Uí Néill "party line" that determines *Lebor Gabála Érenn,* and recensions later than *Lebor Gabála* naturally tend to treat it as unwarrantably authoritative. Fortunately not all Old Irish secular texts are infected with Uí Néill propaganda; especially helpful is a small corpus of tales derived from the kingdom, or province, of Leinster, as well as other stories written down before the intellectual hegemony of the Uí Néill literary school, and further transcribed without meddling.

The situation is not hopeless, but anyone setting out to ascertain the nature of pagan Irish theology must do so from the recognition that not one purely pagan document survives to us. Every single mention of any one of the Tuatha Dé Danann occurs in a manuscript that is the end-product of a series of transcriptions, all of which were the work of Christian clerics. Pagan Greeks and Romans and even Norse managed to write down legends of their gods without the glare of Christianity blurring their outlines. The Irish were not so lucky, but were lucky in that some monkish scribes probably wrote out texts reasonably close to their traditional (oral?) sources, though never, however, with an entirely easy conscience. Many other monks worked hard to discredit Irish pagan mythology, even to the extent of putting into the mouths of such gods as Aengus and Lugh specific denials that they were in fact gods, but rather mortal descendants of Adam. The later an Irish text, the more likely is it to be heavily euhemerised; and especially any text composed later than the *Book of Invasions* is likely to take that weighty forgery as solid authority.

In summary, *The Book of Invasions / Lebor Gabála Érenn* is not an early history of Ireland, but a fiction, and it is not a pre-history of Irish mythology, but a deliberate falsification of Irish mythology. Although a great deal of real mythology has doubtless been fed into it, it is vain to try to reconstruct, from any of its narratives, the shape of any myth for which there is no independent corroboration. To try is as profitable as attempting to reconstruct a goose out of a cleverly molded pâté, even if the pâté happens to be shaped like a goose.

The *Lebor Gabála,* therefore, is not "the best source that we have" (25) for ancient Irish mythology or history; it is about as bad a source as can be imagined. The "history" is a framework of chronology derived from such continental sources as Orosius's *Sex Aetates Mundi (The Six Ages of the World)* into which persons and events from Irish traditional lore, whether mythology or traditional history, have been squeezed by force. Thus the purely mythical Ulster king Conchobar Mac Nessa is given a lifetime contemporary with that of Christ, and consequently all the persons occurring in the stories usually grouped into the "Ulster Cycle" are dated with totally baseless confidence to the first Christian century. Reliance on the historicity of this kind of fabrication leads Peter Smith into assertions that would embarrass a serious scholar. After discussing the highly mythical "Second Battle of Mag Tured [Moytura]" in which the Tuatha Dé Danann expel from Ireland the evil race of Fomoire (Modern Irish *Fomhóraigh*)—a battle that is patently a cosmic struggle between Light and Darkness—Smith notes that "certainly the Second Battle of Moytura does not mark the end of the Fomorians in Irish mythology," since "at the time of the Ulster Cycle, the High King Conaire Mór has three Fomorian hostages" (36). What can he mean by "at the time of the Ulster Cycle"? Does he mean *Lebor Gabála's* first century of Christ? Or does he mean the unknowable prehistoric date

when the mythological Ulster Cycle began to be formed? Or the time
when Ulster Cycle stories first began to be written down? *Lebor Gabála's*
chronology would place the Second Battle of Mag Tured some time
before the Hebrew Exodus, so Smith's assumption of Fomorian survival
from Mag Tured to "the time of the Ulster Cycle" implicitly accepts a
chronological relationship which is purely an artifact of the *Book of Inva-
sions*. Since the Battle and the Fomorians, like Conaire Mór and the
Ulster heroes, have no existence outside myth, there is no chronological
relationship among them. Likewise he notes that the Fianna hero Diar-
maid kills a Fomorian (this by pseudo-dating would be third century
A.D.)—giving Lady Gregory, God help us, as authority. (Lady Gregory
relates this in *Gods and Fighting Men* 294, but does not note her source.)
Actually, even for these assertions his sources are highly dubious, mak-
ing even greater nonsense of what he is trying to say. Conaire Mór can
be placed "at the time of the Ulster Cycle" only because the scribes who
preserved for us the story of that king took mythology at face value and
were little affected by the *Book of Invasions* fabrications. By *Book of
Invasions* standards, Conaire the Great should have lived no later than the
first century before Christ, that is, several generations prior to the life of
Conchobar Mac Nessa (*A.D. 1–33!). But the prime scribe of the story of
his tragic reign lists the names of the contemporary rulers of the major
Irish provinces, including Conchobar over Ulster and Medb over Con-
nacht. That is simply because in story-land Conchobar is always Ulster's
king—unless the point of the story is that at that time he was not;
likewise Medb always rules Connacht. In a saga, "The Wooing of
Étaín"—closely related to the story of Conaire Mór—Conaire's grand-
father, or great-grandfather, Eochaid Airem, "the Ploughman," takes
the kingship of Ireland, and Conchobar Mac Nessa, king of Ulster,
submits to him. This event, therefore, two or three generations before
the lifetime of Conaire, presumably must also be "at the time of the
Ulster Cycle"—in that endlessly elastic Irish first century A.D. Most
absurdly, the successive reigns of Eochaid Airem, Etarscél, and Conaire
Mór must all have taken place not just within Conchobar's putative
thirty-three-year lifespan, but all within the period of his reign as king of
Ulster.

    In brief, *Lebor Gabála* is factual nonsense, and any argument based
upon its authority is equally nonsense. Peter Smith, however, is capable
of developing nonsensical arguments entirely without benefit of that
forgery. For one, part of his argument that Tuatha Dé Danann are not

gods is that "genuine" Irish gods have no character or personality, whereas Tuatha Dé characters are often richly individual. The genuine Irish gods, he says, are to be found in the oaths frequently sworn by pagan persons in Old Irish literature. These invariably take a form such as "I swear by the gods my people swear by!" Such gods are never named and so undeniably lack personality. But it has not occurred to Smith that no Irish pagan person swears in a text written by an Irish pagan scribe. Christian scribes who are busy denying divinity to Lugh are scarcely going to blow the gaff by having someone say "I swear by Lugh!" The scribes, and their readers, know perfectly well that the pagan Irish had gods, and presumably swore by them, and narrative veracity requires those oaths at times to be recorded. But rigorous euhemerism of the actual gods requires their names to be suppressed, and a mere descriptive formula inserted. Does Smith really believe ancient Irish pagans actually swore such circumlocutionary oaths as "I swear by the gods of my tribe"? Modern Christian Irish do not swear "by the God of the Holy Roman Catholic Church." Whatever his thoughts on this matter, Smith reasons that the real gods the ancient Irish worshiped were in fact colorless and characterless, very different from the Tuatha Dé; and at that point he begins to abandon normal reasoning entirely.

It is in the sixth and last chapter of Part 1, "The Tribes of the Goddess Danu," that ignorance and misinformation combine to produce a conclusion quite beyond logic. This begins by positing in pre-Celtic Ireland a primitive race Peter Smith terms the Sídhe. Never mind that the Old Irish word síd, genitive singular and nominative plural síde (the form that he is citing in the recent spelling sídhe), literally means "a mound (inhabited by supernatural beings)." (The proposed Indo-European root is *sed- as in Latin sedere, English sit.) In Old Irish mythology the "mounds" of Ireland—for the most part megalithic (Stone Age) chamber or passage tombs—are inhabited by supernatural beings, all of whom that are named being well-known members of Tuatha Dé Danann. Collectively these people were called aes síde, "mound folk," so modern writers and translators have grown into the habit of calling the mound people Sídhe (literally "mounds"), particularly confusing readers like Smith (and Yeats, and AE, though probably not Synge). Likewise they have taken to translating the word sídhe, when it refers to the mounds, as "elf-mounds" or "fairy mounds," and when it refers to their inhabitants, as "fairies." There are in Irish no fairies who are not literally mounds. The word fairy is not Irish, and there is properly no Irish word for fairy (unless it be the recent *sidheóg, sióg,* with a feminine diminutive, therefore crudely translatable as "Moundette").

Peter Smith has some dim sense of the etymology, at least in so far that he grasps that the "Sídhe" are inextricably connected with the "mounds" and ancient ring-forts and souterrains, but he has decided that the Sídhe were in fact the primitive aborigines of Ireland, who inhabited those "not desirable dwellings" (95), and continued to lurk in them throughout the successive dominations of Ireland by the Tuatha Dé Danann and the *Milesians* (*Lebor Gabála's* term for the Goidil or Gaels). The *Milesians* as a name is another piece of ingenious forgery: the eponymous Míl Espáne, their patriarch, is a slightly gaelicized *miles hispaniensis,* "the Spanish soldier," a cultural gift of St. Isidor of Seville who first proposed, on pseudo-etymological grounds, that the inhabitants of Ireland (*Ibernia*) must have come from Spain (*Iberia*).

The Gaels *qua* Milesians Smith identifies as the Celtic intruders into Ireland, the Sídhe as immeasurably earlier pre-Celtic troglodytes. If the Sídhe were indeed anything like the savages Smith wishes to think them, it is passing strange that already in Old Irish the word *síde* as an adjective had developed the meanings "wondrous, enchanting, charming, delightful" (R.I.A. *Contributions,* fascicule S, 215:58–59 [Dublin, 1959]). The mystery race then is the Tuatha Dé Danann, who, he believes, were definitely not Celts, though the survivors of their defeat intermarried among the Celts, and also not aboriginal primitives. All of this, mind, is speculation about prehistoric reality in Ireland. And Smith's bold solution is that the genuine Tuatha Dé were none other than Phoenician gold-miners, who "set foot in Ireland before the Celts did" (100). "Ancient mine-workings are still to be seen in Ireland," he correctly observes, and adds, less accurately, that "a [gold] mining camp . . . would not leave conspicuous archaeological remains" (100).

Patently Smith knows nothing whatsoever about the prehistoric archaeology of Ireland, and indeed virtually nothing about archaeology. It is true that no Phoenician remains have been found in Ireland, but the country is not a blank in which Phoenicians could have mined gold without trace. Moreover, his vision of "Stone Age" primitives overawed by the magic of Phoenician gold-extraction and smelting betrays a comic-book notion of what the term *Stone Age* means. The high culture of ancient Egypt developed entirely in the Stone Age. The Stone Age is not a specific historical set of dates, but rather a state of technological development prior to the use of hard metals such as bronze and iron. But a pre-bronze technology does not preclude the use of soft metals like gold and silver. Major civilizations of the Old World developed in the Stone Age, and the New World cultures that built the magnificent cities and temples of Mexico, Meso-America, and Peru were technically still in the Stone Age when they were dragged by the Conquistadores not merely into the Iron Age, but into the age of gunpowder and Gutenberg's moveable type. Yet their workmanship in gold and silver is famously marvelous. Three useful terms Smith might add to his vocabulary and understanding are *Paleolithic, Mesolithic,* and *Neolithic.* A fourth I have used already is *Megalithic.*

The first known inhabitants of Ireland arrived after the last great Ice Age, in Boreal Zone VI: 7500–5200 B.C. These were flint quarriers and tool-makers of the Mesolithic (Middle Stone Age). The Old Stone Age had finished in Northern Europe before the first men ventured to Ireland. By 3000 B.C. Ireland was inhabited by Neolithic farmers who had begun to build court-tombs for their dead. These tombs are the historically earliest man-made "mounds" of Old Irish mythology. Are their Neolithic builders also their primitive Stone Age inhabitants whom Smith's Phoenicians overawed?

About 2500 B.C. a new cultural wave arrived in Ireland, the Mega-lithic ("Large Stone") Passage-Grave builders. These people "grouped their graves in cemeteries, their first insular Irish one clustered tightly around imposing central tombs set in commanding positions in the val-ley of the Boyne river."[2] Three massive tumuli—Knowth, Dowth, and Newgrange—each covering an area of about an acre and a half, dominate a cluster of smaller similar tombs in the bend of the Boyne River. New-grange, now fully restored, has a diameter of 80 meters and a height of 15 meters, and contains a passage 19 meters long to a burial chamber 6 meters high. This is the edifice known in Old Irish myth as *Brug na Boinne,* residence of the god Aengus. The structure took incredible skill and hundreds of man-days of work to build; it is a feat of stone-age engineering comparable to the roughly contemporaneous great pyramids of Egypt.

This, also, is the presumable work of Smith's Sídhe primitives, who were abashed by the gold-mining Phoenicians—who could not, even if

2. Michael Herity and George Eogan, *Ireland in Prehistory* (London and Boston: Routledge and Kegan Paul, 1977), 57.

Smith's fantasy were correct—have arrived in Ireland for more than another 1,500 years. Meanwhile the Neolithic age ended and the Bronze Age began in Ireland, probably before the arrival of the first Celts. Which group precisely these latter were, and when they arrived, is quite uncertain. Most likely they were the Érann, a people who inhabited the south coast of Ireland into historical times, and from whom, through some medium, the Greeks ultimately got the name Iernê for the island as a whole. Suggested dates have ranged from 1000 to 100 B.C. The former may well be too early and the latter is definitely too late, at least for the Érann. The Greeks had likely learned the name Iernê before 500, wherefore the Érann must precede that date. Several waves of different Celtic peoples followed, Belgae and Dumnonii and others, ending with the Goidil, whose late descendants created the *Book of Invasions*.

The Celts, all or severally, brought with them the gods they shared with their brethren on the Continent and in Britain: Lugos; Cernunnos, who became Conall Cernach; Vindos ("the White," Welsh Gwynn, after whom Vindobona, now Vienna, is named), who became Fionn mac Cumhaill; as well as a deity known as Maponos (the " 'Great' or 'Divine' Son"), son of Matrona ("the Great Mother," whose name was also that of a river, now the Marne). Maponos may really be a title for Lugos, but in Irish he became Macc in Óc, "The Young Son," son of the river Boyne, and also known as Oengus (Aengus), who very frequently seems interchangeable with Lugh. In neighboring Wales Maponos became Mabon, son of Modron, and probable etymon of the *Mabinogi*.

The Bronze Age probably reached Ireland prior to the first Celts, and native gold mining and gold working began either then or in the late Neolithic, without aid from Phoenicians. About one hundred gold artifacts from the early stages of the Bronze Age survive in Ireland, plus about seven hundred other pieces from the later Bronze Age. Uncountable pieces are known to have been melted down in the nineteenth century, and unguessable quantities in prior centuries. The surviving artifacts are all of designs characteristic of Irish culture in the period, not Phoenician types.

The fantasy of the Tuatha Dé Danann being Phoenician gold miners in Ireland, overawing the primitive aboriginal Sídhe, simply makes no sense. There is no archaeological or other trace of Phoenicians in Ireland, and Ireland has no archaeological blank periods in which they might have quietly slipped in and out. Moreover, there is no evidence that the Phoenicians had reached even the western Mediterranean before 1000 B.C.[3] By the time they might have reached Ireland the Bronze Age and gold working were already in full swing there, with plenty of archaeological evidence for it. The indigenes, whoever they were genetically or linguistically, were the inheritors and perhaps also descendants of the Megalithic tumulus builders, and nothing in the archaeological record suggests that they had culturally regressed to the level of Smith's Sídhe, "a highly primitive, almost feral race" lurking secretively "in waste places and underground chambers" (95). Any such people can scarcely be relevant to any hypothesis about imaginary Phoenicians. And who, one wants to ask Smith, does he think built the underground chambers inhabited by his feral aborigines? Smith has failed to do his obvious homework before advancing his theory.

The sixth and final section of the sixth and final chapter of Part 1 of *Yeats and the Tribes of Danu* is called "Fairy Speech." This begins by conceding that his notion that lost Phoenician gold miners "would be the ancestors of the Tuatha Dé Danann" (100) is "pure speculation." Now, however, Smith asserts "there is a little evidence to support it, which has to do with fairy speech" (100). His chief specimens are two words, collected presumably from modern folk informants by W. Y. Evans Wentz (*The Fairy-Faith in Celtic Countries.* London, 1911), and both said to mean "water." The first, in "the language of the British fairies," is *yyor,* which Smith says, after querying whether in fact *yyor* be not a misprint for *ydor* (Greek ύδορ), is "cognate with Greek, but also with Welsh" (101). If *yyor* is indeed *ydor,* then it is not cognate to Greek, but is Greek. I do not know, however, by what system of comparative philology *yyor* can be demonstrably "cognate" with *ydor.* The Welsh word for *water,* however, is *dwfr, dwr* (cognate with Irish *dobhar*), and I take leave to doubt that this Common Celtic word relates to Greek *[h]ydor.* I find especially difficult the connection of *yyor* with *dwfr.* But this Welsh digression is irrelevant. The Irish "fairy" word for "water" is apparently *hugga,* which philologian Smith states "looks very much like GK. ύδορ, 'water,' again, with lenition of medial *d,* as would be normal in Irish" (101). *Sancta simplicitas!* "Lenition of medial *d!*" But unfortunately lenited medial *d* in Modern Irish never results in the sound /g/, but rather vocalizes, forming a diphthong with the preceding vowel. (In Old

---

3. Donald Harden, *The Phoenicians* (New York: Frederick A. Praeger, 1962), 64.

Irish medial *d* was *ipso facto* lenited, and pronounced /ð/ [voiced /-th-/].)
Is it possible Smith believes the name Midhir with lenited medial *d*, he
cites so often, is pronounced Miggir? It is not. In Old Irish it was pro-
nounced "mithir," in Modern Irish "mee-yir." *Hugga* in fact sounds
much more like a distortion of *uisge,* the common Irish word for "wa-
ter"; but I think, if the reported word has any validity (certainly not in
Fairy Language, but in a formula used by Irish peasants in throwing dirty
water out of doors), it is more likely to be the Irish word *cogar,* "whis-
per!", the actual source of English *hugger-mugger.* Of course, in all this
folly, Smith finds thoroughly acceptable the notion that the Tuatha Dé
must have been Greek-speaking Phoenicians.

The final sentence of this chapter and section: "They [the Tuatha Dé
Danann] are fairies" contradicts the implications of the question with
which Smith opened the first chapter of the section: "But who are the
Tuatha Dé Danaan, the mysterious and splendid race of Ancient Ireland,
the ancestors of the fairies?" (25). The Tuatha Dé Danann can hardly be
the ancestors of the fairies, if the latter are the primitive, almost feral
Sídhe. And the fairies certainly *are* the Sídhe. The Tuatha Dé Danann are
not the *ancestors* of the fairies; they have, over the course of centuries,
through the eroding effect of Christianity, themselves *dwindled into* the
"fairies."

About Part 1 of this book, from its misbegotten title to its risible
conclusion, nothing positive can respectably be said. While it is only
with difficulty I can find anything in it likely to lure a reader or scholar of
Yeats into misconstruing anything in the corpus on the basis of its
pseudo-information, I dread to see hunks of its nonsense purveyed in
other contexts as the latest truth on the "Tribes of Danu."

Part 2 of the book, "Na Daoine Sídhe," is obviously intended to
mean "The Fairy People," which in modern usage it indeed fairly does,
without the gross solecism of the title of Part 1. But here Smith appar-
ently is still reversing himself, for he had ended Part 1 by severing the
Tuatha Dé from the Sídhe, and equating only the former with the
"fairies."

Consistency should require him to argue that the fairies, who are
unquestionably called *na Sídhe* in Irish, must be the survivors of his feral
aboriginal Sídhe, while the Tuatha Dé have either long ago died out or
returned home at last to Phoenicia. But already in Old Irish the Tuatha
Dé and even the Ulster heroes are explicitly identified as *síde.* A colophon
added to the ninth-century saga *Seirgligi Con Culaind (Cú Chulainn's*

Wasting-Sickness) concludes with the sentence: *Conid frisna taidbsib sin atberat na hanéolaig síde ocus áes síde,* "And it is those phantoms the ignorant called *síde* and 'mound folk.'"

Because the material covered in Part 2 of this book, that is, lore concerning fairies, belongs essentially to folk tradition, it has, and can have, no canonical texts to be either mastered or garbled. Its written sources are, of course, of very variable quality and authenticity. Material collected, for instance, by such entities as the Irish Folk Lore Commission is at least genuinely collected from genuine folk. The Folklore Commission method of collecting even allows for some evaluation of the status of the informant and the sources of his or her material. On the other hand, fairy-lore collected by amateurs, especially enthusiasts for the "Fairy Faith," is likely to be deeply tinged by the collectors' predispositions, either literary, stylistic, moral, or credulous. In short, it is a playground for cranks.

Yeatsians cannot conceal from themselves that Yeats certainly wished to believe in the fairies, and so recorded in his two collections of folk and fairy tales and fairy anecdotes printed here and there, stories and beliefs that appealed to him for one or another reason pertinent to the quirks of his mind. But to attempt to organize and rationalize the "fairy facts" as a way of deepening understanding of the uses Yeats made of them is an impossible task. There are no fixed "fairy facts" to deal with, nor in spite of the fervor of many yearners, is there any "Fairy Faith" to study. Many people in many places—including many peasants in Ireland—believe in the existence of fairies. What such believers believe in is various and a certain number of beliefs in common are offset by contradictory beliefs. Also, belief in fairies usually coexists with belief in ghosts and malevolent spirits, and beliefs concerning one are not easily disentangled from beliefs concerning another.

Part 2 of Smith's book, after chapter 7 on "The Fairy Faith in Transition," proceeds to two chapters of pseudo-rigorous definition and classification of types of fairies. Chapter 7, however, is a desperate attempt to bridge the chasm from the Tuatha Dé Danann, the "fairies" of the Ancient Irish fairy faith, to the Sídhe (current spelling *sí*, that Smith has not caught up with), the fairies of more recent Irish fairy beliefs. I refrain from further comment on the quandary vis-á-vis Tuatha Dé and Sídhe he brought upon himself in Part 1.

Two reasons for changes in the fairy faith over the centuries he specifies: the British government and the Roman church. Of the latter he says "even many Early Irish stories betray a Christian as well as a fairy colouring" (106). As I have been insisting, no Early Irish story fails to betray a Christian coloring. There were simply no pagan, or fairy-faith, scribes in business. The rest of this chapter is a simple rehearsal of well-known truisms about Irish fairy beliefs, such as that it is very bad luck to dig up an elf-mound (*sídh*).

Chapter 8, "A First Census of Fairyland," attempts to classify a number of the various kinds of beings believed to constitute types of fairies. First of these is the leprechaun, a kind of sprite widely believed in Irish rural lore to be shoemakers (usually for the other, non-leprechaun, fairies) and also guardians of hidden treasure. They are usually solitary. Smith's discussion of leprechauns enters two areas of would-be erudition: the origin and meaning of their name, and the reason for their association with shoemaking. The results are uneven.

On the matter of the name he cites a number of theories propounded by a selection of chiefly nineteenth-century theorists, rejecting in course the correct answer—metathesis of *lúchorpán*. This latter origin he rejects because it means only "little, littler body" (14). It does not. *Lú* in Old Irish means "small" (in Modern Irish it is the comparative of the word for "little"—whence, I suppose, Smith's "littler"). *Corp* means "body." *Lúchorp*, which also appears in the same eighth-century text in which *lúchorpán* first appears, means "small-body." (See R.I.A. *Contributions* L [1966], 232:15–39.) The word *lúchorpán* ("one with a small body") occurs in several Old Irish texts, including a translation of Orosius's *Sex Aetates Mundi* where it is used to render "pygmy." None of Smith's other candidates for the original of "leprechaun" appears in Old Irish texts, including his favorite, **lugh-chorpán*. The Modern Irish spelling for "leprechaun" is *leipreachán,* derived from *lúchorpán* through the intermediate stages of *luchropán, lucharbán,* and *lupracán.* Metathesis is at work through all stages.

The *lucorpain* [*sic*] who make their first known appearance in Irish literature in the eighth-century *Saga of Fergus Mac Léti* (*Echtra Fergusa maic Léti,* ed. D. Binchy, *Ériu* 16 [1952]: 33–48) are tiny persons (the word *abac,* "dwarf," is used of them individually) who emerge from, and return under, the sea. There is no hint of shoemaking about them, but they provide King Fergus with herbs that enable him to travel underwater. Three hundred years later, towards the end of the eleventh century, somebody developed this nucleus into a long parodistic story called *Aided Fergusa maic Léide* ("The Violent Death of Fergus son of Léide"). In this the three *lúchorpáin* of the eighth-century story have become a complete separate kingdom of *lupraccáin*—a lilliputian travesty, in every detail, of the Court of Ulster in the Red Branch sagas. The story, despite the "violent death" at the end, is clearly intended to be funny: the king *luppracán,* on a visit to King Fergus in Ulster, falls upside down into a pot of oatmeal and becomes a laughingstock for the kitchen staff. It may also have homiletic, or satirical, intentions: the boastings of the tiny king and his court resemble the absurdities of the court of Swift's Lilliput, and thereby put human arrogance into perspective. But likewise the *lupraccáin* are the only "otherworldly" element in this story, thereby occupying the niche traditionally belonging to the Tuatha Dé Danann.

Therefore in this eleventh-century travesty we find both the diminution of the long-obsolete pagan gods to comic dwarves, and also the jelling of the original word *lúchorpán* into the metathesised *lupraccán,* i.e., leprechaun. This text is the first to establish a race of "Wee Folk" in Irish literature, and they are the product of a deliberate attempt to diminish the stature and significance of the Tuatha Dé the author knew in previous Irish literature.

Thereafter the leprechaun belongs to folklore. At what point he became a solitary, treasure-guarding cobbler I cannot say. Why any supernatural creature becomes so specialized is for anthropologists to determine. At any rate, the leprechaun's earliest appearance in English recorded by the O.E.D. (in 1604, under the appellation "lubrican") is merely as an Irish conjurable sprite. There is no way to derive the shoemaking either from the earliest mentions of the creature, or from the word's etymology.

Smith's misguided reading has nonetheless led him to find cobbling in the name, by a very devious kind of sophistry. He adopts as the original form of the word the unattested *lugh-chorpán,* which he says means "little Lugh-body" (it would really mean "one with a Lugh body"). This supposition takes him to the *lugoves,* who are named in Celtic inscriptions both in Switzerland and Spain. It is to the latter, erected on behalf of a guild of shoemakers, that Smith turns, asserting that *lugoves* is a diminutive of *Lugh* [sic] and therefore semantically equivalent to *lugh-chorpán* (114). *Lugoves* is not a diminutive, but the plural of *Lugus/Lugos,* which Mac Cana more plausibly proposes to be "an instance of triplication of the deity which is a familiar feature of Celtic mythology" (Mac Cana 25). Since Lugos was so widely worshiped among the Celts that at least four modern European cities continue to

bear his name, the fact that a guild of Spanish-Celtic shoemakers hon-
ored him offers no sound basis for associating Lug with cobblers. Still
less does it warrant inventing an etymology for *leprechaun* incorporating
his name, quite contrary to the ample evidence. And, as I have noticed,
there is no genuine old evidence associating leprechauns with shoes.
Smith's linguistic adventure, however, brings him to an equation some-
what embarrassing to the thesis of his Part 1: "We have . . . a process of
degeneration from Lugh, who is something like a god . . . to the lep-
rechaun, who lives in a hole beneath a bush" (115). Here we have not
only the admission that a member of the Tuatha Dé is "like a god" (a
Phoenician?) but that he can come to live in "a hole beneath a bush" (like
the primitive aborigines). Smith's final word on the leprechauns is for
once quite accurate: "The leprechaun, then, provides a good example of
the decline of the Tuatha Dé Danann" (115).

Also at least semantically accurate is the first sentence of the next
section, "II. The Cluricaun": "Closely related to the leprechaun is the
cluricaun" (115). It is unnecessary to examine the details of his anatomy
of this creature, for the *clutharachán* is only, through the all-too-common
Irish habit of metathesis, a variant of the *lucharachán,* "puny creature,
pigmy, dwarf; elf."[4] And this *lucharachán* is himself only a predictable
distortion of *lucharpán,* an obvious survivor from the *lúchorpán* in the saga
of Fergus maic Léti. Therefore the cluricaun is etymologically only a
kind of genetic "fairy," whatever supposed distinctive characteristics
informants may have attached to him.

This chapter concludes with discussions of "The Mermaid" and the
"Banshee." The former is, of course, a creature of universal folklore, the
banshee a peculiarly Irish creature. Her designation, *bean Sídhe,* literally
means, as Smith notes "fairy woman" (118), or perhaps more accurately,
"woman of an elf-mound." In Ireland she is a traditional harbinger of
death, and is almost certainly a diminished memory of the Morrigu, the
ancient Irish battlefield goddess. Smith has her basic facts correct, though
muffled in otiose genealogical and onomastic speculations.

Chapter 9, "A Second Census of Fairyland," is a survey of various
ominous or supernatural animals, sampling the usual, chiefly nineteenth-
century, authorities on such matters. Most of these beasts are objects of
superstition rather than of anything that could be construed as a con-

---

4. Niall Ó Dónaill, *Foclóir Gaeilge-Béarla* (Baile Atha Cliath: Oifig an tSoláthair,
1977).

sistent "faith"—the black cats and dogs familiar still at least in the En-glish-speaking world.

Chapter 10 runs over some eschatological folk beliefs, while chapter 11, "The Host of the Air," comes to a phrase actually used by Yeats. A large part of this is a discussion and analysis of the theory that fairies occur as "trooping fairies" and "solitary fairies." To a normally healthy-minded skeptic this theory is not susceptible to criticism, since fairies exist only in folk-belief, and whatever anybody believes is *ipso facto* true in that belief. I have never seen real evidence that any medieval scholastic theologians actually ever disputed the number of angels who can dance on the head of a pin, but this chapter is equally far removed from com-mon sense. Out of the conflicting "evidence" Smith concludes that "there is no distinction whatsoever between the trooping and the solitary fairies. They are one and the same thing" (150).

It is quite one thing to discuss and even analyze the beliefs of people who believe in fairies, that is, to take such beliefs seriously as attributes of the minds and behavior of the believers. It is quite another thing, in serious scholarship, to take the *contents* of such beliefs as ontological, empirical facts. There are simply no verifiable or refutable data; there is not even a coherent received view to be maintained or contested.

W. B. Yeats and the Tribes of Danu comes to us from Colin Smythe as Number 27 in their Irish Literary Studies Series, preceded by works for the most part serious, bearing the names of authors and editors among the most distinguished in the field of Anglo-Irish Studies. This deplora-ble book is a blot on that fair escutcheon.

On the Cornell Yeats

W. B. Yeats. *The Early Poetry*. Volume I: *Mosada* and *The Island of Statues: Manuscript Materials,* ed. George Bornstein.
Ithaca and London: Cornell University Press, 1987. xii + 442 pp.

W. B. Yeats. *Purgatory: Manuscript Materials Including the Author's Final Text,* ed. Sandra F. Siegel.
Ithaca and London: Cornell University Press, 1986. xi + 222 pp.

A review essay by Donald H. Reiman

In 1986 and 1987 there appeared the second and third volumes of the Cornell Yeats, which describe, transcribe, analyze, and reproduce (in part) the manuscripts of, respectively, Yeats's earliest dramatic poems, *Mosada* and *The Island of Statues,* and one of his last two plays, *Purgatory*. To a non-Yeatsian, asked to review the two volumes as a sample of the editorial procedures and general scholarly interest of the Cornell Yeats, this collocation of the manuscripts of the earliest and latest writings of their author provides an opportunity to examine what the publication of Yeats's manuscripts may add to our understanding of his ideational intention and his artistic method, as well as to evaluate the editorial principles being developed for the four related series in the edition—"Plays" (David R. Clark, Series Editor); "Poems" (Richard J. Finneran, Series Editor); "Prose" (George Mills Harper, Series Editor); and "Family Papers" (William M. Murphy, Series Editor). In short, this review will address both the questions of whether this edition was worth undertaking and how well it has been planned and, in its early volumes, executed.

I

Yeats, who inveterately revised and rearranged his poems in his later years, began this habit early. He saved many of his drafts and early transcriptions, and—luckier than many poets—has been blessed with heirs who first faithfully preserved and now are aiding the publication of these treasures. Some poets, doubtless, feel that their first, tentative and often confused scribblings should be destroyed, believing that the survival of these orts could detract from their achievements. But such is the weakness of human nature that students of a poet appreciate him more when they can follow the development of his conception step by faltering step, and many can understand what he intended *only* when they do so. The meaning of a work of art is determined, as the Derridian critic will tell us, by both presence and absence, but it is frequently difficult to identify just what *is* absent in a meaningful sense unless we see it crossed out on a sheet of paper, never to return in later drafts or fair copies. Many readers, in fact, can understand the significance of what is present only when they see it appear for the first time late in the process of composition, or restored to a late draft. Such changes tell us both where the author saw problems with his work and in what direction he sought their solution.

George Bornstein, in the first of two volumes to be devoted to *The Early Poetry,* presents us with the surviving drafts of two early poetic dramas that Yeats published in the *Dublin University Review* in 1885 and 1886. The manuscript evidence confirms Yeats's statement (not observed by the editors of the Yeats *Variorum Edition*) that *Mosada,* though published a year later than *The Island of Statues,* was written earlier. Such a reversal of composition and publication, though common enough with apprentice writings, is interesting in this case, for *Mosada,* in spite of its foreshortening and compression, seems the more mature work of the two. In *Mosada,* Yeats's borrowings are less flagrant and his recognition of the evil powers that dominate both plots is infinitely clearer. Though, as Bornstein notes, there are similarities in themes and characters in the two works and though into both Yeats poured "much that would exfoliate into his own mature art" (4), it seems to me also likely that *Mosada* developed more directly out of Yeats' psyche, while *The Island of Statues* came from his reading.

Three early manuscripts of *Mosada* survive and five of *The Island of Statues,* each manuscript representing a distinct stage of composition. As Bornstein notes, each document contains enough substantive revisions to provide a double helping of developmental stages, six for *Mosada* and ten in all for *The Island of Statues.* The textual authorities, reproduced in the chronological order of their inscription, include three successive manuscripts for *Mosada* (all but one leaf in the library of Trinity College, Dublin). The first is a notebook in which "foliated pages 5–8 and 9–13 represent successive early versions of part of scene 3" (21). This is the same notebook that (as we learn in the description of the manuscripts of *The Island of Statues* on page 127) contains the first draft of that work on the versos of folios 13 through 30 (a reference that also clarifies the ambiguity of the phrase "foliated pages" in the *Mosada* description). In a second notebook of the same general description (there is no formal analysis of the construction of the notebooks, recording the original number of leaves, with their conjugates and quires, or whether these remain intact), there is an intermediate fair copy, with minor revisions, of the full text of *Mosada*. A third manuscript, consisting of unbound foolscap sheets of "unlined" (wove?) paper, contains "a later version of scene 1 and most of scene 2, together with a one-page fragment of scene 3," while an additional "leaf in the National Library of Ireland continues scene 2 almost to the end" (21). All forty-nine pages of these three drafts of *Mosada* are reproduced in facsimile on the left-hand (verso) pages, with diplomatic transcriptions on the facing rectos.

The five surviving manuscripts of *The Island of Statues* include, first, the earliest (untitled) version in the same Trinity College notebook as the earliest drafts for *Mosada;* two subsequent versions in notebooks in the collection of Michael B. Yeats, one entitled "The lady of tuneful guile—a fairy tale in two acts" and the other, "The Island of Statues an Arcadian fairy tale," dated August 1884; three partial revisions of Act 2 in the Michael B. Yeats Collection (one on a loose leaf and the others occupying parts of two separate notebooks); and, most important, the press-copy for the work as it appeared in *Dublin University Magazine,* a document that contains the final corrections and revisions, some in the hand of Yeats and some in that of T. W. Lyster (the "Quaker librarian" of Joyce's *Ulysses*), to whom Yeats submitted his early work for correction.

As in the case of both Coleridge's *Osorio* (later *Remorse*) and Wordsworth's *The Borderers,* a striking change occurs in the names of principal characters. In the manuscripts and 1886 texts of *Mosada,* the Christian monk Ebremar, who first condemns the Moorish girl Mosada to death as a witch without hearing her story, later (after she has poisoned herself to cheat the auto-da-fé) recognizes her and reveals himself as her long-sought-for lover Vallance. Apparently discovering later that Vallance sounds very little like an Arabic or a Spanish name, Yeats changed Ebremar's prior name to Gomez in the 1889 edition. In *The Island of Statues,* the name of Almintor's beloved in the first draft only was Evadne instead of Naschina. Here Bornstein educes two possible antecedents of Yeats's conception, *The Maid's Tragedy* by Beaumont and Fletcher (in which the hero is Amintor and his wife Evadne) and *Evadne; or, The Statue* by Richard Lalor Sheil (1819; a play that Keats saw and mentioned in his journal-letter to his brother George in America). Bornstein may be correct in his judgment that Yeats took little but the soon-abandoned name Evadne (and, possibly, Almintor's name) from either play; he is certainly right in seeing heavy indebtedness to Spenser for the conception of *The Island of Statues* and to Shelley (as well as Keats, Tennyson, and others) for much in the versification and imagery. But the initial coldness and lack of sympathy in Naschina, even with her new name (qualities that may well justify Maud Gonne's preference for the Enchantress of the Island over Naschina) may owe something to the character of Evadne in *The Maid's Tragedy*. Yeats's Evadne-Naschina speaks to her rustic suitors in the opening scenes of Yeats's drama in much the same sarcastic, bantering tone that Beaumont and Fletcher's Evadne uses with Amintor on their wedding night, when she reveals that she will never sleep with him because she is the king's mistress. Yeats seems to have borrowed the harsh qualities of Evadne as well as her name from *The Maid's Tragedy*, and his failure to integrate that borrowing with his Spenserian bucolic setting may have led Yeats—or one of his advisors, such as T. W. Lyster—to realize that the happy ending he had imposed on the play in the early manuscript versions was not, ultimately, true to the spirit of Naschina's character.

II

The Island of Statues, in particular, suggests that young Yeats began his career as a dramatist with a love of good images and good repartee, but without a sense of form. Yeats himself must have sensed—or been apprised of—this failing, for on 7 May 1889 we find him writing to John O'Leary of his "new play," *The Countess Cathleen:* "I think you will like it. . . . The style is perfectly simple and I have taken great care with the construction, made two complete prose versions before writing a line of verse" (L 125). This decision to work out his plots in advance should have stood Yeats in good stead nearly fifty years later in March 1938, when he came to write *Purgatory*, which Richard Ellmann considered "his finest" play (*Yeats: The Man and the Masks*, new edition [New York: W. W. Norton, 1979], 280). In Sandra F. Siegel's edition we find that Yeats began with a prose scenario, but that almost immediately—perhaps before completing the scenario itself—he began to draft portions of the dialogue on the verso of the first leaf of the prose outline and added

two more pages of early draft dialogue. These materials are both re-
produced in facsimile and transcribed, as are two holograph drafts in
verse (from which some scattered leaves are missing). Of four typescript
versions, the last, most fully revised version (National Library of Ireland
MS. 8771, no. 5), contains extensive holograph revisions in addition to
transcriptions of other authorial changes transferred from other type-
scripts. This typescript is reproduced in facsimile almost in full and
completely transcribed, followed by a table of the variants found in the
two partially contemporaneously revised typescripts that form part of
the same National Library of Ireland manuscript, in folders numbered 6
and 4, and then by "Notes on Textual Problems" in these three type-
scripts. Next, Siegel discusses the "Evolution of the Text from TS5 to
the Printed Versions," drawing upon the evidence provided in two sets
of page proofs (Yeats's marked galleys are lost)—the first set corrected
by Yeats and the second, after his death, by Mrs. Yeats and one or more
others. Finally, Siegel writes "Notes on Textual Problems in TS7 and
the Printed Versions" and then adds an appendix reproducing in pho-
tofacsimile both TS7 and the first set of the Longford page proofs.

This evidence, by its mere quantity, shows that writing a play had
become no simpler for Yeats with the passage of time. But more reveal-
ing is the fact that *Purgatory*, like *The Island of Statues*, remains ambiguous
even after its many stages of revision. For, as Siegel notes, different
critics using Yeats's final text have seen the message of *Purgatory* in
diametrically opposed ways. For some critics, noting Yeats's late interest
in eugenics and in an Irish proto-fascist movement, the Old Man who
had, in his youth, killed his father (a groom who had married the lady of
the country estate) and who in the course of the play kills his son with the
same knife is (as he believes himself to be) a cleansing force—a scourge of
God—ridding the world of an accursed, degenerate family. Other crit-
ics, however, see the Old Man as an evil madman. Siegel attempts to
show how Yeats's revisions reveal him changing the nature of the Old
Man: "in the final stage of composition, as Yeats brings his fictional hero
more fully to life, the Old Man loses almost entirely the self-knowledge
he possesses in earlier versions. He is no less preoccupied with purifica-
tion than in earlier versions: on the contrary, as he grows increasingly
ignorant that he is the pollution, he is more intensely preoccupied with
purification—and more powerless" (13). And after Siegel has examined
in some detail the complex interrelations between "On the Boiler" and
Purgatory, she concludes that "The Old Man is neither the hero *A Vision*

proclaims nor the spokesman for Yeats's 'beliefs' but the parodic double of Yeats's own thought" (26).

Coming to *Purgatory* with less knowledge of Yeats's private universe of thought than of the history and spirit of his time and place, I found the play conveying to me a somewhat different message that would render Yeats's drama less exclusively self-referential. Yeats by 1938 was becoming aware of the dark political forces gathering in Europe and, according to Ellmann, he even felt some concern about the verbal support he himself had given the quasi-fascist Irish demagogue General Eoin O'Duffy. When we recall how Sean O'Casey viewed the shadowy world of political violence in *The Shadow of a Gunman*—and think what it has come to since Yeats's time—it may not be too far afield to suggest that the bloody actions of the Old Man represent the spirit of militant political activism in Ireland that had in the past killed its immediate forebears—the landed gentry of the old Protestant ascendency that Yeats admired—and now was beginning to devour its own sons in the continuation of the war by irreconcilables who refused to follow de Valera into constitutional government. This is not to say that the Old Man "symbolizes"—or allegorizes—the IRA, but that the values of violent action that in Yeats's eyes had once become "a terrible beauty" in the Easter Rising of 1916, he now saw as a manifestation of the slouching rough beast that would drown the ceremony of innocence. In *The Playboy of the Western World,* John Millington Synge had ridiculed the Irish penchant for glorifying random violence—even parricide. The Dublin audiences immediately proved Synge's very point by rioting at the Abbey when *Playboy* opened there in 1907. By 1938, this national characteristic could no longer be treated comically. In view of Yeats's other late poems, it seems hardly credible that he would not recognize in the Old Man something far more dangerous than his own flirtations with antidemocratic movements; the Old Man, whether viewed in his youth as the misbegotten son of a groom or in his old age as a restless, landless vagabond outside the law and tradition, represents the element in Irish society that refuses to accept the past or the present and must always resort to violent action in support of an imagined apocalyptic future. Thus I agree with Sandra F. Siegel's estimate of the direction of Yeats's textual revisions, but I think that she interprets them, perhaps, too narrowly in terms of Yeats's private theories, rather than shining on them the light of Irish history and the themes prominent in the Irish theater during Yeats's lifetime.

III

To return to the question of "presence" and "absence" in Yeats's early poems, the significance of the Derridian conception has never been brought home to me so meaningfully as when George Bornstein points out that between the press-copy manuscript of *The Island of Statues* and its first appearance in print (in the *Dublin University Review* from April to July 1885), Yeats added a single stage direction that, as Bornstein writes, "alters the entire meaning of the play by undermining the union of Almintor and Naschina," for the last sentence of the new stage direction reads: "*Close by* Almintor's *side,* Naschina *is standing, shadowless.*" This final stage direction expresses the absence of Naschina's shadow, which no reader could guess without it; this addition thus transforms *Endymion* into *Laodamia* or *Lamia,* for Naschina's lack of a shadow is our only clue that she "has joined the realm of the immortals, that her reunion with Almintor can persist but briefly, and that the antinomies [that Yeats had seemed to struggle to resolve in the play] remain at war with each other" (*Early Poetry* 15). In this case the scholar-critic can call to his support the words of Yeats in a letter discussing the play (*Early Poetry* 16; L 88). But the step-by-step materials of the developing text are not all there for the student of Yeats to see: the stage direction does not exist in the press copy, where the last words are Almintor's triumphant declaration to Naschina: "Until we die within the charmed ring / Of these star studded skies you are the queen" (*Early Poetry* 438). But there the Cornell Yeats volume ends, not carrying forward to the text of the first printing, for which we must turn to the editions done under Yeats's supervision, to the *Variorum Edition,* or to Richard J. Finneran's edition of *The Poems: A New Edition* (1983). Bornstein's volume, lacking both the established text based on the author's final intention and any collation of the final manuscript version with that text, provides only the comment in the introduction (which, in turn, derives from Yeats's 1888 letter to Katharine Tynan) to point us to a major crux that cannot be identified from the manuscripts alone. Those of use who focus upon manuscript sources must always remain aware of their limitations in the case of poems that were published at the author's initiative or under his supervision, and Siegel's decision to include the "The Author's Final Text" of *Purgatory* in her edition seems to be a wise one.

Actually, the Cornell Yeats, like most if not all of the other major editions of manuscript facsimiles now underway, has made a number of compromises. These volumes do not include facsimiles of *all* the relevant manuscripts, and Bornstein—probably constricted by the cost of printing the large number of MSS and transcriptions he has located—does not include or collate the later printed texts. The Cornell Wordsworth prints "reading texts," often based on early and late printed materials, and collates other printed editions, but it also selects among the MSS and reproduces in facsimile and transcribes only the most significant ones. Various facsimile editions published by Garland—*The James Joyce Archive* and *Manuscripts of the Younger Romantics,* for example—attempt to be comprehensive in reproducing the original holograph manuscripts, but do not always provide typed transcriptions or collate the manuscript version with the published texts. These editions see their role as archival—to preserve and disseminate the primary materials so that more critics and students will be moved to become textual critics, to examine for themselves the authoritative textual evidence underlying the decisions made by editors, and to analyze not only the directions of development in the creative process of composition, but also to recognize which parts of the final, authorized text will bear the weight of heavy interpretation and which represent compromises imposed by the exigencies of prosody or represent the staple poetic bridges over which the author traveled to reach his next serious crux.

I mention these variations in principle and practice not only to alert readers using the various series to the differing uses for which they were intended, but also to remind the editors of the Cornell Yeats that they do not seem yet to have stated clearly the rationale that underlies their efforts. This initial lack of an overall program is both understandable and excusable, as individual editors working in four distinct teams develop plans out of their specific and diverse materials and then modify these plans in the light of constraints imposed by the publisher. But now that the early volumes are successfully in print, it would probably be helpful for the future of the project if the editors settled certain basic matters. Is the primary aim of the series to be archival, textual, or critical? In the first case, the individual manuscripts and notebooks should be more thoroughly described, with attention to the construction of notebooks (with identification of missing pages, etc.) as well as to watermarks and other features of the paper, and the interrelations of the different writings found in the same notebook or manuscript more thoroughly analyzed. If the goal is primarily *textual,* then there should be some way to present the new evidence from the MSS in its relation to the shape and readings of the accepted texts, whether this means writing a prose analysis, as Siegel does, tracing the "Evolution of the Text" from the latest manuscript or typescript "to the Printed Versions," or providing a systematic collation of the texts. If the chief goal pursued by the editors is *critical*— that is, to accumulate and highlight the features of the drafts and revisions that bear upon the interpretation of each work (as seems to have been one major aim of the two volumes under review), then the editors must present in greater detail the views of other critics and the biographical or textual evidence drawn from other works that have led those critics to their various opinions. (Obviously, only the most cogent exemplars of each general viewpoint need be summarized.)

Finally, in addition to a clearer sense of purpose on the part of the editorial team, the series will profit from more attention to the details of presentation at the Cornell University Press. Though the editors provide detailed and clear descriptions of their procedures and conventions of transcription (*Early Poetry* 17–20; *Purgatory* 27–28), the Press seems not to have included—what only it can supply—a statement on whether or not all the manuscript facsimiles are actual size, or by what percentage each has been reduced. Though it is impossible to calculate accurately from a printed book page, using only the inevitably approximate dimensions given in the descriptions of the manuscripts, in my rough estimates the facsimiles in *Early Poetry*, I, of notebook leaves of MSS. TCD 3502/1 and TCD 3502/2 seem to have been reduced to about 82 percent of actual size, while the larger loose sheets of MS. TCD 3502/3 seem to have been reduced to a little over 56 percent of their actual size. Another area where the publisher has failed the editors is in an internal book design that is neither convenient for the reader nor attractive in itself. All the transcriptions are crowded into the upper left-hand (gutter) corner of the page, even when Yeats's text is on the lower part of the facing-page facsimile (see, especially, *Purgatory* 72–73, 130–31). If the editors themselves supply the camera-ready copy for the transcriptions, they can give some thought to spacing these in proportion to the space on Yeats's manuscripts or typescripts. Then it would remain the responsibility of the Press to reduce (or blow up) the transcriptions to match the final size of the manuscript facsimiles on the facing pages. Even had the editors supplied unproportional camera-ready copy for the transcriptions, there is no reason why a publisher working with photo-offset materials cannot cut and paste the transcription so that it has some meaningful relationship to the facing facsimiles.

IV

As is often said by reviewers—but here is most sincerely meant by one who has himself encountered (and sometimes succumbed to) similar difficulties—the kinds of minor problems to which I have alluded in the last three paragraphs seem trivial in the face of the great achievement in these two volumes, and such quibbles are further dwarfed by the great promise the edition holds for the future understanding of Yeats. The only question that remains important is whether the investment of time and skill and of financial support for the edition is likely to yield a proportionate dividend through increased interest in and understanding of the life, thought, and art of William Butler Yeats. If my own experience in confronting these two volumes is any indication, I can give that question a wholehearted "Yes" in answer. The Cornell Yeats will, I believe, help generate new interest and enthusiasm for the study of his poetry and dramas—especially those such as the three works presented in these two volumes—on which critics had reached impasses on the basis of the other evidence that was readily available. The manuscript evidence will probably not only solve some of these problems but—even more valuably—raise new questions that the editors cannot resolve in their scholarly apparatus; these new puzzles will, in turn, help to stimulate additional interest in both Yeats's writings and the cruxes of his life that will carry far into the twenty-first century. If Yeats speaks to the concerns of that new era, whatever those concerns may be, he will have an opportunity to win a hearing and to claim a place in the canon of the coming age as exalted as that which he now enjoys in ours.

Reviews

Harold Bloom, ed. *William Butler Yeats*.
Modern Critical Views. New York, New Haven and Philadelphia:
Chelsea House Press, 1986. viii + 232 pp.

Richard J. Finneran, ed. *Critical Essays on W. B. Yeats*.
Critical Essays on Modern British Literature. Boston: G. K. Hall,
1986. viii + 258 pp.

Reviewed by TERENCE DIGGORY

No doubt it would have amused Yeats to see two anthologies of criticism
on his work divide according to the principles that he called the "primary"
and the "antithetical." Having permitted his authors to choose the texts
by which they would be represented, Richard J. Finneran has allowed his
book to be "moulded . . . from without," a characteristically "primary"
condition (AV-B 84). Aside from their holding positions of authority in
the "Yeats industry"—a term Finneran accepts with ironic humility (1)—
Finneran's contributors are united mainly by their devotion to objectivity,
their desire to render an accurate account of Yeats's texts, and their
commitment to acknowledge the sources that shaped those texts as well as
their own. On the other hand, Bloom's contributors, for the most part
distinguished consultants to, rather than executives within the Yeats
industry, are united by a common view of the creative process—not
surprisingly, a view that coincides with that of Harold Bloom. Thus, the
"self-expression" that Yeats held to be characteristically "antithetical"
(AV-B 84) informs Bloom's anthology.

Although dictated by the series in which each volume takes its place,
the titles of these anthologies reflect further differences, which, together
with the editorial apparatus, appear to some extent to reverse the empha-
ses suggested by the selection of contributors. Bloom purports to focus on
Yeats, the end to which the anthologized essays serve as means. An
appendix provides a chronology of Yeats's life, rather thoughtlessly com-
piled from previous versions. For instance, the name and class of the ship
that transported Yeats's body to Ireland are painstakingly recorded, but
the publication of *The Wild Swans at Coole* receives no mention. An
idiosyncratic bibliography of Yeats criticism is also supplied, but Bloom's
attitude toward the criticism is better reflected in his annoying practice of
cutting the notes that appeared in the original versions of the works he

reprints. Bloom's introduction, itself a reprinting of his essay "Yeats, Gnosticism, and the Sacred Void" (Bloom, *Poetry and Repression* [New Haven: Yale University Press, 1976]) continues the attack on "Yeats-idolaters" (9) launched in his earlier *Yeats* (New York: Oxford University Press, 1970). For the most part, however, the essay ignores the critics and extends Bloom's explication of Yeats's "Gnosticism" to a reading of three poems ("The Second Coming," "Byzantium," and "Cuchulain Comforted") according to the six "revisionary ratios" that Bloom proposed in *The Anxiety of Influence* (New York: Oxford University Press, 1973).

Finneran, on the other hand, makes the criticism of Yeats his principal focus. His volume includes no chronology of Yeats's life, and his bibliography acquires a rather narrow integrity by confining itself to an annotated list of "collections of previously published material, not gatherings of original scholarship" (246). With the exception of a few updated references to Finneran's edition of Yeats's *Poems* (P), the notes to the anthologized essays follow the initial printings without alteration. Unfortunately, this means that material since published is cited as unpublished, and abbreviations or acronyms of some titles appear without the key supplied elsewhere in the original context. Finneran's introduction is a survey of Yeats criticism by decade, with special attention to the period from the 1960s to the present, from which both Finneran and Bloom draw their selections. Although he is generally more impartial than Bloom, Finneran also exhibits some blind spots in his introduction. Bloom's *Yeats* is acknowledged only in a footnote; Denis Donoghue is a non-person.

Despite their differences, these collections share two authors, Richard Ellmann and Thomas Whitaker, represented by different selections from *Eminent Domain* (New York: Oxford University Press, 1967) and *Swan and Shadow* (Chapel Hill: University of North Carolina Press, 1964), respectively. The collections also share a general agreement at least about the areas of Yeats's work that are most worthy of attention. Although Paul de Man, in Bloom's anthology, offers provocative readings of some early verse, the poetry that excites most discussion is that of the later period, beginning with the expanded edition of *The Wild Swans at Coole* (1919). In addition to the poems discussed by Bloom, cited above, the major lyrics that receive extended analysis in Bloom's anthology include, in order of first publication, "Nineteen Hundred and Nineteen" (J. Hillis Miller), "Leda and the Swan" (Priscilla Washburn Shaw), "The Tower," "Blood and the Moon," and "Coole Park and

Ballylee, 1931" (the last three discussed by Whitaker). Finneran's contributors focus on "In Memory of Major Robert Gregory" (George Bornstein), "Meditations in Time of Civil War" (Whitaker), "Leda and the Swan," "The Tower" (toth discussed by Bornstein), "Among School Children" (Donald T. Torchiana), "Blood and the Moon," and "A Dialogue of Self and Soul" (both discussed by Daniel A. Harris). Beyond the poetry, due attention is accorded the autobiographical prose (Ian Fletcher for Bloom, Hazard Adams for Finneran) and the plays (Helen Vendler and Denis Donoghue for Bloom, Edward Engelberg and David R. Clark for Finneran).

Overall, Finneran's anthology covers a broader range of topics than does Bloom's. Nothing in Bloom's volume corresponds to Finneran's coverage of Yeats's prosodic technique (Thomas Parkinson), his politics (George Mills Harper), or his links to more recent poetry (Jon Stallworthy). The last topic is reinforced, in Finneran's collection, by Richard Ellmann's seminal study of the Yeats-Pound connection, whereas Bloom characteristically employs Ellmann to explore Yeats's relationship to a precursor, Oscar Wilde. Surprisingly, however, given Bloom's obsession with the theme of literary influence since his 1970 study of Yeats, precursors are not a major preoccupation of Bloom's anthology. Instead, the dominant theme is Yeats's theory of daimons. Represented in Finneran's anthology mainly by James Olney's comparison of Yeats and Jung, that concern is central to at least four of Bloom's selections: one each by Allen R. Grossman and Herbert J. Levine, and two by Bloom himself (chapters from *Yeats,* on *Per Amica Silentia Lunae* and *A Vision*). Unlike many recent studies of this topic, which accept Yeats's daimons on their own terms and place them within an occult tradition, Bloom continues to view them in a literary context, as symbols of that quintessentially romantic concern, the creative imagination. Since, after all, that is what Bloom's theory of "influence" is really about, the reduced attention to influence in his anthology of Yeats criticism proves to be clarifying.

The chronological sequence in which both editors arrange their selections inevitably invites a consideration of the trends in Yeats criticism over the period concerned, as reflected in each volume. By retaining his contributors' notes, Finneran documents more clearly than Bloom how decisively the publication of Bloom's *Yeats* marks a divide between studies published before and after 1970. Bloom provided impetus for a reevaluation of Yeats's place in the tradition of romanticism. Moreover, the "antithetical" theory of tropes that grew out of Bloom's study of Yeats parallels another approach, deconstruction, that gained prominence in the same period. In his anthology of Yeats criticism, Bloom represents the relevance of deconstruction to Yeats studies, or vice versa, with selections from two of his former Yale colleagues, Paul de Man and Hillis Miller. Related to both of these developments, the "antithetical" and the deconstructive, though less sensational than either, is an ongoing redefinition of the basic structural unit relevant to a reading of Yeats.

The earliest essay to appear in either anthology is Hugh Kenner's "The Sacred Book of the Arts" (1955), with which Finneran's collection opens. Reacting against the New Critical view of the poem as self-sufficient object, Kenner's much-anthologized essay persuasively argues that "the unit in which to inspect and discuss his [Yeats's] development is not the poem or sequence of poems but the volume" (11–12). Subsequent developments progress backwards through Kenner's list, though not always in a linear chronological progression. Thus, Finneran's last selection, M. L. Rosenthal's and Sally M. Gall's collaborative study (1983) of "Words for Music Perhaps" and *Last Poems,* takes the sequence as the fundamental unit, while in practice blurring Kenner's distinction between sequence and volume. Most of the anthologized essays take the poem as the fundamental unit, but blur Kenner's distinction between poem and sequence, either by selecting poems that are composed of discrete sections (as a glance at the list of poems above will reveal), or by identifying distinct stages of development within an apparently continuous poem.

Modeling the latter approach on M. H. Abrams's influential essay "Structure and Style in the Greater Romantic Lyric" (in Harold Bloom and Frederick W. Hillis, eds., *From Sensibility to Romanticism* [New York: Oxford University Press, 1965]), Bloom, in his introduction, and Bornstein, in the Finneran collection, are able to explore with unusual precision Yeats's ties to his romantic precursors. Those ties are also at issue when Paul de Man proposes a still narrower structural unit for critical attention. "As in all romantic poetry," de Man writes in Bloom's selection, "the most revealing stylistic unit [for the study of Yeats] will be the image" (184). De Man's focus on the "image," which would lie somewhere off the narrower end of Kenner's scale, further baffles any attempt to view progression along that scale as a chronological sequence. Although published only recently (in de Man, *The Rhetoric of Romanticism* [New York: Columbia University Press, 1984]), and therefore placed next to last in Bloom's anthology, de Man's proposal originally formed part of his doctoral dissertation (1960), making it nearly contemporary with Kenner's "The Sacred Book of the Arts."

As it appears in Bloom's collection, under the title "Imagery in Yeats," de Man's essay focuses on a structure of "conscious self-contemplation" that de Man regards as more characteristic of French symbolist poetry than of anything in English romanticism. In Bloom's edition, the argument concludes with the paradoxical observation: "Later, Yeats will discover his affinities with the *symbolistes,* but his poetry is never closer to theirs than before 1885, when he had little or no knowledge of their work" (187). As it appears in *The Rhetoric of Romanticism,* under the title "Image and Emblem in Yeats," de Man's argument continues for more than eighty pages. This is the only instance in either of the anthologies under review in which the editor has excerpted a portion of a longer work not already designated by the author as a discrete unit. Given the length of de Man's essay, it is understandable that Bloom might not want to print the entire piece, but by cutting it where he does, and by failing to indicate that he has done so, he considerably distorts de Man's principal thesis.

What becomes important in Yeats's career after 1885, in de Man's full account, is not a better informed understanding of the *symbolistes,* but a radical break with their practice, and with the entire "Western poetic tradition." As de Man explains, only thirteen pages after the cut made by Bloom, "this tradition conceives of the *logos* as incarnate and locates divine essence in the object, not in the unmediated *word* of God. Romanticism and symbolism, with their avowed or occult pantheistic overtones and nostalgias, belong in that tradition. But when nature itself is considered a mere sign, or a mouthpiece without actual substance, then one has left the mainstream of the tradition and embarked 'on strange seas of thought'" (*Rhetoric of Romanticism,* 168). Yeats embarked on those seas, according to de Man, when he gave up the practice, employed in his first volume (1889), of grounding his imagery in natural objects, into which subjectivity was subsequently instilled. Seeking a figurative language that is thoroughly subjective at the outset, a "meaning" possessed "by a traditional and not by a natural right" (E&I 147), Yeats turns from "image" to "emblem."

Although Bloom's editing of de Man avoids this turn away from nature, it is a point on which de Man and Bloom are in essential agreement. It is the point that Bloom intends to represent by borrowing from

Yeats the term *antithetical* to designate the separate position of the cre-
ative imagination in opposition to nature (*Yeats* 12–13). Having already
anticipated Bloom in identifying this position with Gnosticism (*Rhetoric
of Romanticism* 170), de Man, after writing his dissertation, also came to
agree with Bloom that that position was already characteristic of the
"true voice" of early romanticism, hitherto obscured by a misunder-
standing in romantic studies ("The Rhetoric of Temporality" [1969],
rpt. de Man, *Blindness and Insight*, 2d ed. [Minneapolis: University of
Minnesota Press, 1983], 207).

Bloom and de Man part company, however, over the question of
what happens after the declaration of imaginative independence. In
Yeats's development, according to de Man, the turn against the "natu-
ral" image is succeeded, in the late work, by a turn against the emblem,
because it can never be sufficiently purged of its dependence on nature.
Since, however, there seems to be no possibility of advancing beyond
this second, deconstructive turn, de Man is forced to conclude "Image
and Emblem in Yeats" with a bleak confession:

> The failure of the emblem amounts to total nihilism. Yeats has
> burned his bridges, and there is no return out of his exploded para-
> dise of emblems back to a wasted earth. Those who look to Yeats
> for reassurance from the anxieties of our own post-romantic predic-
> ament, or for relief from the paralysis of nihilism, will not find it in
> his conception of the emblem. He cautions instead against the dan-
> ger of unwarranted hopeful solutions, and thus accomplishes all that
> the highest forms of language can for the moment accomplish. (*Rhe-
> toric of Romanticism*, 238)

Passages in Bloom's most recent writing on Yeats indicate that he
may be willing to concede Yeats to the deconstructionists. In *A Map of
Misreading* (New York: Oxford University Press, 1975), Bloom claims
that "Yeats could not quite complete" the full imaginative arc that
Bloom prescribes (26), just as "the theorists of deconstruction" are able
to graph that arc through its first two stages, "contraction and destruc-
tion," but omit the third and culminating stage, "antithetical restora-
tion" (5). Similarly, having observed in the "Editor's Note" to his an-
thology of Yeats criticism that "Deconstructive criticism can be said to
explore some of the darker consequences of that inventiveness" that
Yeats claimed for the poets (viii), Bloom proceeds in his introduction to

distinguish Gnosticism in itself from the "consequences" that Yeats deduced from it, and that Bloom finds profoundly disturbing (7).

Nevertheless, so determined is Bloom to hold onto the "hopeful solutions" rejected by de Man, that he gives the last word of his anthology not to de Man, or even to himself, but to Hillis Miller (from Miller, *The Linguistic Moment* [Princeton: Princeton University Press, 1985]), because, Bloom explains, Miller makes "a strong attempt to reconcile the linguistic skepticism of Deconstruction with Yeats's aggressive faith that words alone are certain good" (viii). Bloom's allusion here to one of Yeats's earliest poems, "The Song of the Happy Shepherd" (1885; P 7), sidesteps de Man's contention that linguistic skepticism emerges late in Yeats's career. However, the late poem "Nineteen Hundred and Nineteen" (1921) supplies the basis for Hillis Miller's claims about the unnameable "it" that decenters Yeats's verse. "It" is not to be confused, Miller contends, "with a nihilism of the abyss, the idea that nothing exists at the base but empty and factitious structures of signs. If the *it* is neither thought, nor thing, nor spirit, nor word, it is not nothing either" (203).

To find anything in the two volumes under review that approximates the skepticism that de Man discovers in Yeats, we must turn to Finneran's anthology, and his selection from Daniel A. Harris's *Yeats: Coole Park & Ballylee* (Baltimore: Johns Hopkins University Press, 1974). From a reading of "Blood and the Moon" (1928), Harris concludes that Yeats's "faith in the power of language to establish boundaries has crumpled," and only a "humbled consciousness of community" with his fellow mortals saves Yeats from "utmost nihilism" (188). Harris's study finds a place in Finneran's anthology because it derives its conclusions from a close reading of the poetry rather than from a consciously applied theoretical program. For the same reason, it lends important independent confirmation to the conclusions of de Man, and, again one must add, of Bloom. In referring to the threat of nihilism, Harris acknowledges Bloom's earlier reading of "Blood and the Moon," "where the self-reduction to nihilism is too forceful to be halted, and too eloquent to be discarded" (*Yeats* 380). But instead of his own or de Man's (*Rhetoric of Romanticism,* 137) skeptical readings of the poem, Bloom has chosen for his anthology the more hopeful reading by Thomas Whitaker, with which, in *Yeats,* Bloom quarrels (377–79).

The curious swerve from his own readings that constitutes Bloom's anthology cannot be explained as an attempt to give a hearing to different sides of an issue, because in fact the anthology is remarkably consistent in its presentation of one side. What is curious is that that side does not always reflect Bloom's reading of Yeats's poetry. I would resist, also, too quick an application of a psychoanalytic explanation, for instance, that Bloom is torn between what he knows Yeats to be and what he wants him to be. Again, we would expect greater inconsistency within the anthology itself if this explanation were to apply. Moreover, Bloom's consciousness appears to have such an enormous range that I would hesitate to claim at any point that the boundary of the unconscious had clearly been crossed.

Instead, I would offer an explanation that recognizes another boundary, that between literature and criticism, which recent fashion boasts of having erased. Admittedly, Bloom's own practice as a critic has lent superficial encouragement to that fashion, but his practice in compiling his anthology of Yeats criticism appears to uphold the distinction between literature and the study of literature that he drew in *The Anxiety of Influence:*

> A humanism might still be founded upon a completer *study of liter-*
> *ature* than we have yet achieved, but never upon literature itself, or
> any idealized mirroring of its implicit categories. The strong imag-
> ination comes to its painful birth through savagery and misrepresen-
> tation. The only human virtue we can hope to teach through a more
> advanced study of literature than we have now is the social virtue of
> detachment from one's own imagination, recognizing always that
> such detachment made absolute destroys any individual imagina-
> tion. (86)

Seeking to advance the study of literature thus defined, Bloom has fashioned an anthology about Yeats that defends against Yeats. On the other hand, Finneran's anthology, insofar as his contributors seek to keep Yeats objectively in view, defends against the destruction of the individual imagination.

Brunner, Larry. *Tragic Victory: The Doctrine of Subjective Salvation in the Poetry of W. B. Yeats.*
Troy, N.Y.: Whitston, 1987. viii + 184.

Reviewed by CONNIE K. HOOD

When is a new book not really a new book? When it is actually a dissertation dating from some years earlier and later being published. Larry Brunner's *Tragic Victory: The Doctrine of Subjective Salvation in the Poetry of W. B. Yeats* is, or is based on, his dissertation of 1973 at Duke University (directed by Grover Smith); this review is, in a sense, fourteen years late. While numerous valuable scholarly works have come out of dissertations (Richard Ellmann's *Yeats: The Man and the Masks,* for example), one expects that the publications will normally be developments of and improvements on the academic papers.

The most obvious sign that this is not so in the case of *Tragic Victory* is the absence from the bibliography of any item dated after 1971—some sixteen years before the publication date of the book. Under the circumstances, it is perhaps pointless to complain that Brunner has failed to use as his text *The Poems: A New Edition* (1983) or that he has not relied upon such significant and pertinent works as George Bornstein's *Yeats and Shelley* (1970) and *Transformations of Romanticism in Yeats, Eliot, and Stevens* (1976), though one wonders why he omitted Leonard E. Nathan's *The Tragic Drama of William Butler Yeats* (1965).

In addition to his failure to update his volume's scholarship, Brunner shows many of the usual problems of doctoral dissertations. *Tragic Victory* is too full of quotations carefully garnered from Yeats's work as well as from secondary materials; some of the quotations are, by now, overly familiar. Furthermore, much of the book's doctrine (to be examined shortly) is admittedly heavily inspired by B. L. Reid's *William Butler Yeats: The Lyric of Tragedy* (1961) and Harold H. Watts's "W. B. Yeats: Theology Bitter and Gay" (*South Atlantic Quarterly* 99 [1950]: 359–77); one of Brunner's quotations (77) from Reid contains much of the substance of *Tragic Victory:* Yeats's "gnostic humanism . . . drives him on to assert that man is not only spiritually equal to this fate and able to bear it unbroken, he is spiritually superior to his fate and able to bear it essentially untouched."

The volume has not been proofread with sufficient care by Brunner or the publishers. It has many careless errors, such as *absense* (5, 120), *effects* for *affects* (75, 77), *interpretor* (104), *beings* for *begins* (116), *absure* for *absurd* (129), *essense* (142), *through* for *though* (147), *has* for *was* (144), *Visison* (154), and *Ceasars* (161). In one passage, a line of text has apparently been omitted, since the last word on one line is *possi-* and the first word on the next is *converts* (140). Sometimes passages from Yeats's works contain confusing errors, such as *through* for *though* (88) or *grew* for *drew* (118). For some reason, in most of the inset quotations throughout the volume the first line is slightly further from all the rest than they are from one another, and in one place right-justification fails (148). Although autobiographical passages from Yeats are referred to the English *Autobiographies* (1966), some of the citations match not this edition but the American *Autobiography of William Butler Yeats* (1953) (for example, footnotes 1 and 6 on pages 4–5). Brunner all too frequently quotes without indicating in his text the source or even whether the source is Yeats or secondary (e.g., 26–27n5); in one place (9), he never gives the source of several lines from "The Three Beggars" at all. The index is limited entirely to Yeats's poems, including neither other proper names nor ideas.

Apart from such faults, which mar the volume but need not preclude critical perception, *Tragic Victory* will not be to the taste of all readers in its approach to Yeats. Brunner argues that Yeats envisions life as brief, irrational, amoral, and frustrating—tragic. Accordingly, Yeats retreats into an inner subjectivism, almost a solipsistic position, within which he is the god who orders and structures; he can be the gay hero whose defense against disorder is a stoic coldness, a kind of arrogance. Thus, Yeats seeks a subjective salvation, and this is Brunner's key point. Yet this subjective salvation must not involve total retreat from the outer world; one must never fail to recognize the tragic reality nor veil oneself from its pain and unhappiness. Art must serve "the religious function for which it is intended, winning us to eternity, satisfying our immortal cravings for mastery, self-fulfillment, and freedom" (97).

Perhaps the book's most original, and to some readers irritating, contribution comes at this point. Brunner applies a specifically Christian frame of reference to Yeats's outlook; within this framework, Yeats was good in his *contemptus mundi* but bad in his firm insistence on maintaining his selfhood, in refusing to bow to the majesty of God. This is a highly moral and didactic framework, and the emphasis on it helps to explain why Brunner rarely pays more than lip service to the aesthetics of Yeats's work; as the title might suggest, *Tragic Victory* treats Yeats's work largely as doctrine, generally looks only at small parts of individual poems, and considers whole ones only ideologically.

Occasionally, in fact, one wonders why Brunner chose Yeats and not Eliot for his topic. Sometimes Brunner sounds like T. S. Eliot in "The Function of Criticism" chastising Middleton Murry for his Whiggish devotion to the inner voice, to Romanticism rather than classicism. He quotes with approval this passage from Eliot: "Mr. Yeats's supernatural world was the wrong supernatural world" (168). One may finally ask if Brunner's is a critical endeavor at all, since he concludes by remarking that Yeats's "poetry stands as the record of a protracted struggle toward truth which may serve us well as a guidepost toward our own realization of that Truth which makes for freedom, that Reality which makes for life" (174). Yeats has become an example of spiritual failure, to assist the Christian on his way.

Although Brunner sometimes argues (106) that Yeats never really developed but held his tragic, heroic view of life from the very first, he suddenly discovers development in suggesting that, in his final years, Yeats found his doctrine of subjective salvation had failed him and turned partially toward an objective alternative and that, had he lived long enough, he would "have sought a formulation of experience which would not only include God, but perhaps even center on God" (155). One of the problems of the book is its failure to consider development and the dates of individual poems adequately; "Vacillation" is quoted as example both of ultimate subjectivism (156) and of "How far we have come here from the solipsism and frightful insularity of the self-delighting, self-begotten soul" (163).

There are other problems of interpretation in *Tragic Victory,* particularly regarding Yeats's occultism. Perhaps to strengthen the contrast between Yeats's desolate, godless tragic world and the redeemed one which Brunner wishes he had adopted, Brunner minimizes Yeats's belief in transcendental, other-worldly hopes; as to belief in an inevitable promise of tomorrow, "I suspect that this kind of 'pie in the sky' hopefulness would have been rejected by Yeats out of hand" (61). This leads Brunner to see *A Vision* as "but an elaborate formulation for self-expression" (101) and one which he never really accepted (121). Surely it is more likely that Yeats truly wanted to believe the material of *A Vision* and that he sometimes did so, if not always.

One suspects that many of Yeats's scholarly readers are neither occultists nor Christians, and it is interesting to speculate on why Yeats exercises the fascination he does for such readers. The answer may lie in aspects of Yeats's work which Brunner does not properly appreciate, in Yeats's genuine devotion to his view of the world as opposites. Such a dialectic is a constant tension which allows no easy solutions to life's problems. For Brunner, Yeats's periodic swings from one side of an issue to another suggest a failure of outlook, logical inconsistency; the negative connotations are obvious in Brunner's suggestion that Yeats's "slippery generalities . . . are in fact ill-disguised attempts by Yeats to reassure himself of the validity of the vision he espouses and proclaims in his art" (125). Many readers may find in Yeats's hesitations and charges a greater honesty in confronting aspects of life which genuinely are difficult to solve.

Yeats is neither a transcendentalist beating airy wings into the empyrean nor a Sisyphus smiling in tragic gaiety as he toils uphill; or, better, he is both, and this is his glory. Speaking of two kinds of literary methodology, J. Hillis Miller opposes to the "metaphysical" approaches "those methods which hypothesize that in literature, for reasons which are intrinsic to language itself, metaphysical presuppositions are, necessarily, both affirmed and subverted" (quoted in Vincent B. Leitch, *Deconstructive Criticism* [New York: Columbia University Press, 1983], 190). One of the marks of Yeats's greatness, one of the reasons that he has spoken and continues to speak to modern man, is precisely this double nature, something that Brunner unfortunately misses.

Barbara L. Croft. *"Stylistic Arrangements": A Study of William Butler Yeats's* A Vision.
Lewisburg: Bucknell University Press, 1987. 196 pp.

Reviewed by GEORGE MILLS HARPER

Barbara L. Croft's implied purpose is ambitious and laudable: to compare, contrast, and appraise the relative merits of the two versions of *A Vision*. She suggests in capsule in the title not only her intention but also her critical conviction: "A 'stylistic arrangement' means, not an abstracted pattern of the given but a creative act, an arrangement of experience in the manner of one's own style; when one recalls Yeats's definition of style as a surplus of energy, the playing of strength when the day's work is done, the playful, energetic tone of *A Vision* begins to match Valéry's [definition of cosmogony]" (171). To the careful reader, however, it will be obvious that this critical definition of Yeats's style is more appropriate to the 1937 version than the 1925—at least in Croft's opinion. But it may not be a valid description of either.

Her plan is simple and generally sound: three main chapters are concerned with *A Vision* (both versions), and a fourth is her judgment in favor of the 1937 version based on her perspective of the change in style. The chief interest of Chapter 1 ("An Irish Heresy") lies in Croft's summary and evaluation of "Critical Response and the Question of Belief." Generally sound, this discussion would be more appealing if it were more comprehensive and less dependent on the work of Helen Vendler, Northrop Frye, and Harold Bloom—all provocative but out of date. Chapter 2 is a book-by-book "Comparison of the Systems" of the two versions. Croft's intention is admirable, but the execution is inadequate, primarily because it is far too brief (35 pages). And there are other weaknesses, including questionable assumptions. Having recently traced with some care the composition of the 1925 *Vision,* I am not convinced that it was "simply premature" (57). In fact, I am not at all sure that Yeats could—or would—have made the book "richer" if he had kept it by him "for another year." Almost certainly he would not have made it richer by explications of the Beatific Vision and sexual love (AV-A iii), both of which are directly related to the personal Script, which he was repeatedly warned not to reveal.

Croft also accepts at face value (70) Yeats's statement in the 1937 version that he "knew nothing of the *Four Principles* when I wrote the last Book" (AV-B 187). In fact, he knew as much as he was ever to know: the Automatic Script outlines and defines the Principles in considerable detail. In part he failed to discuss them as he might have because they had strong personal overtones: Husk (originally Physical Body) represents Yeats himself; Passionate Body, Iseult Gonne; Spirit Body, Maud Gonne, and Celestial Body, George Yeats.

The tetradic Body cannot be complete without his "three birds," as Yeats called them. Croft is wrong, I think, in assuming that "the wheel of the Principles is nontemporal" (71). As I understand the Script, two of the Principles (Husk and Passionate Body) are temporal, two (Spirit Body and Celestial Body) nontemporal. Although the Principles represented a basic psychological and cosmic truth to Yeats, he could find little use for the concept in the System. But the blame should not be laid to carelessness or the Frustrators (AV-B 187). Here, as elsewhere, Croft might have avoided questionable assumptions if Yeats's sources had been available to her or even if she had relied more often on *A Critical Edition of Yeats's* A Vision *(1925)*. (I am thinking in particular of an important point about "the Christian implications" of the 1925 version in contrast to the 1937 version [e.g., see 84].) Nevertheless, chapter 2 is useful, but it will need to be revised and expanded when the Automatic Script is available.

More significant to Croft's thesis perhaps is the somewhat fuller discussion in chapter 3 of "A Comparison of the Fiction in the Two Versions of *A Vision*." Basing her argument on Section ix of the "Introduction to 'A Vision,'" Croft accepts without question Yeats's assertion that "The first version of this book . . . fills me with shame" (AV-B 19). If not misleading, as most careful readers of the two versions will conclude, that statement, in the explanation that follows, is certainly a calculated exaggeration. But rather than debate that issue, I want to consider briefly Croft's conclusion, ably argued, that the cover story of version two is more satisfactory because it is better unified in the whole than the literary hoax of the 1925 version. She begins her study of the cover stories by tracing in detail the development of Robartes and Aherne, arriving at last at the provocative conclusion that Yeats has altered their characters to emphasize their antithetical and primary polarities. Although I find that convincing, it is unfortunate that the unpublished Robartes-Aherne dialogues were not available to support and illuminate the argument.

I am not so convinced of the artistic merit of the "Stories of Michael Robartes and His Friends" as an organic part of the whole. In fact, outside of Yeats's brilliant and carefully written introduction (AV-B 8–25), I consider much of the remaining cover material more or less extraneous. To Croft, in contrast, the "Stories of Michael Robartes" are "autobiographical and represent both Yeats's intention to acknowledge, under the veil of fiction, his emotional debts and to assert his convictions regarding determinism and instinct" (127). That, I suggest, is a heavy burden for these "absurdist" stories (Croft's description [148]). Indeed, the very condition of the "manuscript" of A Vision when it was submitted to Macmillan in December 1934 suggests its inorganic character. Connie Hood has described it in her outstanding dissertation, "A Search for Authority: Prolegomena to a Definitive Critical Edition of W. B. Yeats's A Vision (1937)" (University of Tennessee, 1983). She writes, "instead of a single typescript of his new book, Yeats sent to Macmillan as printer's copy three books and a scribal typescript: copy #498 of A Vision (1925), the Cuala editions of A Packet for Ezra Pound and Stories of Michael Robartes, and an original typescript now lost except for a twelve-page fragment and an uncorrected carbon of the entire script" (Hood 48–49). This dissertation might have proved useful to Croft. It is unfortunately only one of several recent studies she failed to consult or to list in her bibliography. As a result she sometimes quotes questionable authorities or out-of-date material.

Chapter 4 focuses on "Style," attempting to prove not only that the "wild new style" of "Stories of Michael Robartes" is complementary to the changed tone of the revised Vision but also that "Yeats had derived [the style] in part from his contemporaries" (135). The most important of these are Jack B. Yeats and Ezra Pound. Croft relates "the seeds of absurdism in Yeats's late plays" (152) to "Stories of Michael Robartes" and by extension to A Vision:

Nevertheless, the comparison of A Vision and absurdism remains a valid means of exploring the tone of Yeats's late work, for he seems to have foreseen in this complex, often frustrating work the problems that the absurdists would later confront. He may have sensed, too, the time coming when the vast poetic statement would seem little more than an eccentricity. (156)

This unsupported assumption that Yeats might lose faith in the validity of his visionary book is, I suggest, entirely wrong. As I have pointed out in *The Making of Yeats's* A Vision: *A Study of the Automatic Script* (London: Macmillan; Carbondale, Ill.: Southern Illinois University Press, 1987), Yeats said the opposite in the strongest possible terms in a draft of the "Introduction" of *A Vision:*

> I will never think any thoughts but these, or some modification or extension of these; when I write prose or verse they must be somewhere present though not it may be in the words; they must affect my judgment of friends and of events . . . . (2:414)

Although Yeats knew that "Some will ask if I believe all that this book contains" (2:414), he remained convinced from October 1917 to the end of his life "that he, George and her Controls were collaborators in the development and structuring of a System by means of which he could interpret 'all thought, all history and the difference between man and man' " (2:417).

Linda Dowling. *Language and Decadence in the Victorian Fin de Siècle.*
Princeton: Princeton University Press, 1986, xvi + 295 pp.

Reviewed by K. P. S. JOCHUM

The literary decadence of the 1890s is a well-explored area. But, as Linda
Dowling's book shows, there is still room for new and valid approaches.
She bases her investigation on a comprehensive discussion of two major
linguistic theories of the eighteenth and nineteenth centuries and their
impact on Decadent poetry and poetic theory through the mediation of
Walter Pater. The first of the theories is Romantic philology. It orig-
inates with Herder and sees "individual languages as the voices of histor-
ical cultures, and language itself as *Volksstimme,* the outward expression
of the inner essence of a nation or people" (15). Herder's "belief in the
identity of words and thought" reappears, with characteristic modifica-
tions, in Wordsworth's "appeal to rural speech and conventional texts"
(20); but at the same time Wordsworth becomes increasingly aware of a
"disturbing autonomy and materiality" in language. Coleridge, a more
important proponent of Romantic philology, holds that a *lingua communis*
is essentially a written language, and it is through literature "that lan-
guage becomes permanent and accessible enough to be held in common
and through time by people otherwise widely different" (27). Cole-
ridge's organic conception of language and culture, his "identification of
literature and civilization" (31), is seen as an important bequest to Vic-
torian culture, where the concept of civilization is lifted onto a na-
tionalistic platform and where the English language assumes the function
of a secularized gospel with which to convert the rest of the world.
Romantic philology has given birth to linguistic nationalism or even
imperialism.

The second theory is that of scientific and comparative philology,
adumbrated in a sense, and quite unintentionally, by Herder and largely
developed by German linguists. Scientific philology undermined Ro-
mantic philology by finding English as a written or literary language to
be "nothing more than an artificial dialect, a petrifaction, a dead tongue"
(5). The Victorians were much disturbed when they learned that "lan-
guage was organized on purely linguistic principles independent of both
men and representation" (61). The new theory threatened the "Victorian
ideal of civilization" because it "divorced language from literature and

valorized sound laws instead of poetic licence" (64). A living language was taken to be identical with living speech, whereas literature was frozen and falsified speech (65). But the sanctioning of oral usage meant to many Victorians a deplorable betrayal of standards, in fact a decay of linguistic and literary values. This is one of the reasons why the appearance of the first volume of the *OED* was greeted with a good deal of criticism.

It is against this background that Pater's works and thinking acquire their full significance. As Dowling sees it, Pater embraced "the relentless insistence of the new philology that literary English is quite literally a dead or moribund language," and he tried "to establish a new mode of writing on its very morbidity, dissolving the antagonistic opposition between philology and literature in a new vision of the writer as a sort of philologist or scholar of words" (111). Pater's principal advice and strategy is "to write English more as a learned language" (124), at the cost of entirely neglecting its spoken form. This neglect is due to Pater's repudiation of the neo-grammatic notion that the life of a language is guaranteed by its living orality. The "living authority" for Pater's euphuism, for his artificial prose style, "can never reside in the mass of speaking men. It resides instead in scholars" (137). The point of decadence is reached when the learned few, the heirs of "Romanticism demoralized by philology" (176), are no longer responsive to the idea of a national language, and when "official culture" has turned away from them (40).

Dowling discusses Pater in some detail, then turns to his less original followers who, even more than their master, insisted on using an artificial language devoid of contact with the living speech, writers such as Aubrey Beardsley, Arthur Machen, George Moore, and Oscar Wilde. It is with these writers that the motif of the "fatal book" assumes dangerous implications. In her fourth chapter, Dowling analyzes the responses of some Nineties poets to Pater's bequest of the artificiality of written, literary language; her chosen examples are Sir Max Beerbohm, William Sharp/Fiona Macleod, Lionel Johnson, Ernest Dowson, Arthur Symons, and John Davidson. The entire fifth and final chapter of about 40 pages is devoted to "Yeats and the Book of the People." This seems a fitting conclusion for several reasons. Yeats was not only affected by the literary decadence; he was also, to some extent, its chronicler; he was the only major writer to survive the Nineties and to emerge, as other critics have observed, at the other end as a contributor to some rather different literary movements. If the Yeats chapter has a legitimate place in the book's argument, it also betrays what seems to me an unsolved problem in the book's overall structure. The linguistic theories discussed earlier certainly have their bearing on Pater who, as an Oxford don, could be expected to be conversant with such problems. As we move towards the end of the century, the writers chosen by Dowling are much less aware of the linguists and grammarians of the preceding one hundred years; Yeats's knowledge of Max Müller is apparently restricted to Müller's mythological investigations, and to the best of my knowledge Herder doesn't figure anywhere in his writings. The pressures felt by Pater when he had to define the linguistic medium in which to write seem to me of a different order from those experienced by Yeats; a point that might bear further investigation.

Dowling is quite right in introducing the complicating Irish factor into the Yeats chapter. The availability of an Irish oral tradition enabled Yeats to maintain a distance from the outworn English literary tradition; but it was a distance characterized by a frequently changing width. Thus Yeats is seen to adopt the written Decadent style when he comes under the influence of the symbolists. But the three stories of *The Secret Rose* foreshadow, in their progression, "the famous stylistic change in his poetry" (267) that manifests itself in the publication of *In the Seven Woods* (1903), where Yeats returns "to the speaking voice of the Irish peasant" (268). Finally, however, the picture of Yeats emerging from this chapter is one of a poet who never really abandoned the "Decadent ideal of elaborate, artificial language" (282) that pervades even such late poems as "Beautiful Lofty Things."

This is all very well, but there are some details, neglected by Dowling, that remove Yeats perceptibly from the linguistic debate of the Victorians and the Decadents. She does not consider Yeats's early folkloristic phase, his habit of collecting legends, stories, and anecdotes among the peasants, fishermen, and servants of the Sligo area and later, together with Lady Gregory, in the cottages of County Galway. Yeats wrote those stories down and published them as *The Celtic Twilight;* they also found their way into several poems throughout his career. The reasons for perpetuating the stories in written form are given in his autobiography and have nothing to do with the Victorian linguistic debate. Yeats considered his stories and poems to be a kind of remuneration, a token of gratitude dedicated to the narrators of the oral tales who, he hoped, would become his ideal audience in a kind of poetic exchange.

(For a pertinent illustration see his poem "The Fisherman.") Yeats could
do this because he thought that both the naive storyteller and the more
sophisticated poet possess a natural command of poetic language; a con-
viction that served as a cornerstone in the national Irish poetic that he
hoped to build. This looks back to Herder rather than to Pater.

A change came when Yeats's interest in occultism grew stronger,
when he found, rightly or wrongly, correspondences between folk be-
liefs and spiritism, a connection that he had been looking for since at least
1889 (see UP1 130). Again this seems to me not quite the same as the
decadent pursuit of the "fatal book." Dowling draws attention to Yeats's
equation of the "poetry of the coteries" with the "true poetry of the
people" (258); but she does not explain, as one might have expected her
to do, what Yeats understood by the "coteries." They are, in my opin-
ion, not the same people as Pater's "scholars."

In sum, then, *Language and Decadence in the Victorian Fin de Siècle* is a
remarkable and thoughtful book. Although the Yeats chapter isn't quite
successful, there is enough matter in it for further study. With the broad
panorama painted in the first three chapters in mind, Dowling's ap-
proach could be extended to more detailed investigations of Yeats's
views on oral and written literature.

Richard Ellmann. *Four Dubliners*.
New York: George Braziller, 1987. 122 pp.

Reviewed by James Olney

This volume, comprised of miniature portraits of Oscar Wilde, W. B. Yeats, James Joyce, and Samuel Beckett and first delivered as lectures at the Library of Congress over a four-year period, comes as a late, gracious gift from Richard Ellmann. The four essays are like a series of grace notes to Ellmann's monumental works on Yeats, Joyce, and Wilde. Ellmann had a genius, here brilliantly displayed, for finding little corners of interest in a subject that would have seemed to others fully explored and exhausted—usually by Ellmann himself—and for turning those little corners into a summary view not only of the room where they are located but of the entire mansion, the complete *oeuvre* of Yeats or Joyce, Wilde or Beckett. An account of a particular period in Wilde's life (his years at Oxford), an analysis of the effects that submitting to the Steinach operation had on Yeats's life and his poetry, a consideration of how Joyce created a couple of encounters in his life that they might be the stuff of his art—these are all transformed under Ellmann's hand to provide synoptic views of the artistic personalities and the careers of the three men. Beckett is rather different, for Ellmann sees him mostly in relation to the other three, his vision and writing being the natural if not necessary outcome of Beckett's responding to certain thematic elements in the work of his three Irish—though mostly Irish-in-exile—predecessors.

That the four men gathered together in this book were all of them Irish, indeed were all Dubliners as the title says, is one thing that makes it possible to talk about them between the covers of a single book, but their nationality or their citizenry is not, as Ellmann presents the "quadrumvirate," the most interesting or the most important characteristic shared by the four. This is rather a certain cast of mind, skeptical, self-critical, detached; and in this respect the portrait of Wilde at Oxford is the perfect lead-off piece. As Ellmann pictures him, Wilde was drawn during his years at Oxford to conflicting opposites, embodied primarily by Pater and Ruskin and figured in another way by his simultaneous attraction to paganism and to Roman Catholicism; rather than give his full loyalty to one or the other, however, Wilde incorporated both into his personality as dialectical elements that produced the stichomythic exchanges of both his life and his drama. "This sudden perception of a truth opposed to the home truth we are all prepared to acknowledge, and just as plausible," Ellmann writes in the final paragraph of his Wildean portrait, "was Wilde's answer to what he called the 'violence of opinion' exhibited as he saw by most of his contemporaries. He traced his own detachment from that violence to Oxford, where he said he had learned 'the Oxford temper,' though it was really his own temper" (37). That this refusal to subscribe to the "violence of opinion" was not solely due to the Oxford experience may be seen in the fact that Yeats, Joyce, and Beckett also declined that violence, yet none of them could explain their detachment by an Oxford education. For Wilde, and surely for the other three as well, Ellmann writes, "The object of life is not to simplify it. As our conflicting impulses coincide, as our repressed feelings vie with those we express, as our solid views disclose unexpected fissures, we are all secret dramatists, whether or not we bring our complexities onto the stage. In this light Wilde's works become exercises in self-criticism as well as pleas for tolerance" (37).

Yeats may have been accused of intolerance by some of those not much taken by his public manner, yet it seems to me that what Ellmann writes of Wilde and of the tolerance that ultimately defined his attitude toward affairs both of life and literature was equally true for Yeats. One thinks of those journal entries in which Yeats was able to reason himself out of indignation with Edmund Gosse in the quarrel with Lady Gregory and Robert Gregory because (or so at least he felt) he saw all around the question, and words that might have been angry turned instead to the task of analysis and understanding. To Robert he drafted a letter of explanation for his inaction, saying, "I want you to understand that I have no instincts in personal life. I have reasoned them all away, and reason acts very slowly and with difficulty and has to exhaust every side of the subject. Above all, I have destroyed in myself, by analysis, instinctive indignation" (Mem 252). In a passage that he deleted from this same draft letter Yeats says, "My mind works like this. When I was younger and more natural my first impulse would have been indignation, but now it was only surprise. I said, why has Gosse done this ridiculous thing. Has he fits of madness? I went over it and over it trying to see what caused it" (Mem 253n2). And in a sentence that speaks volumes about Yeats's refusal of the "violence of opinion" both in his relationships with people and in the typical mode of his poetry, he writes, "Then there is this difficulty, that words are with me a means of investigation, rather than a means of action" (Mem 254). It was for this, that language was with Yeats "a means of investigation, rather than a means of action," that Maud Gonne faulted him in "Easter 1916," but of course in an exactly equal and opposite way it was Maud Gonne's adherence to the "violence of opinion" that so distressed Yeats and caused him finally to turn where "a glad kindness" pleased his eye and mind.

> An intellectual hatred is the worst,
> So let her think opinions are accursed.
> Have I not seen the loveliest woman born
> Out of the mouth of Plenty's horn,
> Because of her opinionated mind
> Barter that horn and every good
> By quiet natures understood
> For an old bellows full of angry wind?
>
> (P 189)

Ellmann pictures Yeats, like Wilde, as someone aware of contrary truths that disallowed fanatical adherence to one or the other. "As Yeats reached his life's end," Ellmann writes, "he recognized that he would never be able to decide between the beatific vision and its obverse. The image of life as cornucopia was relentlessly undermined by the image of life as an empty shell" (62). The sole answer that could satisfy the many-sided mind was to allow the free play of opposites everywhere whether in poem or in life. "A last letter of Yeats took comfort in one thing alone, that man if he cannot know the truth can at least embody it. Not without unconscious pride, he said he would embody it in the completion of his life. What he meant was that the great questions could be given only momentary answers, couched in passionate utterance. Visionaries or not, we are only, as Falstaff says, 'mortal men, mortal men'" (63).

The curse of the "opinionated mind" is not particularly the theme of Ellmann's chapter on Joyce but there can be no doubt of where Joyce, perhaps even more than his three compatriots in this book, stood on the issue. The encounter of Leopold Bloom and the citizen in the "Cyclops" episode of *Ulysses* could well stand as a kind of dramatized statement of belief on the matter of the "violence of opinion" for all four of these Dubliners.

But it's no use, says he. Force, hatred, history, all that. That's not

life for men and women, insult and hatred. And everybody knows
that it's the very opposite of that that is really life.
    What? says Alf.
    Love, says Bloom. I mean the opposite of hatred.

Some of the points of resemblance that Ellmann tries to establish
between Beckett and the other three may seem a bit strained but on this
essential similarity that binds them all together—perhaps as artists rather
than as Irishmen or Dubliners?—he is very good. Comparing Wilde and
Beckett, he could well be making what I take to be the largely unstated
idea behind all of *Four Dubliners*. "A more profound resemblance is the
quality possessed by both men of what might be called self-cancellation.
They cannot think of one possibility without evoking its opposite and
recognizing its equal claim" (108). This it is that keeps them weighing
and balancing, analyzing and investigating, embodying the complexity
of truth rather than screaming a fragmentary or partial truth in the
streets. This spirit of unopinionated, non-violent tolerance was ob-
viously close to Richard Ellmann's own heart, and it is this, together
with his stylistic grace and clarity, that makes one think of him more as a
man of letters than as, in any limiting sense, an academic. *Four Dubliners*
is not his greatest work, nor did Ellmann think it to be, but it is fully
characteristic all the same and a fine volume to have. It is sad to think that
we will not have more like it.

Maeve Good. *W. B. Yeats and the Creation of a Tragic Universe.*
Totowa, N.J.: Barnes & Noble, 1987. [ix] + 176 pp.

Heather C. Martin. *W. B. Yeats: Metaphysician as Dramatist.*
Waterloo, Ontario: Wilfrid Laurier University Press, 1986. [xiv] +
153 pp.

Reviewed by EDWARD ENGELBERG

These are both relatively brief studies and both concern themselves prin-
cipally with Yeats's drama: Good with what she calls Yeats's "Tragic
Universe" and Martin with the relation of the drama to a "metaphysic."
That is where the resemblance ceases. In general, books such as these,
dealing with specific perspectives, are precisely the sort of studies we
should be getting, since the ambitious attempts to write "Yeats" studies
covering all of the poet's work have lately fallen short. However, in the
present case one book succeeds more than the other.

Maeve Good's study reads too much like an unrevised dissertation.
For example, after referring to Harold Bloom's *Yeats* four or five times,
we still read: "Harold Bloom, in his study *Yeats* . . ."; and the sentences
are frustratingly brief. Take, for example, the opening sentences of the
book:

> Yeats's life closes with *The Death of Cuchulain.* He is the subject of
> one of the final meditations on death, "Cuchulain Comforted." He
> has the last word: "No body like / His body has modern woman
> borne" (CP1, 705). He is finally synonymous with the Irish nation
> as its *alter ego* or ideal self (11).

To be sure styles will differ, but these series of short sentences do
have the effect of undermining some better in-depth analyses. On occa-
sion, one has the feeling that premature closure of sentence results in
premature closure of thought. Good's use of previous critical material
also seems a little strained. While she admires Helen Vendler, Harold
Bloom, T. R. Henn, and Thomas Whitaker (among others), every so
often there is what reads like the obligatory disagreement, as if the writer
wishes to make certain that individuality is being asserted. But, once
again, since these differences are often minor in the scheme of the whole,
they draw attention away from the major argument.

Basically that argument is stated clearly enough:

> Harold Bloom, in his study *Yeats,* frequently attacks Yeats for his
> brutality and anti-human stance. . . . I argue that Yeats's presenta-
> tion of the tragic concentrates on this dark element in the tragic
> world, on its terror. (5)

This does not seem to work so much as an argument *against* Bloom as it
is perhaps a re-statement of what Bloom may be objecting to in the
version of the critique Good ascribes to him. There can be little to argue,
I think, on the fact: Yeats does indeed stress the "terror" (in his poems
and prose as well), and whether that constitutes his "tragic universe" is
the question. We recall that Yeats chided Shelley for lacking a "Vision of
Evil," and so his insistence that one stare into reality unflinchingly is very
much a given. Like others before her, Good focuses, and quite rightly,
on Cuchulain. There is a good deal of quoting from Yeats's essays on
tragedy, his comments on the subject of tragedy in other forms—poems,
letters, essays. Yeats, Good asserts, searches for ways of presenting his
tragic conception and arrives, in the first instance, at something like a
shift from realism to a kind of "vision." In the second chapter she deals
with three of the four plays "for dancers": *At the Hawk's Well, The Only
Jealousy of Emer,* and *The Dreaming of the Bones.* Here the author says she
is concerned with their "structure," but I found no overarching concep-
tion of structure emerging. Instead there is a good deal of summary and
many references to this or that critic, with whom there may be either
agreement or disagreement. In the act of validating her general concep-
tion of Yeats's "dark" side, Good concludes that these plays evoke "an
atmosphere of despair, terror, futility and loss" (61)—a description
which to my mind at least makes them sound a bit more like Beckett
than Yeats.

The "Tragic Universe" is seen through *A Vision,* that strange book
which is "entirely amenable to tragedy" (95). This is perhaps the most
interesting chapter because it raises a question still arguable, not resolved:
Did Yeats present us in *A Vision* with a deterministic universe? Did he in
fact trap himself in his own "System"? Good's response is that "antin-
omy, division and conflict" always return us "to cycle, to defeat, to
failure, to time" (96). Perhaps. But one needs to keep in mind that the
very "return" to cycle indicates a temporariness: that is, Yeats's "Sys-
tem" is never static, and if we are mired in defeat one moment we need

only be patient for the gyre to move us eventually to more redemptive positions the next. Indeed we move even into time at whose face Yeats was willing to "spit."

Calvary, The Resurrection, The Words upon the Window-pane, and Purgatory are assigned to the penultimate chapter, and through them Good examines the "Problem of Evil." The chapter is too brief to encompass the subject, and the individual discussions of each play seem rushed. That Purgatory has "the impossibility of forgiveness" at its "centre" (133) is debatable; one would think that forgiveness is far too personalized an emotion for a play that portrays the paradigm of "return" posited earlier. In the end Good seems somewhat to have been trapped in her own overly deterministic interpretations of Yeats, especially when she concedes that throughout the canon "we are conscious of ironies, twists of fate and above all, conflict, exhilaration, and the impetus towards an intense vision which is both self-destructive and a re-creation of the self" (154).

There seems to be a re-discovery of Yeats's anger lately, his pessimism, his rage, even his "hatred" (see Joseph M. Hassett's Yeats and the Poetics of Hate [Dublin: Gill and Macmillan; New York: St. Martin's Press, 1986]), and we should welcome what should need no reminding: Yeats was almost never deluded. He knew early on that our lot on earth was not an easy one; the "redemption" he held out was not to be found in "peace," but in "conflict." But the process of conflict itself, while it costs us, also makes for exhilaration. In that he was Blakean long before he became Nietzschean. This would have been a stronger book had it made these points more deliberately, more leisurely.

Heather Martin's volume is written clearly and with a certain enviable precision, especially considering her difficult subject. To tease out Yeats's "metaphysic" is no easy matter, and though this volume, too, is slim, the author succeeds in making a very creditable case. Once again the plays are the chief texts, and through them Martin intends to trace "'the history of the soul' or spirit. . . ." (xiii). Relying heavily on F. A. C. Wilson (though not always in full agreement), Martin re-traces some well-worn steps. It is not so much any individual comments that startle or surprise, but the organization of Yeats's "metaphysic" is intelligently achieved. Martin presents us with a "system-minded" Yeats in sharp contrast to the figure we have often encountered elsewhere. In short, she argues, Yeats knew what he was about almost from the beginning, and as he grew and developed, he adapted the past and locked it into the ongoing—which really defines the kinetic nature of Yeats's development as a poet. She sees a split Yeats: "skeptical, inquiring" and in rebellion against the "rational" but also willing to embrace the "abstraction" and to "strive for irrational . . . 'truth'" (8). Her quarrels are mostly with Robert Snukal and Suheil Badi Bushrui, and sometimes they border on the too-technical.

The most interesting chapter is titled "'Bitter Memory': Forgetting, Acquiring, and Remembering." It contains this rather provocative sentence: "*The Shadowy Waters* focuses on waiting, killing time, and forgetting" (74)—although again this could pass for a description of *Waiting for Godot*. Yeats's characters are, Martin claims, "torn" between forgetting and remembering, and such a paradigm suits *Purgatory* far better than Good's (although Martin forgoes the opportunity). She reminds us quite correctly that "Those among Yeats's protagonists who attempt to escape this world do so at the risk of gaining, not release from pain and sorrow, but merely oblivion" (83).

In another chapter Martin sorts out, as best as one can, "Chance" and "Choice," and this again deals with the extent of Yeats's determinism, concluding that the two have "merged" (134). In summary we can make choices that "lead . . . up the spheres" but we "cannot . . . choose not to make [choices]" (134). That may seem to be having it both ways, but it far better reflects any proposition that Yeats would be content with leaving us a choice to choose or *not* to choose.

There is, then, some similarity between these two books, for both explore to what extent Yeats's universe is either "tragic" or "free"—or both. Good's book suffers from brevity of development; Martin's book (though sometimes it wanders from its goals) succeeds, in similar brevity, in propounding a strong case for Yeats as Metaphysician.

William H. O'Donnell. *The Poetry of William Butler Yeats: An Introduction*.
New York: Ungar, 1986. xvi + 192 pp.

Reviewed by IAN FLETCHER

Yeats is a difficult and rewarding poet. It is barely surprising then that
there should be a number of primers to the study of his work, though
more surprising perhaps that there should have been comparatively few
over the past quarter of a century. There is A. G. Stock, faintly dull,
highly worthy, who appears in the rather parsimonious bibliography
attached to the present work along with Denis Donoghue, Douglas Ar-
chibald, Balachandra Rajan, and John Unterecker—detailed, stimulat-
ing, and sometimes plain wrong. Richard Morton, arguably the best of
its kind, certainly the most lucid and forcible, goes unmentioned.

    After chapters on the life and (clemently brief) on *A Vision*—a text
like the medieval bible best kept out of profane hands—O'Donnell se-
lects a few poems from each volume and discusses them. The larger
issues of development and the relation of poem to poem within each
volume have in the preliminary essays been already touched upon. The
average number of poems up for analysis is three, dwindling to two in
The Wild Swans at Coole, swelling to four in *The Tower* and *The Winding
Stair,* four from *New Poems,* and no fewer than six from *Last Poems.* Such
intense concentration presumably represents O'Donnell's taste and, like
a number of recent critics, he isolates "Lapis Lazuli" as Yeats's finest
poem. Late works of the masters seem to radiate a certain spectral au-
thority as valediction to art or the distillation of a lifetime's brooding:
Shakespeare, Beethoven, the later Dickens. Yeats kept going pretty well,
unlike most Romantics and Victorians, and the late works have that
impatience with merely technical aptness that Lytton Strachey over-
reacted to in Shakespeare's last plays. One could make an analogy be-
tween the carnal disgusts of a Lear and a Leontes with some of the hasty
old man poems of Yeats's final phase. The relatively trivial ballad "John
Kinsella's Lament for Mrs. Mary Moore" gets its page of exegesis. There
isn't really much to say: the last word can be found in the anecdote about
F. R. Higgins taking the would-be Earl of Ormonde and Nobel Prize
winner (at W. B.'s request) to a pub and being told almost immediately
to remove him: "Higgins, I don't like it. Lead me out again" (*Irish*

307

Literary Portraits, ed. W. R. Rodgers [New York: Taplinger, 1973], 3–4).
As if the old boy hadn't spent his London years visiting the Crown or the
Cheshire Cheese, but that was in another country. Meanwhile to omit
from consideration major poems such as "Meditations in Time of Civil
War" and "Nineteen Hundred and Nineteen" (surely one of the poet's
finest utterances) seems merely perverse. A final chapter discusses the
poet among his contemporaries, a promiscuous assortment: Robert
Bridges, Lionel Johnson, John Masefield, all described as of Yeats's own
generation.

O'Donnell adds his own brief but felicitous comment to the account
of these poems, though it is possible to disagree sometimes either with
his emphases or his interpretation. "Fergus and the Druid" (as revised)
seems a rather better poem than "Adam's Curse," a genuine dramatic
lyric. "Adam's Curse" has three voices all murmuring agreement with
one another, a kind of grumbling middle-aged nostalgia in an Urbino-
like setting. As to the irony, or sarcasm rather, it is self-protective and
the poem retreats into minor ninetyish mode. True, the beloved at length
acquires some presence, but it is shadowy enough. The low-keyed tone
and would-be prosaic diction point forward, which no doubt explains
why the poem is overrated (in context of Yeats's other poems) because it
can be usefully cited as evidence for progress in his art. But there is no
sign here of the ranging dissatisfactions that mark a true advance—the
defamiliarizing of his ambience—only a wistful hymn to dead cere-
monies. Its inclusion is justifiable, but comment on it should be tinged
with astringency. "The Wanderings of Oisin," a splendid narrative, is
not discussed at all.

The commentary on "September 1913" is subtle, but subtly wrong.
O'Donnell suggests that not merely the poet and the middling sensual
modern nationalists are rebuked, but also the heroes themselves who
were always unsuccessful and driven as much by sexual as by political
motives. We could apply this to Robert Emmett and to Lord Edward
FitzGerald, and it was later discovered to be true also for poor old Sir
Roger Casement as he chatted on the shore-o to his natty sailor boy-o;
but is it altogether just to Wolfe Tone? The final note, as criticism has
suggested, is surely one of pity for the cheated dead. On "Easter 1916"
O'Donnell has excellent things to say on the ironies involved in the word
change, though he is oddly faltering about the connotations of *terror* and
beauty, which marry the polarities of Edmund Burke's aesthetics but
draw also on traditions of Romantic nationalism and even Pre-Raphaelit-

ism (Rossetti's "Soul's Beauty"). It is a relief that O'Donnell will have
nothing to do with the Aristotelian pity and terror as proposed by the
ever ingenious Donald Davie. Certainly, as O'Donnell suggests, the
third section of "Easter 1916" contrasts the spontaneous organic life of
nature (an Irish nature, never repeating the same moment twice) with the
stone that diverts the stream of life and, like the stones of Michael's
sheepfold in Wordsworth's "true" pastoral, is assumed into Nature's
permanent forms. But as with his gloss on "delirium" in "September
1913" as unambiguous limiting judgment on the martyrs (their passion
was a wasteful virtue), O'Donnell seems to ignore ambiguity once more,
and the misinterpretation here is serious, when he describes "excess of
love" followed by the word *bewildered* as startlingly negative. "I shall die
for the excess of love I bear for the Gael" was St. Columba's phrase as he
sailed for Scotland from the Irish shore, a phrase encrypted before by
Lionel Johnson and by Padraic Pearse himself, whom it fits all too fully.
Whether O'Donnell is suggesting a West British comment or a simple
doubt or distaste for twentieth-century linguistic and social engineering
is not clear, but the *bewildered* suggests the martyrs as victims—ambigu-
ity lends resonance. Even if Pearse and Co. deceived themselves, the
phrase cannot be purely negative.

Gliding over other readings, one may salute the precise description
of "Byzantium" as deliberately riddling, hypnotically ritualistic and,
despite its subdued narrative structure, jerky in its development. What
remains is the power of the rhetoric in the final stanza. "The Circus
Animals' Desertion" is perhaps still more bitterly humorous than
O'Donnell allows.

Frances Nesbitt Oppel. *Mask and Tragedy: Yeats and Nietzsche, 1902–10.*
Charlottesville: University Press of Virginia, 1987. x + 255 pp.

Reviewed by DAVID S. THATCHER

Uncomfortably close on the heels of Otto Bohlmann's *Yeats and Nietzsche: An Exploration of the Major Nietzschean Echoes in the Writings of William Butler Yeats* (1982) comes a study covering much the same familiar ground and, sadly, falling into the same familiar traps. Frances Nesbitt Oppel's perfunctory description of Bohlmann's book as showing more interest in "philosophy and philosophical echoes than in biography, history, or poetry" (2), is not really accurate, even though his book, unlike hers, seems weighted more towards Nietzsche than to Yeats. In fact, she hardly takes account of Bohlmann's book at all. The challenge, seemingly inescapable, to make clear at the outset in what respects her book differs from his in matters of methodology, scope, and focus has not been taken up, and her references to her predecessor's work are sparse indeed (Bohlmann's name, like many others', does not appear in the less than perfect index). The reader is surely entitled to know what new facts are being brought to light, what fresh insights are being brought to bear, what original conclusions are being reached. It soon emerges that very little of substance has been added to Bohlmann's study and, perhaps even more regrettably, nothing more sophisticated by way of methodology. Bohlmann's reviewers noted that his search for "echoes" tended towards "reductionist simplification" (James Olney), and that, in neglecting studies in the theory of influence (e.g., by Barthes, Foucault and Guillén) the book constitutes a "disappointing display of unjustifiable laziness," giving us the "impression that it could have been written years ago" (Hiroyuki Shima). A casual nod in the direction of Harold Bloom (3) is virtually all Oppel offers on the vexed problem of "influence."

A weakness in theoretical underpinning is accompanied by some rather dismaying lapses from scholarly precision. The first paragraph alone makes one wonder quite how trustworthy a book this will turn out to be. There is, to my knowledge, no evidence to support the claim that Yeats "looked into" *Thus Spake Zarathustra* in the summer of 1902, nor that he read other Nietzsche works in 1903 (it may have been during the last three months of 1902 on receipt of these works from John Quinn). And why is *The Dawn of Day* not mentioned in this list (it *is* mentioned on p. 71)? The largely redundant chapter 2 (which deals in the skimpiest fashion with some Romantic forebears like Hölderlin, Heine, Schopenhauer, Balzac, Byron, Blake and Shelley) contains its quota of glaring errors: for example, the praise (cited on p. 10) Nietzsche gives in 1877 to *Prometheus Unbound* is not to Shelley's work but to Siegfried Lipiner's. And there is throughout the book a chronic rash of misspellings (*Eglington, G. B. Frazer, Sophocle's, Salvatori*), especially of German words (*Forster-Nietzsche, reichdeutschen, Ubermaas, Reichart, Schlecta, Voltz*).

In the course of my review of Bohlmann for this journal (*Yeats* 1 [1983]: 188–91) I observed the author's reluctance to question the judgments of earlier commentators. Oppel, to her credit, is more independent-minded, and often enters the lists on her own behalf. However, I think she sometimes goes wildly astray, as in her speculations about John Quinn's role in the composition of *Where There Is Nothing* (44–46), and is sometimes a little casual, as in her dismissal of Yeats's linking of Nietzsche and William Morris as "somewhat of a red herring" (62). Surely the linking needs exploring, not exploding. The persistent use of phrases like "might well have," "would have," and "must have" suggest a mind ready to risk speculation in the absence of solid evidence, and expressions like "intuition tells me" and "my guess is," though disarmingly arch and disingenuous, are no substitute for persuasive argument.

Oppel claims that "the effect of Nietzsche's thought on Yeats only begins to show in the years 1902 to 1910" and that Nietzsche's presence in Yeats's later work is "ubiquitous" (217). She examines, at greater length than Bohlmann and certainly with more literary sensitivity, critical flair, and stylistic grace, a number of plays which, she thinks, show Yeats working out Nietzschean ideas about the mask and about tragedy, remaking himself in the process of revising his work. For example, *The King's Threshold* (1903) was written during his "initial enthusiasm" for Nietzsche's work: "This enthusiasm inspires most of the play; one finds it in specific 'Nietzscheanisms' in the lines, in the central theme and plot, and in the use of opposition or mask in creating both 'the bony structure' of contrasting characters and the flesh of individual poetic speeches" (134). In this play, as in *The Shadowy Waters* and *On Baile's Strand*, "the revisions work toward clarity of outline, the same forcefulness that characterizes all of Yeats's revisions after he is himself strengthened by

Nietzsche" (150). Oppel also gives a perceptive reading of *The Player Queen*. She is at her most engaging in her readings of such poems as "Adam's Curse," "Never Give All the Heart," and "The Mask." Her commentary on "A Dialogue of Self and Soul," which she terms "perhaps Yeats's greatest tribute to Nietzsche" (231), leads her to claim that "his instilling of moral courage" was one of Nietzsche's greatest contributions to Yeats as man and artist: "This courage . . . helps Yeats to find 'the mask,' to find fruitfulness in the void, and to understand historical cycles, and individual ones, as necessary parts of a whole, continuous design" (232–33).

A frustrating drawback of Oppel's book is that she does not comb Nietzsche's work with sufficient thoroughness. To take one of her two major themes as an example: many references to the "mask" in *Beyond Good and Evil* and *The Gay Science* are ignored, as are commentaries on this theme by such Nietzsche scholars as Ernest Bertram, Karl Jaspers, George Allen Morgan, Harold Aldermann, William D. Williams, and Walter Kaufmann.

If Yeats can declare that "Nietzsche completes Blake and has the same roots" (L 379) when there is no evidence, or even likelihood, that Nietzsche read Blake or had ever heard of him, then the parallels between Nietzsche and Yeats could be explored without restrictive reference to Yeats's extant statements about Nietzsche or his work, even to the annotations in Common's anthology. Although several scholars have found them suggestive, these annotations represent Yeats's immediate and perhaps incompletely considered responses: their very form (fragmentary, cryptic, unsystematic) should make us wary about attaching undue significance to them. The next book exploring the "kinship" between Yeats and Nietzsche (and there is bound to be one sooner rather than later) should, I suggest, ignore or minimize Yeats's documented or putative responses to Nietzsche. It should, that is, eschew every attempt to establish the precise nature and extent of "influence" in favor of a broader approach which would draw upon *all* of Nietzsche's works in order to throw light on Yeats's poems and plays.

Finally, it is worth repeating what a great pity it is that this book makes its appearance without the strictures lodged against Bohlmann's book being noticed, let alone taken to heart. It may be that the pressure to publish, a pressure felt particularly by younger scholars anxious to establish themselves in the academic arena, gave no leisure to contest Bohlmann's ideas at greater length.

Marie Roberts. *British Poets and Secret Societies.*
Totowa, N.J.: Barnes & Noble Books, 1986. [xvi] + 181 pp.

Reviewed by GEORGE MILLS HARPER

The object of this book, according to the author, is to investigate "a
hidden creative underworld; the relationship between poets and secret
societies" (Preface, [xi]). And she has chosen to discuss "five major
poets": Smart, Burns, Shelley, Kipling, and Yeats. Unable to find any
record that Smart was a Freemason, Roberts traces the "evidence . . . in
his poetry, particularly *Jubilato Agno* . . . and *A Song to David*" (10).
Similarly, since Shelley did not belong to any secret organizations,
Roberts is forced to rely on the evidence in his writing, chiefly *St. Irvyne
or the Rosicrucian.* Her brief essay, almost a third of which is devoted to
Peacock's *Nightmare Abbey,* is weak and unconvincing.

Roberts is on firmer ground with Burns, who was initiated into
Freemasonry in 1781 and elected poet laureate of Lodge Canongate Kill-
winning six years later (55). Kipling too became a Mason at an early age
and remained an active member for much of his mature life. Roberts's
essays on Smart, Burns, and Kipling are pedestrian but informative.

The same cannot be said for the essay on Yeats, which contains so
many misconceptions and factual errors that the uninformed reader
should be warned against it. All students of Yeats are, of course, aware
that he was a member of the Theosophical Society from 1887 to 1890,
and of the Golden Dawn (both Inner and Outer Orders) from 1890 to
1922. There is no longer any doubt, surely, that the rituals and doctrines
of the Order remained a powerful influence on Yeats's art and life until
his death. Nothing new or provocative will be found in Roberts's essay,
the disorder and half truths of which could be illustrated from almost any
page. The following is characteristic:

> Certainly he borrowed images for his verse from the Golden Dawn
> such as the twin pillars from the grade of Neophyte, the four ele-
> ments from "The Ritual of the Cross," the dolphin from the Great
> *Hermetic Arcanum,* the *"Hodos Chameliontos"* . . . from the title of a
> Golden Dawn text, the tower from the Tarot pack, and the winding
> stair from Masonic symbolism. (152–53)

Not all wrong, of course, but all partially so. The essay as a whole is marred by inadequate or misleading footnotes and by incorrect quotations, spelling, and punctuation. More disturbing is Roberts's misunderstanding of the primary nature of the Golden Dawn: "The Hermetic-Cabalistic teachings of the Golden Dawn owed much to Rosicrucianism" (134). Elsewhere, she suggests that "the Order had become increasingly immersed in Rosicrucianism" under Dr. Felkin (141). In fact, the Cabalistic teachings obviously *were* Rosicrucian, as Mathers conceived them; and the Second Order (Stella Matutina) *remained* strongly Rosicrucian when Felkin assumed the leadership after the great schism in 1903. On the contrary, Felkin's thinking and teaching became less strictly Rosicrucian as he became immersed in the doctrines of Rudolph Steiner's Anthroposophism.

The student who wishes to understand "the attraction of the poet to the world of secret societies" (126) will not be illuminated by Roberts's inadequate and sometimes misleading book. At one point she implies that the Pre-Raphaelite Brotherhood belongs in her list of secret societies (see p. 4). I am puzzled why a publisher as respectable as Barnes and Noble would lend its name to such an uneven and unreliable book.

M. L. Rosenthal. *The Poet's Art.*
New York: W. W. Norton, 1987. xvi + 160 pp.

Thomas Parkinson. *Poets, Poems, Movements.*
Ann Arbor: UMI Research Press, 1987. ix + 330 pp.

Reviewed by RAEBURN MILLER

Both of these books cover familiar ground in generally familiar ways.
They are less interesting as wholes than for some of their parts. Yet both
are by serious men with long careers of critical achievement, and both
offer enough passages of insight to be worth the attention of anyone
concerned with poetry in our time.

Rosenthal is less forthright than Parkinson in revealing the extent to
which the material of the text has been previously published (he lists at
the end of his acknowledgments nine places in which "certain passages"
have appeared), and he expends greater effort at bringing together the
parts of the book into a unified discussion of the poet's art—into a
consideration of "how the wayward stuff of dream and emotion and
sensuous flickerings is captured and converted into poems" (xii). Unfor-
tunately most of his generalizations on the subject are either obscure or
commonplace. We are told that "in circumstances of murderous repres-
sion, the full import of the imagination's need for full, deep, unsuper-
vised breathing grows brilliantly clear as the supreme value that it is"
(83). And, "The life of a work of art is inseparable from the 'technical'
aspects of its form" (105).

There is also some uncertainty as to the audience these generaliza-
tions are designed to instruct. Rosenthal says the book is "meant for
readers with a lively interest in poetry" (xii), but we are introduced to
"Shakespeare's contemporary, John Donne" (23) and told that " 'read'
and 'reed' have exactly the same pronunciation (an instance of rime
riche)" (139). The tone indeed is generally professorial, as perhaps it
should be, but one feels a certain discomfort in finding such a transition
as, "By an obvious turn of association, these thoughts have suddenly
reminded me of a poem by the American writer James Dickey . . ." (86).

Nevertheless, when Rosenthal moves beyond generalizations to ana-
lyze individual poems, the result is far more rewarding. Some of the
readings (of Larkin's "High Windows," for example, or of some early

lines from *The Prelude*) are more persuasive than others (Auden's "On This Island" or Wordsworth's "Surprised by Joy"), but all are thoughtful, clear, humane, graceful. The examples are carefully varied, including several from languages other than English, material not often drawn upon in Rosenthal's previous work. He mentions several Yeats poems, treating especially "The Tower" and "The People." His pleasure in the line, "Memories of the words of women," is alone worth all the generalizations the book offers about "the poet's art."

As its title indicates, Parkinson's book makes very little attempt to disguise its nature as a collection of essays. The lack of much coherence is suggested by the author's harried explanation of why he included an essay about Burroughs among those on poets—"partly because it fits with the essay on the beat writers in section four and partly because of the extended portrait of Allen Ginsberg with which it opens" (viii). The essays range over a period of forty years; only two are published here for the first time.

Parkinson is a man of taste and sympathy. He has no axes to grind. None of the pieces included are foolish or offensive. And yet none go very far at breaking new ground or providing new understanding. Oddly, the least interesting are those on the California poets, the group Parkinson should be best equipped to deal with. Perhaps the best essay is a short general discussion of "Current Assumptions about Poetry." But aside from that, the four essays on Yeats have special value and appeal. Less substantial, of course, than his books on Yeats, these essays show Parkinson's observations and judgments from several perspectives and over several years. He is equally successful in the discussion of a single poem ("Nineteen Hundred and Nineteen") and in a 21-page overview of the poet. His essay on "Yeats and the Limits of Modernity," originally published in volume 3 of *Yeats,* is a bracing antidote to some current misconceptions about the place of Yeats in contemporary literature.

One minor but irritating aspect of this book is the almost total absence of women poets. Quotations from Stein and di Prima are used as embellishments, and there is a positive reference to H.D., but otherwise all the poets whose work is considered, even in passing, are males.

Whatever deficiencies the book may have, and however uneven the individual essays, there is one consistent virtue that should be noted. Parkinson's style does not call attention to itself (for good or ill) in the way Rosenthal's does, but the book is sprinkled with dozens of memora-

ble formulations and asides that provide an independent source of plea-
sure. The best way to suggest this dimension is to quote a few:

> Would the political history of Ireland hold the attention it now does
> if Yeats had not written? (133)

> It might be more profitable to think of A Vision as being primarily
> concerned with the thought that Yeats wanted to keep out of his
> poetry. (142)

> The beat and beatnik compose a social refusal rather than a revolt.
> (170)

> San Francisco is, for Americans, the city at the end of the world.
> (187)

> When unpredictability becomes a desired norm, the result is a para-
> doxical monotony. (196)

> There is a danger that in reacting against the doctrine of the autono-
> mous poem, current poetics is putting in its place the autonomous
> book and eventually the autonomous man. (218)

> Lowell never learned to think in free verse; it was not his poetic
> cradle language. (227)

> He was self-educated but rarely showed the horrors of unskilled
> labor and he should not have let the job out—he did it very well.
> (263)

> Poetry like all art comes out of courage, the capacity to keep going
> when reason breaks down. (290)

Even if Parkinson offered nothing else, moments like these are
enough to make this a valuable and gratifying book.

Passim: Brief Notices

Mary FitzGerald

This section contains short reviews of books that refer to the life and work of W. B. Yeats only briefly or in passing. Although they are not sufficiently Yeats-oriented to warrant extended review in this annual, they may well be of interest to our readers.

English Literature and History.
[Sotheby's sale catalog for 23–24 July 1987]
London: Sotheby Parke Bernet & Co., 1987.

This sale catalog contains notices of a letter from Yeats to his literary agent, A. P. Watt, and the vastly more important vellum notebook, with title lettered in gold, "The Flame of the Spirit," in which Yeats inscribed seven of his poems, with notations for more to be added, to Maud Gonne on 20 October 1891. Until this transaction it had been in the hands of Maud Gonne's heirs. As Warwick Gould pointed out in an article describing the book and its contents a week before the sale, in the *Times Literary Supplement* (17 July 1987, 770), it is probably "this book" that Maud is urged to take down and read in "When You are Old" (P 41). The sale catalog reproduces the corrected manuscript page on which Yeats inscribed this poem (82), a variant of the text we now have. It is the last verse Yeats wrote in the vellum notebook, though he titled more pages that were finally left blank. Only one of the seven poems was previously unknown to most Yeats scholars (Maud Gonne showed the whole book to Richard Ellmann). The other poems have been published by Yeats, transcribed in the scholarship, or are extant in another manuscript.

"The Flame of the Spirit" was purchased for £31,000 by a bookseller, on behalf of a client who remains anonymous.

Printed Books, Autograph Letters & Manuscripts.
[Christie's sale catalog for 9 December 1987.] New York: Christie's, 1987.

In lot 316, the first of three separate lots, this catalog offers for sale thirty-three items of correspondence sent to various persons, including Ernest Boyd, William Ernest Henley, Henri Davray, F. R. Higgins, and Richard Ashe King. A portion of one such letter is reproduced in the catalog (108). Also included in this set is a letter from George Yeats to Oliver St. John Gogarty in January 1935 discussing Yeats's illness and mentioning that he is in love with a young woman in London, apparently Margot Collis Ruddock (108).

Lot 316A describes autograph letters from Yeats to his father, from 1908–9.

Lot 376, the theatre archive of the actress and founder of the People's National Theatre, Nancy Price, includes five letters and the corrected proof of a song. Yeats is quoted in the catalog discussing the interpretation of Decima in *The Player Queen* (VP 715–760), and the entire text of another letter on the same play is reproduced photographically on page 141.

Peter Conrad. *The History of English Literature: One Indivisible, Unending Book.*
Philadelphia: University of Pennsylvania Press, 1987. x + 740 pp.

Peter Conrad says at the outset of this excellent and intelligent history that he wants to show how all of literature in our language is interrelated: "Thus *Beowulf* is a beginning and also, when Seamus Heaney unearths an echo of Anglo-Saxon song in his peat bog, an end" (vii), and "the great poet of this century, W. B. Yeats, acknowledges no pre-emption and is alive in all of the past at once, now an epic warrior, now a Renaissance prince, now a towering romantic ego" (ix). Consequently, Yeats appears all through the long story, both for his own sake and to interact with the works of Auden, Eliot, Shakespeare, Spenser, Wilde, and the romantics.

Conrad's heady retelling of English literary history (published two years ago in England by J. M. Dent, and only recently released here), is energetic and appealing. It conveys its information with the enthusiasm and delight that only good teachers can muster, and it may profitably be read by seasoned scholars as well as by their students.

Seamus Deane. *A Short History of Irish Literature.*
London, Melbourne, Sydney, Auckland, Johannesburg: Hutchinson; Notre Dame, Ind.: University of Notre Dame Press, 1986. 282 pp.

Seamus Deane, Professor of Modern English and American Literature at University College, Dublin, and master of the long, labyrinthine, and jam-packed paragraph, provides in this book a high-speed chase through the history of Irish literature. Readers of the present *Annual* will probably find that its remarks about Yeats—in chapters about drama and poetry—and about other writers are more important for the ways in which they shed light on the particular and cogent views of Deane than for any new illumination of the literature he discusses.

The pace is simply too rapid: it is not uncommon for seven works or authors to be covered in a single paragraph, and Deane occasionally seems to be corralling examples from all over the range—the wide range—of his interests. But this is not to disparage the achievement. A "short history" is a notoriously difficult thing to write, and Deane should not perhaps be faulted for turning his into a history of ideas with literary examples, some of which are catalogs.

The awareness of time's winged chariot at the heels has occasionally shortchanged the proofreading. Yeatsians and others will note that A. E. F. Horniman loses an initial (her *E*) both in the text and in the index (150, 274), and that Charles Stewart Parnell alters his spelling to match that of the Stuart Pretender (141, 279). There is also the somewhat irritating practice of citing almost all scholarship by author's first initial and last name and omitting names of publishing houses, so that we read of "J. Ronsley (ed.), *Myth and Reality in Irish Literature* (Waterloo 1977)" (253), a sure puzzle to a someone unaware of the Canadian connection.

Denis Donoghue. *We Irish: Essays on Irish Literature and Society.*
New York: Alfred A. Knopf, 1986. ix + 276 pp.

We Irish is predictably peppered with Yeatsian moments, but many of them will already be known to readers of this annual, as this volume mostly collects Donoghue's reviews of Irish books and his earlier essays from other sources, unrevised except for changes "here and there, out of respect for decent observances in the matter of style" and "not . . . brought 'up to date'" (ix)—so that we come to read, for example, a statement about "Yesterday (December 5, 1975)" in a piece on the contemporary Irish situation (148). New to this collection, however, is a chapter called "Yeats, Ancestral Houses, and Anglo-Ireland" (52–66), whose content will not likely surprise those scholars who have followed the progress of Denis Donoghue's falling out with Yeats from the time of his relinquishing of the authorized biography to the present.

He remains out of sympathy with his subject and in this essay adumbrates some of the reasons why, giving us a sort of thumbnail sketch of how he ended up thinking so badly of Yeats:

> When I first read Yeats, Eliot, Pound, and the other major modern poets, I was admonished to respect what was called "the autonomy of the poem." It was not clear to me precisely what I was to respect, except in the . . . [sense] of giving the artist whatever latitude he seems to ask for.
>
> Yeats's poetry, in that context, caused a difficulty at two points[,] the [outlandish] political attitudes implicit or explicit in his last poems . . . [and his] dealings with magic and occult interests generally. (63–64)

This attitude, Donoghue now suggests, has become (has always been?) general all over Ireland:

> In Ireland, it is fair to say, Yeats is resented. . . . [Irish] readers resent his appeal to Irishness, and his assertion that he knows the quality of Irishness when he meets it. That resentment is so inclusive that little or nothing survives in its presence. (66)

To the extent that this generalization may be true—and it is sweepingly overstated—it may help explain the disproportionately small number of Irish scholars who take Yeats as their major figure of study and the almost total absence of Irish graduate students from the research collections that house his manuscripts (including the National Library of Ireland in Dublin). For support, Donoghue can allude to revisionist studies by Seamus Deane and Declan Kiberd as partaking of this anti-Yeats position, which, he admits, is "a political judgment imposed upon poetry" (66). For himself, belying the tone of this chapter and much of his recent writing, he claims that his own stance is "latitudinarian, and I would hold to its concessiveness until a particularly extreme outrage makes me ashamed of it" (66), by which of course he means an outrage allegedly committed by Yeats.

Such is the havoc that has been wrought by the posthumous misplacement of "Under Ben Bulben" as the last of Yeats's poems in place of the mellower and much more instructive "Politics." In Donoghue's school of thought, Yeats's admonition to write of Ascendancy characters is taken literally to mean excluding all other subjects, rather than as insisting that Ascendancy concerns be *included* in the concerns of a modern Ireland. Then all the later work is reread for evidence of class arrogance. The possibility of metaphor is virtually excluded. That this produces monumental distortion goes unnoticed. For example, *Purgatory* cannot be read metaphorically or even allegorically, and so it becomes almost indigestible: "It is only in the context of Yeats's feeling for Ascendancy Ireland that the play becomes tolerable: otherwise, it must appear merely a demand for practical eugenics" (60). It's either/or all the way through for Donoghue.

The hieratic posture does not always serve him well, as when he complains about Trinity College professors R. B. McDowell's and D. A. Webb's use of "far too much" Latin phrasing in their history of TCD—"it is supererogatory to resort to Latin" (175)—while not flinching from flaunting his Irish for the readers of the *New Republic* (269). He cavalierly assumes Samuel Beckett's cooperation with Deirdre Bair's biography (257), Beckett's express statements to the contrary, and Bair's background as a police reporter notwithstanding. (She is widely believed to have interviewed hospital personnel to arrive at the details that Donoghue thinks only Beckett can have provided.) He is similarly astray when he overstates Seamus Heaney's debt to Patrick Kavanagh (268), pounces crankily on his diction (14, 270), and indulges in a sort of Heaney bashing that reminds one of the tenor of his attacks on Yeats: "It is not clear what sacrifices Heaney has made for the sake of being an Irish poet: nothing particularly painful seems to present itself, but I suppose one never knows such things" (12). A little of this goes a long way.

Yeatsians, of course, cannot ignore Donoghue, and there are always the occasional flashes of brilliance that make reading him rewarding. The rough spots in this volume, however, can make one regret the absence of an index.

John Wilson Foster. *Fictions of the Irish Literary Revival: A Changeling Art.* Syracuse, N.Y.: Syracuse University Press; Dublin: Gill and Macmillan, 1987. xx + 407 pp.

The fiction of the Irish literary revival has not received anything like the critical attention accorded its poetry and drama—perhaps, says Foster, because it is "a highly diverse and uncooperative body of work" (xi). Despite the difficulty of managing its diversity, Foster attempts just that in this excellent and protean study. He focuses on all the writers of the period who

> produced an enduring body of literature, and who became dominant figures in contemporary Irish (and in several cases British) literary culture. They [these writers] were associated through their cultural nationalism, their romanticism, their preoccupation with heroism, their interest in folklore and the occult, their attention to the peasantry, their promotion of an ancient Gaelic polity and worldview, and by their repudiation of realism, democracy, individualism, modernization, the bourgeoisie, and cultural union with England. (xi)

The prodigious learning that exemplifies and defends this assertion is gracefully and elegantly manifest throughout the discussion. Foster's complete and thorough grasp of his material is of a kind that is not natural in an age like this, and it is wondrously refreshing. Some of his observations seem inspired, and he has a knack of making unexpected connections between works that strike the reader with the force of revelation.

Yeatsians will be disappointed that it scants the master's novel, but then, as Foster notes, "because the revival encouraged other literary forms at its expense, the novel as a recognizable and autonomous form received a setback at the hands of the revival and its aims and aspirations" (xi). He does, however, handle Yeats's folktales well, though without benefit of consultation with Mary Helen Thuente's *W. B. Yeats and Irish Folklore* (Dublin: Gill and Macmillan; Totowa, N.J.: Barnes and Noble, 1980).

For anyone interested in any aspect of the literature of the Irish Renaissance, this is a book not to be missed. It sheds light all around as well as on its avowed subject matter, and it is uncommonly well written, with very few slips of the pen. (There is one on page 362, where a note refers to a previous citation from AE "above, page 00.") It can even be browsed through, as Foster's one major concession to the diversity of his writers is to handle their works in subdivisions under his main chapter headings, and to exercise some degree of selectivity rather than trying to encompass—and thereby shortchange—them all.

Yeatsians can be especially grateful for the way in which *Fictions of the Irish Literary Revival* enhances our understanding of the literary and cultural world in which Yeats wrote, and for the way in which Foster's emphasis on the least-covered aspect of the period supplies a long-standing need.

Alastair Fowler. *A History of English Literature.*
    Cambridge, Mass.: Harvard University Press, 1987. xii + 395 pp.

Aware of the dangers of crowding too much material into a single volume, Alastair Fowler attempts to impose some limitations on his large area by concentrating on literary forms: "My constant question has been, How have the proportions between the various elements of literature changed?" (ix). He does this commendably if occasionally breathlessly.

Yeats gets his due here, though the comments are very brief and very basic, in the penultimate chapter on "Modernist Poetry and Drama." Fowler says he is writing for "students coming to grips with unfamiliar parts of literature" and to that end he "primarily describes" (ix). This does not, however, prevent him from the occasionally pithy observation, as when he notes that the slow acceptance of modernism in England "had much to do with the fact that many of the writers were not in fact English" (351) and supplies a catalog of names to prove it.

Robert F. Garratt. *Modern Irish Poetry: Tradition and Continuity from Yeats to Heaney.*
    Berkeley, Los Angeles and London: University of California Press, 1986. xii + 322 pp.

Yeats is the starting point for the whole of this book, which focuses on those Irish poets who have inherited his legacy and who, like many sons of famous fathers, have struggled to exist independent of him. Garratt apparently takes the rhetoric of "Under Ben Bulben" seriously, and therefore finds in Yeats a "narrow view of Irish society" with a "restrictive version of continuity and . . . identification with the Protestant Ascendancy" (43), rather than the more generous—and probably more correct—view of the late F. S. L. Lyons, who was intending to argue in the definitive biography that what Yeats really espoused was a pluralistic society. Be that as it may, many of the poets (and not a few critics) who have followed Yeats have perceived his views as Garratt sees them, and his book sheds light on these impressions and on the various tactics the poets have employed to counteract them. Yeats, then, is seen here from the perspective of his influence and the anxiety it has caused among his successors, great and small: James Joyce, Austin Clarke, Patrick Kavanagh, Thomas Kinsella, John Montague, Seamus Heaney, and some more recent Ulster poets.

John Garrett. *British Poetry since the Sixteenth Century: A Students' Guide*.
    Totowa, N.J.: Barnes and Noble, 1987. viii + 248 pp.

The subtitle, *A Students' Guide,* given on the title page but nowhere on the cover, says all that is needed about this book. It is strictly for beginners, and as far as Yeats is concerned, it is for beginners who do not own or cannot find a copy of the poems. Garrett gives the complete texts of "The Lake Isle of Innisfree," "Sailing to Byzantium," and "Politics" before providing close readings of all three poems, with passing allusions to a few others. He cites as his source Richard J. Finneran's *The Poems: A New Edition,* but misquotes the title. In other words, scholars will not need this book.

Edward A. Hagan. *"High Nonsensical Words": A Study of the Works of Standish James O'Grady*.
    Troy, N.Y.: Whitston Publishing Company, 1986. viii + 229 pp.

This compact study takes stock of the enormous influence O'Grady's two-volume *History of Ireland* had on Yeats and others of the Irish revival who were "stirred by the high, noble tone which O'Grady's *History* sounded," because the "Homeric quality of his rendition made them feel heirs to a great tradition" (2–3). It goes well beyond Phillip Marcus's introductory *Standish O'Grady* for Bucknell's Irish Writers Series (1970) by proposing a conscious theory of art in O'Grady, a claim sufficiently demonstrated by analysis of the style, substance, and structure of his work.

Yeats appears sporadically here in the ensuing commentary, and he is often quoted.

Hugh Kenner. *A Sinking Island: The Modern English Writers.*
    New York: Alfred A. Knopf, 1988. [xii] + 292 pp.

A Sinking Island does for England what *A Colder Eye* (New York: Alfred A. Knopf, 1983) did for Ireland, namely to make its literary and cultural history a playground for the fertile wit and clever analysis of Hugh Kenner. Yeats figures only slightly in this volume, primarily in discussions of Ezra Pound or George Bernard Shaw, and here and there whenever a useful comparison or example is needed. Yeatsians will find it unexceptionable rather than controversial, except where Kenner seems to be suggesting that Olivia Shakespear (unnamed, except as Diana Vernon) *resided* at 18 Woburn Buildings with Yeats rather than simply visiting him there (76), and in the faulty transcription of the epigraph to *Responsibilities* (86), which should read "How am I fallen *from* myself . . ." (P 100).

As always with Kenner, the chief joy is the play of ideas across a broad spectrum, teasing the intellect of the reader with fresh and provocative perspectives on modernism and modernists.

James Longenbach. *Modernist Poetics of History: Pound, Eliot, and the Sense of the Past.*
    Princeton: Princeton University Press, 1987. viii + 279 pp.

Walter Pater and W. B. Yeats serve as forerunners for Ezra Pound and T. S. Eliot in this study of the literary approaches to history that characterize modernism. The derivation runs from Pater through Yeats to Pound, and one of the many virtues of this book is that it further documents the extent to which Pound was indebted to Yeats for several of his more important esthetic and philosophical formulations. Eliot derived his own modernist poetics of history partly from both Yeats and Pound.

The book concentrates on Pound's criticism and poetry through 1917 and Eliot's writings through the publication of their joint venture, *The Waste Land* in 1922, explaining ultimately the uses of the past found in the Eliot/Pound poem: "*The Waste Land* remains the ultimate 'poem including history' produced in the twentieth century, and if Yeats was right to present Pater's *La Gioconda* as the first 'modern' poem, then *The Waste Land* may well be the last" (237).

Yeats is mentioned *passim* as the argument develops, but although he is not the primary focus of the discussion, the book amply demonstrates the degree to which he helped shape the modernists' approaches to their cumulative past.

Edna Longley. *Poetry in the Wars.*
Newcastle upon Tyne: Bloodaxe Books, 1986. 264 pp.

Although this study is entirely concerned with poets since Yeats (Edward Thomas, Robert Frost, Louis MacNeice, Keith Douglas, Philip Larkin, Seamus Heaney, Derek Mahon, and Paul Muldoon), it uses Yeats as the starting ground for its discussion of modernism and for an early twentieth-century response to the call for poets to respond to such political outrages as wars.

Yeatsians will not really learn anything new about Yeats from this—unless it is the further documentation of yet more ways in which his example has been alternately a benediction and a challenge for younger poets—but the discussion of the works of his successors shows Edna Longley's customary luminous intelligence and solid grasp of her subject.

John Lucas. *Modern English Poetry from Hardy to Hughes.*
Totowa, N.J.: Barnes & Noble, 1986. 218 pp.

Yeats receives a chapter's worth of consideration in this study, all of it praising him against his British contemporaries, for his verbal strength, his unifying vision, and—primarily—for his willingness to stand up to the times in which he lived and shoulder his "*Responsibilities*." His "ability to intervene in current, critical issues . . . makes Yeats's poetry . . . more valuable than contemporary English poetry" (117). He was steered from the barrenness of an art for art's sake aesthetics by four people: John O'Leary, Maud Gonne, Arthur Symons, and Lady Gregory. The influence of each of these is sketched acceptably enough.

Lucas is almost comically out of patience with English poetry of the period:

> . . . whatever the cause of the explanation, you come face to face with the inescapable truth that the best English poets during the period so far covered in this book cannot feel themselves responsible to the large social issues that engage Yeats.
>
> And if you turn to the more minor poets, you are faced with still more instructive matter. For what you then find is a creation of a "seamless" past whose present "health" is offered in terms that reveal the absurdity of the whole enterprise, and in a language so dead as certainly to imply the entire death of a culture. (115)

The hapless exemplar for this charge is Robert Bridges, whose first poem after his designation as Poet Laureate in 1913 (the same year as his accession to the presidency of the Society for Pure English) is quoted and reviled:

> There, yet again, in 'pure English'—that is, a language drained of any vitality—is the dreary, ridiculous pretence that England is a collection of rural communities, bonded together in Anglican accord. What kind of responsibility is this? To whom? . . . Consider, by contrast, a clutch of [Yeats's] poems which are included in *Responsibilities*. . . . (115–16)

For this earnestness of tone much can be forgiven, though not perhaps the astonishing and unattributed assertion, in parentheses no less, that Yeats "in common with others" thought initially that Robert Gregory "had killed himself. Only later was it discovered that he had been accidentally shot down" (125). Apparently Lucas derives this from a misreading of "An Irish Airman Foresees His Death," and from a misunderstanding of the emphasis on the frequently encountered observation that the initial reports of the circumstances surrounding Gregory's death in combat proved erroneous. It leads him to think that Yeats "needs to proceed tactfully" in "In Memory of Major Robert Gregory" because "to celebrate an act of suicide is not easy" (125). If Lucas means this in some subtle way—say, in the sense that (in Yeats's view) Gregory's choice of combat service in a flying corps when he was really too old to fly *amounted* to a suicidal impulse, then he does not make that sufficiently clear. We will all, no doubt, live to see Gregory's "suicide" solemnly referred to in term papers yet unborn. The same papers will also refer to Yeats's "*Thor* Ballylee," and we can lay the charge for these big and little errors at Lucas's door.

That is unfortunate, because this is a stimulating and enjoyable book, even though it offers Yeatsians nothing in the way of really new (correct) information about Yeats.

F. C. McGrath. *The Sensible Spirit: Walter Pater and the Modernist Paradigm.*
   Tampa: University of South Florida Press, 1986. xi + 299 pp.

In this exquisitely produced volume, printed and bound with a degree of attention to excellence that other publishers might do well to emulate, F. C. McGrath examines the roots of modernism and brings his researches into nineteenth century German philosophy to bear on the traditional approaches. He succeeds in demonstrating the probability that the theories emanating from German idealism came into contact with British empiricism and led to the development of an intellectual and cultural matrix upon which twentieth century writers drew in formulating their new theories of art, paying special attention to Hegel and, of course, to Pater himself.

Yeats figures prominently in the discussion, and many of his poems are considered in these terms, but McGrath chooses Joyce as his chief example, spending the final chapter of his study on a reading of *A Portrait of the Artist as a Young Man.*

James MacKillop. *Fionn mac Cumhaill: Celtic Myth in English Literature.*
   Syracuse, N.Y.: Syracuse University Press, 1986. xv + 256 pp.

This study of the treatment accorded the legendary Finn in English-language literature acknowledges at the outset a deliberate selectivity of sources: "If I had tried to deal with all the citations of Fionn's name, some of them cryptic and ironically allusive, I would be reading still," and so MacKillop restricts himself to narrative portrayals rooted in Irish or Gaelic tradition, a narrowing of focus that left him with "more than a five-foot shelf" of books to deal with (xiv).

On his five-foot shelf is Yeats and George Moore's *Diarmuid and Grania,* which receives somewhat extended consideration, and *The Wanderings of Oisin,* which is treated rather more in passing.

The book as a whole is a helpful summary and discussion of some of the major literary apparitions of Finn.

David Perkins. *A History of Modern Poetry: Modernism and After.* Cambridge and London: Belknap Press of Harvard University Press, 1987. xiii + 694 pp.

This volume brings David Perkins's history of modern poetry up to contemporary times. Yeats figures here as literary forebear to the writers of High Modernism and after, and the study begins significantly with a chapter entitled "The Ascendancy of T. S. Eliot, 1925–1950" (3). Eliot is seen throughout as the major influence on the poets who followed him.

Yeats is mentioned frequently in passing and is given his due as a substantial influence in his own right, but he is not the major focus of Perkins's discussion, which ranges through the works of Dylan Thomas, e. e. cummings, Ezra Pound, Wallace Stevens, and such later writers as Robert Lowell, Richard Wilbur, and John Berryman. It ends with contemporary English poets Charles Tomlinson, Ted Hughes, Geoffrey Hill, and Thom Gunn. Attention is primarily paid to English and American poets, and the absence of Irish poets from Perkins's study accounts in large measure for the lesser emphasis on the influence of Yeats, who was treated at length—though not entirely satisfactorily—in the volume that preceded this one (*A History of Modern Poetry: From the 1890s to the High Modernism Mode* [Cambridge and London: Belknap Press of Harvard University Press, 1976]).